IMMIGRATING TO THE USA

Dan P. Danilov, Attorney

Self-Counsel Press Inc
(a subsidiary of)
International Self-Counsel Press Ltd
USA   Canada

Printed in Canada.

First edition: 1978
Second edition: 1979
Third edition: 1980
Fourth edition: 1983
Fifth edition: 1989
Sixth edition: 1993; Reprinted: 1994
Seventh edition: 1999
Eighth edition: 2002

Canadian Cataloging in Publication Data

Danilov, Dan P., 1927-
    Immigrating to the U.S.A.

    (Self-counsel legal series)
    ISBN 1-55180-402-6

    1. Emigration and immigration law — United States — Popular works. I. Title.
II. Series.
KF4819.6.D35 2002   342.73′082   C2002-911031-9

Self-Counsel Press Inc.
(a subsidiary of)
International Self-Counsel Press Ltd.

1704 N. State Street	1481 Charlotte Road
Bellingham, WA 98225	North Vancouver, BC V7J 1H1
USA	Canada

To the members of my legal staff, with sincere and grateful appreciation for their dedicated assistance in preparing the manuscript for this book.

To my wife, Karen L. Danilov, whose patience and encouragement made it possible for me to devote the many hours necessary for the legal research and publication of this material. To the memory of my mother, Mrs. Mila A. Danilov, for her lifetime support in making it possible for me to complete my legal education and the training to help others less fortunate come to the United States.

Dan P. Danilov

NOTICE TO READERS

Immigration law changes frequently. Every effort is made to keep this publication as current as possible. However, neither the author nor the publisher can accept any responsibility for changes to the law or practice that occur after the printing of this publication. Please be sure that you have the most recent edition.

Note: The filing fees quoted in this book are correct at the date of publication. However, fees are subject to change without notice. For current fees, check with the appropriate government office nearest you. All fees are given in US dollars.

CONTENTS

APPENDIXES

SAMPLES

TABLES

PREFACE

The information in this book has been prepared in concise and general form for people who seek admission into the United States from other countries, and for American citizens and lawful permanent residents who wish to help relatives or friends come to the United States.

It is suggested that you consult your own attorney or an attorney practicing in US immigration and nationality laws for detailed advice concerning the requirements for admission into the United States. More complete information, including up-to-date details about changes in regulations, and necessary applications may be obtained from the nearest US consulate abroad or the US Immigration and Naturalization Service in the United States and other parts of the world (see Appendix 2).

From a Declaration of Principles jointly adopted by a Committee of the American Bar Association and a Committee of Publishers and Associations:

This publication is designed to provide accurate and authoritative information in regard to the subject matter covered. It is sold with the understanding that the publisher is not engaged in rendering legal or other professional service. If legal advice or other expert assistance is required, the services of a competent professional person should be sought.

Dan P. Danilov

INTRODUCTION

The subject of immigration law has always been close to the hearts of many people in the United States, for this is truly a "nation of immigrants." Millions of Americans are the descendants of immigrants who came to the United States from every continent in the world, and today we can trace our heritage to almost every country on the map.

Throughout the history of the United States, US immigration policy has been developed and modified to meet the changing needs of the nation. Shortly after the Declaration of Independence in 1776, Congress provided for qualitative restrictions for the immigration of persons from other countries to the United States, supposedly to ensure the good health and character of aliens entering this country. As the country developed from an agricultural society to an industrial giant, Congress enacted quantitative restrictions on the admission of aliens in order to protect the national economy. The progress of the United States is reflected in continuously changing legislation that sets forth the national policy for the admission or exclusion of millions of persons to the United States. These are some of the highlights in the legislative history of US immigration:

1798 — Alien Act: Gave the president authority to expel aliens whom he perceived to be dangerous to the peace and security of the nation. While the act was qualitative in intent, its existence ran counter to the mood of the American people, resulting in its termination two years later.

1808 — US Constitution, Article I, Section 9: Banned the importation of slaves.

1875 — Qualitative restrictions on immigration: Congress designated categories of aliens (communists, prostitutes, mental and physical incompetents) who were prohibited from entering the United States.

1876 — Landmark US Supreme Court decision: The admission of immigrants to the United States was designated as the sole responsibility of the federal government [Henderson v. Mayor of New York, 92 US 259 (1875)]. All state statutes restricting immigration were declared unconstitutional.

1882 — Chinese Exclusion Act: The increasing importation of low-wage Chinese labor resulted in growing public animosity. Congress banned the future immigration of Chinese laborers into the United States until 1943.

1892 — Amendment to the Chinese Exclusion Act: Required registration of Chinese laborers living in United States and authorized deportation if, after one year, they could not produce a certificate of registration.

1907 — Immigration Act: Expanded existing restrictions on immigration and prohibited entry of aliens over 16 years of age who were unable to read, as well as further restricted the immigration of Orientals to the United States for permanent residence (creating an Asiatic barred zone).

1921 — First quota law: Congress established the first numerical restrictions on immigration — limiting the number of aliens of each nationality who were permitted into the United States to 3 percent of the foreign-born persons of that nationality living in the United States in 1910, and allowing a total of approximately 350,000 immigrants annually. (Aliens residing for one year in an independent country of the Western Hemisphere before admission to the United States were exempt from the quota.)

1924 — National Origins Law: For the first time, Congress established permanent numerical restrictions upon immigration to the United States from all parts of the world (except the Western Hemisphere) under a ceiling of 150,000 per year, with national quotas based on the ethnic composition of the United States in 1920. Prospective immigrants were required to obtain a sponsor in the United States and a visa from a US consulate abroad. Those who entered the United States without a visa and in violation of the law could be deported without any time limitation. Further restrictions were placed on Asian immigration, particularly prohibiting the immigration of all aliens who were ineligible for US citizenship.

1940 — Alien Registration Act: All aliens in the United States were required to register and be fingerprinted. The exclusion and deportation of criminal and subversive groups was expanded.

1943 — Repeal of the Chinese Exclusion Act: Residents of China were permitted to immigrate to the United States.

1945 — War Brides Act: Congress facilitated the immigration of 118,000 spouses and children of members of the US armed forces.

1948 — Displaced Persons Act: This legislation provided for the admission of 400,000 refugees from Germany, Italy, and Austria to the United States.

1952 — Immigration and Nationality Act (commonly called MacCarran-Walter Act): Established the basic (though frequently amended) immigration law of the United States. It consolidated and codified under a single statute all existing laws relating to immigration to the United States. It provided for unrestricted numerical immigration to the United States from Western Hemisphere countries and a national origins quota system. It provided for family reunification, protection of the domestic labor force, and the immigration of persons with needed skills.

1953 — Refugee Relief Act: An additional 214,000 refugees were admitted to the United States.

1965 — Immigration and Nationality Act Amendments: The national origins quota system was repealed by this legislation. A new, eight-category preference system was instituted to reunite families and admit aliens with talents or skills on a "first come, first served" basis in each category. The new law provided an annual limit of 170,000 immigrants from the Eastern Hemisphere with a limit of 20,000 per country, and no preference system. Spouses and children of US citizens and parents of citizens over 21 were exempt from numerical ceilings. Requirements for labor certifications were instituted to control the admission of skilled and unskilled foreign workers. An annual admission of 10,000 refugees was authorized.

1976 — The Immigration and Nationality Act Amendments of 1976: Designed to eliminate the inequities between the treatment of Eastern and Western Hemisphere applicants and extended the eight-category preference system to all Western Hemisphere countries, together with 20,000 per country limit, according to an eight-category preference system that gave priority to persons having —

(a) close family ties with family relatives already in the United States,

(b) labor skills in short supply in the United States, or

(c) refugee status.

However, additional numbers of refugees could be brought into the United States above the numerical limitations by approval of the attorney general, as in the case of refugees from Indo-China.

1978 — The 95th Congress made sweeping changes in immigration legislation, and these became effective in October, 1978. The separate immigration quotas for Eastern and Western Hemispheres are eliminated and replaced by a worldwide numerical limitation of 290,000 persons annually. Children of one US and one non-US parent may retain US citizenship without ever living in the United States, and naturalization is possible for anyone who is over 50 years of age and has been a legal permanent resident for 20 years. Changes were also made in the regulations governing the adoption of foreign children and the status of refugees.

1980 — New Refugee Act: Congress eliminated the seventh preference and allotted 6 percent of this numerical allocation of worldwide visa numbers to the second preference. Distinctions in the definitions of "refugee" and "asylum" provide new procedures for those people to become permanent residents in the United States. Congress authorized up to 50,000 refugees to enter the United States in 1980, 1981, and 1982. The annual worldwide limitation on visa numbers for immigrants to the United States was reduced to 270,000 persons.

1981 — Immigration and Nationality Act Amendments of 1981: Labelled the "INS Efficiency Bill," the legislation raised from 14 to 16 the age limit under which foreign-born adopted children could enter the United States as immediate relatives.

The requirement of applying for permission to reapply for admission into the United States was eliminated for aliens after five years from the date of their deportation.

The validity dates of reentry permits was extended from one year to two years from the date of issue. The annual alien registration requirement was eliminated, but aliens must notify the Immigration and Naturalization Service (INS) in writing of each change of address within ten days of such a change.

Applicants for naturalization are no longer required to provide two witnesses. Senate Bill 1196 amended the Immigration and Nationality Act by approving a 20,000 annual limitation for Taiwan, thereby retaining the 20,000 annual limitation for the People's Republic of China as well.

1986 — Immigration Reform and Control Act of 1986: This new law established the following measures:

(a) Employers who knowingly hired illegal aliens would be subject to civil and criminal penalties.

(b) Illegal aliens who had resided continuously in the United States from before January 1, 1981, until the enactment of the law were granted amnesty and could apply for legalization as Temporary Residents. Eighteen months later, they would qualify to apply for lawful permanent residence.

(c) Illegal aliens who had worked as agricultural workers for 90 days between May 1, 1985, and May 1, 1986, could apply for legal status first as Special Agricultural Workers and, later, as permanent residents.

(d) Spouses of US Citizens and Permanent Alien Residents accorded Conditional Resident Status could, after 21 months, apply to the INS for Permanent Resident Status if the marriage was bona fide and not terminated by divorce. Other changes in the law were enacted to prevent fraudulent marriages by aliens to acquire immigration benefits.

1990 — The Immigration Act of 1990 (known as the Legal Immigration Reform Act for its focus on legal as opposed to illegal immigration): This act increases the number of aliens who may legally immigrate to the United States each year from 270,000 to 675,000 (actually, 700,000 until September 30, 1994). However, for the first time since the 1952 passage of the Immigration and Nationality Act, immediate relatives of US citizens are included in this numerical ceiling (which does not include refugees and those people given asylum). However, immediate relatives will not be subject to any numerical limitations, and special formulas have been worked out to guarantee that family-sponsored immigration will not suffer.

This act increases the number of visas for family members as well as for employment-sponsored immigrants, provided the latter group are bringing talents and skills to this country. It has severely restricted the entry of unskilled workers and has imposed minimum requirements on them. This act separates family and employment-sponsored immigration and creates separate preference categories in each of the two areas. Foreign investors, who fall within the employment categories, can apply for immigrant status if they invest $1 million and hire at least ten US citizens or permanent residents.

Apart from promoting family unification and a skills growth in the United States, the Immigration Act of 1990 has a third goal: to create diversity among the immigrants. This diversity clause will ensure that people from parts of the world that have had relatively low levels of emigration to the United States within the previous five years will now have a greater opportunity to come. A "transition diversity" clause was in place to include a visa lottery as well as measures to provide immigration opportunities for the nationals of Hong Kong, Tibet, and Lebanon.

1991 — The Miscellaneous and Technical Immigration and Naturalization Amendments of 1991: These amendments to the Immigration Act of 1990 and also to some of the previously existing laws clarify issues pertaining to excludability and waivers of excludability. Some of the amendments make it easier to obtain a waiver of excludability if you are the spouse, child, or parent of a US citizen and extreme hardship would occur if you were not admitted into the US. No waivers will be permitted in any circumstances if the applicant has been convicted of murder or if he or she participated in Nazi war crimes. These amendments, most significantly, extend H-1B nonimmigrant visas to foreign medical graduates who fulfill certain educational requirements that allow them to work in clinical positions in the United States.

1993 — North American Free Trade Agreement (NAFTA) Implementation Act: NAFTA superseded the United States Canada Free Trade Agreement Act of September 28, 1988, and established procedures for the temporary entry into the United States of Canadian and Mexican citizen professional businesspersons to render services for remuneration.

1996 — Antiterrorism and Effective Death Penalty Act (AEDPA): This act expedited procedures for the removal of alien terrorists, expanded criteria for deportation for crimes of moral turpitude, permitted the deportation of nonviolent offenders before the completion of their sentence of imprisonment, expedited the process of criminal alien removal, and established deportation procedures for certain criminal aliens who were not permanent residents.

1996 — Personal Responsibility and Work Opportunity Reconciliation Act: This act barred legal immigrants (with certain exceptions) from obtaining food stamps and Supplemental Security Income (SSI), and established screening procedures for current recipients of these programs. The act increased the responsibility of immigrant sponsors by making the affidavit of support legally enforceable, imposed new requirements on sponsors, and required the INS to verify immigration status in order for aliens to receive most federal public benefits.

1996 — Illegal Immigration Reform and Immigrant Responsibility Act (IIRIRA): This act established additional measures to control US borders and to expedite the removal of criminal and other deportable aliens. Often called the Immigration Act of 1996, IIRIRA is notorious because of the many innocent families it has affected. The act has increased penalties for illegal entry to the United States, passport and visa fraud, and failure to leave the country. It has reformed exclusion and deportation procedures by consolidating both into a single removal process. It has also instituted "expedited removal" procedures to speed deportation and alien exclusion through more stringent grounds of admissibility.

The IIRIRA instituted three- and ten-year bars to admissibility for aliens seeking to reenter the United States after having been unlawfully present in the country for over six and twelve months respectively. These three- and ten-year bars were particularly disruptive because of the demise of section 245(i), which "sunset" on January 14, 1998. Section 245(i) was very useful because it allowed out-of-status aliens to adjust their status without having to leave the United States. Now that the law is no longer in effect, out-of-status aliens (with certain exceptions) must leave the United States to adjust their status. However, the new bars to admissibility effectively prevent most out-of-status aliens who leave the United States to adjust their status from reentering the country for three or ten years. Waivers are difficult to obtain.

Fortunately, not all immigration news is bad news. When President Clinton signed into law the October 1998 budget deal, he nearly doubled the number of available H-1B visas. Aliens who have a four-year college degree and a job offer related to their four-year degree, and who are paid at least 95 percent of the prevailing wage may qualify for the valuable H-1B visa.

Note: As this book was going to press, congress was considering changes to the Immigration and Naturalization Service (INS). The proposed changes are the restructuring of the INS into two new agencies — Immigration Enforcement and Citizenship/ Immigration Services. For more information regarding the proposed changes, see the INS Web site <www.ins.gov>.

1
IMMIGRATING TO THE UNITED STATES

1. THE STATUE OF LIBERTY — NEW YORK, USA

Immigration is an experience most Americans have in common, whether recently or in the distant past. Motivation for such an enormous undertaking has varied greatly, for our ancestors came to the United States for all kinds of reasons. Some came to find economic and political opportunities not available in their homelands, others to escape the ravages of war, famine, and persecution of minority religious beliefs. Many came out of pure adventure and some of them stayed. Slaves were the one exception to this pattern: they were the only immigrant group that did not come to the United States of their own free will.

Since October 28, 1886, the first sight of their new home for many immigrants has been the majestic figure of the Statue of Liberty, the cherished symbol of American ideals. Leaving behind all they knew, immigrants by the millions braved the unknown in search of a new life. Fears, hopes, and a host of private anxieties may have accompanied many, but their first glimpse of "the Lady" must have eased their doubts and provided the reassurance they needed. Starting a new life would be difficult, perhaps even cruel, but the statue's imprint remained with them and its message urged them to endure the hardships ahead.

The Statue of Liberty, created by French sculptor Frederic August Bartholdi, was given by the people of France to the people of the United States in recognition of ties first forged during the American Revolution. In her time, she has welcomed more than 50 million people to the country.

2. WHO CAN IMMIGRATE TO THE UNITED STATES?

Anyone can apply to immigrate to the United States. The Congress of the United States has set an annual limit of visas available for any fiscal year. These visas are divided into three categories:

(a) Family-sponsored immigration — including immediate family members of US citizens, a group previously not included in numerical considerations

(b) Employment-based immigration

(c) Diversity immigration

Further divisions are made within these categories to account for more specific criteria within each (see Table 1). The visas are given on a "first come, first served" basis. The US Department of State determined the family and employment preference numerical limits for financial year (FY) 1998 in accordance with the terms of section 201 of the Immigration and Nationality Act (INA). These numerical limitations for FY 1998 were as follows:

★ The worldwide family-sponsored preference limit is 226,000.

★ The worldwide employment-based preference limit is 140,000.

★ Under INA section 202(a), the per-country limit is fixed at 7 percent of the family and employment preference annual limits. For FY 1998, the per-country limit is 25,620.

TABLE 1
CLASSIFICATION FOR IMMIGRANT VISA APPLICANTS

1. Spouse of a US citizen.

2. Parent of a US citizen son or daughter who is over 21 years of age.

3. An unmarried, minor (under the age of 21) son or daughter of a US citizen.

   The first three categories represent those people whose entry into the United States is not restricted by annual numerical limitations.

4. Unmarried son or daughter over the age of 21 of a US citizen. (This benefit applies equally to sons and daughters who were once married, but whose marriage was dissolved by death, divorce, or annulment.)

5. Spouse of a lawful permanent resident alien.

6. Unmarried son or daughter of a lawful permanent resident alien.

7. Married son or daughter of a US citizen.

8. Brother or sister of a US citizen who is over 21 years of age.

   The above categories represent the four preferences within family-sponsored immigration (the families of legal permanent residents are grouped in the second preference).

9. A priority worker (a person of extraordinary ability, an outstanding professor or researcher, or a multinational executive or manager).

10. A professional with an advanced degree or with exceptional ability.

11. A professional without an advanced degree, a skilled worker, or an unskilled worker.

12. A special immigrant who falls into one of the following categories:

    (a) a reinstated citizen

    (b) a returning immigrant

    (c) a religious worker

    (d) a former employee of the Panama Canal Zone

    (e) a foreigner who has worked for a long time for the US government abroad

    (f) a retired officer/employee of an international organization based in the United States who has fulfilled residence requirements in the United States (spouses and children are included)

    (g) a child declared dependent on a US Juvenile Court

    (h) an employee of the US consulate in Hong Kong for at least three years

    (i) a J-1 foreign medical graduate who filed an application for adjustment of status (I-485) with the INS before January 10, 1977, has remained in the United States since then, and was granted a waiver of the two-year foreign residence requirement before January 10, 1978

13. An investor who makes a $1-million investment in establishing or expanding a viable business in the United States that will provide jobs for at least ten qualified US workers (excluding family members), or a $500,000 investment in a depressed area.

    The above categories represent the five preferences of employment-based immigration.

14. A refugee or applicant for asylum.

15. A person who qualifies in terms of Schedule A to be admitted to work in the United States without having to obtain clearance from the Department of Labor. This list includes:

TABLE 1 — Continued

(a) registered, professional nurses and physical therapists

(b) people of exceptional ability in the arts and science

16. A person from an area designated by the attorney general as a low admission region who comes from a low admission state. A special formula will be used to determine who qualifies based on data for the previous five-year period. This person must have a high-school diploma or the equivalent, and two years' work experience or training in the field in which he or she will be working in the United States.

The above category is part of the diversity program of immigration created by the Immigration Act of 1990.

The Immigration Act of 1990 provided a new method of calculating how many people from each part of the world are allowed to immigrate in any year. This calculation distinguishes geographic areas of high immigration and areas of low immigration by how many immigrants from those places have come to the United States during the past five years. Generally, people from areas of low immigration are given preference. This strategy redresses the fact that immigrants from some parts of the world have received a disproportionate number of immigrant visas in the past.

People who live inside the United States can apply for an immigrant visa if they have a relative in the United States who is a US citizen or a lawful permanent resident who can file a Form I-130 Immigrant Petition for Relative, Fiancé(e) or Orphan, for them with the Immigration and Naturalization Service (INS). In certain cases, a Form I-130 may be filed with a US consulate or INS abroad. The approval of a relative visa petition will qualify a person who intends to immigrate to the United States for an immigrant visa at a US consulate in a foreign country.

Other people who do not have relatives in the United States can apply for immigrant visas as priority workers (persons of extraordinary ability, outstanding professors and researchers, or multinational executives or managers), members of the professions holding advanced degrees, aliens of exceptional ability, professionals without advanced degrees, or investors. Foreigners are also eligible to apply for immigration if they are capable of performing specified skilled or unskilled labor that is not of a temporary or seasonal nature and for which a shortage of employable and willing persons exists in the United States.

Labor certifications are required for almost all immigrants whose applications are based on employment. The exceptions are priority workers who intend to enter the labor market and do not have relatives to file relative visa petitions for them, and those whose professions or qualifications have been precertified by the Department of Labor and who are therefore eligible for a "Schedule A" Labor Certification Waiver.

The Refugee Act of 1980 distinguishes between those who are refugees and those who seek asylum. People outside of the United States may be admitted as refugees. People physically present in the United States or at a land border or port of entry to the United States at the time of seeking refuge may apply for asylum within one year of entry. The term refugee has been broadened to fit the definition of the United Nations Convention and Protocol relating to the status of refugees.

People who wish to immigrate to the United States from abroad must apply for immigrant visas at a US consulate in the foreign country of their residence, with some exceptions, and must comply with all the laws and regulations of the Immigration and Nationality Act and its amendments. At the discretion of the INS, qualified applicants who have been "inspected and admitted" into the United States may apply for adjustment of status in order to become permanent residents.

If you have been living and working legally in the United States, it is usually possible to file a Form I-485 Application to Register Permanent Residence or Adjust Status. You will also be eligible to file this form if you are an immediate family member of a US citizen, even if you have been working illegally in the country, if you initially entered the United States with inspection.

There are no limits placed on the number of people who come to the United States as permanent residents if they are the immediate relatives of US citizens over 21 years of age. Immediate relatives include spouses, parents, and unmarried children under 21 years old. Because this number is now included in the total number of immigrants who will be admitted in any given fiscal year, the availability of family visas for any year will be determined by subtracting the number of immediate family visas issued in the previous fiscal year from the total number of available family visas. But, according to the new law, a minimum of 226,000 family-sponsored immigrant visas will always be available, even if it means reducing the number of visas available in other categories.

Limits are placed on the number of visas that can be given out to individuals in each preference category in a given year. The categories of immigration and the breakdown of each group into numerically restricted preference groups are discussed in chapter 2. Sample 2 in chapter 2 shows a visa availability bulletin.

In general terms, if you intend to immigrate in one of these categories, you must either —

(a) have a relative in the United States who will file a visa petition on your behalf, or

(b) have made arrangements to be employed and your employment has been approved by the Department of Labor, unless you are exempt from this requirement, as is the case with priority workers and those people whose professions or occupations are on Schedule A.

Even if you satisfy the above criteria, you may still be ineligible to get an immigrant visa if you do not qualify in terms of the grounds of inadmissibility, or general rules of admissibility to the United States. These rules deny entry to people who are likely to have a negative effect on the lives of others in terms of their health, economic circumstances, or past criminal records.

Grounds of inadmissibility in terms of health are applied to those suffering from a communicable disease of public health significance, such as infectious tuberculosis; those suffering from a physical or mental disorder that would render them a threat to the property, safety, or welfare of others; and drug abusers or addicts.

Grounds of inadmissibility in terms of economic criteria include people who are likely to become public charges; people attempting to enter the country to work in skilled or unskilled jobs for which there is no demand and for which the Department of Labor has not issued labor certifications; and medical graduates of schools that are not approved by the Department of Health and Human Services and who are, therefore, deemed not competent to work in the United States. This restriction does not apply to doctors of international acclaim or to doctors who wish to enter the United States as investors.

Criminal and moral grounds for inadmissibility and removal apply to a wide range of people, including members of the Nazi or Communist Party or any affiliated organizations and those who have committed crimes for which there was a jail penalty of at least one year. Finally, there are grounds of inadmissibility that relate primarily to INS regulations. For example, if you attempt to enter the country fraudulently, using false or stolen papers, you are considered inadmissible.

In some cases, you will be able to obtain a waiver for a ground of inadmissibility if the reason you are requesting this waiver is for family reunification. If, for example, you are suffering from an HIV infection, you may be allowed to enter provided you show a means of support and agree to obtain immediate treatment in the United States. See chapter 4 for more information.

The fees payable for a formal immigrant application and for the issuance of a visa are approximately $350.* The visa is valid for four months from the date it is issued. As there can be no advance determination of when a visa will be issued, applicants are advised not to make any final travel arrangements, not to dispose of their property, and not to give up their jobs until visas have been issued to them.

Your immigrant visa, once current, does not confer US citizenship on you but it does entitle you to enter the United States during its validity period and to live and work in the United States.

All children need visas except those born after a visa has been issued. The parent should then have the child's birth certificate. Also, the child should have a valid passport or be included on the parent's passport.

Generally, your personal property and automobile may be imported duty free into the United States if intended for your personal use. There is no restriction on the amount of US currency or foreign currency that you may bring in. You may not, however, import gold rings, bullion, and gold-coin jewelry without a permit from US Customs. Some countries also restrict how much of their currency can be taken out. Be sure to check this before you leave and declare everything to US Customs at the port of entry, especially cash of more than US$10,000. If items are not declared and are then discovered, you may face criminal charges and forfeiture.

3. WELCOME TO THE USA

Once you arrive in the United States, you cannot qualify to become a citizen until you have resided in the United States for five years and applied for naturalization. While in the United States, you are subject to the same laws and legal obligations as citizens and this means you have to pay tax on your worldwide income. See the "US Tax Guide for Aliens" for details. If you move, you will be required to notify the INS of your current address within ten days of obtaining your new address. Appendix 2 lists the addresses of the INS offices. Contact the one nearest you for forms and information.

When you are admitted to the United States on an immigrant visa, you will receive a plastic card. These cards were traditionally green and were called green cards. Unlike recent pink cards, the new green card actually does have a slightly green tint, and not only has visible security features that make it easier for employers to verify the new card's authenticity, but also has other less visible security features that can be identified by INS personnel, thus reducing counterfeiting and tampering. Unlike the previous laminated paper cards, the new permanent resident card is a plastic document similar to a credit card. It has a digital fingerprint and photograph that are actually part of the card. The new card also features a hologram depicting the Statue of Liberty, the letters "USA" in large print, an outline of the United States, and the INS seal. The back of the card, called

*All fees quoted are correct at the time of printing but are subject to change without notice. Please contact your local authority to confirm fees before proceeding.

Form I-551, features an optical memory stripe which contains a laser-engraved version of the information contained on the front of the card, including the cardholder's photograph, name, signature, date of birth, and alien registration number. This laser-etched information cannot be erased or altered. Much of the same information, along with the cardholder's fingerprint, is digitally encoded in the stripe and can only be read by INS officers using a high-tech scanner.

This card is important proof of your lawful residence in the United States. No sample is shown in this book because it is illegal to reproduce this card without authorization. You are required to carry it with you at all times if you are 18 years or older. If you have not received your card within six months of being "inspected and admitted" at a US port of entry, see your nearest INS office.

A reentry permit or travel document is similar to an I-551 card for the purpose of showing your lawful residence in the United States. The reentry permit is meant to be used by lawful permanent residents who have to leave the United States. Think of the reentry permit as a "passport" for lawful permanent residents of the United States. If you are planning on extended travel abroad, apply for a reentry permit while you are still in the United States (see Sample 1). The fee is $110. A reentry permit is valid for two years only. You can renew your reentry permit while you are abroad if you apply for a renewal at an INS office or certain US consulates before the expiry date.

You will then be allowed to reenter the United States as a lawful permanent resident.

In the Cold War era, you were required to get the permission of the INS before traveling in communist countries in order for your reentry permit or I-551 card to be valid for readmission to the United States. This is no longer the case for most countries, but when you apply for a reentry permit, or if you plan to travel abroad to countries that have no formal ties with the United States, it is wise to check with the INS before you leave to find out if any special procedures are necessary.

Before going overseas for lengthy periods of time, a lawful permanent resident is also required to obtain a "sailing permit" from the US Internal Revenue Service (IRS) stating that all taxes have been paid. Inheritance taxes for surviving spouses of lawful permanent residents are considerably higher than those for US citizens. It is suggested that permanent residents should apply for naturalization (US citizenship) as soon as they qualify in order to minimize the payment of inheritance taxes.

If you are going to be out of the United States for a short period of time, either on vacation or business, you will need to show a valid I-551 card in order to be readmitted as a lawful permanent resident. Under the 1996 Immigration Act, however, any lawful permanent resident leaving the United States for six months or more is subject to forfeiture of his or her lawful permanent resident status.

SAMPLE 1
FORM I-131 APPLICATION FOR TRAVEL DOCUMENT

U.S. Department of Justice
Immigration and Naturalization Service

OMB No. 1115-0005
Application for Travel Document

START HERE - Please Type or Print

Part 1. Information about you.

| Family Name AGU | Given Name Sharon | Middle Initial D. |

Address - C/O N/A

Street # and Name 2303 One Union Square | Apt. # None

City Seattle | State or Province Washington

Country King | Zip/Postal Code 98101

Date of birth (month/day/year) 6-12-71 | Country of Birth England

Social Security # 822-23-9087 | A # 92-867-098

Part 2. Application Type (check one).

a. ☒ I am a permanent resident or conditional resident of the United States and I am applying for a Reentry Permit.

b. ☐ I now hold U.S. refugee or asylee status and I am applying for a Refugee Travel Document.

c. ☐ I am a permanent resident as a direct result of refugee or asylee status, and am applying for a Refugee Travel Document.

d. ☐ I am applying for an Advance Parole to allow me to return to the U.S. after temporary foreign travel.

e. ☐ I am outside the U.S. and am applying for an Advance Parole.

f. ☐ I am applying for an Advance Parole for another person who is outside the U.S. *Give the following information about that person:*

Family Name N/A | Given Name | Middle Initial

Date of birth (month/day/year) | Country of Birth

Foreign Address - C/O

Street # and Name | Apt. #

City | State or Province

Country | Zip/Postal Code

Part 3. Processing Information

Date of Intended departure (Month/Day/Year) 8-24-02 | Expected length of trip 6 months

Are you, or any person included in this application, now in exclusion or deportation proceedings?
☒ No   ☐ Yes, at (give office name)

If applying for an Advance Parole Document, skip to Part 7.

Have you ever been issued a Reentry Permit or Refugee Travel Document?
☒ No   ☐ Yes, (give the following for the last document issued to you)

Date Issued | Disposition (attached, lost, etc.)

Form I-131 (Rev. 12/10/91) N

Continued on back.

FOR INS USE ONLY

Returned | Receipt

Resubmitted

Reloc Sent

Reloc Rec'd

☐ Applicant Interviewed on

Document Issued
☐ Reentry Permit
☐ Refugee Travel Document
☐ Single Advance Parole
☐ Multiple Advance Parole
Validity to

If Reentry Permit or Refugee Travel Document
☐ Mail to Address in Part 2
☐ Mail to American Consulate
☐ Mail to INS overseas office
AT

Remarks:
☐ Document hand delivered
On | By

Action Block

To Be Completed by
Attorney or Representative, if any
☒ Fill in Box if G-28 is attached to represent the applicant

VOLAG# SEA 0000 05

ATTY State License # WSBA # 170

Part 3. Processing Information. (continued)

Where do you want this travel document sent? (check one)

a. ☒ Address in Part 2. above
b. ☐ American Consulate at (give City and Country, below)
c. ☐ INS overseas office at (give City and Country, below)

City   Country

If you checked b. or c., above, give your overseas address: N/A

Part 4. Information about the Proposed Travel.

Purpose of trip, *If you need more room, continue on a separate sheet of paper*	List the countries you intend to visit.
I would like to visit an ashram outside of Bombay, India. Then I would like to visit friends in Amsterdam and Barcelona.	India, The Netherlands, Spain

Part 5. Complete only if applying for a Reentry Permit.

Since becoming a permanent resident (or during the last five years, whichever is less) how much total time have you spent outside the United States?

☐ less than 6 months   ☐ 2 to 3 years
☒ 6 months to 1 year   ☐ 3 to 4 years
☐ 1 to 2 years   ☐ more than 4 years

Since you became a Permanent Resident, have you ever filed a federal income tax return as a nonresident, or failed to file a federal tax return because you considered yourself to be a nonresident? (If yes, give details on a separate sheet of paper).   ☐ Yes   ☐ No

Part 6. Complete only if applying for a Refugee Travel Document.

Country from which you are a refugee or asylee:

If you answer yes to any of the following **questions**, explain on a separate sheet of paper.

Do you plan to travel to the above named country?   ☐ Yes   ☐ No

Since you were accorded Refugee/Asylee status, have you ever: returned to the above-named country; applied for an/or obtained a national passport, passport renewal, or entry permit into this country; or applied for an/or received any benefit from such country (for example, health insurance benefits)?   ☐ Yes   ☐ No

Since being accorded Refugee/Asylee status, have you, by any legal procedure or voluntary act, re-acquired the nationality of the above-named country, acquired a new nationality, or been granted refugee or asylee status in any other country?   ☐ Yes   ☐ No

Part 7. Complete only if applying for an Advance Parole.   N.A.

On a separate sheet of paper, please explain how you qualify for an Advance Parole and what circumstances warrant issuance of Advance Parole. Include copies of any documents you wish considered(See instructions.)

For how many trips do you intend to use this document?   ☐ 1 trip   ☐ More than 1 trip
If outside the U.S., at right give the U.S. consulate or INS office you wish notified if this application is approved.

Part 8. Signature.   *Read the information on penalties in the instructions before completing this section. You must file this application while in the United States if filing for a reentry permit or refugee travel document.*

I certify under penalty of perjury under the laws of the United States of America that this petition, and the evidence submitted with it, is all true and correct. I authorize the release of any information from my records which the Immigration and Naturalization Service needs to determine eligibility for the benefit I am seeking.

Signature *Sharon D. Agu*	Date 5-11-02	Daytime Telephone # (206) 522-8034

Please note: If you do not completely fill out this form, or fail to submit the required documents listed in the instructions, you may not be found eligible for the requested document and this application will have to be denied.

Part 9. Signature of person preparing form if other than above. (sign below)

I declare that I prepared this application at the request of the above person and it is based on all information of which I have knowledge.

Signature	Print Your Name LAW OFFICES OF DAN P. DANILOV	Date 5-11-02
Firm Name and Address	SUITE 2303 ONE UNION SQUARE SEATTLE, WASHINGTON 98101-3143 U.S.A. TELEPHONE: (206) 624-6868 FAX: (206) 624-0812	Daytime Telephone #

Page 2

2
FAMILY-BASED IMMIGRATION

This chapter discusses how US citizens or lawful permanent residents can bring their relatives into the United States.

There is a numerical visa quota for people who wish to come to the United States as immigrants. In financial year (FY) 1998, family-based immigration accounted for 226,000 of the total visas issued. This number includes immediate relatives, who are included in a numerical quota.

1. WHO IS AN IMMEDIATE RELATIVE?

Immediate relatives are the children, spouse, and parents of a US citizen. A US citizen must be at least 21 years of age in order to sponsor his or her parents. The term *child* (when referring to preferences) usually means an unmarried person under 21 years of age who is a legitimate or legally legitimatized child.

Widows or widowers of US citizens may apply if they submit their petition within two years of their spouse's death and they have not remarried during this time. For the purposes of becoming an immigrant in the immediate relative category, children are defined as natural-born (legitimate), adopted, step-children, or legitimated, and can be sponsored for immigration if they meet all the criteria of the category that applies to them.

When a US citizen parent sponsors a child younger than the age of 21 for a green card, the child is considered an immediate relative. The child can process a green card application without being subject to a backlog.

"Aging out" becomes a concern for children who turn 21 before they complete the processing of their green cards. If the child does turn 21 while in this process, he or she is automatically converted to the family-first preference category as an adult child of a US citizen. The problem with this category is that it is backlogged by several years.

The US Congress recently passed a bill called the Child Status Protection Act. The bill addresses the problem of aging out and means that the child's age would be considered at the time when the Form I-130 Petition is filed, and not on the date that this Petition has been approved by the INS, or the date of the application for Immigrant Visa.

You must prepare and file a separate application for each immediate relative who wishes to immigrate, as there is no derivative status for accompanying members to apply for immigrant visas, as in other preference classifications. There is no restriction on how many immediate relatives can be admitted each year.

2. NON-IMMEDIATE RELATIVES

Non-immediate relatives are admitted into the United States according to a preference system on a "first come, first served" basis, as described below. The list of availability of immigrant visas is published monthly by the visa office of the Department of State in Washington, DC (see Sample 2).

2.1 First preference

First preference visas are for unmarried sons or daughters, over 21 years of age, of US citizens: 23,400 visas are available in any fiscal year, plus unused fourth preference visas.

2.2 Second preference

Second preference visas are for spouses, minor children, and unmarried sons and daughters of legal permanent residents of the United States. This preference is divided into three categories with a total of 114,200 visas available each year, plus any excess over the floor level of 226,000, as well as unused first preference visas.

    (a) Spouses and minor children of legal permanent residents (exempt or subject to per-country limit). Seventy-seven percent of all the visas in the second preference will go to this category. Seventy-five percent of this number will not be subject to per-country limitations.

    (b) NA-3 Visas for children born overseas may be admitted to the USA at a port of entry on Form 181 within two years of the child's birth. The NA-3 Visa is a "way around" the Second Preference Visa Petition processing, which is "backlogged" for serveral years.

    (c) Legalization beneficiaries — spouses and children of legalized aliens (persons granted permanent residence under IRCA and special agricultural workers (SAWs)

    (d) Unmarried sons and daughters aged 21 or over. Twenty-three percent of second preference visas are for this category.

2.3 Third preference

Third preference visas are for married sons and daughters of US citizens: 23,400 visas are available, plus any numbers not used by the first two preferences.

2.4 Fourth preference

Fourth preference visas are for brothers and sisters of US citizens (US citizen sponsors must be 21 years of age or over): 65,000 visas are available each year, plus any unused allocations from the first three preferences. A native-born or naturalized citizen of the United States can petition for his or her brother or sister from any country.

3. THE IMMIGRATION PROCESS

While this section describes the standard process for immigrating as a relative, slight variations in the procedure will arise when the immigrant is a fiancé or fiancée, when the relative has already been deported, or when the relative is suffering from a disease, mental disorder, or defect which results in exclusion.

We will start with the simplest procedure first. As in all cases, carefully read all the forms that you are going to complete and be sure that the information you give is as accurate as possible.

3.1 Form I-130 Immigrant Petition and supporting documents

In order to sponsor relatives to immigrate, the lawful permanent resident or the US citizen has to file a petition. This petition is called the Form I-130 Petition for Alien Relative (see Sample 3).

This form asks the government to let the beneficiary (the foreign relative) have a visa. Supporting documents must be filed by the petitioner, and the beneficiary (the person on whose behalf the petition is filed) is also responsible for filing a Form DS-230 Application for Immigrant Visa and Alien Registration (see Sample 4) and numerous supporting documents.

When filing a Form I-130, certain documentary evidence is needed to establish the relationship between the petitioner (called the sponsor) and the foreign relative (sometimes called the applicant or the beneficiary).

These documents include the following:

    (a) Birth or baptismal certificates for both petitioner and beneficiary if

SAMPLE 2
LIST OF AVAILABILITY OF IMMIGRANT VISAS

AVAILABILITY OF IMMIGRANT VISA NUMBERS FOR: NOVEMBER 2002

FAMILY-SPONSORED AND EMPLOYMENT-BASED CATEGORIES	ALL CHARGEABILITY AREAS EXCEPT THE COUNTRIES SEPARATELY LISTED	MEXICO	PHILIPPINES
FAMILY-SPONSORED CATEGORIES:			
F1 Unmarried Sons and Daughters of US Citizens	15 Mar 99	01 Jun 91	01 Feb 90
F2A Spouses and Unmarried Children of Permanent Residents-Subject to Per Country Limit	15 Aug 97	01 Mar 95	15 Aug 97
F2B Unmarried Sons and Daughters (21-years of Age or older) of Permanent Residents	01 Mar 94	22 Oct 91	01 Mar 94
F3 Married Sons and Daughters of U.S. Citizens	15 Nov 96	15 Aug 92	01 Nov 89
F4 Brothers & Sisters of Adult U.S. Citizens	01 Nov 90	15 Aug 90	01 Nov 81

	ALL CHARGEABILITY AREAS EXCEPT THE COUNTRIES SEPARATELY LISTED	INDIA	MEXICO	PHILIPPINES
EMPLOYMENT-BASED CATEGORIES:				
E1 Priority Workers	C	C	C	C
E2 Professionals Holding Advanced Degree or Persons of Exceptional Ability	C	C	C	C
E3 Skilled Workers and Professionals	C	C	C	C
EW Other Workers (Unskilled Workers)	C	C	C	C
E4 Certain Special Immigrants	C	C	C	C
E4 Certain Religious Workers (SR)	C	C	C	C
E5 Employment Creation (Investors)	C	C	C	C
E5 Employment Creation (Investors in Targeted Employment Areas)	C	C	C	C

NOTE:
C = Current; U = Unavailable; Cut-off – The cut-off date for an **oversubscribed** category is the priority date of the first applicant who could not be reached within the statutory limits. Only applicants who have priority dates earlier than the cut-off date may be allotted a number.

FAMILY-SPONSORED AND EMPLOYMENT-BASED CATEGORIES
UNDER THE IMMIGRATION ACT OF 1990

Following is a description of the new preference system under the "Immigration Act of 1990," as well as other changes in Title 1 (Immigrants) of this Act.

FAMILY-SPONSORED IMMIGRATION
New Categories of Family-Sponsored Immigrants:

F1 -   **1st Preference**
Unmarried sons and daughters of U.S. citizens (23,400 visa numbers + "spilldown" (unused visas) from family 4th preference allocation).

F2A -   **2nd Preference** (Exempt or Subject to Per County Limit)
(a) Spouses and minor children of Permanent Residents (114,200 visas + excess over the 226,000 floor + spilldown from family 1st preference allocation, but at least 77% of the visas must go to spouses and minor children). Exempt: Until the waiting lines for all countries are about equal, 75% of the F2A visas go to those who have waited longest in line, regardless of their place of birth. These are exempt from the per country visa limits. The remaining 25% are allocated to people from all countries in the normal fashion.

F2B -   **2nd Preference**
(b) Unmarried sons and daughters of Permanent Residents (114,200 visas + excess over the 226,000 floor + spilldown from family 1st preference allocation, - 23% of the F 2 visas go to this category).

F3 -   **3rd Preference**
Married sons and daughters of U.S. citizens (23,400 + spilldown from family 1st and 2nd preference allocations).

F4 -   **4th Preference**
Brothers and sisters of adult U.S. citizens (65,000 + spilldown from family 1st and 2nd preference allocations).

EMPLOYMENT-BASED IMMIGRATION
New Categories of Employment-Based Immigrants:

E1 -   **Priority Workers** (approximately 40,000 + spilldown from employment-based category 4 & 5 allocations)

(a) Aliens with "Extraordinary Ability" in Arts, Sciences, Education, Business or Athletics
Requires:
(i) Sustained national or international acclaim,
(ii) Recognized achievements with extensive documentation,
(iii) Intent to work in area of ability, and
(iv) Contribution that would "substantially benefit prospectively" the U.S.
In effect, reserved for the finest in any given field.

(b) Outstanding Professors and Researchers
Requires:
(i) International recognition as outstanding in a specific field,
(ii) At least 3 years experience in teaching or research position. (Does not discuss effect of failure to receive tenure after entry).
(iii) Certain corporate researchers may qualify.

(c) Multinational Executives and Managers
Requires:
Overseas employment with sponsor for at least one year within the three years preceding application, and intent to continue to work for that employer (or subsidiary or affiliate).

E2 -   **Professionals Holding Advanced Degrees (or equivalent) or Persons of "Exceptional Ability"** (40,000 + spilldown from employment-based category 1 allocation):
Requires:
for "exceptional ability," that the alien's presence "substantially benefit" the U.S. Allows the job offer and the labor certification requirement to be waived by the Attorney General. Stipulates that "exceptional ability" requires more than a mere degree or license.

E3 -   **Skilled Workers and Professionals Holding Baccalaureate Degrees, and "Other Workers"** (40,000 + spilldown from employment-based category 1&2 allocations, with a cap of 10,000 for "unskilled workers" - EW category).

E4 -   **Special Immigrants**
Includes ministers of religion and religious workers, certain employees of U.S. government, former employees of the Panama Canal Company and their families, certain foreign medical graduates, retired employees of international organizations and their families, and alien minors dependant on a juvenile court - (approximately 10,000 visas)

E5 -   **Employment-Creation (Investors)**
Includes those with $1 million U.S. investment in capital and who employ 10 or more U.S. persons (approximately 7,000 visas) and aliens in Targeted Employment Areas who invest at least $500,000 and who employ 10 or more U.S. persons (approximately 3,000 visas) (no spilldown).

DIVERSITY IMMIGRATION
Immigrant Visa Lottery Program
DV-1   55,000 visas are available each year from Fiscal Year 95 on for natives of almost every country in the world (adversely affected countries). This is a permanent diversity (visa lottery) program.

THE WORLD-WIDE AND PER-COUNTRY NUMERICAL LEVELS ARE AS FOLLOWS:

WORLD-WIDE LEVEL
Overall Numbers. Introduces an overall cap on world-wide immigration. Transition visas are provided for certain groups in the first three years, with diversity visas coming later.

	Family	Employment	Transitional Diversity	Transitional-LB Beneficiaries	Permanent Diversity	Total
FY 92-94	465,000	140,000	40,000+	55,000*		700,000
FY 95	480,000	140,000			55,000 +	675,000

* Families of Legalized Aliens   + For Adversely Affected Countries

PER COUNTRY LEVEL
The foreign state annual maximum limit can not be less than 25,620

FAMILY-SPONSORED IMMIGRATION. For the first three fiscal years, 465,000 visas are allocated to family-based immigration, and 480,000 visas thereafter. Any unused employment-based visas "spilldown" to the family immigration total.

Immediate Relatives. The definition of immediate relative does not change: spouses and minor children of U.S. citizen and parents are not themselves numerically limited, they are included in the family immigration total until only 226,000 visas remain for the standard family categories. Once the "floor" is reached, immediate relatives are no longer counted toward the family cap.

EMPLOYMENT-BASED IMMIGRATION. Employment-based visas are set at 140,000 annually, plus any spilldown from family total.

they are brothers and sisters with the same parents

(b) Marriage certificate

(c) Divorce papers

(d) Form G-325 Biographic Information for alien spouse and citizen spouse or lawful permanent resident spouse

(e) Two photos (with right ear showing) of alien spouse and new citizen spouse or lawful permanent resident spouse

(f) Evidence of US citizenship or Form I-551 Alien Registration Receipt Card of petitioner (US passports accepted)

If any of the above documents are lost or destroyed, secondary evidence may be presented in the form of sworn affidavits from other people, attesting to the necessary facts and circumstances of the family relationships.

If the petitioner and his or her foreign relative are represented by a lawyer, the petitioner would file a Form G-28 Notice of Entry of Appearance as Attorney or Representative (see Sample 5) along with the petition and the supporting documents listed above.

If the I-130 application is rejected, Form EOIR-29 Notice of Appeal to the Board of Immigration Appeals of Decision of the District Director is used to appeal the decision (see Sample 6).

Note that all of the above documents except the US Citizenship Certificate and the I-551 card may be submitted as certified copies if the original documents are first presented for inspection to an officer of the State Department. Application packages should be submitted to the INS Regional Adjudication Center (RAC) that serves the area where the sponsors live.

The person filing the petition on behalf of his or her relative must pay a filing fee of $130 (cash or US postal money order) when applying for the visa. The beneficiary who files the Application for Immigration Visa and Alien Registration must also pay a fee.

3.2 Form I-797 Notice of Action

After the Form I-130 Petition is approved, the INS sends a Form I-797 Notice of Action to the National Visa Processing Center, which then transmits this information to the petitioner (the permanent resident alien or US citizen), and to the US consulate in the foreign country where the beneficiary will apply for an immigrant visa.

The applicant who desires to immigrate must then contact the US consulate in his or her country where detailed instructions and information regarding procedure will be given.

The instructions are usually provided in the language of the country where the US consulate is located.

As soon as an applicant can comply with all of the requirements for an immigrant visa and notifies the US consulate that all the necessary documents have been assembled, a visa appointment date will be made. On that date, the applicant can apply in person for an immigrant visa.

3.3 Form DS-230 Application for Immigrant Visa and Alien Registration

All applicants are required to establish that they qualify for an immigrant visa by signing *under oath and before a us consul* Form DS-230 Application for Immigrant Visa and Alien Registration. You must fill out this form carefully and accurately but do not sign it until you are actually before the US consul. It is like the covering document that refers to all the other documents filed in support of the foreign relative's application. Every item must be filled out completely. The applicant must have a complete medical examination by a designated physician before applying in person at the consulate.

U.S. Department of Justice
Immigration and Naturalization Service

OMB #1115-0054

Petition for Alien Relative

DO NOT WRITE IN THIS BLOCK - FOR EXAMINING OFFICE ONLY

A#	Action Stamp	Fee Stamp

Section of Law/Visa Category
- [ ] 201(b) Spouse - IR-1/CR-1
- [ ] 201(b) Child - IR-2/CR-2
- [ ] 201(b) Parent - IR-5
- [ ] 203(a)(1) Unm. S or D - F1-1
- [ ] 203(a)(2)(A)Spouse - F2-1
- [ ] 203(a)(2)(A) Child - F2-2
- [ ] 203(a)(2)(B) Unm. S or D - F2-4
- [ ] 203(a)(3) Married S or D - F3-1
- [ ] 203(a)(4) Brother/Sister - F4-1

Petition was filed on: _____ (priority date)
- [ ] Personal Interview
- [ ] Pet. [ ] Ben. " A" File Reviewed
- [ ] Field Investigation
- [ ] 203(a)(2)(A) Resolved
- [ ] Previously Forwarded
- [ ] I-485 Filed Simultaneously
- [ ] 204(g) Resolved
- [ ] 203(g) Resolved

Remarks:

A. Relationship   You are the petitioner; your relative is the beneficiary.

1. I am filing this petition for my:
[X] Husband/Wife [ ] Parent [ ] Brother/Sister [ ] Child

2. Are you related by adoption?
[ ] Yes [ ] No

3. Did you gain permanent residence through adoption?
[ ] Yes [ ] No

B. Information about you

1. Name (Family name in CAPS) (First) (Middle)
GOMEZ-Salas   Jose   NMN

2. Address (Number and Street) (Apt.No.)
12345 State Street

(Town or City) (State/Country) (Zip/Postal Code)
Seattle   WA   USA   98000

3. Place of Birth (Town or City) (State/Country)
Nogales   Sonora   MEXICO

4. Date of Birth (Month/Day/Year)
10/27/1958

5. Gender
[X] Male [ ] Female

6. Marital Status
[X] Married [ ] Single [ ] Widowed [ ] Divorced

7. Other Names Used (including maiden name)
none

8. Date and Place of Present Marriage (if married)
05/05/1998   Seattle,   WA

9. Social Security Number (if any)
123-45-6789

10. Alien Registration Number
#A 000 000 000

11. Name(s) of Prior Husband(s)/Wive(s)
none

12. Date(s) Marriage(s) Ended

13. If you are a U.S. citizen, complete the following:
My citizenship was acquired through (check one):
- [ ] Birth in the U.S.
- [X] Naturalization. Give certificate number and date and place of issuance.
  #2222222   07/04/1997   Seattle,   WA
- [ ] Parents. Have you obtained a certificate of citizenship in your own name?
  [ ] Yes. Give certificate number, date and place of issuance. [ ] No

14a. If you are a lawful permanent resident alien, complete the following: Date and place of admission for, or adjustment to, lawful permanent residence and class of admission.

14b. Did you gain permanent resident status through marriage to a United States citizen or lawful permanent resident?
[ ] Yes [X] No

C. Information about your relative

1. Name (Family name in CAPS) (First) (Middle)
GOMEZ   Maria   NMN

2. Address (Number and Street) (Apt. No.)
c/o 12345 State Street

(Town or City) (State/Country) (Zip/Postal Code)
Seattle   WA   USA   98000

3. Place of Birth (Town or City) (State/Country)
Nogales   Sonora   MEXICO

4. Date of Birth (Month/Day/Year)
04/02/1956

5. Gender
[ ] Male [X] Female

6. Marital Status
[X] Married [ ] Single [ ] Widowed [ ] Divorced

7. Other Names Used (including maiden name)
Maria GALLARDO (Maiden name)

8. Date and Place of Present Marriage (if married)
05/05/1998   Seattle,   WA

9. Social Security Number (if any)
none

10. Alien Registration Number
none

11. Name(s) of Prior Husband(s)/Wive(s)
none

12. Date(s) Marriage(s) Ended

13. Has your relative ever been in the U.S.?
[X] Yes [ ] No

14. If your relative is currently in the U.S., complete the following:
He or she arrived as a::
(visitor, student, stowaway, without inspection, etc.) B-2 Visitor

Arrival/Departure Record (I-94)
0 0 0 ■ 0 0 0 0 0 0 0 1

Date arrived (Month/Day/Year)
01-03-02

Date authorized stay expired, or will expire, as shown on Form I-94 or I-95
07-02-02

15. Name and address of present employer (if any)
none

Date this employment began (Month/Day/Year)

16. Has your relative ever been under immigration proceedings?
[X] No [ ] Yes Where _____ When _____
[ ] Removal [ ] Exclusion/Deportation [ ] Recission [ ] Judicial Proceedings

INITIAL RECEIPT ___ RESUBMITTED ___ RELOCATED: Rec'd ___ Sent ___ COMPLETED: Appv'd ___ Denied ___ Ret'd ___

Form I-130 (Rev. 06/05/02) Y

C. Information about your alien relative (continued)

17. List husband/wife and all children of your relative.
(Name) (Relationship) (Date of Birth) (Country of Birth)

NONE

18. Address in the United States where your relative intends to live.
(Street Address) (Town or City) (State)
12345 State Street Seattle WA

19. Your relative's address abroad. (Include street, city, province and country)
124 Avenue San Pedro Ciudad Juarez Chihuahua MEXICO none
Phone Number (if any)

20. If your relative's native alphabet is other than Roman letters, write his or her name and foreign address in the native alphabet.
(Name) Address (Include street, city, province and country):

21. If filing for your husband/wife, give last address at which you lived together. (Include street, city, province, if any, and country):
12345 State Street Seattle WA USA From: (Month) (Year) 05/2002 To: (Month) (Year) Present

22. Complete the information below if your relative is in the United States and will apply for adjustment of status
Your relative is in the United States and will apply for adjustment of status to that of a lawful permanent resident at the office of the Immigration and Naturalization Service in Seattle WA . If your relative is not eligible for adjustment of status, he or she
(City) (State)
will apply for a visa abroad at the American consular post in Ciudad Juarez MEXICO
(City) (Country)

NOTE: Designation of an American embassy or consulate outside the country of your relative's last residence does not guarantee acceptance for processing by that post. Acceptance is at the discretion of the designated embassy or consulate.

D. Other information

1. If separate petitions are also being submitted for other relatives, give names of each and relationship.
No other petitions

2. Have you ever filed a petition for this or any other alien before? ☐ Yes ☑ No
If "Yes," give name, place and date of filing and result.

WARNING: INS investigates claimed relationships and verifies the validity of documents. INS seeks criminal prosecutions when family relationships are falsified to obtain visas.

PENALTIES: By law, you may be imprisoned for not more than five years or fined $250,000, or both, for entering into a marriage contract for the purpose of evading any provision of the immigration laws. In addition, you may be fined up to $10,000 and imprisoned for up to five years, or both, for knowingly and willfully falsifying or concealing a material fact or using any false document in submitting this petition.

YOUR CERTIFICATION: I certify, under penalty of perjury under the laws of the United States of America, that the foregoing is true and correct. Furthermore, I authorize the release of any information from my records which the Immigration and Naturalization Service needs to determine eligibility for the benefit that I am seeking.

E. Signature of petitioner.
Jose Gomez Salas Date 11/2002 Phone Number 206/555-1212

F. Signature of person preparing this form, if other than the petitioner.
I declare that I prepared this document at the request of the person above and that it is based on all information of which I have any knowledge.
Print Name DAN P. DANILOV Signature Dan P. Danilov Date 06/2002
Address LAW OFFICES OF DAN P. DANILOV Suite 2302 One Union Sq., Seattle G-28 ID or VOLAG Number, if any.

Form I-130 (Rev. 06/05/02) Y Page 2

SAMPLE 4
FORM DS-230 APPLICATION FOR IMMIGRANT VISA AND ALIEN REGISTRATION

OMB APPROVAL NO. 1405-0015
EXPIRES: 05/31/2004
ESTIMATED BURDEN: 1 HOUR*
(See Page 2)

U.S. Department of State
APPLICATION FOR IMMIGRANT VISA AND ALIEN REGISTRATION

PART I - BIOGRAPHIC DATA

INSTRUCTIONS: Complete one copy of this form for yourself and each member of your family, regardless of age, who will immigrate with you. Please print or type your answers to all questions. Mark questions that are Not Applicable with "N/A". If there is insufficient room on the form, answer on a separate sheet using the same numbers that appear on the form. Attach any additional sheets to this form.

WARNING: Any false statement or concealment of a material fact may result in your permanent exclusion from the United States.

This form (DS-230 PART I) is the first of two parts. This part, together with Form DS-230 PART II, constitutes the complete Application for Immigrant Visa and Alien Registration.

1. Family Name	First Name	Middle Name
GOMEZ	Maria	NMN

2. Other Names Used or Aliases *(If married woman, give maiden name)*
Maria GALLARDO (Maiden name)

3. Full Name in Native Alphabet *(If Roman letters not used)*

4. Date of Birth *(mm-dd-yyyy)*	5. Age	6. Place of Birth		
		(City or town)	(Province)	(Country)
04/02/1956	46	Nogales	Sonora	MEXICO

7. Nationality *(If dual national, give both)*	8. Gender	9. Marital Status
Mexican	☐ Male ☒ Female	☐ Single *(Never married)* ☒ Married ☐ Widowed ☐ Divorced ☐ Separated Including my present marriage, I have been married __1__ times.

10. Permanent address in the United States where you intend to live, if known *(street address including zip code). Include the name of a person who currently lives there.*

Mr. Jose GOMEZ-Salas
12345 State Street
Seattle, WA 98000

Telephone number:

11. Address in the United States where you want your Permanent Resident Card *(Green Card) mailed, if different from address in item #10 (include the name of a person who currently lives there).*

Same

Telephone number:

12. Your Present Occupation

Housewife

13. Present Address *(Street Address) (City or Town) (Province) (Country)*

12345 State Street
Seattle, WA 98000

Telephone number: Home 206/555-5555   Office   none

14. Name of Spouse *(Maiden or family name)*	First Name	Middle Name
GOMEZ-Salas	Jose	NMN

Date *(mm-dd-yyyy)* and place of birth of spouse: 10/27/1958   Nogales, Sonora, MEXICO

Address of spouse: *(If different from your own):*   same

Spouse's occupation: **Economist**   Date of marriage *(mm-dd-yyyy):* 05/05/1998

15. Father's Family Name	First Name	Middle Name
GALLARDO	Jorge	NMN

16. Father's Date of Birth *(mm-dd-yyyy)*	Place of Birth	Current Address	If deceased, give year of death
06/10/1917	Ciudad Juarez, MX	deceased	1994

17. Mother's Family Name at Birth	First Name	Middle Name
TORRES	Maria	NMN

18. Mother's Date of Birth *(mm-dd-yyyy)*	Place of Birth	Current Address	If deceased, give year of death
03/25/1924	Ciudad Juarez, MX	deceased	1997

DS-230 Part I
05-2001

THIS FORM MAY BE OBTAINED FREE AT CONSULAR OFFICES OF THE UNITED STATES OF AMERICA
PREVIOUS EDITIONS OBSOLETE

Page 1 of 4

19. List Names, Dates and Places of Birth, and Addresses of ALL Children.

NAME	DATE (mm-dd-yyyy)	PLACE OF BIRTH	ADDRESS (If different from your own)
NONE			

20. List below all places you have lived for at least six months since reaching the age of 16, including places in your country of nationality. Begin with your present residence.

CITY OR TOWN	PROVINCE	COUNTRY	FROM/TO (mm-yyyy)
Seattle	WA	USA	1/98 – Present
Ciudad Juarez	Chihuahua	MEXICO	03/72 – 12/97

21a. Person(s) named in 14 and 19 who will accompany you to the United States now.

21b. Person(s) named in 14 and 19 who will follow you to the United States at a later date.

22. List below all employment for the last ten years.

EMPLOYER	LOCATION	JOB TITLE	FROM/TO (mm-yyyy)
none			

In what occupation do you intend to work in the United States? Housewife

23. List below all educational institutions attended.

SCHOOL AND LOCATION	FROM/TO (mm-yyyy)	COURSE OF STUDY	DEGREE OR DIPLOMA
none			

Languages spoken or read: Spanish   English   French

Professional associations to which you belong: none

24. Previous Military Service ☐ Yes ☒ No

Branch: _____ Dates (mm-dd-yyyy) of Service: _____

Rank/Position: _____ Military Speciality/Occupation: _____

25. List dates of all previous visits to or residence in the United States. (If never, write "never") Give type of visa status, if known. Give INS "A" number if any.

FROM/TO (mm-yyyy)	LOCATION	TYPE OF VISA	"A" NO. (If known)
01/02/1998 Present	Seattle, WA USA	B-2	n/a

SIGNATURE OF APPLICANT *Maria Gomez*   DATE (mm-dd-yyyy)

Privacy Act and Paperwork Reduction Act Statements

The information asked for on this form is requested pursuant to Section 222 of the Immigration and Nationality Act. The U.S. Department of State uses the facts you provide on this form primarily to determine your classification and eligibility for a U.S. immigrant visa. Individuals who fail to submit this form or who do not provide all the requested information may be denied a U.S. immigrant visa. If you are issued an immigrant visa and are subsequently admitted to the United States as an immigrant, the Immigration and Naturalization Service will use the information on this form to issue you a Permanent Resident Card, and, if you so indicate, the Social Security Administration will use the information to issue you a social security number and card.

*Public reporting burden for this collection of information is estimated to average 1 hour per response, including time required for searching existing data sources, gathering the necessary data, providing the information required, and reviewing the final collection. In accordance with 5 CFR 1320 5(b), persons are not required to respond to the collection of this information unless this form displays a currently valid OMB control number. Send comments on the accuracy of this estimate of the burden and recommendations for reducing it to: U.S. Department of State (A/RPS/DIR) Washington, D.C. 20520.

DS-230 Part I

Page 2 of 4

U.S. Department of State

APPLICATION FOR IMMIGRANT VISA AND ALIEN REGISTRATION

OMB APPROVAL NO. 1405-0015
EXPIRES: 05/31/2004
ESTIMATED BURDEN: 1 HOUR*

PART II - SWORN STATEMENT

INSTRUCTIONS: Complete one copy of this form for yourself and each member of your family, regardless of age, who will immigrate with you. Please print or type your answers to all questions. Mark questions that are Not Applicable with "N/A". If there is insufficient room on the form, answer on a separate sheet using the same numbers that appear on the form. Attach any additional sheets to this form. The fee should be paid in United States dollars or local currency equivalent, or by bank draft.

WARNING: Any false statement or concealment of a material fact may result in your permanent exclusion from the United States. Even if you are issued an immigrant visa and are subsequently admitted to the United States, providing false information on this form could be grounds for your prosecution and/or deportation.

This form (DS-230 PART II), together with Form DS-230 PART I, constitutes the complete Application for Immigrant Visa and Alien Registration.

26. Family Name	First Name	Middle Name
GOMEZ	Maria	NMN

27. Other Names Used or Aliases (If married woman, give maiden name)

Maria GALLARDO (maiden name)

28. Full Name in Native Alphabet (If Roman letters not used)

29. Name and Address of Petitioner

Jose GOMEZ-Salas
12345 State Street
Seattle,   WA   98000

Telephone number:

30. United States laws governing the issuance of visas require each applicant to state whether or not he or she is a member of any class of individuals excluded from admission into the United States. The excludable classes are described below in general terms. You should read carefully the following list and answer YES or NO to each category. The answers you give will assist the consular officer to reach a decision on your eligibility to receive a visa.

EXCEPT AS OTHERWISE PROVIDED BY LAW, ALIENS WITHIN THE FOLLOWING CLASSIFICATIONS ARE INELIGIBLE TO RECEIVE A VISA. DO ANY OF THE FOLLOWING CLASSES APPLY TO YOU?

a. An alien who has a communicable disease of public health significance; who has failed to present documentation of having received vaccinations in accordance with U.S. law; who has or has had a physical or mental disorder that poses or is likely to pose a threat to the safety ☐ Yes ☒ No

b. An alien convicted of, or who admits having committed, a crime involving moral turpitude or violation of any law relating to a controlled substance or who is the spouse, son or daughter of such a trafficker who knowingly has benefited from the trafficking activities in the past five years; who has been convicted of 2 or more offenses for which the aggregate sentences were 5 years or more; who is coming to the United States to engage in prostitution or commercialized vice or who has engaged in prostitution or procuring within the past 10 years; who is or has been an illicit trafficker in any controlled substance; who has committed a serious criminal offense in the United States and who has asserted immunity from prosecution; who, while serving as a foreign government official and within the previous 24-month period, was responsible for or directly carried out particularly severe violations of religious freedom; or whom the President has identified as a person who plays a significant role in a severe form of trafficking in persons, who otherwise has knowingly aided, abetted, assisted or colluded with such a trafficker in severe forms of trafficking in persons, or who is the spouse, son or daughter of such a trafficker who knowingly has benefited from the trafficking activities within the past five years. ☐ Yes ☒ No

c. An alien who seeks to enter the United States to engage in espionage, sabotage, export control violations, terrorist activities, the overthrow of the Government of the United States or other unlawful activity; who is a member of or affiliated with the Communist or other totalitarian party; who participated in Nazi persecutions or genocide; who has engaged in genocide; or who is a member or representative of a terrorist organization as currently designated by the U.S. Secretary of State. ☐ Yes ☒ No

d. An alien who is likely to become a public charge. ☐ Yes ☒ No

e. An alien who seeks to enter for the purpose of performing skilled or unskilled labor who has not been certified by the Secretary of Labor; who is a graduate of a foreign medical school seeking to perform medical services who has not passed the NBME exam or its equivalent; or who is a health care worker seeking to perform such work without a certificate from the CGFNS or from an equivalent approved independent credentialing organization. ☐ Yes ☒ No

f. An alien who failed to attend a hearing on deportation or inadmissibility within the last 5 years; who seeks or has sought a visa, entry into the United States, or any immigration benefit by fraud or misrepresentation; who knowingly assisted any other alien to enter or try to enter the United States in violation of law; who, after November 30, 1996, attended in student (F) visa status a U.S. public elementary school or who attended a U.S. public secondary school without reimbursing the school; or who is subject to a civil penalty under INA 274C. ☐ Yes ☒ No

Privacy Act and Paperwork Reduction Act Statements

DS-230 Part II   PREVIOUS EDITIONS OBSOLETE   Page 3 of 4

g. An alien who is permanently ineligible for U.S. citizenship; or who departed the United States to evade military service in time of war. ☐ Yes ☒ No

h. An alien who was previously ordered removed within the last 5 years or ordered removed a second time within the last 20 years; who was previously unlawfully present and ordered removed within the last 10 years or ordered removed a second time within the last 20 years; who was convicted of an aggravated felony and ordered removed; who was previously unlawfully present in the United States for more than 180 days but less than one year who voluntarily departed within the last 3 years; or who was unlawfully present for more than one year or an aggregate of one year within the last 10 years. ☐ Yes ☒ No

i. An alien who is coming to the United States to practice polygamy; who withholds custody of a U.S. citizen child outside the United States from a person granted legal custody by a U.S. court or intentionally assists another person to do so; who has voted in the United States in ☐ Yes ☒ No

j. An alien who is a former exchange visitor who has not fulfilled the 2-year foreign residence requirement. ☐ Yes ☒ No

k. An alien determined by the Attorney General to have knowingly made a frivolous application for asylum. ☐ Yes ☒ No

l. An alien who has ordered, carried out or materially assisted in extrajudicial and political killings and other acts of violence against the Haitian ☐ Yes ☒ No
people; who has directly or indirectly assisted or supported any of the groups in Colombia known as FARC, ELN, or AUC; who through abuse of a governmental or political position has converted for personal gain, confiscated or expropriated property in Cuba, a claim to which is owned by a national of the United States, has trafficked in such property or has been complicit in such conversion, has committed similar acts in another country, or is the spouse, minor child or agent of an alien who has committed such acts; who has been directly involved in the establishment or enforcement of population controls forcing a woman to undergo an abortion against her free choice or a man or a woman to undergo sterilization against his or her free choice; or who has disclosed or trafficked in confidential U.S. business information obtained in connection with U.S. participation in the Chemical Weapons Convention or is the spouse, minor child or agent of such a person.

31. Have you ever been charged, arrested or convicted of any offense or crime? ☐ Yes ☒ No
(If answer is Yes, please explain)

32. Have you ever been refused admission to the United States at a port-of-entry? ☐ Yes ☒ No
(If answer is Yes, please explain)

33a. Have you ever applied for a Social Security Number (SSN)?	33b. CONSENT TO DISCLOSURE: I authorize disclosure of information from this form to the Immigration and Naturalization Service (INS), the Social Security Administration (SSA), such other U.S. Government agencies as may be required for the purpose of assigning me an SSN and issuing me a Social Security card, and I authorize the SSA to share my SSN with the INS.
☐ Yes Give the number _____ ☒ No	
Do you want the Social Security Administration to assign you an SSN (and issue a card) or issue you a new card (if you have an SSN)? You must answer "Yes" to this question and to the "Consent To Disclosure" in order to receive an SSN and/or card.	☒ Yes ☐ No
☐ Yes ☐ No	The applicant's response does not limit or restrict the Government's ability to obtain his or her SSN, or other information on this form, for enforcement or other purposes as authorized by law.

34. WERE YOU ASSISTED IN COMPLETING THIS APPLICATION? ☒ Yes ☐ No

(If answer is Yes, give name and address of person assisting you, indicating whether relative, friend, travel agent, attorney, or other)

LAW OFFICES OF DAN P. DANILOV, Suite 2303 One Union Sq., Seattle, WA 98101

DO NOT WRITE BELOW THE FOLLOWING LINE
The consular officer will assist you in answering item 35.
DO NOT SIGN this form until instructed to do so by the consular officer

35. I claim to be:

☐ A Family-Sponsored Immigrant   ☐ I derive foreign state chargeability under Sec. 202(b) through my _____   ☐ Preference: _____
☐ An Employment-Based Immigrant
☐ A Diversity Immigrant   ☐ Numerical limitation:_____
☐ A Special Category *(Specify)* _____   *(foreign state)*
(Returning resident, Hong Kong, Tibetan, Private Legislation, etc.)

I understand that I am required to surrender my visa to the United States Immigration Officer at the place where I apply to enter the United States, and that the possession of a visa does not entitle me to enter the United States if at that time I am found to be inadmissible under the immigration laws.
I understand that any willfully false or misleading statement or willful concealment of a material fact made by me herein may subject me to permanent exclusion from the United States and, if I am admitted to the United States, may subject me to criminal prosecution and/or deportation.
I, the undersigned applicant for a United States immigrant visa, do solemnly swear (or affirm) that all statements which appear in this application, consisting of Form DS-230 Part I and Part II combined, have been made by me, including the answers to items 1 through 35 inclusive, and that they are true and complete to the best of my knowledge and belief. I do further swear (or affirm) that, if admitted into the United States, I will not engage in activities which would be prejudicial to the public interest, or endanger the welfare, safety, or security of the United States; in activities which would be prohibited by the laws of the United States relating to espionage, sabotage, public disorder, or in other activities subversive to the national security; in any activity a purpose of which is the opposition to or the control, or overthrow of, the Government of the United States, by force, violence, or other unconstitutional means.
I understand that completion of this form by persons required by law to register with the Selective Service System (males 18 through 25 years of age) constitutes such registration in accordance with the Military Selective Service Act.
I understand all the foregoing statements, having asked for and obtained an explanation on every point which was not clear to me.

_____
Signature of Applicant

Subscribed and sworn to before me this _____ day of _____ at: _____

_____
Consular Officer

DS-230 Part II

THIS FORM MAY BE OBTAINED FREE AT CONSULAR OFFICES OF
THE UNITED STATES OF AMERICA

Page 4 of 4

U.S. Department of Justice
Immigration and Naturalization Service

Notice of Entry of Appearance as Attorney or Representative

Appearance - An appearance shall be filed on this form by the attorney or representative appearing in each case. Thereafter, substitution may be permitted upon the written withdrawal of the attorney or representative of record or upon notification of the new attorney or representative. When an appearance is made by a person acting in a representative capacity, his personal appearance or signature shall constitute a representation that under the provisions of this chapter he is authorized and qualified to represent. Further proof of authority to act in a representative capacity may be required. **Availability of Records** - During the time a case is pending, and except as otherwise provided in 8CFR 103.2(b), a party to a proceeding or his attorney or representative shall be permitted to examine the record of proceeding in a Service office. He may, in conformity with 8 CFR 103.10, obtain copies of Service records or information therefrom and copies of documents or transcripts of evidence furnished by him. Upon request, he/she may, in addition, be loaned a copy of the testimony and exhibits contained in the record of proceeding upon giving his/her receipt for such copies and pledging that it will be surrendered upon final disposition of the case or upon demand. If extra copies of exhibits do not exist, they shall not be furnished free on loan; however, they shall be made available for copying or purchase of copies as provided in 8 CFR 103.10.

In re: **Maria GOMEZ**	Date	**06/10/2002**
	File No.	**None**

I hereby enter my appearance as attorney for (or representative of), and at the request of, the following named person(s):

Name **Maria** **GOMEZ**	☐ Petitioner ☒ Beneficiary	☐ Applicant

Address (Apt. No.) (Number & Street) c/o **12345 State Street**	(City) **Seattle**	(State) **WA**	(ZIP Code) **98000**

Name **Jose** **GOMEZ-Salas**	☒ Petitioner ☐ Beneficiary	☐ Applicant

Address (Apt. No.) (Number & Street) **12345 State Street**	(City) **Seattle**	(State) **WA**	(ZIP Code) **98000**

Check applicable Item(s) below:

☒ 1. I am an attorney and a member in good standing of the bar of the Supreme Court of the United States or of the highest court of the following State, territory, insular possession, or District of Columbia **Washington** **Washington State Supreme Court** and am not under a court or administrative agency
Name of Court
order suspending, enjoining, restraining, disbarring, or otherwise restricting me in practicing law.

☐ 2. I am an accredited representative of the following named religious, charitable, social service, or similar organization established in the 'United States and which is so recognized by the Board:

☐ 3. I am associated with _____
the attorney of record who previously filed a notice of appearance in this case and my appearance is at his request. *(If you check this item, also check item 1 or 2 whichever is appropriate.)*

☒ 4. Others (Explain fully.)

SIGNATURE *Dan P. Danilov*	COMPLETE ADDRESS Law Offices of Dan P. Danilov Suite 2303 One Union Square Seattle WA 98101-3192
NAME (Type or Print) **DAN P. DANILOV, Esquire**	TELEPHONE NUMBER 206/624-6868 206/624-0812(FAX)

PURSUANT TO THE PRIVACY ACT OF 1974, I HEREBY CONSENT TO THE DISCLOSURE TO THE FOLLOWING NAMED ATTORNEY OR REPRESENTATIVE OF ANY RECORD PERTAINING TO ME WHICH APPEARS IN ANY IMMIGRATION AND NATURALIZATION SERVICE SYSTEM OF RECORDS:
DAN P. DANILOV, Esquire
_____
(Name of Attorney or Representative)
THE ABOVE DISCLOSURE IS IN CONNECTION WITH THE FOLLOWING MATTER:

Form I-130 Petition for Alien Relative

Name of Person Consenting **Jose GOMEZ-Salas**	Signature of Person Consenting *Jose Gomez-Salas*	Date **6/10/2002**

(NOTE: Execution of this box is required under the Privacy Act of 1974 where the person being represented is a citizen of the United States or an alien lawfully admitted for permanent residence.)

This form may not be used to request records under the Freedom of information Act or the Privacy Act. The manner of requesting such records is contained in 8CFR 103.10 and 103.20 Et.SEQ.

Form G-28 (09-26-00)Y

SAMPLE 6
FORM EOIR-29 NOTICE OF APPEAL TO THE BOARD OF IMMIGRATION
APPEALS OF DECISION OF DISTRICT DIRECTOR

NOTICE OF APPEAL TO THE BOARD OF IMMIGRATION APPEALS
OF DECISION OF DISTRICT DIRECTOR

In the Matter:

JONESS, Roberto L., Bene.
JONESS, Samantha L., Pet.

Fee Stamp

File Number: A 00   —   000   —   000

1. I hereby appeal to the Board of Immigration Appeals from the decision of the District Director, ___Nebraska Service Center___ District, dated ___03/12/200-___ , in the above entitled case.

2. Specify reasons for this appeal and continue on separate sheets if necessary. If the factual or legal basis for the appeal is not sufficiently described the appeal may be summarily dismissed.

3. I ☐ do ☒ do not desire oral argument before the Board of Immigration Appeals in Falls Church, Virginia.

4. I ☒ am ☐ am not <u>filing a separate written brief or statement.</u>

Samantha Joness
Petitioner

Dan P. Danilov
Signature of Appellant
(or attorney or representative)

DAN P. DANILOV, Esquire
(print or type name)

___03/17/200-___
Date

Law Offices of Dan P. Danilov

Suite 2303 One Union Square

Seattle,   WA 98101-3192
Address *(number, street, city, state, Zip code)*

FORM EOIR-29
JAN. 89

INSTRUCTIONS

1. **Filing.** This notice of appeal must be filed with the Office of the Immigration and Naturalization Service (INS) having administrative control over the Record of Proceeding within 15 calendar days *(or 18 calendar days if mailed)* after service of the decision of the District Director. The Notice of Appeal is not to be forwarded directly to the Board of Immigration Appeals (BIA).

2. **Fees.** A fee of one hundred and ten dollars *($110)* must be paid for filing this appeal. It cannot be refunded regardless of the action taken on the appeal. *(Only a single fee need be paid if two or more persons are covered by a single decision.)* DO NOT MAIL CASH. ALL FEES MUST BE SUBMITTED IN THE EXACT AMOUNT. Payment by check or money order must be drawn on a bank or other institution located in the United States and be payable in United States Currency. If appellant resides in Guam, check or money order must be payable to the "Treasurer of Guam." If appellant resides in the Virgin Islands, checks or money order must be payable to the "Commissioner of Finance of the Virgin Islands." All other appellants must make the check or money order payable to the "Treasurer of the United States." When check is drawn on account of a person other than the appellant, the name and "A" number of the appellant must be entered on the face of the check. If appeal is submitted from outside the United States, remittance may be made by bank international money order or foregoing draft drawn on a financial institution in the United States and payable to the "Treasurer of the United States" in United States currency. Personal checks are accepted subject to collectibility. An uncollected check will render the appeal form and any document issued pursuant thereto invalid.

3. **Counsel.** In presenting and prosecuting this appeal, the INS may be represented by appropriate counsel. An appellant may be represented at no expense to the Government by counsel or other duly authorized representative. A separate notice of appearance must be filed with this notice of appeal.

4. **Briefs.** When a brief is filed, it shall be submitted to the Office of the Immigration and Naturalization Service having administrative control over the Record of Proceeding in this matter within the time designated by the District Director. A copy shall be served on the opposing party. The District Director, or the BIA, for good cause, may extend the time of filing a brief or reply brief. The BIA in its discretion may authorize the filing of briefs with it, in which event the opposing party shall be allowed a specified time to respond.

5. **Oral argument.** No personal appearance by the appellant or counsel is required. The BIA will consider every case on the record submitted, whether or not oral representations are made. Oral argument may be requested. If approved, oral argument in any case should not extend beyond fifteen *(15)* minutes, unless additional time is granted by the BIA pursuant to a request made in advance of the hearing. No interpreters are furnished by the Government for the argument before the BIA.

   An appellant will not be released from detention or permitted to enter the United States to present oral argument to the BIA personally. The appellant, however, may make arrangements to have someone represent him/her before the BIA. Unless such arrangements are made at the time the appeal is taken, the Board will not calendar the case for argument.

6. **Summary dismissal of appeals.** The BIA may deny oral argument and summarily dismiss any appeal in which (i) the party concerned fails to specify the reasons for his/her appeal on the reverse side of this form, (ii) the only reason specified by the party concerned for his/her appeal involves a finding of fact or conclusion of law which was conceded by him/her at the hearing, (iii) the appeal is from an order that grants the party concerned the relief which he/she requested, or (iv) if the BIA is satisfied from a review of the record, that the appeal is frivolous or filed solely for the purpose of delay.

If any of the requirements apply to you, be sure to include the additional information on a separate sheet and file it with your biographical detail form.

3.4 Supporting documents

The Application for Immigrant Visa and Alien Registration is available at any US consulate abroad. Generally, the application must be accompanied by the following documentary evidence:

(a) Passport

(b) Birth certificate

(c) Police certificate

(d) Four photos

(e) Evidence of support or employment in United States (Form I-864 Affidavit of Support)

(f) Proof of Marriage

    (i) Marriage certificate

    (ii) Evidence of termination of any former marriages, certified divorce decree, or certified death certificate, if applicable, with seals.

(g) Medical examination form

(h) Form I-724 Application for Permission to Reapply for Admission, if applicable

(i) Courts records, if applicable

(j) Military card, if applicable

(k) Form DS-230 Application for Immigrant Visa and Alien Registration (see Sample 4)

(l) Certified English translations of all foreign documents

3.4.a Passport

You must have a passport with a validity date for at least six months beyond the date of the immigrant visa. The requirements for obtaining a passport vary from country to country.

3.4.b Birth certificate

You must produce your birth certificate. If you are not in your country of birth and do not have one, contact your country's embassy for information.

In Canada, apply to the Department of Vital Statistics located in the parliament buildings in each provincial capital city. A small fee is charged. In Quebec, a records search is also needed. In addition, you should ask that the certificate include your parents' names. In all cases, indicate that the birth certificate is needed for the use of a US consulate.

In Mexico, all birth certificates must be authenticated by the State Civil Registrar at the central archives in the capital city of the state in which the birth occurred. Two authenticated copies of the birth certificate must be submitted to the consulate along with two certified English translations. The consulate can direct you to someone who is capable of providing certified translations.

In the People's Republic of China, birth certificates may be obtained from the place of birth. They must be authenticated by a US consul.

If you were adopted, you must file two copies of your decree in addition to your birth certificate.

If you now use a name that differs in any respect from the name on the birth certificate, you must submit a notarized statement explaining the reasons for the difference.

If a birth certificate is unobtainable for some reason, substitute documents, like a baptismal certificate issued with the seal of the church, may be accepted. In any event, contact the US consulate before arriving with substitute birth evidence as they may provide names and addresses of where to write for the proper documentation.

US passports are accepted as evidence of US citizenship.

3.4.c Police certificate

You require one police certificate for each member of the family over 16 years of age. Unless otherwise instructed, you must have one for all places of residence (i.e., every city or town in which each person has resided for at least six months since the age of 16).

The certificate issued for your last place of residence must have been issued no longer than six months before the date on which your visa application is made.

In Canada, obtain your certificate from the RCMP, whose central headquarters are in Ottawa. It is easiest to go to your local police station and tell them what you want. The consulate that informed you that a petition from a sponsor on your behalf has been approved may supply you with a form letter of introduction for this purpose.

Your fingerprints will be taken in duplicate at the local police station. You will then forward them to RCMP headquarters in Ottawa, Ontario, along with information concerning all previous addresses.

In the United States, have your fingerprints taken on a precoded chart at the nearest police station and show some identification. Send the fingerprint chart back to the INS or the US consulate abroad for referral to the FBI.

In other countries, see your own embassy or consulate for this information. If you have problems, contact the nearest US consulate.

3.4.d Photos

You must provide three photographs in color (1" x 1") showing the applicant in a frontal portrait with the right ear showing.

3.4.e Evidence of support or employment in United States

A new Form I-864 Affidavit of Support must be filed by the sponsoring US citizen or lawful permanent resident to show that the foreign relative will not become a "public charge" (see Sample 7). Usually, in the sponsoring situation, the petitioner is the lawful permanent resident or US citizen. If the sponsor cannot meet the required income level, another person(s) may be a joint sponsor(s). The joint sponsor(s) has the same liabilities as the principal sponsor.

The new affidavit of support is indefinitely binding on the sponsor after the foreign national beneficiary has entered the United States until the sponsored person dies, leaves the United States permanently, becomes a US citizen, or is credited with 40 employment quarters. See Form I-864 for complete instructions and obligations. The US government is authorized to seek reimbursement from the sponsor or joint sponsors for any public benefits paid to the foreign relative. The sponsor or joint sponsors who file Affidavit(s) of Support must file one or more of the following forms of proof to substantiate the statements made in the affidavit and demonstrate sufficient resources to support the immigrant at 125 percent of the federal poverty level for the sponsor's total family size, including the foreign national beneficiary (see the attachment to Form I-864 for the required income level):

(a) Copies of his or her last income tax return

(b) A statement in duplicate from his or her employer, preferably on company stationery, showing the salary, length, and permanency of employment

(c) A statement in duplicate from an officer of a bank regarding his or her account, showing the date the account was opened and the present balance

(d) Any other information, such as title to real property or a list of bonds or stocks held by him or her that discloses the serial numbers, face value, and name of the record owners

If the person making the Affidavit of Support is married, then the affidavit must

OMB No.1115-0214

U.S. Department of Justice
Immigration and Naturalization Service

Affidavit of Support under Section 213A of the Act

START HERE - Please Type or Print

Part 1. Information on Sponsor (You)

Last Name	First Name	Middle Name
GOMEZ-Salas	Jose	

Mailing Address (Street Number and Name)	Apt/Suite Number
12345 State Street	

City	State or Province
Seattle	WA

Country	Zip/Postal Code	Telephone Number
USA	98000	206/555-5555

Place of Residence if different from above (Street Number and Name)	Apt/Suite Number
Same as above	

City	State or Province

Country	Zip/Postal Code	Telephone Number

Date of Birth (Month, Day, Year)	Place of Birth (City, State, Country)	Are you a U.S. Citizen?
10/27/1958	Nogales, Sonora, MEXICO	☒ Yes ☐ No

Social Security Number	A-Number (If any)
123-45-6789	A00 000 000

FOR AGENCY USE ONLY

This Affidavit   Receipt

[ ] Meets

[ ] Does not meet

Requirements of Section 213A

Part 2. Basis for Filing Affidavit of Support

I am filing this affidavit of support because   (check one):

a. ☒ I filed/am filing the alien relative petition.

b. ☐ I filed/am filing an alien worker petition on behalf of the intending immigrant, who is related to me as my _____ .
(relationship)

c. ☐ I have ownership interest of at least 5% of _____ .
(name of entity which filed visa petition)
which filed an alien worker petition on behalf of the intending immigrant, who is related to me as my _____ .
(relationship)

d. ☐ I am a joint sponsor willing to accept the legal obligations with any other sponsor(s).

Officer's Signature

Location

Date

Part 3. Information on the Immigrant(s) You Are Sponsoring

Last Name	First Name	Middle Name
GOMEZ	Maria	

Date of Birth (Month, Day, Year)	Sex:	Social Security Number (If any)
04/02/1956	☐ Male ☒ Female	None

Country of Citizenship	A-Number (If any)
MEXICO	None

Current Address (Street Number and Name)	Apt/Suite Number	City
c/l 12345 State Street		Seattle

State/Province	Country	Zip/Postal Code	Telephone Number
WA	USA	98000	206/555-5555

List any spouse and/or children immigrating with the immigrant named above in this Part: (Use additional sheet of paper if necessary.)

Name	Relationship to Sponsored Immigrant			Date of Birth			A-Number (If any)	Social Security (If any)
	Spouse	Son	Daughter	Mo.	Day	Yr.		
None							N/A	N/A

Form I-864 (Rev. 11/05/01)Y

Part 4. Eligibility to Sponsor

To be a sponsor you must be U.S. citizen or national or lawful permanent resident. If you are not the petitioning relative, you must provide proof of status. To prove status, U.S. citizens or nationals must attach a copy of a document proving status, such as a U.S. passport, birth certificate, or certificate of naturalization, and lawful permanent residents must attach a copy of both sides of their Alien Registration Card (Form I-551).

The determination of your eligibility to sponsor an immigrant will be based on an evaluation of your demonstrated ability to maintain an annual income at or above 125 percent of the Federal poverty line (100 percent if you are a petitioner sponsoring your spouse or child and you are on active duty in the U.S. Armed Forces). The assessment of your ability to maintain an adequate income will include your current employment, household size, and household income as shown on the Federal income tax returns for the 3 most recent tax years. Assets that are readily converted to cash and that can be made available for the support of sponsored immigrants if necessary, including any such assets of the immigrant(s) you are sponsoring, may also be considered.

The greatest weight in determining eligibility will be placed on current employment and household income. If a petitioner is unable to demonstrate ability to meet the stated income and asset requirements, a joint sponsor who can meet the income and asset requirements is needed. Failure to provide adequate evidence of income and/or assets or an affidavit of support completed by a joint sponsor will result in denial of the immigrant's application for an immigrant visa or adjustment to permanent resident status.

A. Sponsor's Employment

I am:
1. ☐ Employed by _____ (Provide evidence of employment)
   Annual salary $ _____ or hourly wage $ _____ (for _____ hours per week)
2. ☒ Self employed __d/b/a Facility Structres__ (Name of business)
   Nature of employment or business __Temporary construction site buildings//fencing__
3. ☐ Unemployed or retired since _____

B. Sponsor's Household Size

Number

1. Number of persons (related to you by birth, marriage, or adoption) living in your residence, including yourself. (Do NOT include persons being sponsored in this affidavit.) — **1**
2. Number of immigrants being sponsored in this affidavit (Include all persons in Part 3.) — **1**
3. Number of immigrants NOT living in your household whom you are still obligated to support under a previously signed affidavit of support using Form I-864. — **0**
4. Number of persons who are otherwise dependent on you, as claimed in your tax return for the most recent tax year. — **0**
5. Total household size. (Add lines 1 through 4.) **Total 2**

List persons below who are included in lines 1 or 3 for whom you previously have submitted INS Form I-864, if your support obligation has not terminated.
(If additional space is needed, use additional paper)

Name	A-Number	Date Affidavit of Support Signed	Relationship
None	N/A	N/A	N/A

Form I-864 (Rev. 11/05/01)Y Page 2

Part 4. Eligibility to Sponsor   *(Continued)*

C. Sponsor's Annual Household Income

Enter total unadjusted income from your Federal income tax return for the most recent tax year below. If you last filed a joint income tax return but are using only your *own* income to qualify, list total earnings from your W-2 Forms, *or, if* necessary to reach the required income for your household size, include income from other sources listed on your tax return. If your *individual* income does not meet the income requirement for your household size, you may also list total income for anyone related to you by birth, marriage, or adoption currently living with you in your residence if they have lived in your residence for the previous 6 months, or any person shown as a dependent on your Federal income tax return for the most recent tax year, even if not living in the household. For their income to be considered, household members or dependents must be willing to make their income available for support of the sponsored immigrant(s) and to complete and sign Form I-864A, Contract Between Sponsor and Household Member. A sponsored immigrant/household member only need complete Form I-864A if his or her income will be used to determine your ability to support a spouse and/or children immigrating with him or her.

You must attach evidence of current employment and copies of income tax returns as filed with the IRS for the most recent 3 tax years for yourself and all persons whose income is listed below. See "Required Evidence" in Instructions. Income from all 3 years will be considered in determining your ability to support the immigrant(s) you are sponsoring.

☐ I filed a single/separate tax return for the most recent tax year.
☒ I filed a joint return for the most recent tax year which includes only my own income.
☐ I filed a joint return for the most recent tax year which includes income for my spouse and myself.
    ☐ I am submitting documentation of my individual income (Form W-2 and 1099).
    ☐ I am qualifying using my spouse's income; my spouse is submitting a Form I-864A.

Indicate most recent tax year	2002 *(tax year)*
Sponsor's individual income	$ 225,000
or	
Sponsor and spouse's combined income *(If spouse's income is to be considered, spouse must submit Form I-864A.)*	$
Income of other qualifying persons. *(List names; include spouse if applicable. Each person must complete Form I-864A.)*	
_____	$
_____	$
_____	$
Total Household Income	$ 225,000

Explain on separate sheet of paper if you or any of the above listed individuals are submitting Federal income tax returns for fewer than 3 years, or if other explanation of income, employment, or evidence is necessary.

D. Determination of Eligibility Based on Income

1.   ☒ I am subject to the 125 percent of poverty line requirement for sponsors.
     ☐ I am subject to the 100 percent of poverty line requirement for sponsors on active duty in the U.S. Armed Forces sponsoring their spouse or child.
2.   Sponsor's total household size, from Part 4.B., line 5   **2**   .
3.   Minimum income requirement from the Poverty Guidelines chart for the year of   **2002**   is $ **14,925** for this household size.   *(year)*

If you are currently employed and your household income for your household size is equal to or greater than the applicable poverty line requirement (from line D.3.), you do not need to list assets (Part 4.E. and 5) or have a joint sponsor (Part 6) unless you are requested to do so by a Consular or Immigration Officer. You may skip to Part 7, Use of the Affidavit of Support to Overcome Public Charge Ground of Admissibility **Otherwise, you should continue with Part 4.E.**

Part 4. Eligibility to Sponsor   *(Continued)*

E. Sponsor's Assets and Liabilities

Your assets and those of your qualifying household members and dependents may be used to demonstrate ability to maintain an income at or above 125 percent (or 100 percent, if applicable) of the poverty line *if* they are available for the support of the sponsored immigrant(s) and can readily be converted into cash within 1 year. The household member, other than the immigrant(s) you are sponsoring, must complete and sign Form I-864A, Contract Between Sponsor and Household Member. List the cash value of each asset *after* any debts or liens are subtracted. Supporting evidence must be attached to establish location, ownership, date of acquisition, and value of each asset listed, including any liens and liabilities related to each asset listed. See "Evidence of Assets" in Instructions.

Type of Asset	Cash Value of Assets *(Subtract any debts)*
Saving deposits	$ 30000
Stocks, bonds, certificates of deposit	$ 100000
Life insurance cash value	$ 50000
Real estate	$ 300000
Other *(specify)*	$
Total Cash Value of Assets	$ 480000

Part 5. Immigrant's Assets and Offsetting Liabilities

The sponsored immigrant's assets may also be used in support of your ability to maintain income at or above 125 percent of the poverty line   *if* the assets are or will be available in the United States for the support of the sponsored immigrant(s) and can readily be converted into cash within 1 year.

The sponsored immigrant should provide information on his or her assets in a format similar to part 4.E. above. Supporting evidence must be attached to establish location, ownership, and value of each asset listed, including any liens and liabilities for each asset listed. See "Evidence of Assets" in Instructions.

Part 6. Joint Sponsors

If household income and assets do not meet the appropriate poverty line for your household size, a joint sponsor is required. There may be more than one joint sponsor, but each joint sponsor must individually meet the 125 percent of poverty line requirement based on his or her household income and/or assets, including any assets of the sponsored immigrant. By submitting a separate Affidavit of Support under Section 213A of the Act (Form I-864), a joint sponsor accepts joint responsibility with the petitioner for the sponsored immigrant(s) until they become U.S. citizens, can be credited with 40 quarters of work, leave the United States permanently, or die.

Part 7. Use of the Affidavit of Support to Overcome Public Charge Ground of Inadmissibility

Section 212(a)(4)(C) of the Immigration and Nationality Act provides that an alien seeking permanent residence as an immediate relative (including an orphan), as a family-sponsored immigrant, or as an alien who will accompany or follow to join another alien is considered to be likely to become a public charge and is inadmissible to the United States unless a sponsor submits a legally enforceable affidavit of support on behalf of the alien. Section 212(a)(4)(D) imposes the same requirement on employment-based immigrant, and those aliens who accompany or follow to join the employment-based immigrant, if the employment-based immigrant will be employed by a relative, or by a firm in which a relative owns a significant interest. Separate affidavits of support are required for family members at the time they immigrate if they are not included on this affidavit of support or do not apply for an immigrant visa or adjustment of status within 6 months of the date this affidavit of support is originally signed. The sponsor must provide the sponsored immigrant(s) whatever support is necessary to maintain them at an income that is at least 125 percent of the Federal poverty guidelines.

I submit this affidavit of support in consideration of the sponsored immigrant(s) not being found inadmissible to the United States under section 212(a)(4)(C) (or 212(a)(4)(D) for an employment-based immigrant) and to enable the sponsored immigrant(s) to overcome this ground of inadmissibility. I agree to provide the sponsored immigrant(s) whatever support is necessary to maintain the sponsored immigrant(s) at an income that is at least 125 percent of the Federal poverty guidelines. I understand that my obligation will continue until my death or the sponsored immigrant(s) have become U.S. citizens, can be credited with 40 quarters of work, depart the United States permanently, or die.

Form I-864 (Rev. 11/05/01)Y Page 4

Part 7. Use of the Affidavit of Support to Overcome Public Charge Grounds *(Continued)*

Notice of Change of Address.

Sponsors are required to provide written notice of any change of address within 30 days of the change in address until the sponsored immigrant(s) have become U.S. citizens, can be credited with 40 quarters of work, depart the United States permanently, or die. To comply with this requirement, the sponsor must complete INS Form I-865. Failure to give this notice may subject the sponsor to the civil penalty established under section 213A(d)(2) which ranges from $250 to $2,000, unless the failure to report occurred with the knowledge that the sponsored immigrant(s) had received means-tested public benefits, in which case the penalty ranges from $2,000 to $5,000.

> *If my address changes for any reason before my obligations under this affidavit of support terminate, I will complete and file INS Form I-865, Sponsor's Notice of Change of Address, Within 30 days of the change of address. I understand that failure to give this notice may subject me to civil penalties.*

Means-tested Public Benefit Prohibitions and Exceptions.

Under section 403(a) of Public Law 104-193 (Welfare Reform Act), aliens lawfully admitted for permanent residence in the United States, with certain exceptions, are ineligible for most Federally-funded means-tested public benefits during their first 5 years in the United States. This provision does not apply to public benefits specified in section 403(c) of the Welfare Reform Act or to State public benefits, including emergency Medicaid; short-term, non-cash emergency relief; services provided under the National School Lunch and Child Nutrition Acts; immunizations and testing and treatment for communicable diseases; student assistance under the Higher Education Act and the Public Health Service Act; certain forms of foster-care or adoption assistance under the Social Security Act; Head Start programs; means-tested programs under the Elementary and Secondary Education Act; and Job Training Partnership Act programs.

Consideration of Sponsor's Income in Determining Eligibility for Benefits.

If a permanent resident alien is no longer statutorily barred from a Federally-funded means-tested public benefit program and applies for such a benefit, the income and resources of the sponsor and the sponsor's spouse will be considered (or deemed) to be the income and resources of the sponsored immigrant in determining the immigrant's eligibility for Federal means-tested public benefits. Any State or local government may also choose to consider (or deem) the income and resources of the sponsor and the sponsor's spouse to be the income and resources of the immigrant for the purposes of determining eligibility for their means-tested public benefits. The attribution of the income and resources of the sponsor and the sponsor's spouse to the immigrant will continue until the immigrant becomes a U.S. citizen or has worked or can be credited with 40 qualifying quarters of work, provided that the immigrant or the worker crediting the quarters to the immigrant has not received any Federal means-tested public benefit during any creditable quarter for any period after December 31, 1996.

> *I understand that, under section 213A of the Immigration and Nationality Act (the Act), as amended, this affidavit of support constitutes a contract between me and the U.S. Government. This contract is designed to protect the United States Government, and State and local government agencies or private entities that provide means-tested public benefits, from having to pay benefits to or on behalf of the sponsored immigrant(s), for as long as I am obligated to support them under this affidavit of support. I understand that the sponsored immigrants, or any Federal, State, local, or private entity that pays any means-tested benefit to or on behalf of the sponsored immigrant(s), are entitled to sue me if I fail to meet my obligations under this affidavit of support, as defined by section 213A and INS regulations.*

Civil Action to Enforce.

If the immigrant on whose behalf this affidavit of support is executed receives any Federal, State, or local means-tested public benefit before this obligation terminates, the Federal, State, or local agency or private entity may request reimbursement from the sponsor who signed this affidavit. If the sponsor fails to honor the request for reimbursement, the agency may sue the sponsor in any U.S. District Court or any State court with jurisdiction of civil actions for breach of contract. INS will provide names, addresses, and Social Security account numbers of sponsors to benefit-providing agencies for this purpose. Sponsors may also be liable for paying the costs of collection, including legal fees.

Form I-864 (Rev. 11/05/01)Y Page 5

Part 7. Use of the Affidavit of Support to Overcome Public Charge Grounds   *(Continued)*

I acknowledge that section 213A(a)(1)(B) of the Act grants the sponsored immigrant(s) and any Federal, State, local, or private agency that pays any means-tested public benefit to or on behalf of the sponsored immigrant(s) standing to sue me for failing to meet my obligations under this affidavit of support. I agree to submit to the personal jurisdiction of any court of the United States or of any State, territory, or possession of the United States if the court has subject matter jurisdiction of a civil lawsuit to enforce this affidavit of support. I agree that no lawsuit to enforce this affidavit of support shall be barred by any statute of limitations that might otherwise apply, so long as the plaintiff initiates the civil lawsuit no later than ten (10) years after the date on which a sponsored immigrant last received any means-tested public benefits.

Collection of Judgment.

I acknowledge that a plaintiff may seek specific performance of my support obligation. Furthermore, any money judgment against me based on this affidavit of support may be collected through the use of a judgment lien under 28 U.S.C. 3201, a writ of execution under 28 U.S.C. 3203, a judicial installment payment order under 28 U.S.C. 3204, garnishment under 28 U.S.C. 3205, or through the use of any corresponding remedy under State law. I may also be held liable for costs of collection, including attorney fees.

Concluding Provisions.

I, __Jose Gomez-Salas__ , *certify under penalty of perjury under the laws of the United States that:*

    (a) *I know the contents of this affidavit of support signed by me;*
    (b) *All the statements in this affidavit of support are true and correct;*
    (c) *I make this affidavit of support for the consideration stated in Part 7, freely, and without any mental reservation or purpose of evasion;*
    (d) *Income tax returns submitted in support of this affidavit are true copies of the returns filed with the Internal Revenue Service; and*
    (e) *Any other evidence submitted is true and correct.*

Jose Gomez-Salas   06/10/2002
(Sponsor's Signature)   *(Date)*

Subscribed and sworn to *(or affirmed)* before me this
__8th__ day of __August__ , __2002__
         (Month)   *(Year)*
at __Seattle, WA__

My commission expires on __12/10/2004__

_____
(Signature of Notary Public or Officer Administering Oath)
__Notary Public__
(Title)

Part 8. If someone other than the sponsor prepared this affidavit of support, that person must complete the following:

I certify under penalty of perjury under the laws of the United States that I prepared this affidavit of support at the sponsor's request, and that this affidavit of support is based on all information of which I have knowledge.

Signature	Print Your Name	Date	Daytime Telephone Number
	DAN P. DANILOV, Esquire		206/624-6868

Firm Name and Address
  Law Offices of Dan P. Danilov
  Suite 2303 One Union Square, Seattle, WA 98101-3192

Form I-864 (11/05/01)Y Page 6

U.S. Department of Justice
Immigration and Naturalization Service

OMB #1115-0214
Poverty Guidelines

2002 Poverty Guidelines*

Minimum Income Requirement For Use in Completing Form I-864

For the 48 Contiguous States, the District of Columbia, Puerto Rico, the U.S. Virgin Islands, and Guam:

Sponsor's Household Size	100% of Poverty Line For sponsors on active duty in the U.S. Armed Forces who are petitioning for their spouse or child	125% of Poverty Line For all other sponsors
2	$11,940	$14,925
3	15,020	18,775
4	18,100	22,625
5	21,180	26,475
6	24,260	30,325
7	27,340	34,175
8	30,420	38,025
	Add $3,080 for each additional person.	Add $3,850 for each additional person.

	For Alaska:		For Hawaii:	
Sponsor's Household Size	100% of Poverty Line For sponsors on active duty in the U.S. Armed Forces who are petitioning for their spouse or child	125% of Poverty Line For all other sponsors	100% of Poverty Line For sponsors on active duty in the U.S. Armed Forces who are petitioning for their spouse or child	125% of Poverty Line For all other sponsors
2	$14,930	$18,662	$13,740	$17,175
3	18,780	23,474	17,280	21,600
4	22,630	28,286	20,820	26,025
5	26,480	33,098	24,360	30,450
6	30,330	37,910	27,900	34,875
7	34,180	42,722	31,440	39,300
8	38,030	47,534	34,980	43,725
	Add $3,850 for each additional person.	Add $4,812 for each additional person.	Add $3,540 for each additional person.	Add $4,425 for each additional person.

Means-tested Public Benefits

Federal Means-tested Public Benefits. To date, Federal agencies administering benefit programs have determined that Federal means-tested public benefits include Food Stamps, Medicaid, Supplemental Security Income (SSI), Temporary Assistance for Needy Families (TANF), and the State Child Health Insurance Program (CHIP).

State Means-tested Public Benefits. Each State will determine which, if any, of its public benefits are means-tested. If a State determines that it has programs which meet this definition, it is encouraged to provide notice to the public on which programs are included. Check with the State public assistance office to determine which, if any, State assistance programs have been determined to be State means-tested public benefits.

Programs Not Included: The following Federal and State programs are *not* included as means-tested benefits: emergency Medicaid; short-term, non-cash emergency relief; services provided under the National School Lunch and Child Nutrition Acts; immunizations and testing and treatment for communicable diseases; student assistance under the Higher Education Act and the Public Health Service Act; certain forms of foster-care or adoption assistance under the Social Security Act; Head Start programs; means-tested programs under the Elementary and Secondary Education Act; and Job Training Partnership Act programs.

* These poverty guidelines remain in effect for use with the Form I-864 Affidavit of Support from April 1, 2002 until new poverty guidelines go into effect in the Spring of 2003.

Form I-864P (3/18/02)N

be signed by both husband and wife. If the sponsor making the affidavit is a self-employed businessperson, he or she should submit copies of the income tax return filed for the previous year and the report of a commercial rating concern.

Generally, the Affidavit of Support should be presented to the consular office as soon as possible after it is signed. If more than a year has passed from the date it was formally signed in front of a notary public, the consulate will refuse to accept it.

Information sheets on Form I-864 are available to visa applicants who expect to have their sponsors file an Affidavit of Support. These information sheets should be forwarded to the sponsor so that his or her affidavit will be effective.

If an applicant has a job offer where a relative is either the petitioner or has sufficient ownership interest (5 percent or more) in the petitioning entity, that relative must also file a Form I-864.

3.4.f Proof of Marriage

The petitioner must file a marriage certificate if he or she is bringing in a husband or wife. It must be a certificate issued from a civil, rather than a church, registry. All marriage certificates should have a seal affixed.

In Canada, write to the Department of Vital Statistics for the province in which the marriage took place. Indicate that it is required for US consular purposes and give full details of the date, place, and parties to the wedding.

In the United States, contact the Vital Statistics Department in the state capital for a certified copy of the marriage certificate.

In Mexico, marriage certificates, like birth certificates, must be authenticated by the State Civil Registrar at the central archives in the capital city of the state where the marriage occurred.

If either the sponsoring relative or the incoming beneficiary is divorced or widowed, he or she must present proof of the termination of the marriage. Two authenticated copies of the divorce papers must be submitted along with two certified English translations.

If you are divorced or separated and have children who are single and under 18 years of age, you must present documents showing who has legal custody of the children. If the children are not coming into the country with the parent, you must file an affidavit that says who is going to be financially responsible for the children and who is looking after them. You should also provide an affidavit indicating that, if the children wish to immigrate at a later date, an Affidavit of Support will be provided by you and your present spouse on their behalf.

Mexican divorces that took place after 1971 are not legal in the United States and there are no legal divorces in Brazil, Columbia, Argentina, and the Philippines.

3.4.g Medical examination form

All immigrant visa applicants need to be medically examined at their own expense. This applies regardless of age. If the applicant is 15 or older, he or she must have a chest x-ray and a blood test.

The new immigration law of 1996 requires immigrant applicants to present evidence of vaccinations against mumps, measles, rubella, polio, tetanus, diphtheria, pertussis, type-B influenza, and type-B hepatitis. Special waivers are available for individuals if the vaccination would not be medically appropriate or would be contrary to the alien's religious or moral beliefs.

The report of the examination must be on Form I-693 Medical Examination of Aliens Seeking Adjustment of Status, which is provided by the consulate (see Sample 8). It must be signed by an approved physician. A list of approved physicians can be obtained from your consulate. Usually, the consulate will give you a letter of instructions to your examining physician which will explain what is required.

SAMPLE 8
FORM I-693 MEDICAL EXAMINATION OF ALIENS SEEKING ADJUSTMENT OF STATUS

U.S. Department of Justice
Immigration & Naturalization Service

OMB #1115-0134

Medical Examination of Aliens Seeking Adjustment of Status

(Please type or print clearly)

I certify that on the date shown I examined:

1. Name (Last in CAPS)

(First)   (Middle Initial)

2. Address (Street number and name)   (Apt. number)

(City)   (State)   (Zip Code)

3. File number (A number)

4. Sex
   ☐ Male   ☐ Female

5. Date of birth (Month/Day/Year)
   / /

6. Country of birth

7. Date of examination (Month/Day/Year)
   / /

General Physical Examination: I examined specifically for evidence of the conditions listed below. My examination revealed;

☐ No apparent defect, disease, or disability.   ☐ The conditions listed below were found (check all boxes that apply).

Class A Conditions

☐ Chancroid   ☐ Hansen's disease, infectious   ☐ Mental defect   ☐ Psychopathic personality
☐ Chronic alcoholism   ☐ HIV infection   ☐ Mental retardation   ☐ Sexual deviation
☐ Gonorrhea   ☐ Insanity   ☐ Narcotic drug addiction   ☐ Syphilis, Infectious
☐ Granuloma inguinale   ☐ Lymphogranuloma venereum   ☐ Previous occurrence of one   ☐ Tuberculosis, active
     or more attacks of insanity

Class B Conditions

☐ Hansen's disease, not infectious   ☐ Tuberculosis, not active

☐ Other physical defect, disease or disability (specify below).

Examination for Tuberculosis - Tuberculin Skin Test

☐ Reaction_____mm   ☐ No reaction   ☐ Not Done

Doctor's name (please print)   Date read

Examination for Tuberculosis - Chest X-Ray Report

☐ Abnormal   ☐ Normal   ☐ Not done

Doctor's name (please print)   Date read

Serologic Test for Syphilis

☐ Reactive Titer (confirmatory test performed)   ☐ Nonreactive

Test Type

Doctor's name (please print)   Date read

Serologic Test for HIV Antibody

☐ Positive (confirmed by Western blot)   ☐ Negative

Test Type

Doctor's name (please print)   Date read

Immunization Determination (DTP, OPV, MMR, Td-Refer to *PHS Guidelines* for recommendations.)

☐ Applicant is currently for recommended age-specific immunizations.   ☐ Applicant is not current for recommended age-specific immunizations and I have encouraged that appropriate immunizations be obtained.

REMARKS:

Civil Surgeon Referral for Follow-up of Medical Condition

☐ The alien named above has applied for adjustment of status. A medical examination conducted by me identified the conditions above which require resolution before medical clearance is granted or for which the alien may seek medical advice. Please provide follow-up services of refer the alien to an appropriate health care provider. The actions necessary for medical clearance are detailed on the reverse of this form.

Follow-up Information:

The alien named above has complied with the recommended health follow-up.

Doctor's name and address (please type or print clearly)   Doctor's signature   Date

Application Certification

I certify that I understand the purpose of the medical examination, I authorize the required tests to be completed, and the information on this form refers to me.

Signature   Date

Civil Surgeon Certification:

My examination showed the applicant to have met the medical examination and health follow-up requirements for adjustment of status.

Doctor's name address (please type or print clearly)   Doctor's signature   Date

I-693

The Immigration and Naturalization Service is authorized to collect this information under the provisions of the Immigration and Nationality Act and the Immigration Reform and Control Act of 1986, Public Law 99-603

Form I 693 (Rev. 09/01/87) N   ORIGINAL: INS A-FILE

Medical Clearance Requirements
for Aliens Seeking Adjustment of Status

Medical Condition	Estimate Time For Clearance	Action Required
*Suspected Mental Conditions	5 - 30 Days	The applicant must provide to a civil surgeon a psychological or psychiatric evaluation from a specialist or medical facility for final classification and clearance.
Tuberculin Skin Test Reaction and Normal Chest X-Ray	Immediate	The applicant should be encouraged to seek further medical evaluation for possible preventive treatment.
Tuberculin Skin Test Reaction and Abnormal Chest X-Ray or Abnormal Chest X-Ray (Inactive/Class B)	10 - 30 Days	The applicant should be referred to a physician or local health department for further evaluation. Medical clearance may not be granted until the application returns to the civil surgeon with documentation of medical evaluation for tuberculosis.
Tuberculin Skin Test Reaction and Abnormal Chest X-Ray or Abnormal Chest X-Ray (Active of Suspected Active/Class A)	10 - 300 Days	The applicant should obtain an appointment with physical or local health department. If treatment for active disease is started, it must be completed (usually 9 months) before a medical clearance may be granted. At the completion of treatment, the applicant must present to the civil surgeon documentation of completion. If treatment is not started, the applicant must present to the civil surgeon documentation of medical evaluation for tuberculosis.
Hansen's Disease	30 - 210 Days	Obtain an evaluation from a specialist of Hansen's disease clinic. If the disease is indeterminate or Tuberculoid, the applicant must present to the civil surgeon documentation of medical evaluation. If disease is Lepromotous or Borderline (dimorphous) and treatment is started, the applicant must complete at least 6 months and present documentation to the civil surgeon showing adequate supervision , treatment, and clinical response before a medical clearance is granted.
**Venereal Diseases	1 - 30 Days	Obtain an appointment with a physician or local public health department. An applicant with a reactive serologic test for syphilis must provide to the civil surgeon documentation of evaluation for treatment. If any of the venereal diseases are infectious, the applicant must present to the civil surgeon documentation of completion of treatment.
Immunizations Incomplete	Immediate	Immunizations are not required, but the applicant should be encouraged to go to physician or local health department for appropriate immunizations
HIV Infection	Immediate	Post - test counseling is not required, but the applicant should be encouraged to seek appropriate post-test counseling.

*Mental retardation; insanity; previous attack of insanity; psychopathic personality, sexual deviation or mental defect; narcotic drug addition; and chronic alcoholism.

**Chancroid; gonorrhea; granuloma inguinale; lymphogranuloma venereum; and syphilis.

Form I-693 (Rev. 09/01/87) N

When you arrive at the doctor's office, you must produce official documents (usually a passport) that have your picture attached. After the doctor examines you, he or she will keep one of the three copies of the form for his or her own files and give you two copies to forward or deliver by hand to the consulate where you are going to have your visa interview.

If you are found to be suffering from a dangerous contagious disease such as active tuberculosis, or a serious mental or physical defect, you will be told that other arrangements will have to be made, such as the filing of a Form I-601 Application for Waiver of Grounds of Excludability which requires a filing fee of $195 (see Sample 9) or begin a course of treatment.

3.4.h Form I-212 Application for Permission to Reapply for Admission into the United States after Deportation or Removal

If you were previously deported from the United States, you will have to file a Form I-212 Application for Permission to Reapply for Admission into the United States after Deportation or Removal, and pay the $195 filing fee. If you are applying for entry into the United States after ten years from your removal, it is no longer necessary to file a Form I-212.

You must file all documents relating to your deportation along with your Form I-212. You should also file a statement indicating any special circumstances that the INS should take into account. If you were deported more than ten years ago or if you left voluntarily, this section does not apply.

3.4.i Other documents

Any other documents required by the US consulate, such as fingerprint charts, must be presented.

3.5 Paying fees

When paying fees, do not mail cash. It is best to pay by certified check or money order.

If you are applying from the Virgin Islands, make the check or money order payable to the Commissioner of Finance, Virgin Islands.

If you live in Guam, the check or money order must be payable to the Treasurer, Guam.

All other applicants should make the check or money order payable to the Immigration and Naturalization Service. Personal checks are not acceptable.

3.6 Getting ready for the visa interview

You must be prepared to produce at the interview before the US consul all the usual documents and any that are applicable to a special case. Therefore, it is very important that you come prepared. If you have only one copy of a document (a marriage certificate, for example) make two photocopies and bring them along with the original to the consular officer. The original must accompany the photocopy; it will be returned to you.

Everyone who is to be immigrating with you must bring three color photographs of themselves 1" x 1" with right ear showing. If children's pictures are not contained on their parents' passports, a separate passport for each of them must be produced.

Remember that you do not sign your Application for Immigrant Visa and Alien Registration form until you can do it in front of the consular officer. This form must be completed in duplicate for each member of your family who plans to immigrate with you.

The interview and signing of the applications are done under oath before the US consul. Any false statements can result in the cancellation of the immigrant visa at any time in the future. There is no statute of limitations for perjury.

U. S. Department of Justice
Immigration and Naturalization Service

Application for Waiver of Ground of Excludability

DO NOT WRITE IN THIS BLOCK

Fee Stamp

☐ 212 (a) (1) ☐ 212 (a) (10)
☐ 212 (a) (3) ☐ 212 (a) (12)
☐ 212 (a) (6) ☐ 212 (a) (19)
☐ 212 (a) (9) ☐ 212 (a) (23)

A. Information about applicant

1. Family Name (Surname In CAPS) (First) (Middle)
   DUNSTON Ralph Williams
2. Address (Number and Street) (Apartment Number)
   134 – South 15th Street
3. (Town or City) (State/Country) (Zip/Postal Code)
   Vancouver B.C. CANADA V6J 2X2
4. Date of Birth (Month/Day/Year)   5. INS File Number
   11/16/1951   **A- 00 000 000**
6. City of Birth   7. Country of Birth
   Cape Race   **CANADA**
8. Date of Visa Application   9. Visa Applied for at:
   10/22/1998   **Vancouver, B.C. CANADA**

10. Applicant was declared inadmissible to the United States for the following reasons: (List acts, convictions, or physical or mental conditions. If applicant has active or suspected tuberculosis, page 2 of this form must be fully completed.)

11. Applicant was previously in the United States, as follows:

City and State	From (Date)	To (Date)	INS Status

12. Applicant's Social Security Number (if any)

B. Information about relative, through whom applicant claims eligibility for a waiver

1. Family Name (Surname in CAPS) (First) (Middle)
   DUNSTON Sally Jane
2. Address (Number and Street) (Apartment Number)
   200 Seaside Plaza #4531
3. (Town or City) (State/Country) (Zip/Postal Code)
   Seattle WA USA 98000
4. Relationship to applicant   5. INS Status
   Wife   **US-Citizen**

C. Information about applicant's other relatives in the U.S.
(List only U.S. citizens and permanent residents)

1. Family Name (Surname in CAPS) (First) (Middle)
   none
2. Address (Number and Street) (Apartment Number)
3. (Town or City) (State/Country) (Zip/Postal Code)
4. Relationship to applicant   5. INS Status

1. Family Name (Surname in CAPS) (First) (Middle)
2. Address (Number and Street) (Apartment Number)
3. (Town or City) (State/Country) (Zip/Postal Code)
4. Relationship to applicant   5. INS Status

1. Family Name (Surname in CAPS) (First) (Middle)
2. Address (Number and Street) (Apartment Number)
3. (Town or City) (State/Country) (Zip/Postal Code)
4. Relationship to applicant   5. INS Status

Signature (of applicant or petitioning relative)   *Sally Jane Dunston*
Relationship to applicant   Date
Wife   **11/2002**

Signature (of person preparing application, if not the applicant or petitioning relative). I declare that this document was prepared by me at the request of the applicant or petitioning relative, and is based on all information of which I have any knowledge.

Signature

Address   Date
10/2002

FOR INS USE ONLY. DO NOT WRITE IN THIS AREA.	Initial receipt	Resubmitted	Relocated		Completed		
			Received	Sent	Approved	Denied	Returned

Form I-601 (Rev. 01/16/02)Y

To be Completed for Applicants with
Active Tuberculosis or Suspected Tuberculosis

A. Statement by Applicant

Upon admission to the United States I will:

1. Go directly to the physician or health facility named in Section B;

2. Present all X-rays used in the visa medical examination to substantiate diagnosis;

3. Submit to such examinations, treatment, isolation and medical regimen as may be required; and

4. Remain under the prescribed treatment or observation whether on inpatient or outpatient basis, until discharged.

Signature of Applicant
_____

Date
_____

B. Statement by Physician or Health Facility

(May be executed by a private physician, health department, other public or private health facility or military hospital.)

I agree to supply any treatment or observation necessary for the proper management of the alien's tuberculosis condition.

I agree to submit Form CDC 75.18, "Report on Alien with Tuberculosis Waiver," to the health officer named in Section D:

1. Within 30 days of the alien's reporting for care, indicating presumptive diagnosis, test results and plans for future care of the alien; or

2. 30 days after receiving Form CDC 75.18, if the alien has not reported.

Satisfactory financial arrangements have been made. (This statement does not relieve the alien from submitting evidence, as required by consul, to establish that the alien is not likely to become a public charge.)

I represent (enter an "X" in the appropriate box and give the complete name and address of the facility below.)

☐ 1. Local Health Department
☐ 2. Other Public or Private Facility
☐ 3. Private Practice
☐ 4. Military Hospital

Name of Facility (please type or print)
_____

Address (Number and Street)   (Apartment Number)
_____

City, State and Zip Code
_____

Signature of Physician   Date
_____

C. Applicant's Sponsor in the U.S.

Arrange for medical care of the applicant and have the physician complete Section B.

If medical care will be provided by a physician who checked box 2 or 3, in Section B, have Section D completed by the local or State Health Officer who has jurisdiction in the U.S. area where the applicant plans to reside.

If medical care will be provided by a physician who checked box 4, in Section B, forward this form directly to the military facility at the address provided in Section B.

Address in the U.S. where the alien plans to reside.
_____

Address (Number and Street)   (Apartment Number)
_____

City, State and Zip Code
_____

D. Endorsement of Local or State Health Officer

Endorsement signifies recognition of the physician or facility for the purpose of providing care for tuberculosis. If the facility or physician who signed his or her name in Section B is not in your health jurisdiction and not familiar to you, you may want to contact the health officer responsible for the jurisdiction of the facility or physician prior to endorsing.

Endorsed by: Signature of Health Officer
_____

Date
_____

Enter below the name and address of the Local Health Department where the "Notice of Arrival of Alien with Tuberculosis Waiver" should be sent when the alien arrives in the U. S.

Official Name of Department
_____

Address (Number and Street)   (Apartment Number)
_____

City, State and Zip Code
_____

If further assistance is needed, contact the INS office with jurisdiction over the intended place of U.S. residence of the applicant.

Form I-601 (Rev. 01/16/02)Y Page 2

U. S. Department of Justice
Immigration and Naturalization Service

**Application for Waiver of
Ground of Excludability**

DO NOT WRITE IN THIS BLOCK	
☐ 212 (a) (1) ☐ 212 (a) (10)	Fee Stamp
☐ 212 (a) (3) ☐ 212 (a) (12)	
☐ 212 (a) (6) ☐ 212 (a) (19)	
☐ 212 (a) (9) ☐ 212 (a) (23)	

A. Information about applicant

1. Family Name (Surname In CAPS)　(First)　(Middle)
   DUNSTON　　Ralph　　Williams

2. Address (Number and Street)　(Apartment Number)
   134 – South 15th Street

3. (Town or City)　(State/Country)　(Zip/Postal Code)
   Vancouver　B.C.　CANADA　V6J 2X2

4. Date of Birth *(Month/Day/Year)*　5. INS File Number
   11/16/1951　　A- 00 000 000

6. City of Birth　　7. Country of Birth
   Cape Race　　　CANADA

8. Date of Visa Application　9. Visa Applied for at:
   10/22/1998　　Vancouver B.C. CANADA

10. Applicant was declared inadmissible to the United States for the
following reasons: (List acts, convictions, or physical or mental conditions.
If applicant has active or suspected tuberculosis, page 2 of this form must
be fully completed.)

11. Applicant was previously in the United States, as follows:
   City and State　　From (Date)　　To (Date)　　INS Status

12. Applicant's Social Security Number (if any)

**B. Information about relative, through whom applicant claims
eligibility for a waiver**

1. Family Name (Surname in CAPS)　(First)　(Middle)
   DUNSTON　　Sally　　Jane

2. Address (Number and Street)　(Apartment Number)
   200 Seaside Plaza　　#4531

3. (Town or City)　(State/Country)　(Zip/Postal Code)
   Seattle　WA　98000

4. Relationship to applicant　5. INS Status
   Wife　　　　　US Citizen

C. Information about applicant's other relatives in the U.S.
(List only U.S. citizens and permanent residents)

1. Family Name (Surname in CAPS)　(First)　(Middle)
   none

2. Address (Number and Street)　(Apartment Number)

3. (Town or City)　(State/Country)　(Zip/Postal Code)

4. Relationship to applicant　5. INS Status

1. Family Name (Surname in CAPS)　(First)　(Middle)

2. Address (Number and Street)　(Apartment Number)

3. (Town or City)　(State/Country)　(Zip/Postal Code)

4. Relationship to applicant　5. INS Status

1. Family Name (Surname in CAPS)　(First)　(Middle)

2. Address (Number and Street)　(Apartment Number)

3. (Town or City)　(State/Country)　(Zip/Postal Code)

4. Relationship to applicant　5. INS Status

INS Use Only: Additional Information and Instructions

Signature and Title of Requesting Officer

Address　　　　　　Date

**This office will maintain only a folder relating to the
applicant pursuant to A.M. 2712.01**

AGENCY COPY

Form I-601 (Rev. 01/16/02)Y Page 3

Be prepared to pay about $350 for the visa application and issuance fees for each person. Do not bring personal checks; pay in cash, certified checks, or money orders. Even if you are ineligible to receive the visa, you will not have your visa application fee refunded. These fees apply to each visa; each person immigrating, regardless of age, requires a separate visa and fee.

It is likely that you will receive your visa on the same day as the interview but some applicants may have to return to the consulate at a later date. In any event, do not give up your job or make travel arrangements until you obtain your visa. The visa usually is valid for four months and during that time it is to be used to apply for admission into the United States.

If you are unable to keep the appointment for the visa interview, call at once and make arrangements for a new appointment. Your application and any supporting petitions will lapse if you do not have the interview within one year of the scheduled appointment.

4. SPOUSES

Although applications on behalf of spouses generally follow the same procedures as all other applications for immediate relatives, the following additional information should be read with care.

4.1 Immigration Marriage Fraud Amendments of 1986

This act was passed to try to eliminate a common practice among foreigners wishing to live permanently in the United States: marrying a US citizen to ease their own immigration into the United States. Today, a US citizen who marries a foreigner abroad and wishes to bring him or her into the country must file Form I-130 Petition for Alien Relative, with the Immigration and Naturalization Service (see Sample 3), which will entitle the foreign spouse to enter the country after final approval by the US consulate. However, unlike other immigrants, foreign spouses of US citizens are subject to a two-year conditional clause on their permanent residence. This means a foreign spouse can enter the United States, live here, and work here, but, before he or she can become an unconditional permanent resident, he or she and his or her US spouse must apply to the INS to remove the conditional status on the immigrant visa.

4.2 Circumstances under which conditional status is terminated

The conditional status of a foreign spouse will be terminated if, before two years have passed —

(a) the marriage was officially annulled (other than through the spouse's death),

(b) the INS learns that the marriage was fraudulent and the foreigner paid his or her US spouse to obtain entry into the country, or

(c) the foreign spouse and his or her US partner do not petition the INS within 90 days of the second anniversary of being granted conditional residence, or they do not show up at the INS interview scheduled to take place once this petition has been received (unless good cause is shown).

4.3 Petitioning to remove conditional status

Within 90 days of the second anniversary of the granting of conditional residence, the US citizen and his or her foreign spouse must jointly file a Form I-751 Petition to Remove the Conditions on Residence (see Sample 10) along with a filing fee of $145. If the parties cannot file a joint application, the foreign spouse can still apply and submit information as to why his or her US spouse was unable to comply. This waiver is also filed on Form I-751 and has the same filing fee.

U.S. Department of Justice
Immigration and Naturalization Service

Petition to Remove the Conditions on Residence

OMB No. 1115-0145

START HERE - Please Type or Print

FOR INS USE ONLY

Returned	Receipt

Part 1. Information about you.

Family Name	Given Name	Middle Initial
SMITH	William	B.

Resubmitted

Address - C/O:

Street Number and Name	Apt. #
94 Terrace Drive	#48

Reloc Sent

City	State or Province
Seattle	WA

Country	ZIP/Postal Code
USA	98004

Reloc Rec'd

Date of Birth (month/day/year)	Country of Birth
03/03/1960	Jamaica

Social Security # (if any)	A#
011-02-0333	22 222 222

Conditional residence expires on
(month/day/year)   05/20/1992

☐ Applicant Interviewed

Mailing address if different from address listed above:
n/a

Street Number and Name	Apt. #

City	State or Province

Country	ZIP/Postal Code

Remark

Part 2. Basis for petition *(check one).*

a. ☒ My conditional residence is based on my marriage to a U.S. citizen or permanent resident, and we are filing this petition together.
b. ☐ I am a child who entered as a conditional permanent resident and I am unable to be included in a Joint Petition to Remove the Conditional Basis of Alien's Permanent Residence (Form I-751) filed by my parent(s).

My conditional residence is based on my marriage to a U.S. citizen or permanent resident, but I am unable to file a joint petition and I request a waiver because: (check one)

c. ☐ My spouse is deceased.
d. ☐ I entered into the marriage in good faith, but the marriage was terminated through divorce/annulment.
e. ☐ I am a conditional resident spouse who entered into the marriage in good faith, or I am a conditional resident child, who has been battered or subjected to extreme cruelty by my citizen or permanent resident spouse or parent.
f. ☐ The termination of my status and removal from the United States would result in an extreme hardship.

Action

Part 3. Additional information about you.

Other Names Used (including maiden name):	Telephone #
Bill SMITH	206/555-5555

Date of Marriage	Place of Marriage
02/05/1990	Kingston, Jamaica

If your spouse is deceased, give the date of death.
(month/day/year)   n/a

• Are you in removal or deportation proceedings?   ☐ Yes ☒ No

• Was a fee paid to anyone other than an attorney in connection with this petition?   ☐ Yes ☒ No

To Be Completed by Attorney or Representative, if any

☒ Fill in box if G-28 is attached to represent the applicant

VOLAG#   SEA 2468 13

ATTY State License #
249816

Continued on back.

Form I-751 (Rev. 06/05/02)Y Page 1

Part 3. Additional information about you. (continued)

- Since becoming a conditional resident, have you ever been arrested, cited, charged, indicted, convicted, fined or imprisoned for breaking or violating any law or ordinace (excluding traffic regulations), or committed any crime for which you were not arrested? ☐ Yes ☒ No

- If you are married, is this a different marriage than the one through which conditional residence status was obtained? ☐ Yes ☒ No

- Have you resided at any other address since you became a permanent resident? *(If yes, attach a list of all addresses and dates.)* 05/20/1990 – 11/01/1991 44 First Avenue, #12 Anytown, NJ 07000 ☒ Yes ☐ No

- Is your spouse currently serving with or employed by the U.S. government and serving outside the United States? ☐ Yes ☒ No

Part 4. Information about the spouse or parent through whom you gained your conditional residence.

Family Name	SMITH	Given Name	Janet	Middle Initial	R.	Phone Number	206/555-6666

Address	94 Terrace Drive, #4B Seattle WA 98004

Date of Birth (month/day/year)	03/03/1960	Social Security # (if any)	222-44-9999	A#	30 500 700

Part 5. Information about your children. *List all your children. Attach another sheet(s) if necessary.*

Name	Date of Birth (month/day/year)	If in U.S., give A number, current immigration status and U.S. address.	Living with you?
1. Frederick SMITH	05/03/1984	#A3 009 888 Conditional Permanent Res. living with me	☒ Yes ☐ No
2. June JOHNSON	06/03/1981	Not in United States	☐ Yes ☒ No
3.			☐ Yes ☐ No
4.			☐ Yes ☐ No

Part 6. Signature. *Read the information on penalties in the instructions before completing this section. If you checked block "a" in Part 2, your spouse must also sign below.*

I certify, under penalty of perjury under the laws of the United States of America, that this petition and the evidence submitted with it is all true and correct. If conditional residence was based on a marriage, I further certify that the marriage was entered into in accordance with the laws of the place where the marriage took place and was not for the purpose of procuring an immigration benefit. I also authorize the release of any information from my records that the Immigration and Naturalization Service needs to determine eligibility for the benefit sought.

Signature *William Smith*	Print Name William SMITH	Date 11/02
Signature of Spouse *Janet Smith*	Print Name Janet SMITH	Date 11/02.

Please note: If you do not completely fill out this form or fail to submit any required documents listed in the instructions, you cannot be found eligible for the requested benefit and this petition may be denied.

Part 7. Signature of person preparing form, if other than above.

I declare that I prepared this petition at the request of the above person and it is based on all information of which I have knowledge.

Signature *Dan P. Danilov*	Print Name DAN P. DANILOV	Date 10/2002
Firm Name and Address	LAW OFFICES OF DAN P. DANILOV Suite 2303 One Union Square -- Seattle, WA 98101	

Form I-751 (Rev. 05/26/02) Y Page 2

When Form I-751 is filed, this automatically extends the foreigner's status for six to twelve months, during which an interview with the INS is usually held to determine whether or not permanent residence will be granted.

In the following circumstances the INS will allow the foreigner to remain in the United States as a permanent resident even if his or her marriage is no longer valid:

(a) The foreigner will experience extreme hardship if he or she is removed and this hardship only became manifest during the conditional residency.

(b) The foreigner married his or her US spouse in good faith but this marriage ended in divorce.

(c) The marriage took place in good faith, but the foreign spouse has been the victim of physical or other abuse. Any such claims must be substantiated by reports from clinical workers in the appropriate fields of psychology, sociology, psychiatry, or by other relevant documents such as police or court records.

The foreign spouse can still submit Form I-751 if he or she is not in the United States as long as he or she returns to the United States for the interview with the INS.

4.4 Documents in support of Form I-751

When a couple submits the joint petition to remove the conditions on permanent residence, they must also submit various documents to demonstrate that their marriage is not fraudulent. Some of the documents that will help to establish the validity of the marriage include —

(a) bank statements showing combined assets,

(b) documents showing joint ownership of property,

(c) lease showing joint tenancy,

(d) birth certificates of children,

(e) affidavits of third parties attesting to the validity of the marriage (e.g., from religious leaders, organizations to which both spouses belong), and

(f) other relevant documents such as letters from family members or other personal papers that show that the marriage is valid.

4.5 The rights of a US citizen and his or her foreign spouse

To what extent may the INS investigate a marriage? This question arises when a US citizen and his or her spouse have to appear before the INS at the interview that will determine whether or not unconditional permanent residence is granted to the foreign spouse. The more documentation you submit in support of the validity of your marriage, the smoother your interview will be. However, remember that the US citizen and his or her spouse have certain rights during an INS interview.

The rights and privileges of a US citizen and his or her spouse are as follows:

(a) They are entitled to representation by an attorney at all times.

(b) They must have the opportunity to cross-examine adverse witnesses.

(c) They are entitled to receive prior warning of the Fifth Amendment privilege against self-incrimination.

(d) All investigative reports are to be disclosed to them.

(e) All evidence that the immigration officials will rely on must be formally introduced at the hearing (in other words, it must pass the laws governing the admissibility of evidence before the court will consider it).

A petition to remove conditional status cannot be denied (i.e., the court could not refuse to hear it) just because the couple exercised the Fifth Amendment privilege or because the marriage in question is interracial or interdenominational. In addition, differences in national origin or age are not valid reasons for denying a petition. Removals are normally placed on hold while the petition is being evaluated.

Reasonable advance notice must be given to the couple, setting out the procedure that will be followed and informing the couple of the rights available to them. These interviews are also sometimes recorded on video.

There are also rules for the general conduct of immigration officers. Immigration officers are prohibited from doing the following:

(a) Searching the body or personal property of the petitioner or beneficiary without first making a lawful arrest

(b) Asking for fingerprints or photographs from a US citizen petitioner when there is no bona fide question as to his or her identity

(c) Asking questions about intimate details of the marital relationship (except as to whether the marriage was consummated)

4.6 Legal Immigration and Family Equity Act (LIFE): V and K Visas

LIFE created a V visa to allow spouses and unmarried children (under the age of 21) of permanent residents to live and work in the United States while their immigration cases are pending. This act was passed to bring families together.

To be considered for the V visa, the foreign spouse must have been waiting for permanent residence for at least three years or more from the time the INS received a second preference petition filed on his or her behalf. The V visa is available to all foreign spouses of a permanent resident. Even if a foreign spouse has been living unlawfully in the United States for more than 180 days, he or she can still apply to change status without returning home. Likewise, the spouses of US citizens now can qualify for a new K-3 visa, together with minor children.

4.7 Suppose you want to marry in the United States

When a US citizen wishes to bring in his or her fiancé or fiancée, the person who comes to the United States to marry is granted a nonimmigrant class K-1 visa and any children are granted a class K-2 nonimmigrant visa.

Suppose James Larson wants to bring Vivian Des Vria to the United States in order to marry her. In order to establish a K-1 visa classification for Vivian, James has to file Form I-129F Petition for Alien Fiancé(e) (see Sample 11). If Vivian has any children under 21 who are to accompany her to the United States, they have to be described in the petition.

According to the Immigration Marriage Fraud Amendment Act of 1986, the US citizen spouse is required to have met his or her foreign spouse within two years of applying for an entry visa on his or her behalf. Many petitions are denied if the couple has not met, unless information can be provided to show that this meeting did not take place for religious, cultural, or other legitimate reasons.

James would file the petition with the INS Regional Adjudication Center for his area. The center would look it over and approve or reject it. If the petition is approved, the INS office notifies the National Visa Center, which forwards the approved petition to the US consulate for the area where Vivian lives. The consulate notifies Vivian that the petition filed by her husband-to-be has been approved and that she should go to their offices within four months to pick up all the necessary forms and receive instructions on how to apply for her visa.

Vivian will have to assemble the following documents:

(a) A valid passport. Any children accompanying her should be included on her passport or should have separate passports.

(b) Her birth certificate

(c) If she was previously married, evidence of the termination of the previous marriage unless James' petition indicates that these documents are already filed

(d) A police certificate. If she has lived in any other area for longer than six months after she turned 16, she has to obtain police certificates from those areas as well. If any children accompanying Vivian are over 16 but under 21, she must have police certificates for them, as well.

(e) A medical report

(f) A sworn statement that she and her fiancé are free to marry and that she intends to marry James within 90 days of her arrival in the United States.

Once all these documents are obtained and in order, a consular official will schedule an appointment and interview Vivian and any children who will accompany her to see if they are eligible for a "K1/K2" category nonimmigrant visa.

If all goes well, the visa will be issued for free and is valid for one entry into the United States. Vivian must marry James within 90 days of her arrival in the United States, and after the marriage she may apply to the INS office at their place of residence for adjustment of status to establish a record of entry for conditional permanent residence classification, if she is otherwise admissible.

If a valid marriage does not occur between Vivian and James within 90 days after entry, Vivian must leave the United States or she will be subject to removal proceedings. Vivian may not apply for a change to any other nonimmigrant status, and she cannot apply for any extension of stay. If the couple decides not to marry but Vivian wishes to marry another US citizen, she must leave the country and apply again.

SAMPLE 11
FORM I-129F PETITION FOR ALIEN FIANCÉ(E)

OMB No. 1115-0071

U.S. Department of Justice
Immigration and Naturalization Service

Petition for Alien Fiancé(e)

DO NOT WRITE IN THIS BLOCK		
Case ID#	Action Stamp	Fee Stamp
A#		
G-28 or Volag #		
The petition is approved for status under Section 101(a)(15)(k). It is valid for four months from date of action.		AMCON: _____ ☐ Personal Interview ☐ Previously Forwarded ☐ Document Check ☐ Field Investigations
Remarks:		

A. Information about you.

1. Name (Family name in CAPS) (First) (Middle)
CAMPBELL   Sally   Jane

2. Address (Number and Street) (Apartment Number)
200 Seaside Plaza   #4531

(Town or City) (State/Country) (Zip/Postal Code)
Seattle   WA   98000

3. Place of Birth (Town or City) (State/Country)
Jacksonville   OR   USA

4. Date of Birth (Mo/Day/Yr) 03/07/1957
5. Sex ☐ Male ✔ Female
6. Marital Status ☐ Married ☒ Single ☐ Widowed ☐ Divorced

7. Other Names Used (including maiden name)
none

8. Social Security Number (if any) 000 00 0000
9. Alien Registration Number (if any) none

10. Names of Prior Husband/Wives none
11. Date(s) Marriages(s)

12. If you are a U.S. citizen, complete the following:
My citizenship was acquired through (check one)

☒ Birth in the U.S.   ☐ Naturalization
   Give number of certificate, date and place it was issued

☐ Parents
Have you obtained a certificate of citizenship in your own name?
   ☐ Yes   ☐ No
If "Yes," give number of certificate, date and place it was issued.

13. Have you ever filed for this or any other alien fiancé(e) before? ☐ Yes ☒ No
If you checked "yes," give name of alien, place and date of filing, and result.
n/a

B. Information about your alien fiancé(e).

1. Name (Family name in CAPS) (First) (Middle)
DUNSTON   Ralph   Williams

2. Address (Number and Street) (Apartment Number)
134 – South 15th Street

(Town or City) (State/Country) (Zip/Postal Code)
Vancouver   B.C.   CANADA   V6J 2X2

3. Place of Birth (Town or City) (State/Country)
Cape Race   Newfoundland   CANADA

4. Date of Birth (Mo/Day/Yr) 11/16/1951
5. Sex ☒ Male ☐ Female
6. Marital Status ☐ Married ☒ Single ☐ Widowed ☐ Divorced

7. Other Names Used (including maiden name)
none

8. Social Security Number (if any) none
9. Alien Registration Number (if any) none

10. Names of Prior Husbands/Wives none
11. Date(s) Marriages(s)

12. Has your fiancé(e) ever been in the U.S.? ☒ Yes ☐ No

13. If your fiancé(e) is currently in the U.S., complete the following:
He or she last arrived as a (visitor, student, exchange alien, crewman, stowaway, temporary worker, without inspection, etc.)

n/a

Arrival/Departure Record (I-94)   **Date arrived (Month/Day/Year)** n/a

Date authorized stay expired, or will expire, as shown on Form I-94
n/a

	INITIAL	RESUBMITTED	RELOCATED		COMPLETED		
			Rec'd	Sent	Approved	Denied	Returned

Form I-129F (Rev.11/20/01) Y Page 1

B. Information about your alien fiancé(e) (Continued) .

14. List all children of your alien fiancé(e) (if any)

(Name)	(Date of Birth)	(Country of Birth)	(Present Address)
NONE			

15. Address in the United States where your fiancé(e) intends to live

(Number and Street)	(Town or City)	(State)
200 Seaside Plaza, #4531	Seattle	WA

16. Your fiancé(e)'s address abroad

(Number and Street)	(Town or City)	(Province)	(Country)	(Phone Number)
134 – South 15th Street	Vancouver	British Columbia	CANADA	604/555-1234

17. If your fiancé(e)'s native alphabet uses other than Roman letters, write his or her name and address abroad in the native alphabet:

(Name)	(Number and Street)	(Town or City)	(Province)	(Country)

18. Is your fiancé(e) related to you? ☐ Yes ☒ No
If you are related, state the nature and degree of relationship, e.g., third cousin or maternal uncle, etc.

19. Has your fiancé(e) met and seen you? ☒ Yes ☐ No

Describe the circumstances under which you met. If you have not personally met each other, explain how the relationship was established, and explain in detail any reasons you may have for requesting that the requirement that you and your fiancé(e) must have met should not apply to you. **We met during a sailing regatta in Victoria, B.C. in 1993 – we have spent 6 weeks sailing in Bahamas every year since**

20. Your fiancé(e) will apply for a visa abroad at the American Consulate in   Vancouver, B.C.   CANADA
  (City)   (Country)

(Designation of a consulate outside the country of your fiancé(e)'s last residence does not guarantee acceptance for processing by that consulate. Acceptance is at the discretion of the designated consulate.)

C. Other information

If you are serving overseas in the Armed Forces of the United States, please answer the following:

I presently reside or am stationed overseas and my current mailing address is   n/a

I plan to return to the United States on or about   n/a

Penalties: You may, by law, be imprisoned for not more than five years, or fined $250,000, or both, for entering into a marriage contract for the purpose of evading any provision of the immigration laws and you may be fined up to $10,000 or imprisoned up to five years, or both, for knowingly and willfully falsifying or concealing a material fact or using any false document in submitting this petition.

Your Certification:
I am legally able to and intend to marry my alien fiancé(e) within 90 days of his or her arrival in the United States. I certify, under penalty of perjury under the laws of the United States of America, that the foregoing is true and correct. Furthermore, I authorize the release of any information from my records which the Immigration and Naturalizaton Service needs to determine eligibility for the benefit that I am seeking.

Signature *Sally Jane Campbell*   (Date) 11/02.   (Phone Number) 206/555-5555

Signature of Person Preparing Form, If Other Than Above:

I declare that I prepared this document at the request of the person above and that it is based on all information of which I have any knowledge.

Print Name DAN P. DANILOV   (Address) Suite 2302   (Signature) *Dan P. Danilov*   (Date) 11/2002.
    One Union Sq.
G-28 ID   249816   Seattle, WA 98101   Volag   SEA 2468 13

Form I-129F (Rev. 11/20/01)Y Page 2

3
EMPLOYMENT-BASED IMMIGRATION

1. THE PREFERENCE CATEGORIES

There are a total of 140,000 visas available annually for employment-based immigration, plus any visas that are unused in the family preference categories. There are five employment-based preference categories.

1.1 First preference

First preference visas are for priority workers: 40,000 visas are available plus unused fourth and fifth preference visas. This preference is divided into three levels:

(a) People of extraordinary ability

(b) Outstanding professors and researchers

(c) Multinational executives and managers

1.2 Second preference

Second preference visas are for members of the professions who have advanced degrees or for people of exceptional ability: 40,000 visas are available plus any unused from the first preference.

1.3 Third preference

Third preference visas are for skilled workers, professionals, and other workers (skilled and unskilled): 40,000 visas are available (of which only 10,000 are for unskilled workers), plus unused first and second preference visas.

1.4 Fourth preference

Fourth preference visas are for special immigrants: 10,000 visas are available each year (with a 5,000 limitation on religious workers). Returning US legal permanent residents are included in this preference but are not subject to numerical limitations; neither are former US citizens seeking reinstatement of citizenship. Special immigrants will be discussed in greater detail in chapter 4.

1.5 Fifth preference

Fifth preference visas are for investors: 10,000 visas are available each year of which 3,000 are set aside for the creation of employment in areas that have been targeted by the US government as areas of slow growth. This category is described in detail in chapter 6.

The list of availability of immigrant visas is published monthly by the visa office of the Department of State in Washington, DC (see Sample 2).

2. LABOR CERTIFICATION

All immigrants in the employment-based preferences must obtain an approved Form I-140 Immigrant Petition for Alien Worker before they can apply for an immigrant visa or adjustment of status (if they are already in the United States with legal non-immigrant status). Those in the first preference category can file this form themselves. All others will have to get the form completed and signed by a prospective employer.

Generally, people applying in the second and third preference categories (professionals with advanced degrees or people of exceptional ability and professional, skilled, and other workers in short supply, respectively) ordinarily must obtain clearance from the Department of Labor in the form of a labor certification before they can submit Form I-140 Immigrant Petition for Alien Worker. The Form I-140 filing fee is $135.

There are, however, certain categories of people who are exempt from the labor certification requirement. These people have what is known as Schedule A occupations or professions, which are in short supply in the United States or which would otherwise benefit the country economically, scientifically, culturally, or in terms of education.

People applying for immigration within the employment-based first preference do not need job offers nor do they need prior approval by the US Department of Labor before their visa applications can be approved.

2.1 Getting labor certification

To get a labor certification, a worker has to have a job offer or Schedule A status. The certification is evidence —

(a) that there are not sufficient US workers at the place where the alien wishes to work who are able, willing, and qualified; and

(b) that the employment of the applicant will not adversely affect the wages and working conditions of workers in the United States similarly employed.

All those who need labor certification in order to apply for immigration must submit in duplicate Form ETA 750 Application for Alien Employment Certification, Part A — Offer of Employment, from a prospective employer in the United States and Part B — Statement of Qualifications of Alien (see Sample 12).

Both copies of the two parts of the form, together with documentary evidence, must be filed at the local State Employment Service office for registration and entry into a job bank. After being screened, these forms are sent to the US Department of Labor in the area where the immigrant will be employed. Here they will decide whether a labor certification will be issued.

By the time the Department of Labor makes its initial decision, the employer is expected to have fulfilled his or her requirements. In addition to correctly completing all the application forms for the employee's labor certification, the employer must also advertise the job in question. The employer must be able to prove to the Department of Labor that a legitimate job search was undertaken in the domestic market before a foreign employee was offered the job.

It is not unusual for a labor certification to be denied because certain requirements have not been adequately met. For example, an employer may need to advertise the job further in the appropriate media before a labor certification will be issued. This is particularly relevant in times of high unemployment in the country.

2.2 When labor certification is denied

If the labor certification is denied, the Department of Labor will send the employer a Notice of Findings outlining the reasons for this denial. The employer has 35 days from the date of receiving this Notice of Findings to provide additional information that could change the outcome. If the Department of Labor does not overturn its denial, the employer will have another 35 days after receiving their most recent notice of denial in which to request a judicial administrative review. The case will then be heard by the Board of Alien Labor Certification Appeals (BALCA).

If a worker's labor certification is denied and he or she chooses not to take any of the steps indicated above, the employer may submit another application for labor certification for the same job after waiting six months. The worker can, however, apply for another labor certification for a different job — either with the same or another employer — immediately after the initial application is denied.

OMB Approval No. 44-R1301

U.S. DEPARTMENT OF LABOR
Employment and Training Administration

APPLICATION
FOR
ALIEN EMPLOYMENT CERTIFICATION

IMPORTANT! READ CAREFULLY BEFORE COMPLETING THIS FORM
PRINT legibly in ink or use a typewriter. If you need more space to answer questions on this form, use a separate sheet. Identify each answer with the number of the corresponding question. SIGN AND DATE each sheet in original signature.

To knowingly furnish any false information in the preparation of this form and any supplement thereto or to aid, abet, or counsel another to do so is a felony punishable by $10,000 fine or 5 years in the penitentiary, or both (18 U.S.C. 1001).

PART A. OFFER OF EMPLOYMENT

1. Name of Alien (Family name in capital letter, First, Middle, Maiden)
Jerome J. Johansen

2. Present Address of Alien (Number, Street, City and Town, State ZIP Code or Province, Country)
16505 Meridian Avenue North
Seattle, WA 98107

3. Type of Visa (If in U.S.)
H-1

The following information is submitted as evidence of an offer of employment.

4. Name of Employer (Full name of organization)
Markson Landers and Associates, Inc.

5. Telephone (Area Code and Number)
(206) 455-5555

6. Address (Number, Street, City or Town, Country, State, ZIP Code)
6000 Union Plaza Center
Seattle, WA 98104

7. Address Where Alien Will Work (if different from item 6)
6000 Union Plaza Center
Seattle, WA 98104

8. Nature of Employer's Business Activity	9. Name of Job Title	10. Total Hours Per Week		11. Work Schedule (Hourly)	12. Rate of Pay	
		a. Basic	b. Overtime		a. Basic	b. Overtime
Manufacturer of chemicals and related products	CHEMICAL ENGINEER	40	None	8:00 a.m. 5:00 p.m.	$ 40,000 per anum.	$ NONE per hour

13. Describe Fully the Job to be Performed (Duties)

Designs equipment and develops processes for manufacturing chemicals and related products utilizing principles and technology of chemistry, physics, mathematics, engineering and related physical and natural sciences: Conducts research to develop new and improved chemical manufacturing processes, Designs, plans layout, and oversees workers engaged in constructing, controlling, and improving equipment to carry out chemical processes on commercial scale. Analyzes operating procedures and equipment and machinery functions to reduce processing time and cost. Designs equipment to control movement, storage, and packaging of solids, liquids, and gases.

14. State in detail the MINIMUM education, training, and experience for a worker to perform satisfactorily the job duties described in item 13 above.

15. Other Special Requirements

NONE

EDU-CATION (Enter number of years)	Grade School	High School	College	College Degree Required (specify)
	6	4	4	B.S.
				Major Field of Study Chemical Engineering

TRAIN-ING	No. Yrs.	No. Mos.	Type of Training
	0	0	0

EXPERI-ENCE	Job Offered		Related Occupation Number		Related Occupation (specify)
	Yrs.	Mos.	Yrs.	Mos.	NONE
	5	0	0	0	

16. Occupational Title of Person Who Will Be Alien's Immediate Supervisor ▶ ▶ VICE-PRESIDENT

17. Number of Employees ▶ 0 Alien will Supervise

◀ ENDORSEMENTS (Make no entry in section - for government use only)

Date Forms Received

L.O.	S.O.
R.O.	N.O.
Ind. Code	Occ. Code
Occ. Title	

Replaces MA 7-50A, B and C (Apr. 1970 edition) which is obsolete.

ETA 750 (Oct. 1979)

18. COMPLETE ITEMS ONLY IF JOB IS TEMPORARY			19. IF JOB IS UNIONIZED *(Complete)*	
a. No. of Openings To Be Filled By Aliens Under Job Offer	b. Exact Dates You Expect To Employ Alien		a. Number of Local	b. Name of Local
	From	To		N/A
N/A	N/A	N/A	N/A	c. City and State
				N/A

20. STATEMENT FOR LIVE-AT-WORK JOB OFFERS *(Complete for Private Household Job ONLY)*

a. Description of Residence		b. No. Persons Residing at Place of Employment				c. Will free board and private room not shared with anyone be provided?	("X" one)
("X" one)	Number of Rooms	Adults		Children	Ages		☐ YES ☐ NO
☐ House	N/A	N/A	BOYS	N/A	N/A	N/A	
☐ Apartment			GIRLS	N/A	N/A		

21. DESCRIBE EFFORTS TO RECRUIT U.S. WORKERS AND THE RESULTS. *(Specify Sources of Recruitment by Name)*

Advertisement placed in The Seattle Times for three consecutive days. Notice posted in two conspicuous places for ten consecutive business days - NO RESPONSES RECEIVED.

22. Applications require various types of documentation. Please read PART II of the instructions to assure that appropriate supporting documentation is included with your application.

23. EMPLOYER CERTIFICATIONS

By virtue of my signature below, I HEREBY CERTIFY the following conditions of employment.

a. I have enough funds available to pay the wage or salary offered the alien.

b. The wage offered equals or exceeds the prevailing wage and I guarantee that, if a labor certification is granted, the wage paid to the alien when the alien begins work will equal or exceed the prevailing wage which is applicable at the time the alien begins work.

c. The wage offered is not based on commissions, bonuses, or other incentives, unless I guarantee a wage paid on a weekly, bi-weekly or monthly basis.

d. I will be able to place the alien on the payroll on or before the date of the alien's proposed entrance into the United States.

e. The job opportunity does not involve unlawful discrimination by race, creed, color, national origin, age, sex, religion, handicap, or citizenship.

f. The job opportunity is not:

(1) Vacant because the former occupant is on strike or is being locked out in the course of a labor dispute involving a work stoppage.

(2) At issue in a labor dispute involving a work stoppage.

g. The job opportunity's terms, conditions and occupational environment are not contrary to Federal, State or local law.

h. The job opportunity has been and is clearly open to any qualified U.S. worker.

24. DECLARATIONS

DECLARATION OF EMPLOYER ➤ Pursuant to 28 U.S.C. 1746, I declare under penalty of perjury the foregoing is true and correct.

SIGNATURE	DATE
Warren S. Landers	April 15, 199–

NAME *(Type or Print)*	TITLE
WARREN S. LANDERS	VICE-PRESIDENT

AUTHORIZATION OF AGENT OF EMPLOYER ➤ I HEREBY DESIGNATE the agent below to represent me for the purposes of labor certification and I TAKE FULL RESPONSIBILITY for accuracy of any representations made by my agent.

SIGNATURE OF EMPLOYER	DATE
W. S. Landers	April 15, 199–

NAME OF AGENT *(Type or Print)*	ADDRESS OF AGENT *(Number, Street, City, State, ZIP Code)*
DAN P. DANILOV, Esquire	LAW OFFICES OF DAN P. DANILOV Suite 2303 - One Union Square Seattle, WA 98101-3192

PART B. STATEMENT OF QUALIFICATIONS OF ALIEN

FOR ADVICE CONCERNING REQUIREMENTS FOR ALIEN EMPLOYMENT CERTIFICATION: *If alien is in the U.S., contact nearest office of Immigration and Naturalization Service. If alien is outside U.S., contact nearest U.S. Consulate.*

IMPORTANT: READ ATTACHED INSTRUCTIONS BEFORE COMPLETING THIS FORM.

Print legibly in ink or use a typewriter. If you need more space to fully answer any questions on this form, use a separate sheet. Identify each answer with the number of the corresponding question. Sign and date each sheet.

1. Name of Alien *(Family name in capital letters)*	First name	Middle name	Maiden name
JOHANSEN,	Jerome	J.	

2. Present Address *(No., Street, City or Town, State or Province and ZIP Code*	Country	3. Type of Visa *(If in U.S.)*
16505 Meridian Avenue North		H-1
Seattle, Washington 98107		

4. Alien's Birthdate *(Month, Day, Year)*	5. Birthplace *(City or Town, State or Province)*	Country	6. Present Nationality or Citizenship *(Country)*
May 16, 1953	Oslo, NORWAY		NORWAY

7. Address in United States Where Alien Will Reside
16505 Meridian Avenue North
Seattle, Washington 98107

8. Name and Address of Prospective Employer if Alien has job offer in U.S.	9. Occupation in which Alien is Seeking Work
Markson Landers and Associates, Inc. 6000 Union Plaza Center Seattle, Washington 98107	CHEMICAL ENGINEER

10. "X" the appropriate box below and furnish the information required for the box marked

		City in Foreign Country	Foreign Country
a. ☐	Alien will apply for a visa abroad at the American Consulate in ———		

		City	State
b. ☒	Alien is in the United States and will apply for adjustment of status to that of a lawful permanent resident in the office of the Immigration and Naturalization Service at ———	SEATTLE	WASHINGTON

11. Names and Addresses of Schools, Colleges and Universities Attended *(include trade or vocational training facilities)*	Field of Study	FROM Month	FROM Year	TO Month	TO Year	Degrees or Certificates Received
Gurchen High School Oslo, Norway	General Studies	Sept.	1969	June	1972	Graduation Cert.
University of Norway Oslo, Norway	Chemical Engineering	Sept.	1973	June	1976	B.S. Degree in Chemical Engineering

SPECIAL QUALIFICATIONS AND SKILLS

12. Additional Qualifications and Skills Alien Possesses and Proficiency in the use of Tools, Machines or Equipment Which Would Help Establish if Alien Meets Requirements for Occupation in item 9.
NONE

13. List Licenses *(Professional, journeyman, etc.)*
NONE

14. List Documents Attached Which are Submitted as Evidence that Alien Possesses the Education, Training, Experience, and Abilities Represented
SEE ATTACHED DOCUMENTARY EVIDENCE

Endorsements	DATE REC. DOL
	O.T. & C.
(Make no entry in this section — FOR Government Agency USE ONLY)	

(Items continued on next page)

15. WORK EXPERIENCE. *List all jobs held during past three (3) years. Also, list any other jobs related to the occupation for which the alien is seeking certification as indicated in item 9.*

a. NAME AND ADDRESS OF EMPLOYER

Lundsted and Associates
Oslo, Norway

NAME OF JOB	DATE STARTED Month Year	DATE LEFT Month Year	KIND OF BUSINESS
Chemical Engineer	January, 198–	December, 199–	Manufacturer of Chemicals and related products

DESCRIBE IN DETAILS THE DUTIES PERFORMED, INCLUDING THE USE OF TOOLS, MACHINES, OR EQUIPMENT	NO. OF HOURS PER WEEK
Designs equipment and develops processes for manufacturing chem.	40

and related products utilizing principles and technology of chemistry, physics, math-

ematics, engineering, and related physical and natural sciences: Conducts research to

~~develop new and improved chemical manufacturing processes.~~

b. NAME AND ADDRESS OF EMPLOYER

NAME OF JOB	DATE STARTED Month Year	DATE LEFT Month Year	KIND OF BUSINESS

DESCRIBE IN DETAIL THE DUTIES PERFORMED, INCLUDING THE USE OF TOOLS, MACHINES, OR EQUIPMENT	NO. OF HOURS PER WEEK

c. NAME AND ADDRESS OF EMPLOYER

NAME OF JOB	DATE STARTED Month Year	DATE LEFT Month Year	KIND OF BUSINESS

DESCRIBE IN DETAIL THE DUTIES PERFORMED, INCLUDING THE USE OF TOOLS, MACHINES, OR EQUIPMENT	NO. OF HOURS PER WEEK

16. DECLARATIONS

DECLARATION OF ALIEN ▶ ▶ *Pursuant to 28 U.S.C. 1746, I declare under penalty of perjury the foregoing is true and correct.*

SIGNATURE OF ALIEN	DATE
Jerome J. Johansen	April 15, 199–

AUTHORIZATION OF AGENT OF ALIEN ▶ ▶ *I hereby designate the agent below to represent me for the purposes of labor certification and I take full responsibility for accuracy of any representations made by my agent.*

SIGNATURE OF ALIEN	DATE
Jerome J. Johansen	April 15, 199–

NAME OF AGENT (Type or print)	ADDRESS OF AGENT (No., Street, City, State, ZIP Code)
LAW OFFICES OF DAN P. DANILOV	**LAW OFFICES OF DAN P. DANILOV** SUITE 2303-ONE UNION SQUARE SEATTLE, WASHINGTON 98101-3143 U.S.A. TELEPHONE: (206) 624-6868 FAX: (206) 624-0812

Because of the time and effort invested in a labor certification case, the sponsoring employer would be wise to consider the new, fast-track method of labor certification, called "Reduction in Recruitment" labor certification. Not only is Reduction in Recruitment labor certification much faster than the "slow track" process, a properly prepared case is also more often successful. The problem with the slow track labor certification process is that it can take over three years to complete. Reduction in Recruitment is a greatly speeded up process which, if successful, allows the foreign national to obtain a green card in just over one year from the date the application is submitted. Reduction in Recruitment requests are normally granted where the employer can establish a "pattern of recruitment" spread over six months immediately preceding the application. The authority for Reduction in Recruitment is provided by 20 CFR section 656.21(i), which states:

> The Certifying Officer may reduce the employer's recruitment efforts required by sections 656.21(f) and/or 656.21(g) of this part if the employer satisfactorily documents that the employer has adequately tested the labor market with no success at least at the prevailing wage and working conditions.

An employer who wants to ask for Reduction in Recruitment must do so with a cover letter when the employer files the labor certification application. The Reduction in Recruitment application needs to include:

(a) evidence of the posting of a preapplication notice consistent with the requirements of 20 CFR section 656.20(g), showing that the employer made "good faith" efforts within the six months preceding the application to recruit US workers for the job, at least at the prevailing wage and working conditions, through recruitment sources normal for the occupation; and

(b) any additional information that the employer believes will support the argument that additional recruitment will not be successful. Reduction in Recruitment requests are normally granted where the employer can establish a pattern of recruitment spread over the six months immediately preceding the application.

3. FORM I-140 IMMIGRANT PETITION FOR ALIEN WORKER

After the forms are reviewed and a labor certification is granted, the employer or prospective employer can then file a Form I-140 Immigrant Petition for Alien Worker with the INS Regional Adjudication Center in the area where the foreign worker will be employed (see Sample 13). Keep in mind that having an approved labor certification does not mean that the INS will automatically approve an I-140 petition.

The certifying officer has the discretion to excuse a failure on the part of the employer to comply fully with all the requirements if the officer has determined that the labor market has not been sufficiently tested to warrant a finding that US workers are unavailable and that there would be no adverse effect.

4. FORM DS-230 APPLICATION FOR IMMIGRANT VISA AND ALIEN REGISTRATION

After the Form I-140 Immigrant Petition for Alien Worker is approved by the INS, a Notice of Approval is forwarded to the Transitional Immigrant Visa Processing Center for transmittal to the employer and to the US consulate abroad where the applicant can then file the Form DS-230 Application for Immigrant Visa and Alien Registration for himself or herself and accompanying immediate family members (see Sample 4).

SAMPLE 13
FORM I-140 IMMIGRANT PETITION FOR ALIEN WORKER

<table>
<tr><td>U.S. Department of Justice
Immigration and Naturalization Service</td><td colspan="2">OMB No.1115-0061
Immigrant Petition for Alien Worker</td></tr>
</table>

START HERE - Please Type or Print	FOR INS USE ONLY

Part 1.   Information about the person or organization filing this petition.

If an individual is filing, use the top name line. Organizations should use the second line.

Family Name	Given Name	Middle Initial

Company or Organization **Markson Landers and Associates, Inc.**

Address - Attn: **Mr. Warren S. Landers**

Street Number and Name **6000 Union Plaza Center**	Room

City **Seattle**	State or Province **Washington**

Country **U.S.A.**	Zip/Postal Code **98104**

E-mail Address: **landersw@markson.com**

IRS Tax # **500-56-7009**	Social Security # (if any) **458-98-7890**

Receipt (FOR INS USE ONLY)

Part 2.   Petition type.

1. This petition is being filed for (check one)
   - a. ☐ An alien of extraordinary ability
   - b. ☐ An outstanding professor or researcher
   - c. ☐ A multinational executive or manager
   - d. ☒ A member of the professions holding an advanced degree or an alien of exceptional ability (who is **NOT** seeking a National Interest Waiver.)
   - e. ☐ A skilled worker (requiring at least two years of specialized training or experience) or professional (Item F- no longer available)
   - g. ☐ Any other worker (requiring less than two years of training or experience)
   - i. ☐ An alien applying for a national interest waiver (who **IS** a member of the professions holding an advanced degree or an alien of exceptional ability)

Classification
- ☐ 203 (b)(1)(A) Alien of Extraordinary Ability
- ☐ 203 (b)(1)(B) Outstanding Professor or Researcher
- ☐ 203 (b)(1)(C) Multi-national executive or manager
- ☐ 203 (b)(2) Member of professional w/adv. degree or of exceptional ability
- ☐ 203 (b)(3)(A)(i) Skilled Worker
- ☐ 203 (b)(3)(A)(ii) Professional
- ☐ 203 (b)(3)(A)(iii) Other worker

Certification
- ☐ National Interest Waiver (NIW)
- ☐ Schedule A, Group I
- ☐ Schedule A, Group II

Priority Date	Consulate

Remarks

Action Block

Part 3.   Information about the person you are filing for.

Family Name **JOHANSEN**	Given Name **Jerome**	Middle Initial **J.**

Address - C/O   **N/A**

Street # and Name **16505 Meridian Avenue North**	Apt. # **N/A**

City **Seattle**	State or Province **Washington**

Country **U.S.A.**	Zip/Postal Code **98107**

E-mail Address: **johansenj@coldmail.com**

Date of Birth (Month/Day/Year) **05/16/1953**	Country of Birth **Norway**

Social Security # (if any) **None**	A# (if any) **None**

If in the U.S.	Date of Arrival (Month/Day/Year) **12/16/2000**	I-94# **000000000 01**
	Current Nonimmigrant Status **H-1**	Expires on (Month/Day/Year) **02/04/2000**

Form I-140 (Rev. 12/04/01)N

Part 4.   Processing Information.

Please complete the following for the person named in Part 3: (Check one)

☒ Alien will apply for a visa abroad at the American
Consulate in: City: **Oslo**   Foreign Country: **Norway**

☐ Alien is in the United States and will apply for adjustment of status to that of lawful permanent resident.

Alien's Country of Nationality: _____

Alien's country of current residence or, if now in the U.S., last permanent residence abroad: **U.S.A**

If you provided a U.S. address in Part 3, print the person's foreign address: **Old South Road, Route 84 Oslo, Norway N51 49 585**

If the person's native alphabet is other than Roman letters, write the person's foreign name and address in the native alphabet:

Are you filing any other petitions or applications with this one?   ☒ No   ☐ Yes-attach an explanation
Is the person you are filing for in removal proceedings?   ☒ No   ☐ Yes-attach an explanation
Has any immigrant visa petition ever been filed by or on behalf of this person?   ☒ No   ☐ Yes-attach an explanation

If you answered yes to any of these questions, please provide the case number, office location, date of decision and disposition of the decision on a separate piece of paper.

Part 5.   Additional information about the petitioner.

Type of petitioner (Check one)
☒ Employer   ☐ Self   ☐ Other (Explain, e.g., Permanent Resident, U.S. Citizen or any other person filing on behalf of the alien.)

If a company, give the following: **Manufacturer of chemicals and related products**			NAICS Code:	3 3 6 8 8 0
Type of business				

Date Established **1920**	Current # of employees **500**	Gross Annual Income **$8,000,000,000**	Net Annual Income **$2,000,000,000**

If a individual, give the following: Occupation **N/A**		Annual Income **N/A**

PART 6.   Basic information about the proposed employment.

Job title **CHEMICAL ENGINEER**	SOC Code	1 4 - 8 4 5 3

Nontechnical description of job   **Design and development of chemical related products and equipment**

Address where the person will work if different from address in Part 1.   **Same address**

Is this a full-time position?:	☒ Yes ☐ No (hours per week _____)	Wages per week $ **$890.78**

Is this a permanent position?:	☒ Yes ☐ No	Is this a new position? ☒ Yes ☐ No

Part 7.   Information on the spouse and all children of the person you are filing for.

List husband/wife and all children related to the individual for whom the petition is being filed.   Provide an attachment of additional family members, if needed.

(Name)		(Relationship)	(Date of Birth)	(Country of Birth)
N/A	**N/A**	**N/A**	**N/A**	**N/A**

Form I-140 (Rev. 12/04/01)N Page 2

Part 8.   Signature.   *Read the information on penalties in the instructions before completing this section. If someone helped you prepare this petition, he or she must complete Part 9.*

I certify, under penalty of perjury under the laws of the United States of America, that this petition and the evidence submitted with it are all true and correct. I authorize the release of any information from my records which the Immigration and Naturalization Service needs to determine eligibility for the benefit I are seeking.

Petitioner's Signature	Print Name	Date	Daytime Telephone No.
Warren S. Landers	Warren S. Landers	August 10, 2002	206/555-9765

E-mail Address: landersw@markson.com

Please Note: *If you do not completely fill out this form or fail to submit required documents listed in the instructions, you may not be found eligible for the requested benefit and this petition may be denied*

Part 9.   Signature of person preparing form, if other than above. *(Sign below)*

I declare that I prepared this petition at the request of the above person and it is based on all information of which I have knowledge.

Signature	Print Name	Date	Daytime Telephone No.
Dan P. Danilov	Dan P. Danilov	August 10, 2002	206/624-6868

Firm's Name and Address   **Law Offices of Dan P. Danilov**
Suite 2303 - One Union Square, Seattle, WA 98101-3192

E-mail Address: dpdanilov@aol.com

To Be Completed by *Attorney or Representative, if any.*
☒ Fill in box if G-28 is attached to represent the petitioner.

VOLAG No. **SEA 0000 05**	ATTY State License No. **WSBA # 170**

Attorney or Representative Signature:
Note: In the event of a Request for Evidence (RFE) may the INS contact you by Fax or E-mail: ☒ Yes   ☐ No

Fax Number: **206/624-0812**	E-mail Address: **dpdanilov@aol.com**

Form I-140 (Rev. 12/04/01)N Page 3

If the foreign employee is already in the United States working under nonimmigrant status authorized by the INS, he or she can file for an adjustment of status using Form I-485 Application to Register Permanent Residence or Adjust Status to qualify for permanent residence in the United States (see Sample 14).

5. SUPPORTING DOCUMENTS

The following documentary evidence must be produced by professional (both those with advanced degrees and those without) and skilled or unskilled workers in short supply in the United States:

(a) Licenses held by the applicant which give evidence of proficiency in a profession, trade, or occupation

(b) Certified copies of school records showing periods of attendance, major field of study, and degrees or diplomas awarded

(c) Copies of licenses or other official permission granted to the applicant to practice a trade or profession in a country that has found the applicant to be qualified

(d) Affidavits or published material are recommended as evidence of the applicant's technical training or specialized experience. These affidavits must be signed and dated by someone familiar with the applicant's work, such as former employers or recognized experts. The affidavit must identify the person who is making it and show the capacity in which that person is testifying. The affidavit must show the place and dates of the training or experience involved and specify the details of duties performed, the tools and equipment used, and the amount of any kind of supervision given and received

(e) Certified English translations of all foreign-language documents, attesting to the accuracy of the translation and the competency of the translator

6. SCHEDULE A APPLICANTS

The US Employment Service has determined that in certain occupations there are not sufficient US workers who are willing, qualified, and available to do the work. It has therefore precertified these occupations, and foreign workers coming to the United States to work in these fields do not have to obtain labor certifications before applying for immigration. Instead, they can apply for labor certification waivers based on Schedule A precertification.

Two groups qualify under Schedule A:

(a) Group I: Physical therapists and professional, registered nurses — previously, physical therapists did not need licenses to get a waiver. However, the US State Department now requires that immigrant physical therapists get certification from the appropriate certifying agency before the alien can adjust status.

Nurses must have already obtained their state licenses and must be graduates of US or Canadian nursing schools, or must have passed the Commission on Graduates of Foreign Nursing Schools examination (CGFNS).

(b) Group II: People of exceptional ability in the arts or sciences — people must be famous in at least two countries in order to qualify. Substantial proof must be submitted attesting to exceptional ability. Books, publications, articles, magazines, awards, and personal affidavits, as well as any other relevant documentation, must be submitted with the waiver application.

SAMPLE 14

**FORM I-485 APPLICATION TO REGISTER PERMANENT RESIDENCE
OR ADJUST STATUS**

U.S. Department of Justice
Immigration and Naturalization Service

OMB No. 1115-0053
**Form I-485, Application to Register
Permanent Residence or Adjust Status**

START HERE - Please Type or Print

FOR INS USE ONLY

Part 1. Information about you.

Family Name	Given Name	Middle Initial

Address - C/O

Street Number and Name	Apt. #

City

State	Zip Code

Date of Birth (month/day/year) / /	Country of Birth

Social Security #	A # (if any)

Date of Last Arrival (month/day/year)	I-94 #

Current INS Status	Expires on (month/day/year)

Returned	Receipt
———	
———	
Resubmitted	
———	
———	
Reloc Sent	
———	
———	
Reloc Rec'd	
———	
———	
☐ Applicant Interviewed	

Part 2. Application Type. *(Check one)*

I am applying for adjustment to permanent resident status because

a. ☐ an immigrant petition giving me an immediately available immigrant visa number has been approved. (Attach a copy of the approval notice-- or a relative, special immigrant juvenile, or special immigrant military visa petition filed with this application that will give you an immediately available visa number, if approved.)

b. ☐ My spouse or parent applied for adjustment of status or was granted lawful permanent residence in an immigrant visa category that allows derivative status for spouses and children.

c. ☐ I entered as a K-1 fiance(e) of a U.S. citizen whom I married within 90 days of entry, or I am the K-2 child of such a fiance(e) [Attach a copy of the fiance(e) petition approval notice and the marriage certificate.]

d. ☐ I was granted asylum or derivative asylum status as the spouse or child of a person granted asylum and am eligible for adjustment.

e. ☐ I am a native or citizen of Cuba admitted or paroled into the U.S. after January 1, 1959, and thereafter have been physically present in the U.S. for at least one year.

f. ☐ I am the husband, wife, or minor unmarried child of a Cuban described in (e) and am residing with that person, and was admitted or paroled into the U.S. after January 1, 1959, and thereafter have been physically present in the U.S. for at least on year.

g. ☐ I have continuously resided in the U.S. since before January 1, 1972.

h. ☐ Other basis of eligibility. Explain. (If additional space is needed, use a separate piece of paper.)

_____

I am already a permanent resident and am applying to have the date I was granted permanent residence adjusted to the date I originally arrived in the U.S. as a nonimmigrant or parolee, or as of May 2, 1964, whichever date is later, and: *(Check one)*

i. ☐ I am a native or citizen of Cuba and meet the description in (e), above.

j. ☐ I am the husband, wife or minor unmarried child of a Cuban, and meet the description in (f), above.

Section of Law

☐ Sec. 209(b), INA
☐ Sec. 13, Act of 9/11/57
☐ Sec. 245, INA
☐ Sec. 249, INA
☐ Sec. 1 Act of 11/2/66
☐ Sec. 2 Act of 11/2/66
☐ Other _____

Country Chargeable

Eligibility Under Sec. 245

☐ Approved Visa Petition
☐ Dependent of Principal Alien
☐ Special Immigrant
☐ Other _____

Preference

Action Block

To Be Completed by Attorney or Representative, if any
☐ Fill in box if G-28 is attached to represent the applicant
VOLAG#
ATTY State License #

Continued on back.

Form I-485 (Rev. 02/07/00)N Page 1

Part 3. Processing Information

A. City/Town/Village of Birth	Current occupation
Your mother's first name	Your father's first name

Give your name exactly how it appears on your Arrival/Departure Record (Form I-94)

Place of last entry into the U.S. (City/State)	In what status did you last enter? *(Visitor, Student, exchange alien, crewman, temporary worker, without inspection, etc.)*
Were you inspected by a U.S. Immigration Officer? ☐ Yes ☐ No	
Nonimmigrant Visa Number	Consulate where Visa was issued
Date Visa was issued (month/day/year)	Sex: ☐ Male ☐ Female	Marital Status ☐ Married ☐ Single ☐ Divorced ☐ Widowed

Have you ever before applied for permanent resident status in the U.S.?   ☐ No   ☐ Yes If you checked "Yes," give date and place of filing and final disposition.

B. List your present husband/wife, all of your sons and daughters (if you have none, write "none". If additional space is needed, use separate paper).

Family Name	Given Name	Middle Initial	Date of Birth (month/day/year)
Country of Birth	Relationship	A #	Applying with you? ☐ Yes ☐ No
Family Name	Given Name	Middle Initial	Date of Birth (month/day/year)
Country of Birth	Relationship	A #	Applying with you? ☐ Yes ☐ No
Family Name	Given Name	Middle Initial	Date of Birth (month/day/year)
Country of Birth	Relationship	A #	Applying with you? ☐ Yes ☐ No
Family Name	Given Name	Middle Initial	Date of Birth (month/day/year)
Country of Birth	Relationship	A #	Applying with you? ☐ Yes ☐ No
Family Name	Given Name	Middle Initial	Date of Birth (month/day/year)
Country of Birth	Relationship	A #	Applying with you? ☐ Yes ☐ No

C. List your present and past membership in or affiliation with every political organization, association, fund, foundation, party, club, society, or similar group in the United States or in other places since your 16th birthday. Include any foreign military service in this part. If none, write "none". Include the name(s) of organization(s), location(s), dates of membership from and to, and the nature of the organization(s). If additional space is needed, use a separate piece of paper.

Form I-485 (Rev. 02/07/00)N Page 2

Part 3. Processing Information   *(Continued)*

Please answer the following questions. (If your answer is "Yes" on any one of these questions, explain on a separate piece of paper. Answering "Yes" does not necessarily mean that you are not entitled to register for permanent residence or adjust status).

1. Have you ever, in or outside the U.S.:
   a. knowingly committed any crime of moral turpitude or a drug-related offense for which you have not been arrested?   ☐ Yes   ☐ No
   b. been arrested, cited, charged, indicted, fined, or imprisoned for breaking or violating any law or ordinance, excluding traffic violations?   ☐ Yes   ☐ No
   c. been the beneficiary of a pardon, amnesty, rehabilitation decree, other act of clemency or similar action?   ☐ Yes   ☐ No
   d. exercised diplomatic immunity to avoid prosecution for a criminal offense in the U.S.?   ☐ Yes   ☐ No

2. Have you received public assistance in the U.S. from any source, including the U.S. government or any state, county, city, or municipality (other than emergency medical treatment), or are you likely to receive public assistance in the future?   ☐ Yes   ☐ No

3. Have you ever:
   a. within the past 10 years been a prostitute or procured anyone for prostitution, or intend to engage in such activities in the future?   ☐ Yes   ☐ No
   b. engaged in any unlawful commercialized vice, including, but not limited to, illegal gambling?   ☐ Yes   ☐ No
   c. knowingly encouraged, induced, assisted, abetted or aided any alien to try to enter the U.S. illegally?   ☐ Yes   ☐ No
   d. illicitly trafficked in any controlled substance, or knowingly assisted, abetted or colluded in the illicit trafficking of any controlled substance?   ☐ Yes   ☐ No

4. Have you ever engaged in, conspired to engage in, or do you intend to engage in, or have you ever solicited membership or funds for, or have you through any means ever assisted or provided any type of material support to, any person or organization that has ever engaged or conspired to engage, in sabotage, kidnapping, political assassination, hijacking, or any other form of terrorist activity?   ☐ Yes   ☐ No

5. Do you intend to engage in the U.S. in:
   a. espionage?   ☐ Yes   ☐ No
   b. any activity a purpose of which is opposition to, or the control or overthrow of, the Government of the United States, by force, violence or other unlawful means?   ☐ Yes   ☐ No
   c. any activity to violate or evade any law prohibiting the export from the United States of goods, technology or sensitive information?   ☐ Yes   ☐ No

6. Have you ever been a member of, or in any way affiliated with, the Communist Party or any other totalitarian party?   ☐ Yes   ☐ No

7. Did you, during the period March 23, 1933 to May 8, 1945, in association with either the Nazi Government of Germany or any organization or government associated or allied with the Nazi Government of Germany, ever order, incite, assist or otherwise participate in the persecution of any person because of race, religion, national origin or political opinion?   ☐ Yes   ☐ No

8. Have you ever engaged in genocide, or otherwise ordered, incited, assisted or otherwise participated in the killing of any person because of race, religion, nationality, ethnic origin, or political opinion?   ☐ Yes   ☐ No

9. Have you ever been deported from the U.S., or removed from the U.S. at government expense, excluded within the past year, or are you now in exclusion or deportation proceedings?   ☐ Yes   ☐ No

10. Are you under a final order of civil penalty for violating section 274C of the Immigration Act for use of fraudulent documents or have you, by fraud or willful misrepresentation of a material fact, ever sought to procure, or procured, a visa, other documentation, entry into the U.S., or any other immigration benefit?   ☐ Yes   ☐ No

11. Have you ever left the U.S. to avoid being drafted into the U.S. Armed Forces?   ☐ Yes   ☐ No

12. Have you ever been a J nonimmigrant exchange visitor who was subject to the two-year foreign residence requirement and not yet complied with that requirement or obtained a waiver?   ☐ Yes   ☐ No

13. Are you now withholding custody of a U.S. Citizen child outside the U.S. from a person granted custody of the child?   ☐ Yes   ☐ No

14. Do you plan to practice polygamy in the U.S.?   ☐ Yes   ☐ No

Continued on back   Form I-485 (Rev. 02/07/00)N Page 3

Part 4. Signature. *(Read the information on penalties in the instructions before completing this section. You must file this application while in the United States.)*

I certify, under penalty of perjury under the laws of the United States of America, that this application and the evidence submitted with it is all true and correct. I authorize the release of any information from my records which the INS needs to determine eligibility for the benefit I am seeking.

Selective Service Registration. The following applies to you if you are a man at least 18 years old, but not yet 26 years old, who is required to register with the Selective Service System: I understand that my filing this adjustment of status application with the Immigration and Naturalization Service authorizes the INS to provide certain registration information to the Selective Service System in accordance with the Military Selective Service Act. Upon INS acceptance of my application, I authorize INS to transmit to the Selective Service System my name, current address, Social Security number, date of birth and the date I filed the application for the purpose of recording my Selective Service registration as of the filing date. If, however, the INS does not accept my application, I further understand that, if so required, I am responsible for registering with the Selective Service by other means, provided I have not yet reached age 26.

Signature	Print Your Name	Date	Daytime Phone Number

Please Note: *If you do not completely fill out this form, or fail to submit required documents listed in the instructions, you may not be found eligible for the requested document and this application may be denied.*

Part 5. Signature of person preparing form if other than above. *(Sign Below)*

I declare that I prepared this application at the request of the above person and it is based on all information of which I have knowledge.

Signature	Print Your Name	Date	Daytime Phone Number

Firm Name and Address

Form I-485 (Rev. 02/07/00)N Page 4

Employers must write on Form ETA 750 Application for Alien Employment Certification that the foreign employee is eligible for a labor certification waiver under Schedule A, Group I or Group II (whichever applies) and that it is not necessary to provide evidence that they tried to recruit US workers for the job.

In order to qualify for an immigrant visa or adjustment of status to a permanent resident in the United States under Schedule A, you must file two copies of the Form ETA 750 Application for Alien Employment Certification (see Sample 12) with a US consulate abroad or with an INS Regional Adjudication Center (RAC) in the United States. If you are a physical therapist, the hospital or other institution where you work may simultaneously file a Form I-140 Immigrant Petition for Alien Worker (see Sample 13) with the RAC in the area where you will be employed.

If you are in the United States working on a nonimmigrant visa and you are adjusting your status to that of permanent residence, you may also file Form I-485, Application to Register Permanent Residence or Adjust Status (see Sample 14) for yourself and your family members at the same time, if visa numbers are available. You must also submit a letter from your employer indicating that you will be employed as described in the job offer.

Each applicant must fill out his or her own form; children under 14 must have their guardian sign for them. A $50 fingerprinting fee must be paid and biographical information must also be filed.

In addition to the supporting documents discussed under section **5.** above, Schedule A, Group II applicants should also submit documents that testify to the universal acclaim and national or international recognition accorded to him or her. These should show receipt of a nationally or internationally recognized prize or award for excellence of a specific product or performance, or for outstanding achievement

which shows that the applicant is a member of a national or international association requiring outstanding achievement of its members as judged by recognized national or international experts in a specific discipline or field of endeavor.

Published material by or about the applicant should also be submitted and identified by name, address, and date of publication.

7. INFORMATION FOR EMPLOYERS PLANNING TO EMPLOY FOREIGN WORKERS

7.1 Agencies involved

Three federal government agencies have specific responsibilities in processing papers for an alien to enter this country to work. These three agencies are —

(a) the Department of State: consulates and embassies,

(b) the Department of Justice: Immigration and Naturalization Service (INS), and

(c) the Department of Labor (DOL): State Employment Service.

The Department of Labor is concerned with the protection of wages, working conditions, and job opportunities for the legal resident labor force. Therefore, before the DOL approves the entry of an alien to work, it must be convinced that there are no workers already in that area of the country available for the job and that the employment of the alien will not adversely affect the wages and working conditions of the workers in the United States similarly employed.

If there is anything that you do not understand about filling out forms, contact the local State Employment Service office. If prospective employees have any questions concerning their right to work, they should contact the INS.

However, after you have submitted an application to the local State Employment

Service office, do not contact them in an effort to speed them up. If they need more information, they will contact you. The workers processing the requests are slowed down by the many telephone calls received from people who have submitted requests. Your request will be processed as soon as possible.

7.2 The Application for Alien Employment Certification

If you want to bring a foreign worker into the country or employ a foreigner who is already here and a labor certification is necessary (see section **2.** above), you must complete and file two copies of ETA 750 Application for Alien Employment Certification (see Sample 12). The prospective employee must sign both copies of Part B — Statement of Qualifications. You file the application with the local office of the State Employment Service for the area where the work will be performed.

Before filling out the form, carefully read the instructions. Some of the items on the form look so simple that many people do not bother to read the instructions, but this can lead to problems. For example, the employee's surname must be given in capital letters (e.g., JONES) followed by the first name, middle name, and maiden name, if applicable. Failure to do this could result in the misplacement of a case file. It is a simple matter, but it is surprising how many people fail to enter the name correctly. So, look at every item in the instructions and fill in the forms carefully.

The forms are processed in a local State Employment Service office and, in some cases, are forwarded to Washington, DC, where the application is either approved or denied.

Employment Services staff may suggest changes to the completed forms to ensure that the forms are correctly filled out. If any changes are necessary, you must initial and date each one. If changes are made in several significant items, such as rate of pay, hours of work, education, experience, or job duties, you may be requested to file new forms.

7.3 Advertising the job

You are required to advertise the job so that qualified US workers may be referred to you if they are available. If you advertise before submitting your ETA 750 form, be sure to document those advertisements by keeping tear sheets or other original proof.

After you submit the ETA 750 form, the State Employment Service will advertise the job through its computer bank. Under the old, slow-track method of labor certification, you must also advertise for three consecutive business days in a publication designated by the State Employment Service and post the job opening in the place of employment. Notices must be —

(a) posted by the employer for at least ten consecutive business days,

(b) clearly visible and unobstructed while posted, and

(c) posted in conspicuous places, where the employer's US workers readily can read the posted notice on the way to or from the place of employment.

In certain occupations in which there is a nationwide surplus of workers, you will have to list the job through the Inter-Area Clearance System so that other areas where there could be a supply of qualified US workers can be notified.

The certifying officer is allowed to reduce for good cause shown some of the recruitment efforts otherwise required.

An application that is inactive for 45 days in local office files due to your failure to provide requested documentation will be returned to you and, if resubmitted, will be considered a new application for filing purposes.

The pay you offer the foreign worker must be at least as much as the prevailing wage for the occupation in the area. For example, some employers may pay $12 an hour for a job and other employers may pay $13. However, if the majority of workers are being paid $13 an hour, the employer must offer the foreign worker a minimum of 95 percent of the prevailing wage.

7.4 Employing domestics, farm workers, and entertainers

If you are submitting an application for a live-in household domestic service worker, you must file a written contract. Your prospective employee's documentation must be prepared according to the instructions sheet of the ETA 750 Application for Alien Employment Certification. If any changes are made in the contract, they should be initialed by you and the worker. An agent cannot initial these.

The reason that a household worker is needed to live on the premises must be explained. If justification is the ill health of a member of the household, a doctor's statement to this effect must be submitted in three copies.

The information on all forms and attachments must be the same. For instance, if the rate of pay is $450 for a 40-hour week on one form, it must be the same on all other forms, contracts, etc. In requests for a live-in household domestic service worker, the dollar rate "plus room and board" must be stated. For example, "$450 a week, plus room and board."

Agricultural workers fall into a category of nonimmigrants that require labor certification before even this temporary visa will be granted. The application procedure is exactly the same, but there are a few additional details. If you are submitting an application for an agricultural worker, you must submit proof of advertising in a local newspaper within 60 days prior to application filing and the applicants must have been instructed to report to the local Employment Service office. The opening must be extended to other states through the Inter-Area Clearance System.

If the application is for a person in the entertainment field, you must include with the application a copy of the contract and evidence of prearranged employment (a 12-month itinerary). This type of request is sent from the local office to a special office in New York City for determination.

8. OCCUPATIONS DESIGNATED FOR SPECIAL HANDLING

Certain job categories have been designated by the Department of Labor for special handling within the labor certification process. College teachers or professors, sheepherders, and performing artists with exceptional ability are able to get labor certification based on their levels of work experience. In most occupations, US workers have to be offered a job if they meet the minimum requirements for this job. However, foreign applicants in the special occupations mentioned above may be hired above US applicants if they have the same level of experience or more experience than their US counterparts. The employer must provide specific reasons why the foreign worker is more qualified for the job than the US worker. The regulations state that employers of people in these categories must provide documentation that they selected the foreign worker pursuant to a competitive recruitment and selection process through which the alien was found to be more qualified than any of the US workers who applied for the job.

4
OTHER CLASSIFICATIONS OF IMMIGRANTS*

1. SPECIAL IMMIGRANTS

Special immigrants now fall into the fourth preference within the employment-based immigration category. There is a limit of 10,000 visas a year for this category; however, two groups of special immigrants are not subject to this numerical restriction. They are —

(a) legal permanent residents who are returning to live in the United States, and

(b) former citizens who are seeking to be reinstated as citizens.

Others that may be admitted without labor certification within the special immigrant category include the following:

(a) An employee, or an honorably retired former employee, of the US government abroad who has performed faithful service for a total of 15 years or more, subject to approval by the secretary of state

(b) A minister of religion or a professional or nonprofessional religious worker who has been a member for at least two years of a religious organization that has a legitimate, nonprofit affiliate in the United States and who will be coming to work in the same capacity.

(c) A medical doctor who graduated abroad and has been working in the United States with a state license on either a J or H visa since January 9, 1978, or before. A doctor on a J visa must have a two-year foreign residence waiver or a "no-objection"

letter from his or her government. Foreign medical graduates will be discussed in greater detail further in this chapter.

(d) An employee of the Canal Zone government or Panama Canal Company who lived in the area on or before April 1, 1979, and worked at least one year by October 1, 1979. Panamanians who worked for the US government in this area for at least 15 years before October 1, 1979, are also eligible in this group.

(e) A former employee of an international organization based in the United States who worked on a G-4 visa for at least 15 years, and who was present in the United States for at least half of the 7 years before applying for permanent residence. (Retirees must apply within six months of their retirement.)

(f) A minor, declared a dependent of the US juvenile court system or recommended for long-term foster care in the United States. You may not sponsor your family for immigration if you get an I-551 card in this way.

2. ADOPTED FOREIGN CHILDREN

Unfortunately, the State Department cannot assist you in adopting a foreign child. If the adoption takes place in a foreign country, that country's laws apply. If it takes place in the United States, the law of the state applies.

---

*Parts of this chapter were taken from an article prepared by Dan P. Danilov, Allen E. Kaye, and Laurier B. McDonald.

An adopted child, or one about to be adopted, must be documented as an immigrant. Contact the US consular office nearest the child's place of residence to find out what visa requirements must be met. There is a difference in procedure for orphans and non-orphans.

2.1 Non-orphans

Children are defined as non-orphans when they have already been adopted. A foreign child will receive an immediate relative classification provided he or she was under 16 years of age when adopted and has been in the legal custody of and living with the adoptive parent for at least two years after the adoption. If the child cannot meet these requirements, there will be a delay in the issuing of an immigrant visa. The adoptive parents must be able to prove that they had legal custody for two years after the legal adoption. In cases where the adopted child as well as his or her natural parent live with the adoptive parent, the latter must be able to prove parental authority.

2.2 Orphans

Children are defined as orphans when both their parents have died or abandoned them or the sole surviving parent has given them up completely because he or she is unable to support them properly. The parent in this situation must have irrevocably released the child in writing for adoption and immigration. A genuine orphan who lives outside the United States and is under age 16 when the adoption petition is filed may be adopted by a US citizen and brought into the United States as an immediate relative immigrant. A single US citizen parent must be at least 25 years old before he or she can petition to bring an adopted orphan child into the country.

If you are going to adopt a child who will be coming to the United States, you have to show that you complied with the pre-adoption requirements of your state. See your nearest INS office for petition forms and instructions.

There is no limit on the number of children that may be adopted by US citizens, subject to the approval of a home study by an adoption agency in the United States.

Foreign-born children under 16 years of age who have been adopted by US citizens may apply for naturalization when they enter the United States for permanent residence. Non-orphan adopted children of US permanent residents can become family-sponsored second preference immigrants.

Adopted children may not sponsor their natural parents for immigration, unless they did not get their I-551 cards through their adoptive parents, or unless they got their I-551 cards through marriage and their adoptive parents are no longer alive.

3. REFUGEES

Every year, the president, in consultation with Congress, sets the annual quota for refugees for the following fiscal year. The number of refugees who may be admitted into the United States for financial year 1998 has been set at 83,000. The term refugee includes any person who is outside the United States and cannot return to his or her country due to persecution, the threat of persecution, or the pattern or practice of persecution, based on his or her race, religion, nationality, political opinions, or membership of a particular group.

Additional visas can be issued for "emergency or humanitarian reasons" in the public interest. People admitted in these circumstances are known as parolees. Unlike those with full refugee status, parolees may live and work in the United States but have to have their status renewed each year. Parolees are not guaranteed permanent residence in the United States and their status may be revoked at any time.

Unlike refugee status, which can only be granted from outside the United States, asylum status can be granted to people who might otherwise have qualified as refugees, but who are already in the United

States or at its borders. After April 1, 1998, applicants for asylum must apply within one year of entry to the United States. Otherwise they have to either show changed country conditions, or provide a good reason why they were unable to apply within one year of entry.

All refugees admitted become eligible for permanent residence after one year. There is no limit to the number of I-551 cards issued annually to refugees who are found admissible into the country. There is no limit to the number of qualified people granted asylum every year, but only 5,000 permanent residence visas are available to asylum applicants each year. Also, before granting an asylee permanent residence, the INS will consider whether the conditions that gave rise to this status are still effective in that person's country. In some cases, an asylee will have to wait several years for his or her I-551 card and during this wait, the conditions in his or her country may change, thereby canceling his or her eligibility, as has happened in the case of Russia, Poland, and other East European countries.

4. DIVERSITY IMMIGRANTS

The Immigration Act of 1990 introduced a new category of immigrants: immigrants of countries from which immigration to the United States has been traditionally low. This two-pronged program involves a diversity transition program and a diversity immigration program.

4.1 Transition program

Fifty-five thousand visas were available in the transition program's visa lottery, aimed at giving the nationals of certain countries an advantage in gaining US immigration. Forty percent of these visas were earmarked for Irish nationals. Ten thousand immigrant visas were available to the nationals of Hong Kong.

4.2 Immigration program

As of October 1, 1994, there have been 55,000 immigrant visas available to the nationals of countries that had low levels of US immigration during the previous five years. A special formula is used to calculate which regions are low-admission regions and which are high-admission regions and, within these regions, which are low- and high-admission states. Only the nationals of low-admission states from either low- or high-admission regions will be eligible for these visas. Each eligible state will be able to receive 3,850 visas a year or 7 percent of the total available number.

All diversity immigrants must have a high-school diploma (or its equivalent) and must have worked in a trade or occupation that needed at least two years' training or experience for two years during the five years preceding a visa application.

The above groups of immigrants do not need an affidavit of support, nor do they have to meet any requirements of the US Department of Labor before they are granted immigrant status. However, all other immigrants must obtain a labor certification or be exempt from the requirement of a labor certification in order to qualify for an immigrant visa.

5. FOREIGN MEDICAL GRADUATES

Graduates of foreign medical schools who want to be admitted as immigrants under employment-based first preference (priority workers people of outstanding ability, outstanding professors, or researchers) or second preference (people with advanced degrees or of exceptional ability) categories, must take and pass the Federation Licensing Examination (FLEX), or either of its equivalents: Parts I, II, and III of the National Board of Medical Examiners' (NBME) certifying examinations or Steps 1, 2, and 3 of the new US Medical Licensing Examination (USMLE). As of 1995, the USMLE has been the only qualifying examination that enables foreign medical graduates to work in the United States.

5.1 H-1B nonimmigrant visas

Passing one of these examinations is one of the prerequisites for foreign medical graduates to be granted H-1B nonimmigrant visas in order to practice medicine in the United States. Before the Immigration Act of 1990 and its amendments tabled in the Miscellaneous and Technical Immigration and Naturalization Amendments of 1991, foreign doctors could only get H-1B visas to conduct research or to teach at the invitation of a public or nonprofit private educational or research facility. See Table 2 for a list of common nonimmigrant visa classifications for foreign medical graduates.

5.2 J-1 exchange visitor visas

Foreign doctors can also get J-1 exchange visitor visas, which enable them to receive or impart graduate medical training or education and to work in the clinical setting as required by this education or training program. As in the case of H-1B visas, doctors visiting the United States on J-1 visas must be competent in written and oral English and must pass the FLEX, NBME, or USMLE. If they are studying or training in the United States, it can only be at an accredited medical school or affiliated hospitals.

5.3 Adjusting status

It will be easier for a doctor who has been working on an H-1B visa to adjust his or her status to permanent residence than it will be for a doctor who has been working in the United States on a J-1 visa. This is because adjustment of status is not allowed for J-1 visa holders unless they have a hardship waiver on the two-year foreign residence requirement or a no-objection letter from their government, neither of which doctors are likely to obtain.

5.4 Fluency in English

Foreign doctors must be fluent in written and oral English in order to work in the United States. They are required to take a shortened version of the Test of English as a Foreign Language (TOEFL) examination at the time of taking their US licensing examination.

An information booklet and application to write the qualifying examination to work in the United States is available from most US consular posts and from:

Educational Commission for
  Foreign Medical Graduates
3624 Market Street, 4th Floor
Philadelphia, PA 19104-2685
USA
Telephone: (215) 386-5900
Web site: www.ecfmg.org

5.5 Special immigrant status for alien physicians

As described earlier, foreign medical doctors may get special immigrant status if they —

(a) have graduated from a medical school or have qualified to practice medicine in a foreign state;

(b) were fully and permanently licensed and were practicing medicine in a state on January 9, 1978;

(c) entered the United States as a nonimmigrant with an H or J visa before January 10, 1978; and

(d) have been continuously present in the United States in the practice or study of medicine since the date of entry.

Temporary trips abroad to visit family do not break the continuous presence or practice requirement.

In order for foreign medical graduates who came to the United States on exchange visitor visas after January 10, 1977, for

TABLE 2
COMMON NONIMMIGRANT VISA CLASSIFICATIONS
FOR FOREIGN MEDICAL GRADUATES

1. Temporary Workers (H-1B) whose work will include teaching or research, pursuant to an invitation from a public or private nonprofit institution or agency, or the practice of medicine, if the foreigner graduated from a medical school in the United States or passed the Department of Health and Human Service's stipulated entrance examination, and has a good command of oral and written English.

   The immediate family of the H-1B nonimmigrant physician may accompany or join him or her in H-4 status.

2. Exchange visitor visa (J-1), if the physician is a graduate of a US medical school or has passed the required entrance examination, and has a good command of oral and written English.

graduate medical education or training to obtain immigrant visas, they must fulfill the two-year foreign residence requirement by returning to their home country for two years or obtaining a waiver of this requirement.

Others who came before January 10, 1977, are subject to this requirement only if their profession or occupation is listed on the Skills List for their country or if they were governmentally funded.

There are three types of waivers of the two-year foreign residence requirement:

(a) Exceptional hardship to a US citizen or permanent resident spouse or child

(b) Satisfactory proof that persecution would be imposed at home

(c) An interested US government agency request

Letters of no objection from foreign governments stating that they have no objections to their medical graduate nationals not returning home after receiving medical education and training in the United States are not usually available to foreign medical graduates.

5.6 Nurses

Foreign professional licensed nurses who have passed their state licensing examinations are eligible to apply for immigration to the United States and will be able to obtain a labor certification waiver and adjust status — as long as the nurse has received certification from the Commission of Graduates of Foreign Nursing School (CGFNS). Nurses are listed on what is known as Schedule A, which lists professions that are in short supply in the United States and for which qualified workers do not need approval by the Department of Labor.

5

NORTH AMERICAN FREE TRADE AGREEMENT (NAFTA)

The North American Free Trade Agreement (NAFTA) is a treaty of trade and commerce. This treaty provides that Canadians and Mexicans may now enter the United States under a new classification, the TN (for Treaty National). This classification is available for professional persons coming to perform occupations that are included on the schedule listed in Table 3.

To qualify under the TN classification, a Canadian or Mexican citizen must meet the minimum qualifications to engage in the profession, including all licenses, and must have a bona fide offer of employment within the qualifying profession.

A letter from a prospective US employer that confirms a job offer for a Canadian or Mexican citizen may be sufficient evidence for admission. However, in case of doubt, an alien seeking entry under TN should be prepared to produce diplomas, licenses, and other evidence. The first-time application fee for a Canadian citizen making an application for a TN visa at a port of entry is $50. A renewal costs $50 if the Canadian makes a new application at a port of entry, or more if he or she applies using Form I-129, Petition for Nonimmigrant Worker, while remaining in the United States. If a Canadian applies for readmission at a port of entry with an unexpired Form I-94, and a letter from an employer stating that the Canadian citizen's services are needed by the same employer for a period of time beyond what is authorized on the I-94, the Canadian citizen will be admitted for a new period of time upon paying a $50 fee. If a Canadian applies at a port of entry with an unexpired Form I-94, and a letter indicating that either —

(a) the Canadian citizen's former employer will be substituted by a different employer, or

(b) the Canadian citizen has acquired an additional employer,

upon paying a $50 fee, the Canadian will be issued a new I-94 with a new expiration date. It should be noted that, unless Canadian citizens wish to work in the United States, they are generally exempt from visa requirements.

Canadian citizens seeking to enter the United States in any of the following classifications must establish that they are coming to the United States on a temporary basis and not to reside permanently.

Applicants will generally be admitted for a period of one year. Those admitted as L-1 or H-1 may be admitted for an initial period of up to three years.

The spouse and children of persons admitted under the above classifications may be admitted for one year in the B-2 Visitor for Pleasure classification. Such dependents may not accept employment in the United States unless they qualify for an appropriate classification in their own right. The non-Canadian spouses and children of Canadian citizens qualifying for entry will generally require visas for admission into the United States.

Canadian citizens entering in one classification may seek change of status to another classification or apply for extensions of stay from within the United States or by departing and applying for a new admission period and classification. Extensions of stay are generally granted in increments of one year for an indefinite period, except

TABLE 3
SCHEDULE OF TREATY NATIONAL PROFESSIONS (CANADA & MEXICO)

The United States Code of Federal Regulations (CFR), specifically 8 CFR section 214.6(c), includes a listing of the occupations agreed upon by the three signatory countries to NAFTA.

"Appendix 1603.D.1 to Annex 1603 of the NAFTA. Pursuant to the NAFTA, an applicant seeking admission under this section shall demonstrate business activity at a professional level in one of the professions set forth in Appendix 1603.D.1 to Annex 1603. The professions in Appendix 1603.D.1 and the minimum requirements for qualification for each are as follows:[1]

- Accountant: Baccalaureate or Licenciatura degree; or CPA, CA, CGA, or CMA
- Architect: Baccalaureate or Licenciatura degree; or state/provincial license[2]
- Computer Systems Analyst: Baccalaureate or Licenciatura degree; or post-secondary diploma[3] or post-secondary certificate[4] and three years' experience
- Disaster relief insurance claims adjuster (claims adjuster employed by an insurance company located in the territory of a party, or an independent claims adjuster): Baccalaureate or Licenciatura degree and successful completion of training in the appropriate areas of insurance adjustment pertaining to disaster relief claims; or three years' experience in claims adjustment and successful completion of training in the appropriate areas of insurance adjustment pertaining to disaster relief claims
- Economist: Baccalaureate or Licenciatura degree
- Engineer: Baccalaureate or Licenciatura degree; or state/provincial license
- Forester: Baccalaureate or Licenciatura degree; or state/provincial license
- Graphic Designer: Baccalaureate or Licenciatura degree; or post-secondary diploma or post-secondary certificate and three years' experience
- Hotel Manager: Baccalaureate or Licenciatura degree in hotel/restaurant management; or post-secondary diploma or post-secondary certificate in hotel/restaurant management and three years' experience in hotel/restaurant management
- Industrial Designer: Baccalaureate or Licenciatura degree; or post-secondary diploma or post-secondary certificate, and three years' experience
- Interior Designer: Baccalaureate or Licenciatura degree; or post-secondary diploma or post-secondary certificate, and three years' experience
- Land Surveyor: Baccalaureate or Licenciatura degree or state/provincial/federal license
- Landscape Architect: Baccalaureate or Licenciatura degree
- Lawyer (including Notary in the province of Quebec): LLB, JD, LLL, BCL, or Licenciatura degree (five years); or membership in a state/provincial bar
- Librarian: MLS or BLS (for which another Baccalaureate or Licenciatura degree was a prerequisite)
- Management Consultant: Baccalaureate or Licenciatura degree; or equivalent professional experience as established by statement or professional credential attesting to five years' experience as a management consultant, or five years' experience in a field of specialty related to the consulting agreement
- Mathematician (including Statistician): Baccalaureate or Licenciatura degree
- Range Manager/Range Conservationist: Baccalaureate or Licenciatura degree
- Research Assistant (working in a post-secondary educational institution): Baccalaureate or Licenciatura degree

TABLE 3 — Continued

- Scientific Technician/Technologist:[5]
  (a) Theoretical knowledge of any of the following disciplines: agricultural sciences, astronomy, biology, chemistry, engineering, forestry, geology, geophysics, meteorology, or physics; and
  (b) the ability to solve practical problems in any of those disciplines, or the ability to apply principles of any of those disciplines to basic or applied research
- Social Worker: Baccalaureate or Licenciatura degree
- Sylviculturist (including Forestry Specialist): Baccalaureate or Licenciatura degree
- Technical Publications Writer: Baccalaureate or Licenciatura degree, or post-secondary diploma or post-secondary certificate, and three years' experience
- Urban Planner (including Geographer): Baccalaureate or Licenciatura degree
- Vocational Counselor: Baccalaureate or Licenciatura degree

MEDICAL/ALLIED PROFESSIONALS

- Dentist: DDS, DMD, Doctor en Odontologia or Doctor en Cirugia Dental or state/provincial license
- Dietitian: Baccalaureate or Licenciatura degree, or state/provincial license
- Medical Laboratory Technologist (Canada)/Medical Technologist[6] (Mexico and the United States): Baccalaureate or Licenciatura degree; or post-secondary diploma or post-secondary certificate, and three years' experience
- Nutritionist: Baccalaureate or Licenciatura degree
- Occupational Therapist: Baccalaureate or Licenciatura degree; or state/provincial license
- Pharmacist: Baccalaureate or Licenciatura degree; or state/provincial license
- Physician (teaching or research only): MD Doctor en Medicina; or state/provincial license
- Physiotherapist/Physical Therapist: Baccalaureate or Licenciatura degree; or state/provincial license
- Psychologist: State/provincial license; or Licenciatura degree
- Recreational Therapist: Baccalaureate or Licenciatura degree
- Registered Nurse: State/provincial license or Licenciatura degree
- Veterinarian: DVM, DMV, or Doctor en Veterinaria; or state/provincial license

SCIENTISTS

- Agriculturist (including Agronomist): Baccalaureate or Licenciatura degree
- Animal Breeder: Baccalaureate or Licenciatura degree
- Animal Scientist: Baccalaureate or Licenciatura degree
- Apiculturist: Baccalaureate or Licenciatura degree
- Astronomer: Baccalaureate or Licenciatura degree
- Biochemist: Baccalaureate or Licenciatura degree
- Biologist: Baccalaureate or Licenciatura degree

TABLE 3 — Continued

- Chemist: Baccalaureate or Licenciatura degree
- Dairy Scientist: Baccalaureate or Licenciatura degree
- Entomologist: Baccalaureate or Licenciatura degree
- Epidemiologist: Baccalaureate or Licenciatura degree
- Geneticist: Baccalaureate or Licenciatura degree
- Geochemist: Baccalaureate or Licenciatura degree
- Geologist: Baccalaureate or Licenciatura degree
- Geophysicist (including Oceanographer in Mexico and the United States): Baccalaureate or Licenciatura degree
- Horticulturist: Baccalaureate or Licenciatura degree
- Meteorologist: Baccalaureate or Licenciatura degree
- Pharmacologist: Baccalaureate or Licenciatura degree
- Physicist (including Oceanographer in Canada): Baccalaureate or Licenciatura degree
- Plant Breeder: Baccalaureate or Licenciatura degree
- Poultry Scientist: Baccalaureate or Licenciatura degree
- Soil Scientist: Baccalaureate or Licenciatura degree
- Zoologist: Baccalaureate or Licenciatura degree

TEACHER
- College: Baccalaureate or Licenciatura degree
- Seminary: Baccalaureate or Licenciatura degree
- University: Baccalaureate or Licenciatura degree

1. A businessperson seeking temporary employment under this appendix may also perform training functions relating to the profession, including conducting seminars.

2. The terms "state/provincial" and "state/provincial/federal license" mean any document issued by a state, provincial, or federal government, as the case may be, or under its authority, but not by a local government, that permits a person to engage in a regulated activity or profession.

3. "Post-secondary diploma" means a credential issued, on completion of two or more years of post-secondary education, by an accredited academic institution in Canada or the United States.

4. "Post-secondary certificate" means a certificate issued, on completion of two or more years of post-secondary education at an academic institution, by the federal government of Mexico or a state government in Mexico, an academic institution recognized by the federal government or a state government, or academic institution created by federal or state law.

5. A businessperson in this category must be seeking temporary entry for work in direct support of professionals in agricultural sciences, astronomy, biology, chemistry, engineering, forestry, geology, geophysics, meteorology, or physics.

6. A businessperson in this category must be seeking temporary entry to perform in a laboratory chemical, biological, hematological, immunologic, microscopic, or bacteriological tests and analyses for diagnosis, treatment, or prevention of diseases.

that L-1 and H-1 admissions are usually limited to five or six years.

Entry in any of the following classifications may be sought at ports of entry without advance arrangements, except that E-1 and E-2 classifications require visas, and L-1, H-1, H-2, and H-3 classifications require petitions. Such petitions may be presented at ports of entry at time of application for entry.

Further information may be obtained by visiting or calling the office of any US Immigration and Naturalization Service.

L-1, H-1, H-2, and H-3 petitions as well as TN admissions fees range from $50 to $265. Fees must be paid in US funds and exact change is advised.

1. B-1 VISITOR FOR BUSINESS

A visitor for business is a person engaged in international trade of goods or services or in investment activities.

A businessperson may enter to buy goods, take orders for goods to be shipped from abroad, attend meetings or trade shows, or negotiate contracts. However, the source of any remuneration (salaries, commission, etc.) must be from outside the United States.

Persons listed below, as well as those performing similar functions, may be admitted as B-1:

★ Technical, scientific, and statistical researchers

★ Harvester owners directing crews

★ Market researchers and analysts

★ Sales representatives and agents taking orders or negotiating contracts for goods or services but not delivering goods or providing services

★ Truck or bus operators delivering goods or transporting groups. No goods or passengers may load in United States for delivery in United States.

★ Customs brokers exporting goods

★ Installers, repair or maintenance personnel performing installation or repair of imported machinery during the life of a warranty or service agreement

★ Professionals (engineers, lawyers, etc.), managers, computer specialists, insurers, bankers, investment brokers, public relations and advertising personnel, tour and travel guides and agents, translators or interpreters

The above list is not all-inclusive. For an evaluation of a particular activity, contact an Immigration and Naturalization Service (INS) office.

Note, as well, the following points:

(a) The salary must be paid from abroad.

(b) A long-term presence in the United States is not intended under the B-1 classification.

(c) Service and repair personnel may only enter to repair or install machinery imported from abroad for which the employer holds a warranty or service contract.

2. E-1 TREATY TRADER

A treaty trader is a foreign national representing a foreign company carrying on trade with the United States. The US office must do over 50 percent of its business with the foreign country.

Trade means the exchange, purchase, or sale of goods or services. Goods are tangible commodities or merchandise having intrinsic value, excluding money, securities, and negotiable instruments. Services are economic activities with outputs other than tangible goods. Such activities include but are not limited to banking, insurance, transportation, communications, data processing, advertising, accounting, design and engineering, management consulting, and tourism.

3. E-2 TREATY INVESTOR

A treaty investor is a foreign national directing or developing a business in which he or she has invested substantial capital. Substantial capital is not a narrowly defined term. Rather, the amount of investment required may vary from one type of business to another, or with other circumstances.

The funds invested must be "at risk." Thus, funds may not merely be invested in stocks or bonds to qualify. The investment must be of sufficient amount to insure a certain element of control of the business.

Shares of a company owned by lawful permanent resident aliens of the United States, even though foreign nationals, may not be considered in determining majority foreign ownership.

Aliens may only be classified as E-1 or E-2 if their duties are executive, managerial, or supervisory in nature, or they possess specific technical expertise to perform service on intricate or complex products sold in the course of trade between the United States and the treaty country.

An alien under an E-1 or E-2 visa may change employers upon the authorization of the INS, provided the new employer is a qualifying treaty trader or investor company.

4. H-1B WORKER

A person in this category is a professional or person of "distinguished merit and ability" coming to perform a special occupation that requires a person of such qualifications.

A special occupation is defined as an occupation that requires, as a minimum educational attainment, a baccalaureate-level college degree for entry into the profession. Some professions may require advanced degrees for professional standing.

5. H-2 TEMPORARY WORKER

An H-2 temporary worker may be employed in any field or occupation, provided there is a shortage of workers in this field in the area of the United States where the alien will be employed.

A shortage of workers must be certified by the Department of Labor. Alien labor certification is applied for through the State Employment Service of the state where the alien will be employed.

Employers are advised that the certification procedures require advertising and other steps, and may take several months to complete. A visa petition must also be filed with the INS along with the approved labor certification.

6. H-3 TRAINEE

A person may be brought into the United States by an employer to receive experience and training. The H-3 classification requires that a formal, structured classroom training program be in existence, and that any productive employment be merely incidental to the training program and not the purpose of coming to the United States. The H-3 visa can be approved at the border or at preflight posts before entering the country, as long as the INS officials have the necessary form. The author recently changed the status of an F-1 student already in the United States to that of an H-3 trainee.

7. L-1 INTRACOMPANY TRANSFEREE

A Canadian citizen may be transferred to an existing company or to establish a company in the United States that is the parent of, subsidiary of, or affiliated with a foreign company.

The person being transferred must have been employed with the foreign company for at least the immediate prior year in a position that was managerial, executive, or required specialized knowledge of a proprietary nature for the efficient operation of the company. The new position in the United States must also be managerial, executive, or require specialized knowledge as indicated above.

The foreign parent, subsidiary, or affiliated company must remain in operation while the person is in the United States; that is, aliens cannot be transferred to the US company to close or relocate the foreign branch.

An L-1 intracompany transferee need not be employed in the United States on a full-time basis, and may alternate duties in the United States and Canada. However, the transferee must be involved in productive duties in the United States. A person may not merely participate in meetings, conferences, or training and qualify for intracompany classification.

6
IMMIGRANT INVESTORS

The Immigration Act of 1990 created an employment-based immigration preference for foreign investors in the United States. There have been, as a result, 10,000 immigrant visas available annually in the fifth preference (E5) category. Of this number, 3,000 visas have been set aside for people who will be investing in areas where unemployment is one-and-a-half times the national average or more.

1. REQUIREMENT OF INVESTMENT

Foreigners wishing to make a business investment in the United States may qualify for an immigrant visa if they will be establishing a new commercial enterprise, investing money in that enterprise, and employing at least ten US workers full time.

The financial investment required depends on the area where the investment is being made. For example, in areas of high unemployment where the US government wishes to boost the economy and create jobs, it may be possible to obtain immigrant status with an investment of $500,000. To further encourage investors to consider these high unemployment areas, 3,000 visas are set aside for investors in these target areas.

In areas where employment levels are higher than the national average, it may be necessary to invest as much as $1 million in order to qualify for investor status. The INS will determine the size of the investment necessary to qualify for immigrant status in the area where you plan to start or expand a business.

The ten workers employed does not include the investors and their families or any other foreign workers employed on nonimmigrant visas. It includes citizens and legal permanent residents and other categories of people legitimately entitled to work on a permanent basis in the United States.

2. KIND OF ENTERPRISE

About the meaning of the term *investment of capital* the Board of Immigration Appeals has said "neither an idle bank account nor a speculative land holding qualifies, as the regulation contemplates an investment in a business venture which is productive of some service or commodity." In other words, the investment must be used for purposes such as —

    (a) the formation of a corporation,

    (b) the purchase or rental of office or factory space,

    (c) the purchase of equipment,

    (d) the recruiting of employees,

    (e) the solicitation of business, or

    (f) the signing of business agreements.

3. WHERE CAN THE MONEY COME FROM?

The money that a prospective immigrant investor applies toward an enterprise located in the United States must be his or her own in the sense that he or she must be able to exercise control over it and possess it.

If the prospective investor appears to have obtained control over the money through a paper or sham transaction, and never had actual possession of the funds, then it would not be acceptable for computing the value of the investment in the United States.

How the money was acquired is taken into account when considering whether the proposed investment is contemplated and whether its success is honestly contemplated. For example, a person with a history of low-paying employment and no probable personal assets would have to show convincing evidence of how the money was acquired, even if he or she had more money to invest.

If a prospective immigrant investor were to present several promissory notes indicating that he or she had borrowed substantial amounts of money from relatives, the consular officer would be entitled to look into and ask about the financial capabilities of the lending family members. They would have to have enough financial ability to continue advancing loans of this size.

4. HOW CAN THE MONEY BE INVESTED?

The investment should not consist of, for example, a mortgage advanced on a fairly low down payment, because the down payment will be considered the investment. There must be clear evidence of an outlay of capital of the total amount in the acquisition or establishment of a business.

In a wholesale distributorship corporation, invoices for the purchase of goods for immediate resale would not constitute acceptable evidence of investment. These would simply be taken as one-time costs for a single transaction.

In addition, it should be pointed out that the purchase of land in itself does not constitute evidence of an investment. Land can be purchased on terms and therefore its purchase is not always evidence of an investment of the required amount.

Neither does part-time plowing or absentee ownership of farm land provide evidence of investment intent, nor does an agreement to purchase stock satisfy the requirements for investment. The investment should be in one specific enterprise in order to be considered valid; it can't be invested in different stocks, for example.

A partial commitment of capital would be acceptable if it is going to a specific enterprise where a substantial investment will be involved. In this situation, the prospective investor must show that he or she has the rest of the funds and that they are being spent on the investment. For example, the investor could purchase a business for $250,000 and show that this is a fair valuation. He or she should then show a signed contract calling for an initial payment of $150,000 with the balance to be paid in 90 days, along with evidence that he or she has sufficient money to complete the contract within the time period.

In this situation, the business must actually exist. It cannot simply exist on paper and have no property or assets. For this reason, the act of incorporation with a transfer of funds to the corporation account through the purchase of stock would not be considered an acceptable investment.

Keep in mind that the applicant for an investor immigrant visa has the burden of proof to demonstrate that he or she is a legitimate investor and is, therefore, exempt from the labor certification requirement. It is to the applicant's advantage to be as active as possible in the United States.

The prospective immigrant must meet a "reasonable" standard of proof. In other words, satisfactory documentation of the proposed investment must be presented to the consular officer. There must be direct, credible evidence of the transfer of funds under the possession and control of the prospective immigrant. When considered as a whole, the record should be reasonably supportive of the alleged investment.

5. THE APPLICATION PROCEDURE

Foreign investors planning on immigrating to the United States must submit Form I-526 Immigrant Petition by Alien Entrepreneur (see Sample 15). This form must be submitted to a US consulate abroad or, if the applicant is already in the United States, to either the Texas or California Service Center which has jurisdiction over the area where the investment is being made. The filing fee for Form I-526 has been raised from $350 to $400.

The information contained in this application must include details of the investment and be accompanied by extensive documentation to prove the financial viability of this investment. This application procedure takes the place of the Labor Certification and Form I-140 Immigrant Petition for Alien Worker that are required by most other employment-based immigrants.

Some of the documents that might be filed with the INS or US consulate in support of a fifth preference investor visa include the following:

(a) Certification of stock issuance

(b) Check vouchers

(c) Corporate resolutions electing officers

(d) Business forms

(e) Contracts

(f) Bank statements

(g) Invoices

(h) Classified advertisements or other evidence of recruiting efforts

The filing of these applications will establish a priority date for the applicant under the fifth preference category and qualify him or her to apply for an immigrant visa when a visa number is available. There has been low demand for these visas to date and this preference category is expected to remain current for some time.

Once Form I-526 has been approved, the foreign investor can then submit his or her application for an immigrant visa, if applying from abroad, or for an adjustment of status, if applying from within the United States.

When a visa number is available and the applicant receives a visa appointment date, all of the usual documentation, such as passports, photographs, medical examination forms, police certificate, and fingerprints, must be filed at the US consulate. An interview will also be held under oath with a consular officer.

Investors already living in the United States may adjust their status to permanent residents at the discretion of the INS by also filing Form I-485 Application to Register Permanent Residence or Adjust Status (see Sample 14).

6. CONDITIONAL STATUS OF INVESTOR IMMIGRANTS

All foreign investors who get their I-551 cards through investment will be subject to a two-year conditional permanent resident status. In the same way that the foreign spouses of US citizens have to apply for a removal of their conditional permanent resident status after two years, investors, too, have to comply with this requirement.

Within 90 days immediately before the second anniversary of obtaining an I-551 card, an investor has to submit Form I-829 Petition by Investor to Remove Conditions plus a filing fee of $395 to the Regional Service Center where he or she submitted Form I-526. The petition must provide information and be accompanied by documentation to show —

(a) he or she established a commercial enterprise,

(b) he or she invested or is involved in the process of investing the amount of capital specified by the INS, and

(c) the investment or enterprise is viable.

The effect of filing the I-829 is much the same as filing an I-751 Petition to Remove Condition on Residence, in that the receipt for the filed Form I-829, together with your I-551, extends your temporary lawful

U.S. Department of Justice
Immigration and Naturalization Service

OMB #1115-0081

Immigrant Petition by Alien Entrepreneur

START HERE - Please Type or Print	FOR INS USE ONLY	

Part 1. Information about you.

Family Name BENEDICT	Given Name Juan	Middle Initial R.

Address - In Care of: n/a	

Street # and Name 1510 Battleground Avenue	Apt #

City or town Morven	State or Province North Carolina

Country USA	Zip or Postal Code 56003

Date of Birth (Month/Day/Year) 03/01/1935	Country of Birth Brazil

Social Security # 000 00 0000	A# 00 000 000

If In the U.S	Date of Arrival (Month/Day/Year) 05/05/2002	I-94# 000 000000 01
	Current Nonimmigrant Status B-1/2	Expires on (Month/Day/Year) 08/01/2003

FOR INS USE ONLY:
Returned
Receipt
Resubmitted
Reloc Sent
Reloc Rec'd
☐ Applicant Interviewed

Part 2. Application type (Check one).

a. [x] This petition is based on an investment in a commercial enterprise in a targeted employment area for which the required amount of capital invested has been adjusted downward.

b. ☐ This petition is based on an investment in a commercial enterprise in an area for which the required amount of capital invested has been adjusted upward.

c. ☐ This petition is based on an investment in a commercial enterprise which is not in either a targeted area or in an upward adjustment area.

Part 3. Information about your investment.

Name of Commercial Enterprise Invested In GLASS PACK, Inc.

Street Address
1510 Battleground Ave., Morven, N.C. 56003

Phone # 219/555-2691	Business Organized as (Corporation, partnership, etc ...) Incorporation

Kind of Business
(Example: Furniture Manufacturer) Glass finishing

Date established (Month/Day/Year) 12/12/2002	IRS Tax # UBI# 94-12908432

Date of your initial investment (Month/Day/Year) 10/12/2002	Amount of your initial investment $1,000,000.00 +

Your total capital investment in enterprise to date $ 50,000.00	Percentage of enterprise you own 100%

If you are not the sole investor in the new commercial enterprise, list on separate paper the names of all other parties (natural and non-natural) who hold a percentage share of ownership of the new enterprise and indicate whether any of these parties is seeking classifications as an alien entrepreneur. Include the name, percentage of ownership and whether or not the person is seeking classification under section 203(b)(5). none

If you indicated in Part 2 that the enterprise was in a targeted employment area or in an upward adjustment area, give the location at right.

	County	State
	Morven	N.C.

Action Block

To Be Completed by
Attorney or Representative, if any
☒ Fill in box if G-28 is attached to represent the applicant

VOLAG# SEA 2468 13
ATTY State License # 249816

Continued on back.

Form I-526 (Rev. 11/30/01)Y Page 1

Part 4. Additional information about the enterprise.

Type of enterprise *(check one):*

[XX] new commercial enterprise resulting from the creation of a new business.
[ ] new commercial enterprise resulting from the purchase of an existing business.
[ ] new commercial enterprise resulting from a capital investment in an existing business.

Assets:

Total amount in U.S. bank account	$ 600,000.00
Total value of all assets purchased for use in the enterprise	$ 350,000.00
Total value of all property transferred from abroad to the new enterprise	$ 150,000.00
Total of all debt financing	$ ----
Total stock purchases	$ ----
Other (explain on separate paper) rent/utilities/salaries	$ 100,000.00
Total	$1100,000.00

Income:

When you made investment	Gross $ 1,000,000.00	Net $ 150,000.00 (estimated annually)
Now	Gross $	Net $

Net worth   When you made investment $ _____   Now $ _____

Part 5. Employment creation information.

Number of full-time employees In Enterprise in U.S. (excluding you, spouse, sons and daughters)

When you made your initial investment __15 employees__   Now __11 employees__   Difference __4__

How many of these new jobs were created by your investment? __15__   How many additional now jobs will be created by your additional investment? __40__

What is your position, office or title with the new commercial enterprise?
Owner/President/Manager

Briefly describe your duties, activities and responsibilities. I will run/direct company's general operations and focus on its financial operations. I will provide initial training for assistant manager and approx. ten technicians. I have already established need for company by contacting related industry and factory within area. My old suppliers continue to provide me w/part of equipment and most spare parts. I have potential buyers from all over world including U.S.

Your Salary $80,000 per annual   Cost of Benefits $20,000 annually

Part 6. Processing information.

Check One:

[x] The person named In Part 3 is now in the U.S. and an application to adjust status to permanent resident will be filed if this petition is approved.

[ ] If the petition is approved, and the person named in Part 3 wishes to apply for an immigrant visa abroad, complete the following for that person:

Country of Nationality : ____n/a____

Country of current residence or , if now in the U.S., last permanent residence abroad: n/a

If you provided a U.S. address in Part 3, print the person's foreign address: n/a

If the person's native alphabet is other than Roman letters, write the foreign address in the native alphabet:

Is an application for adjustment of status attached to this petition?	[x] Yes	[ ] No
Are you in exclusion or deportation proceedings?	[ ] Yes (If yes, explain on separate paper)	[x] No
Have you ever worked in the U.S. without permission?	[ ] Yes (Explain on separate paper)	[x] No

Part 7. Signature. *Read the information on penalties in the instrucitons before completing this section.*

I certify under penalty of perjury under the laws of the United States of America that this petition, and the evidence submitted with it, is all true and correct. I authorize the release of any information from my records which the Immigration and Naturalization Service needs to determine eligibility for the benefit I am seeking.

Signature _(signed)_   Date 11/2002

Please Note: *If you do not completely fill out this form, or fail to submit required documents listed in the instructions, you may not be found eligible for the requested document and this application may be denied.*

Part 8. Signature of person preparing form, if other than above. (Sign below)

I declare that I prepared this application at the request of the above person and it is based on all information of which I have knowledge.

Signature _(signed)_   Print Your Name   DAN P. DANILOV   Date

Firm Name and Address   LAW OFFICES OF DAN P. DANILOV
Suite 2303 One Union Sq., Seattle,   WA   98101

Form I-526 (Rev. 11/30/01)Y Page 2

permanent resident status. If you travel outside the United States during this period, you may present your card and the filing receipt to be readmitted. If an interview takes place, the INS must inform the investor within 90 days of this interview whether or not the petition was successful.

7. DENYING PERMANENT RESIDENCE

The INS will not grant full permanent residence to investors who

(a) do not file a petition to remove conditional status (unless they can show good cause or extenuating circumstances),

(b) fail to attend the interview without good cause,

(c) provide false information that is revealed during the interview,

(d) made the investment purely to evade immigration laws,

(e) did not establish a commercial enterprise,

(f) did not make an investment and are not in the process of making an investment,

(g) are not sustaining their investments as commercial enterprises, or

(h) did not meet the requirements of the fifth preference category.

8. OVERTURNING A DENIAL

If the attorney general, by way of an INS official, finds that an investor is ineligible for immigrant status because of failure to meet a requirement, the government must prove ineligibility. However, if the investor has only failed to file a petition to remove conditional status or fails to appear at an interview, the investor has to establish his or her eligibility. In the first case, there will probably be litigation and the investor will have to hire a lawyer. In the second case, it is likely that an investor will be allowed to submit a petition or reschedule an interview.

7
STUDENTS AND EXCHANGE VISITORS

1. F-1 VISA FOR ACADEMIC AND LANGUAGE STUDENTS

If you are a foreign student who wishes to pursue academic or language studies in the United States, you may apply for a nonimmigrant student visa, called an F-1 visa, at a US consulate. You will be eligible for an F-1 visa if you intend to study in a full-time program that will lead to a degree. It should be noted that, as of November 30, 1996, the new immigration law (IIRIRA) prohibited any foreign student from receiving an F-1 student visa if the foreign student was coming to the United States to attend a public school, kindergarten through grade 8, or a publicly funded adult education program. Students in grades 9 through 12 at a public school must pay the unsubsidized, per capita costs of education in advance to be eligible for an F-1 student visa, and are limited to a period not to exceed one year. Students at private schools do not have the one-year limitation. F-1 students who fail to maintain a full-time course of study fall out of legal status immediately.

Before an F-1 visa is granted, you must have the following:

(a) A passport valid for at least six months beyond your intended stay in the United States. (See Table 4 for a list of countries that have entered into an agreement with the United States that their passports will be recognized as valid for six months beyond the expiration date.)

(b) A Form I-20 A-B Certificate of Eligibility for Nonimmigrant Student (see Sample 16) from a US school approved by the Immigration and Naturalization Service (INS), which declares that you have been accepted as a student.

(c) Proof that you will be able to support yourself while a full-time student in the United States. This may take the form of a sponsor who is a US citizen or lawful permanent resident or the documentation of funds sufficient for your support. The person responsible for supporting you should complete and submit an Affidavit of Support.

(d) Proof that you have the educational qualifications to pursue your intended course of study. This can consist of transcripts showing grades and the nature of courses taken. In addition, you must be able to understand English well enough to study at your intended school. A statement from the school that special tutoring provisions have been established for the non-English-speaking student or that the school offers the full course of study in a language that you understand may be necessary if you do not speak English.

(e) Proof that you intend to leave the United States upon completion of your education and that you have a residence abroad that you do not intend to abandon and to which you will return.

Canadian nationals do not require passports if they are coming to study in the United States. They do need to show approved Forms I-20 A-B or M-N certificates as well as proof of their citizenship to the INS border official in order to gain entry into the United States.

2. M-1 VISA FOR VOCATIONAL AND NONACADEMIC STUDENTS

This visa is available to foreign students for vocational and other nonacademic studies. The same prerequisites and limitations that apply to F-1 students visas apply to M-1 students. There is a slight difference in the application procedure in that M-1 students apply on Form I-20 M-N.

3. J-1 VISA FOR EXCHANGE VISITORS

Other students may apply for J-1 nonimmigrant visas as exchange visitors. The applicants must present a Form IAP-66 Certificate of Eligibility for Exchange Visitor (J-1) Status, which is evidence of acceptance by an educational institution approved by the US Information Agency for Exchange Visitors (see Sample 17). In addition, the applicant must also present all of the documents noted in section **1.**, except, of course, Form I-20 Certificate of Eligibility for F-1 students.

If the consular officer does not feel that the prospective student or exchange visitor really intends to return to his or her home country, it may be necessary for the student or exchange visitor to post a bond with the attorney general.

If students or exchange visitors intend to study English exclusively, they may be admitted to the United States even though no credit is given for this study. However, the applicant must be otherwise qualified to study English, and the school where the learning is to take place must be properly qualified and equipped to offer a full course in the English language. The applicant must also be accepted to study English by the school involved.

The J-1 exchange visitor program is operated by the United States Information Agency for the purpose of providing qualified aliens with opportunities for study, research, teaching, and clinical training in the United States. The program aims to promote international relations by bringing foreign exchange visitors into the United States under approved programs in order that they may acquire skills to be used in their home countries.

One of the most important aspects of the J-1 program is that many but not all exchange visitors are subject to a foreign residence requirement, which requires the foreign national to return to his or her country of last residence for two years after finishing his or her studies before being permitted to return to the United States. This foreign residence requirement must be either fulfilled or waived before the foreign national can qualify for any subsequent immigration benefit, including a change of status. Whether the foreign residence requirement can be avoided or waived is frequently the most important factor of a foreign national's consideration whether to come to the United States as an exchange visitor.

4. DEPENDENTS OF STUDENTS OR EXCHANGE VISITORS

The families and children of nonimmigrant students may accompany or follow the principal F-1, M-1, or J-1 student or visitor as spouses and children of students and exchange visitors. (They will travel on F-2, M-2, or J-2 visas.) Under no circumstances will the spouses and children be allowed to precede the student or exchange visitor into the United States. When they follow the student or exchange visitor into the United States, they must show the consular officer and the immigration officer a certified copy of the Certificate of Eligibility that was issued to the student.

J-2 spouses are permitted to work in the United States if permission is received from the US Information Agency administering the program. However, the spouse's work may not be taken as the sole support of the exchange visitor.

TABLE 4
COUNTRIES WHOSE PASSPORTS ARE VALID
FOR SIX MONTHS BEYOND EXPIRATION DATE

Algeria

Antigua and Barbuda

Argentina

Australia

Austria (Reisepass only)

Bahamas

Bangladesh

Barbados

Belgium

Brazil

Canada

Chile

Colombia

Costa Rica

Côte d'Ivoire (Ivory Coast)

Cuba

Cyprus

Czech Republic

Denmark

Dominican Republic

Ecuador

Egypt

Ethiopia

Finland

France

Germany

Greece

Grenada

Guinea

Hong Kong

Hungary

Iceland

India

Ireland

Israel

Italy

Jamaica

Japan

Jordan

Korea

Kuwait

Laos

Lebanon

Liechtenstein

Luxembourg

Madagascar

Malaysia

Malta

Mauritius

Mexico

Monaco

Netherlands

New Zealand

Nicaragua (Diplomatic and official passports only)

Nigeria

Norway

Oman

Pakistan

Panama

Paraguay

Peru

Philippines

Poland

Portugal

Qatar

Russia

Senegal

Singapore

Slovak Republic

Slovenia

South Africa

Spain

Sri Lanka

St. Kitts and Nevis

St. Lucia

St. Vincent and the Grenadines

Sudan

Suriname

Sweden

Switzerland

Syria

Taiwan

Thailand

Togo

Trinidad and Tobago

Turkey

Tunisia

United Arab Emirates

United Kingdom

Uruguay

Venezuela

U.S. Department of Justice	Certificate of Eligibility for Nonimmigrant (F-1) Student	OMB No. 1115-0051
Immigration and Naturalization Service	Status - For Academic and Language Students	
Please Read Instructions on Page 2		Page 1

This page must be completed and signed in the U.S. by a designated school official.

1. Family Name (surname)
   BUCHOLZ

   First (given) name (do not enter middle name)
   Bjorn

Country of birth **Germany**	Date of birth (mo./day/year) **12/10/1976**
Country of citizenship **Germany**	Admission number (Complete if known)

   For Immigration Official Use

Visa issuing post	Date Visa issued

   Reinstated, extension granted to:

2. School (school district) name
   Liberty High School, Smalltown District

   School official to be notified of student's arrival in U.S. (Name and Title)
   Jane Welcome, Principal

   School address (include zip code)
   123 Lincoln Ave., Smalltown, AZ 12345

   School code (including 3-digit suffix, if any) and approval date
   214F **445K10**   approved on **01/22/2002**

3. This certificate is issued to the student named above for:
   (Check and fill out as appropriate)
   a. ☒ Initial attendance at this school
   b. ☐ Continued attendance at this school
   c. ☐ School transfer.
      Transferred from _____
   d. ☐ Use by dependents for entering the United States.
   e. ☐ Other _____

4. Level of education the student is pursuing or will pursue in the United States:
   (check only one)
   a. ☐ Primary   e. ☐ Master's
   b. ☒ Secondary   f. ☐ Doctorate
   c. ☐ Associate   g. ☐ Language training
   d. ☐ Bachelor's   h. ☐ Other

5. The student named above has been accepted for a full course of study at this school, majoring in **English Language**

   The student is expected to report to the school no later than (date)
   Sept 1 and complete studies not later than (date) **June 15**
   The normal length of study is **10 months**

6. ☐ English proficiency is required:
   ☒ The student has the required English proficiency
   ☐ The student is not yet proficient, English instructions will be given at the school.
   ☐ English proficiency is not required because _____

7. This school estimates the student's average costs for an academic term of
   10 (up to 12) months to be:
   a. Tuition and fees $ **0.00**
   b. Living expenses $ **1000.00**
   c. Expenses of dependents $ **0.00**
   d. Other(specify): $ **0.00**
   Total $ **1,000.00**

8. This school has information showing the following as the student's means of support, estimated for an academic term of **10** months (Use the same number of months given in item 7).
   a. Student's personal funds $ **1000.00**
   b. Funds from this school $ _____
      (specify type)
   c. Funds from another source $ _____
      (specify type and source)
   d. On-campus employment (if any) $ _____
   Total $ **1,000.00**

9. Remarks: _____

10. School Certification: I certify under penalty of perjury that all information provided above in items 1 through 8 was completed before I signed this form and is true and correct; I executed this form in the United States after review and evaluation in the United States by me or other officials of the school of the student's application, transcripts or other records of courses taken and proof of financial responsibility, which were received at the school prior to the execution of this form; the school has determined that the above named student's qualifications meet all standards for admission to the school; the student will be required to pursue a full course of study as defined by 8 CFR 214.2(f)(6); I am a designated official of the above named school and I am authorized to issue this form.

Jane Welcome	Jane Welcome	Principal	08/10/2002	Smalltown, AZ
Signature of designated school official	Name of school official (print or type)	Title	Date issued	Place issued (city and state)

11. Student Certification: I have read and agreed to comply with the terms and conditions of my admission and those of any extension of stay as specified on page 2. I certify that all information provided on this form refers specifically to me and is true and correct to the best of my knowledge. I certify that I seek to enter or remain in the United States temporarily, and solely for the purpose of pursuing a full course of study at the school named on page 1 of this form. I also authorize the named school to release any information from my records which is needed by the INS pursuant to 8 CFR 214.3(g) to determine my nonimmigrant status.

Bjorn Bucholz	Bjorn Bucholz	August 10, 2002	8/10/02	
Signature of student	Name of student		Date	
Thomas Bucholz	Thomas Bucholz	3 Struss Street, Kiel	Germany	08/10/2002
Signature of parent or guardian if student is under 18	Name of parent/guardian (Print or type)	Address(city)	(State or province) (Country)	(Date)

Form I20 A-B/I20ID(Rev 04-27-88)N

For official use only
Microfilm Index Number

SAMPLE 17
FORM IAP-66 CERTIFICATE OF ELIGIBILITY
FOR EXCHANGE VISITOR (J-1) STATUS

United States Information Agency
EXCHANGE VISITOR PROGRAM SERVICES, GC/V
CERTIFICATE OF ELIGIBILITY FOR EXCHANGE VISITOR (J-1) STATUS

( ) Male
(X) Female

THE PURPOSE OF THIS FORM IS TO:

1. **AGU**　　　　**Maria**　　　　**Sharon**
(FAMILY NAME OF EXCHANGE VISITOR)　　(FIRST NAME)　　(MIDDLE NAME)

1 (X) Begin a new program ( ) Accompanied by _____ immediate family members

born **07**　**19**　**37**　**Manila**　　　　**Philippines**
(Mo)　(Day)　(Yr)　　(City)　　　　　(Country)

2 ( ) Extend an on-going program.

a citizen of ___**PHILIPPINES**___　　___**RP**___　a legal permanent resident of _____
(Country)　　　(Code)

3 ( ) Transfer to a different program.

___**PHILIPPINES**___　　___**RP**___　whose position in that country is　**Member of**
(Country)　　　(Code)

4 ( ) Replace a lost IAP-66 form; amend a previous IAP-66 form.

Religious Order engaged in Education　　**352**
(Pos. Code)

5 ( ) Permit visitor's immediate family (_____ members) to enter U.S. separately

U.S. address　**Western Hospital**
354 Virginia Avenue
Seattle, WA 98103

6 ( ) Reinstatement request to USIA.

2. Will be sponsored by____**Assiciation for Clinical Pastoral Education Organization**
____to participate in Exchange Visitor Program No. __**P**__ __**2**__ __**3388**__ which is still valid and is officially described as follows.

A program to provide professional courses in clinical pastoral education, consisting of courses of study, lectures, seminars, and practical training at selected centers in the United States for qualified foreign students or trainees, to enable such foreign nationals to pursue education and training in the field and to promote the general interests of international exchange.

3. This form covers the period from __**5**__ __**1**__ __**01**__ to __**8**__ __**1**__ __**02**__ Exchange Visitor are permitted to travel abroad & maintain status (e.g. obtain a new visa) under duration of the program as indicated by the dates on this form.

4. The category of this visitor is 1( ) Student, 2( ) Trainee, 3 ( ) Teacher, 4 ( ) Professor, 5 ( ) International Visitor, 6 ( ) Alien Physician, 7 ( ) Government Visitor, 8 ( ) Research Scholar, 9 ( ) Short-Term Scholar, 10 ( ) Specialist, 11 ( ) Camp Counselor. The specific field of study, research, training or professional activity is **9220** verbally described as follows: **Pastoral trainee in a program of CPE to obtain practical skill in pastoral care.**
(Subj/Field Code)

12 ( ) Summer Travel/Work

5. During the period covered by this for, the total estimated financial support (in U.S. $) is to be provided to the exchange visitor by:

a. ( ) The Program Sponsor in item 2 above　　$_____

This Program Sponsor has [ ] has not [X] (check one) received funding for international exchange from one or more U.S. Government Agency(ies) to support this exchange visitor. If any U.S. Government Agency(ies) provided funding, indicate the Agency(ies) by code below.

Financial support from organizations other than the sponsor will be provided by one or more of the following:

b1.( ) U.S. Government Agency(ies) _____ (Agency Code). $_____ ; b2._____ (Agency Code). $_____
c1.( ) International Organization(s) _____ (Int. Org. Code). $_____ ; c2._____ (Int. Org. Code). $_____
d. ( ) The Exchange Visitor's Government　$_____
e. ( ) The binational Commission of the visitor's Country　$_____
f. (X) All other organizations providing support　$**15,000.00**
g. ( ) Personal funds　$_____

(If necessary, use above spaces for funding by multiple U.S. Agencies or Intl. Organizations)

6. I.N.S. OR U.S.I.A USE

7. **John H. WONG**　　　　**ADMINISTRATOR**
(Name of Official Preparing Form)　　(Title)
1549 University Street, Suite 103, Seattle, WA 98101
(Address)

John Wong
(Signature of Responsible Officer or Alternate R.O)　**08/10/2002**
(Date)

PRELIMINARY ENDORSEMENT OF CONSULAR OR IMMIGRATION OFFICER REGARDING SECTION 212 (e) OF THE I.N.S.

1. (Name)
(Title)

have determined that this alien in the above program.
1. ( ) is not subject to the two year residence requirement
2. ( ) is subject based on — A ( ) government financing and/or
　　　　　　　　　　　　B ( ) the Exchange visitor skills list and/or
　　　　　　　　　　　　C ( ) PL-94 484 as amended

(Signature of Officer)　　(Date)
The United States information Agency reserves the right to make the final determination

8. STATEMENT OF RESPONSIBLE OFFICER FOR RELEASING SPONSOR (FOR TRANSFER OF PROGRAM)

Date _____ Transfer of this exchange visitor from program No._____ sponsored by _____ to the program specified in item (2) is necessarily or highly desirable and is in conformity with the objectives of the Mutual Educational and Cultural Exchange Act of 1961.

(Signature of Officer)　　(Date)

IAP-66 (1-97)

5. GENERAL INFORMATION FOR STUDENTS, EXCHANGE VISITORS, AND THEIR FAMILIES

5.1 Arriving in the United States

When you arrive at a port of entry into the United States as a student or exchange visitor, you will be "inspected" by an immigration officer. If you are found to be admissible into the United States, you will be issued a Form I-94 Arrival-Departure Record which shows the length of time you are authorized to stay in the United States (see Sample 20 in chapter 8).

5.2 Length of stay

Foreign students are admitted to the United States (on F-1, M-1, and J-1 visas) for designated periods of time only and/or for the duration of their studies.

5.3 Transferring to another school/program

Students or exchange visitors must attend the school of their original choice — the institution that issued the Certificate of Eligibility. If you do not attend this school or transfer to another school without notifying the INS and obtaining their permission, your student or exchange visitor visa is automatically canceled. If this happens, you can be removed.

After you have enrolled in the original school and have been a full-time student, you can apply for a transfer to a different school or to another full-time educational program at the same school. Before the transfer takes place, you must submit another completed Form I-20 A-B Certificate of Eligibility for Nonimmigrant Student issued by the new school (or the same school, if it is for a transfer to another department or another program) to the INS for approval.

It is up to the designated school officials to advise the INS when foreign students are no longer enrolled in the school or when significant changes in status occur.

All nonimmigrant students must notify the INS of any change of address within ten days. The address must also be reported to the INS every three months, regardless of any changes.

6. EMPLOYMENT IN THE UNITED STATES

6.1 Practical training

Students and exchange visitors are permitted to work in the United States as part of the practical requirements of their courses of study. There are various limitations regarding time allowed for practical training. In most cases, a 12-month maximum is allowed but this depends on the program and the structure of the courses. The designated school official who administers the student program on behalf of the INS will be in a position to provide details on practical training limitations.

6.2 On-campus employment

Students in F-1 status may be employed on campus during their first year of study. They may not work more than 20 hours a week.

6.3 Off-campus employment

After their first year, students in good standing who can demonstrate unforeseen economic necessity that occurred after they arrived in the United States (for example, the cutting off of foreign funds, devaluation of foreign currency, tuition increases, or child support) may apply for authorization to work off campus. Even if the INS approved a student work authorization, he or she will not be permitted to work more than 20 hours a week during term time.

6.4 Exchange visitors

Exchange visitors who are not students are permitted to work if the program in which they are involved is accredited by the US Information Agency and employment is a component of this program. Examples of this would be medical doctors coming to US hospitals as exchange visitors, or foreign employees of a US based oil company coming to work for the parent company as an exchange visitor. There are various organizations and institutions accredited by the US Information Agency that are able to approve J-1 visas for foreign staff.

7. WHO CAN BECOME A LAWFUL PERMANENT RESIDENT WITH A J-1 VISA?

Some, but not all, J-1 exchange visitors are able to apply for an adjustment of status to permanent residents in the United States. These students and their spouses and children (if applicable) must first comply with the two-year foreign residence requirements before they can apply for an immigrant visa, unless they obtain a waiver from the INS.

Generally, exchange visitors who participated in exchange programs that were wholly or partially financed, either directly or indirectly, by the US government, or by the government of their country of nationality or last residence, must comply with the two-year foreign residence requirement.

They will also have to comply with the two-year foreign residence requirement if they come from countries that the US government has designated as needing people with the skills they will acquire as a result of the J-1 program. This designation is made when the visa is issued or when the students obtain exchange visitor status on admission to the United States.

The two-year foreign residence requirement may be waived if exchange visitors can show that they are married to a lawful permanent resident or US citizen or that they have an unmarried minor child who is a lawful permanent resident or US citizen, and that complying with the two-year foreign residence requirement would cause the spouse or child extreme hardship.

Exchange students can also obtain the waiver by establishing that they would be persecuted because of race, religion, or political opinion if they were forced to return to their country. Another possible way of obtaining a waiver is if the home or resident country tells the secretary of state that it has no objection to the waiver requested by the exchange visitor.

To apply for a waiver of the foreign residence requirement, the student or visitor must file a Form I-612 Application for Waiver of the Foreign Residence Requirement of Section 212(e) of the Immigration and Nationality Act, As Amended (see Sample 18). A filing fee of $195 must be submitted with this application, along with all supporting documents (e.g., birth certificates of spouse and children). If the waiver is requested on the basis of hardship to a US citizen spouse or children, it is important to sufficiently document the hardship. Obtaining a "family impact study" from a licensed psychologist is advised.

Documents should be originals; if you want an original returned, submit it with a photocopy. Under no circumstances should you make a copy of a Certificate of Naturalization or Citizenship: to do so is illegal.

In all circumstances, the secretary of state must approve the waiver and make a favorable recommendation to the attorney general.

SAMPLE 18
FORM I-612 APPLICATION FOR WAIVER OF THE FOREIGN RESIDENCE REQUIREMENT

OMB No 1115-0059

Application for Waiver of the Foreign Residence Requirement of Section 212(e) of the Immigration and Nationality Act, as amended

U. S. Department of Justice
Immigration and Naturalization Service

This application must be typewritten or printed legibly in black ink with block letters.

Fee Stamp

1. Name (Last in CAPS)	First	Middle	If you are a married woman, give your maiden
LEMANS	Sarthe	Du	n/a

2. Mailing Address (Apt. No.)	(Number and Street)	(Town or City)	(State or Province)	(Country)	(Zip Code, if in U.S.)
911 Daytona Bank Road		Wilimington	Delaware	USA	13245

Present or last U.S. residence	(Number and Street)	(City)	(State)	(ZIP Code)
same as above				

3. Date of Birth	Country of Birth	Country of Nationality	Country of Last Foreign Residence
06/08/1957	France	France	France

Alien Registration Number, If Known   none

4. I believe I am subject to the foreign residence requirements because: (Check appropriate box(es))

A. ☒ I participated in an exchange program which was financed by an agency of the U.S. Government or the government of the country of my nationality or last foreign residence for the purpose of promoting international educational, and cultural exchange.

B. ☐ An agency of the Government of the U.S. or the government of the country of my nationality or last foreign residence gave me a grant (such as a Fullbright grant), stipend or allowance for the purpose of participation in an exchange program. Name of U.S. Government agency or foreign country _____ .

C. ☐ I became an exchange visitor after the Secretary of State designated the country of my nationality or last foreign residence as clearly requiring the services of persons with my specialized knowledge or skill.

D. ☐ I entered the United States as, or my status was changed to that of, an exchange visitor on or after January 10, 1977 to participate in graduate medical education or training.

5. I am applying for waiver of the foreign residence requirement on the ground that: (Check appropriate box(es))

A. ☒ My departure from the United States would impose exceptional hardship on my United States citizen or lawful permanent resident spouse or child.

B. ☐ I cannot return to the country of my nationality or last foreign residence because I would be subject to persecution on account of race, religion or political opinion.

IMPORTANT: If you have checked "A" under number 5, you must attach to this application a statement dated and signed by you giving a *detailed explanation* of the basis for your belief that compliance by you with the two-year foreign residence requirement of Section 212(e) of the Immigration and Nationality Act, as amended, would impose exceptional hardship on your spouse or child who is a citizen of the United States or a lawful permanent resident thereof. Without such statement your application is incomplete. You must include in the statement all pertinent information concerning the income and savings of yourself and your spouse. There should also be attached such documentary evidence as may be available to support the allegations of hardship.

If you have checked "B" under number 5, you must attach a statement dated and signed by you setting forth in detail the reason(s) you believe that you cannot return to the country of your nationality or last foreign residence because you would be subject to persecution on account of race, religion or political opinion. There should also be attached such documentary evidence as may be available to support the allegations of persecution.

6. If married, check appropriate box(es):   (See Instruction No. 4)   n/a - wife is US Citizen

A. ☐ My spouse is included in this application.   B. ☐ My spouse is filing a separate application for waiver.

RECEIVED	TRANS. IN	RET'D TRANS. OUT	COMPLETED

Form I-612 (Rev. 11/30/01)Y Page 1

7. List all program numbers and names of *all* program sponsors.

    G-I-1   (administered by IIE)
    Field Code 4900 - Public Administration, General

8. Major field of activity (*Check one*)			9. Occupation
☐ (1) Agriculture	☐ (4) Engineering	☐ (7) Natural And Physical Sciences	**Pers. Admin.**
☐ (2) Business Administration	☐ (5) Humanities	☐ (8) Social Sciences	
☐ (3) Education	☐ (6) Medicine	☒ (9) Other	

10. Date and port of last arrival in the United States as participant in a designated exchange program.

    02/12/1995   Seattle, WA

11. If you are now abroad, give date of departure from U.S.		12. Number of prior marriages of applicant	0
n/a		If married, number of prior marriages of applicant's spouse	0

13. Name of spouse	Date and Country of birth	Nationality	Country of last foreign residence
Rose LEMANS	04/13/1960 US	US	n/a

14. Names of children	Date and Country of birth	Nationality	Country of last foreign residence
Melissa LEMANS	08/13/1996 US	US	n/a

15. If you checked "A" under number 5 on page 1 of this form, furnish the following information concerning your spouse or one of your children who is a citizen of the United States and who you believe would suffer exceptional hardship if you resided outside the United States for 2 years following your departure from this country.

    If United States citizenship of spouse or child was acquired through naturalization, give the following:

Name of United States citizen spouse or child:	United States citizenship of spouse or child was acquired through (*check one*)
Rose LEMANS and Melissa LEMANS	☒ Birth in the United States ☐ Naturalization ☐ Parent(s)

Number of naturalization certificate	Date of naturalization	Place of naturalization
n/a	n/a	n/a

If United States citizenship of spouse or child was acquired through parent(s), has spouse or child obtained a certificate of citizenship?   **n/a**

If so, give number of certificate   **n/a**   If not, submit evidence in accordance with instruction 6(a) (2).

16. If you checked "A" under number 5 on page 1 of this form, and you do not have a spouse or child who is a citizen of the United States, furnish the following information concerning your spouse or one of your children who is a lawful permanent resident of the United States and who you believe would suffer exceptional hardship if you resided outside the United States for two years following your departure from this country.

Name of lawful resident alien spouse or child:	Alien Registration Number
n/a	n/a

Date, place and means of admission for lawful permanent residence:

    n/a

I certify under penalty of perjury under the laws of the United States of America that the foregoing is true and correct.

Executed on   **11/2002**   **Wilmington, DE**   *(Signature of applicant)*
    (Date)   *(Place)*

Signature of person preparing form, if other than applicant: I declare that this document was prepared by me at the request of the applicant and is based on all information of which I have any knowledge:

                                                (Signature)

LAW OFFICES OF DAN P. DANILOV
Suite 2303 One Union Sq., Seattle, WA 98101 **10/2002**   **Attorney**
(Address of person preparing form, if other than applicant)   *(Date)*   *(Occupation)*

Form I-612 (Rev.11/30/01)Y Page 2

8
NONIMMIGRANT VISAS FOR TEMPORARY VISITS TO THE UNITED STATES*

1. TYPES OF NONIMMIGRANT VISAS

Any of the nonimmigrant visas listed in Table 5 may be issued to an applicant to allow him or her to make one or more entries into the United States. The applicant must ask the US consulate for a single or multiple entry visa into the United States when he or she first applies for a visa.

Table 5 shows the classifications of nonimmigrant visas, their type, and the length of time they allow the visa holder to stay in the United States.

2. QUALIFYING FOR A VISITOR'S VISA

Visitor's visas are issued to people who want to come to the United States for business or pleasure for a short time. Among the other nonimmigrant categories are those for people who want to enter the United States on a temporary basis as students, participants in exchange programs, performing artists, professional employees, or representatives of foreign governments.

In order to obtain a visitor's visa, you, the applicant, must show that you are eligible to receive one. The US consular officer is responsible for deciding what type of visa you require and for deciding whether or not you are eligible for it, unless you are applying for a visa that will enable you to work. If this is the case, you will first have to submit a petition to the INS and, if it is granted, the INS will then contact the US consul dealing with your case and give the go-ahead to issue you a visa.

In order to qualify for a visitor's visa, you have to show that you have a residence in a foreign country that you do not intend to abandon and that you wish to enter the United States for a specific period of time. Your purpose must be for business or pleasure. If you want to work in the United States or remain there indefinitely, you will be denied a visitor's visa.

You are ineligible to receive any kind of nonimmigrant visa if you —

(a) suffer from a contagious disease such as tuberculosis,

(b) have suffered a serious mental illness,

(c) have a criminal record,

(d) are a drug addict or trafficker, or

(e) have previously sought to obtain a visa by misrepresentation or fraud.

In addition, if you are or have been a member of a totalitarian (communist) or fascist organization (or an affiliate), you will be ineligible to receive a visa. In some cases, you may apply for a waiver of inadmissibility, but waivers are usually granted only for the sake of family unity in immigration cases.

3. APPLYING FOR A VISITOR'S VISA

To obtain a visitor's visa, you must complete Form DS-156 Nonimmigrant Visa Application and have your passport endorsed for travel to the United States (see Sample 19). The passport must be valid for at least six months beyond the period of stay in the

---

*Parts of this chapter are reproduced by permission from an article by Allen E. Kaye.

TABLE 5
TYPES OF NONIMMIGRANT VISAS

Classifications	Type	Durations and Extensions
A-1, A-2, & A-3	Diplomatic — Foreign government official or employee, family and servants	Issued for duration of diplomatic service
B-1	Temporary visitor for business extensions	Up to one year with six-month
B-2	Temporary visitor for pleasure — (cannot work in United States)	Valid for six months' stay — extensions allowed
C-1	Alien in transit States and elsewhere	For traveling in the United
C-2	Alien in transit to UN HQ	In transit
D	Crewmen of vessels or aircraft	Temporary stay
E-1	Treaty trader, spouse, and children	One-year intervals — extensions of one-year intervals while treaty trade status is maintained
E-2	Treaty investor, spouse,	One-year intervals — extensions of and children one-year intervals while treaty trade status is maintained
F-1	Student	For "Duration of Studies" (up to eight years)
F-2	Spouse or child of student	Same as F-1
G-1, G-2, G-3, and G-4	Recognized foreign member of government, etc.	Duration of government services
G-5	Attendants, servants, and personal employees of G-1 G-4	Admitted for three years with two-year renewal
H-1A	Registered nurses	Currently unavailable until Congressional renewal
H-1B	People in specialty occupations requiring at least a bachelor's decree or equivalent on-the-job experience	Admitted for up to three years with a maximum extension of three years given in one- or two-year increments. May also attend school if incidental to employment.
H-2A	Temporary agricultural workers	Admitted for duration of temporary or seasonal job — one-year extensions available to a maximum stay of three years
H-2B	Temporary workers in all other fields where jobs are themselves temporary	Admitted for duration of temporary or seasonal job (as stated on labor certification) — one-year extensions available to a maximum stay of three years

TABLE 5 — Continued

Classifications	Type	Durations and Extensions
H-3	Temporary or alien trainee	One-year intervals — usually with a one-year extension granted. Must be out of the US for six months after this two-year period in order to apply for extension, change of status, or readmission.
H-4	Spouse or child of H-1, H-2, and H-3	Same as H-1, H-2, and H-3
I	Representative of foreign information media, spouse, and children	Duration of stay with one-year extensions available indefinitely
J-1	Exchange visitor or student	Students admitted for duration of studies plus 18 months for practical training; business and industrial trainees are admitted for 18 months; teachers and scholars have a three-year limit; professors and researchers may stay for longer periods — extensions can be obtained
J-2	Spouse and children of exchange visitor/student	Same as J-1
K-1	Alien fiancé or fiancée of US citizen	Admission for 90 days to get married
K-2	Children of alien fiancé or fiancée of US citizen	Same as K-1
L-1	Intracompany transferee	Visa issued for up to three years — one-year extensions possible. Maximum stay — five years.
L-2	Spouse and children of intracompany transferee	Same as L-1
M-1	Vocational and other nonacademic student	Admitted for time necessary to complete course plus 30 days, or for one year — whichever is less — extensions may be sought
M-2	Spouse or children of vocational and other nonacademic student	Same as M-1
N-1, N-2	Parents and children of G-4 special immigrants	Three-year visas with three-year renewals
O-1	People of extraordinary ability in the arts, sciences, business, education, or athletics	Admitted for the duration necessary for the performances, programs, or other endeavors in which they will be working

TABLE 5 — Continued

Classifications	Type	Durations and Extensions
O-2	People accompanying O-1 and assisting them in their athletic or artistic performances based on their critical skills and experience	Same as for O-1
O-3	Spouses and children of O-1 and O-2	Same as for O-1 and/or O-2
P-1	Internationally recognized athletes and entertainers	Athletes admitted up to five years with another five-year extension, entertainers admitted for duration of performances
P-2	Entertainers who are part of a cultural exchange program with the US	Admitted on reciprocal basis with foreign country for duration of program
P-3	Artists and entertainers in culturally unique group performances	Admitted for duration of performances
P-4	Spouses and children of P-1, P-2, and P-3 visa holders	Same as P-1, P-2, or P-3
Q-1	International cultural visitor	Admitted for maximum of 15 months
Q-2	Spouse and children of Q-1	Same as Q-1
R-1	Ministers and religious workers of recognized religions	Admitted for maximum period of five years
R-2	Spouse and children of R-1	Same as R-1

S visas:

The S visa classification provides for the admission of two classes of aliens to the United States. The first class (S-1) involves aliens who possess reliable information critical to a federal or state government investigation and/or prosecution of an individual in a criminal organization or enterprise. The attorney general determines which aliens qualify for the S-1 visa, and there is an annual numerical limitation of 100 for this class.

The second class (S-2) involves aliens who possess critical information sought by certain federal authorities, who might be placed in danger for supplying such information, and who are eligible for the terrorism information reward. In this case, the secretary of state and the attorney general would determine which aliens qualify. An annual limitation of 25 is imposed.

This section also provides for a derivative spouse and children within the discretion of the attorney general for the S-1 visa and the attorney general and the secretary of state for the S-2 visa.

Anticipating that aliens otherwise qualifying for S visa issuance may be ineligible under one of the INA section 212(a) grounds of ineligibility, Congress has added waiver provisions specifically for the S visa classification. Aliens classified as S-1 or S-2 are prohibited from changing status to another nonimmigrant visa classification. However, INA section 245 has been amended to provide for the adjustment of status for aliens in S status to permanent resident status under certain circumstances.

United States. You must also provide a color photograph. If children under 16 years of age are accompanying you on your passport, they do not need pictures.

You must also produce evidence substantiating the purpose of your proposed trip. For example, if you are traveling to the United States on business, a letter from your firm indicating the purpose and length of the trip and its intention to pay all or most of your costs is required. Your firm must also make an undertaking that you will not be paid in the United States other than to cover your expenses. Anyone traveling on a B-1 visa must be paid his or her salary abroad.

If you are visiting for pleasure, you can submit your itinerary and explain why you will return to your home country afterwards. Family obligations, a job, and home ownership are all factors that show you intend to return. If you lack sufficient funds for your stay in the United States, you will need to submit a letter or statement from a close relative or family friend indicating that they will be financially responsible for you while you are visiting.

If you obtained a visitor's visa for a prior trip, let the consulate know, as your application can be processed faster.

There is no charge for filing an application for a visitor's visa. The charge for issuing one will be the same as the fee charged US citizens visiting your country.

Keep in mind that people who have visitor's visas are not allowed to accept employment in the United States. You should also note that the validity period shown on the visa applies to the period of time in which you may use the visa to enter the United States. It does not reflect the length of time you may spend in the United States. The length of your permitted stay is the period designated by the US immigration officer on your I-94 card (see Sample 20) when you are inspected at the port of entry.

Visas do not guarantee you the right to enter the United States. You are still subject to inspection at the port of entry. The US immigration officer there has the power to refuse to admit you.

Visas are not transferable. Once you have one, it is yours, so do not give it to someone else.

If your visa is denied, you may present new evidence in order to obtain one. However, the consular officers are not compelled to reexamine the matter until the new evidence is produced.

4. ENTERING THE UNITED STATES WITH NONIMMIGRANT VISAS

Tourists visiting the United States for pleasure (on nonimmigrant B-2 visas) or business (on nonimmigrant B-1 visas) are usually granted entry for not more than six months. In most cases, B-2 visitors who are found admissible are issued at the point of entry into the country Form I-94 Arrival-Departure Record that permits them an initial stay of six months, regardless of how much time is requested. Visitor's visas cannot be issued to people already in the United States; they are only issued by US consulates.

A six-month extension of temporary stay may be granted if, before his or her stay expires, the visitor applies on Form I-539 Application to Extend/Change Nonimmigrant Status (see Sample 21) and pays a fee of $140. It should be noted that applications for extensions beyond one year from the date of entry are rarely granted, and that, because the processing time for an extension request is normally measured in months rather than weeks, the request should be made as soon as possible. Under the tough new immigration laws, the foreign national is better off knowing whether an extension request will be granted before the foreign national's initial status expires.

However, a timely filed and non-frivolous application to extend or change status

SAMPLE 19
FORM DS-156 NONIMMIGRANT VISA APPLICATION

U.S. Department of State
NONIMMIGRANT VISA APPLICATION

Approved OMB 1405-0018
Expires 08/31/2004
Estimated Burden 1 hour
See Page 2

PLEASE TYPE OR PRINT YOUR ANSWERS IN THE SPACE PROVIDED BELOW EACH ITEM

1. SURNAMES *(As in Passport)*

2. FIRST AND MIDDLE NAMES *(As in Passport)*

3. OTHER SURNAMES USED *(Maiden, Religious, Professional, Aliases)*

4. OTHER FIRST AND MIDDLE NAMES USED

5. DATE OF BIRTH *(mm-dd-yyyy)*

6. PASSPORT NUMBER

7. PLACE OF BIRTH

Country	City	State/Province

8. NATIONALITY

9. SEX
☐ Male
☐ Female

10. NATIONAL IDENTIFICATION NUMBER

11. MARITAL STATUS
☐ Married ☐ Single (Never Married) ☐ Widowed ☐ Divorced ☐ Separated

12. HOME ADDRESS *(Include apartment number, street, city, state or province, postal zone, and country)*

13. HOME TELEPHONE NUMBER

14. E-MAIL ADDRESS

15. PRESENT OCCUPATION *(If retired, write "retired")*

16. NAME AND STREET ADDRESS OF PRESENT EMPLOYER OR SCHOOL
(Postal box number unacceptable)

17. BUSINESS TELEPHONE NUMBER

18. BUSINESS FAX NUMBER

19. WHAT IS THE PURPOSE OF YOUR TRIP?

20. AT WHAT ADDRESS WILL YOU STAY IN THE U.S.?

21. WHEN DO YOU INTEND TO ARRIVE IN THE U.S.?

22. HOW LONG DO YOU INTEND TO STAY IN THE U.S.?

23. WHO WILL PAY FOR YOUR TRIP?

24. NAMES AND RELATIONSHIPS OF PERSONS TRAVELING WITH YOU
(NOTE: A separate application for a visa must be made for each traveler, regardless of age.)

DO NOT WRITE IN THIS SPACE

B-1/B-2 MAX	B-1 MAX	B-2 MAX

OTHER _____ MAX
Visa Classification

MULT OR _____
Number of Applications

MONTHS _____
Validity

ISSUED/REFUSED

ON _____ BY _____

UNDER SEC. 214(b) 221(g)

OTHER _____ INA

REFUSAL REVIEWED BY _____

25. DO YOU INTEND TO WORK IN THE U.S.?
☐ YES ☐ NO
If YES, give name and complete address of U.S. employer.

26. DO YOU INTEND TO STUDY IN THE U.S.?
☐ YES ☐ NO
If YES, give name and complete address of school.

27. HAVE YOU EVER BEEN IN THE U.S.?
☐ YES ☐ NO

WHEN? _____

FOR HOW LONG? _____

DO NOT WRITE IN THIS SPACE

37 mm x 37 mm

PHOTO

staple or glue photo here

DS-156
08-2001

PREVIOUS EDITIONS OBSOLETE

Page 1 of 2

28. HAVE YOU EVER BEEN ISSUED A U.S. VISA?

☐ YES   ☐ NO

WHEN? _____

WHERE? _____

WHAT TYPE OF VISA? _____

29. HAVE YOU EVER BEEN REFUSED A U.S. VISA?

☐ YES   ☐ NO

WHEN? _____

WHERE? _____

WHAT TYPE OF VISA? _____

30. HAS YOUR U.S. VISA EVER BEEN CANCELLED OR REVOKED?

☐ YES   ☐ NO

WHEN? _____

WHERE? _____

31. HAS ANYONE EVER FILED AN IMMIGRANT VISA PETITION ON YOUR BEHALF?

☐ YES   ☐ NO

32. ARE ANY OF THE FOLLOWING PERSONS IN THE U.S., OR DO THEY HAVE U.S. LEGAL PERMANENT RESIDENCE OR U.S. CITIZENSHIP?
Mark YES or NO and indicate that person's status in the U.S. *(i.e., U.S. legal permanent resident, U.S. citizen, visiting, studying, working, etc.)*.

☐ YES ☐ NO   Husband/Wife _____

☐ YES ☐ NO   Fiance/Fiancee _____

☐ YES ☐ NO

☐ YES ☐ NO   Father/Mother _____

☐ YES ☐ NO   Son/Daughter _____

Brother/Sister _____

33. IMPORTANT: ALL APPLICANTS MUST READ AND CHECK THE APPROPRIATE BOX FOR EACH ITEM.

A visa may not be issued to persons who are within specific categories defined by law as inadmissible to the United States *(except when a waiver is obtained in advance)*. Is any of the following applicable to you?

- Have you ever been arrested or convicted for any offense or crime, even though subject of a pardon, amnesty or other similar legal action? Have you ever unlawfully distributed or sold a controlled substance (drug), or been a prostitute or procurer for prostitutes?   ☐ YES ☐ NO

- Have you ever been refused admission to the U.S., or been the subject of a deportation hearing, or sought to obtain or assist others to obtain a visa, entry into the U.S., or any other U.S. immigration benefit by fraud or willful misrepresentation or other unlawful means? Have you attended a U.S. public elementary school on student (F) status or a public secondary school after November 30, 1996 without reimbursing the school?   ☐ YES ☐ NO

- Do you seek to enter the United States to engage in export control violations, subversive or terrorist activities, or any other unlawful purpose? Are you a member or representative of a terrorist organization as currently designated by the U.S. Secretary of State? Have you ever participated in persecutions directed by the Nazi government of Germany; or have you ever participated in genocide?   ☐ YES ☐ NO

- Have you ever violated the terms of a U.S. visa, or been unlawfully present in, or deported from, the United States?   ☐ YES ☐ NO

- Have you ever withheld custody of a U.S. citizen child outside the United States from a person granted legal custody by a U.S. court, voted in the United States in violation of any law or regulation, or renounced U.S. citizenship for the purpose of avoiding taxation?   ☐ YES ☐ NO

- Have you ever been afflicted with a communicable disease of public health significance or a dangerous physical or mental disorder, or ever been a drug abuser or addict?   ☐ YES ☐ NO

A YES answer does not automatically signify ineligibility for a visa, but if you answered YES to any of the above, or if you have any questions about the above, a personal appearance at this office is recommended. If an appearance is not possible at this time, attach a statement of facts in your case to this application.

34. WAS THIS APPLICATION PREPARED BY ANOTHER PERSON ON YOUR BEHALF?   ☐ YES ☐ NO

(If answer is YES, then have that person complete item 35.)

35. Application Prepared By: NAME: _____

ADDRESS: _____

Relationship to Applicant: _____

Signature of Person Preparing Form: _____ DATE *(mm-dd-yyyy)* _____

36. I certify that I have read and understood all the questions set forth in this application and the answers I have furnished on this form are true and correct to the best of my knowledge and belief. I understand that any false or misleading statement may result in the permanent refusal of a visa or denial of entry into the United States. I understand that possession of a visa does not automatically entitle the bearer to enter the United States of America upon arrival at a port of entry if he or she is found inadmissible.

APPLICANT'S SIGNATURE _____

DATE *(mm-dd-yyyy)* _____

Privacy Act and Paperwork Reduction Act Statements

INA Section 222(f) provides that visa issuance and refusal records shall be considered confidential and shall be used only for the formulation, amendment, administration, or enforcement of the immigration, nationality, and other laws of the United States. Certified copies of visa records may be made available to a court which certifies that the information contained in such records is needed in a case pending before the court.

Public reporting burden for this collection of information is estimated to average 1 hour per response, including time required for searching existing data sources, gathering the necessary data, providing the information required, and reviewing the final collection. You do not have to provide the information unless this collection displays a currently valid OMB number. Send comments on the accuracy of this estimate of the burden and recommendations for reducing it to: U.S. Department of State, A/RPS/DIR, Washington, D.C. 20520-1849.

DS-156

Page 2 of 2

Admission Number

02085b422 00

Immigration and
Naturalization Service

**I-94
Arrival Record**

1. Family Name
2. First (Given) Name — Birth Date (Day/Mo/Yr)
3. Country of Citizenship — Sex (Male or Female)
4. Passport Number — Airline and Flight Number

LAND

5. Country Where You Live — City Where You Boarded
6. City Where Visa Was Issued — Date Issued (Day/Mo/Yr)
7. Address While in the United States (Number and Street)
8. City and State

Departure Number

02085b422 00

Immigration and
Naturalization Service

**I-94
Departure Record**

14. Family Name
15. First (Given) Name — Birth Date (Day/Mo/Yr)
16. Country of Citizenship

STAPLE HERE

See Other Side

---

18. Occupation

19. Waivers

20. INS File

A -

21. INS FCO

22. Petition Number

23. Program Number

24. ☐ Bond

25. ☐ Prospective Student

26. Itinerary/Comments

27. TWOV Ticket Number

Warning -A nonimmigrant who accepts unauthorized employment is subject to deportation.

Important - Retain this permit in your possession; *you must surrender it when you leave the U.S.* Failure to do so may delay your entry into the U.S. in the future. You are authorized to stay in the U.S. only until the date written on this form. To remain past this date, without permission from immigration authorities, is a violation of the law.

Surrender this permit when you leave the U.S.:
- By sea or air, to the transportation line;
- Across the Canadian border, to a Canadian Official;
- Across the Mexican border, to a U.S. Official.

Students planning to reenter the U.S. within 30 days to return to the same school, see "Arrival-Departure" on page 2 of Form I-20 prior to surrendering this permit.

Record of Changes

Port:

Date:

Carrier:

Flight #/Ship Name:

Departure Record

For sale by the Superintendent of Documents, U.S. Government Printing Office
Washington, D.C. 20402

SAMPLE 21
FORM I-539 APPLICATION TO EXTEND/CHANGE NONIMMIGRANT STATUS

OMB #1115-0093; Expires 7/31/04

U.S. Department of Justice
Immigration and Naturalization Service

Application to Extend/Change Nonimmigrant Status

START HERE - Please Type or Print

FOR INS USE ONLY

Part 1. Information about you.

Family Name **BENEDICT**	Given Name **Ernest**	Middle Initial **A.**

Address-
In Care of- **N/A**

Street Number and Name **1510 - 14th Avenue South**   Apt. #

City **Seattle**	State **WA**	Zip Code **98105**	Daytime Phone# **206/586-9786**

Country of Birth **Bolivia**	Country of Citizenship **Bolivia**

Date of Birth (MM/DD/YYYY) **07/04/1971**	Social Security # (if any) **568-89-3475**	A# (if any) **79-895-687**

Date of Last Arrival Into the U.S. **02/17/2002**	I-94# **000 000000 08**

Current Nonimmigrant Status **B-2**	Expires on (MM/DD/YYYY) **12/31/2003**

FOR INS USE ONLY columns:

Returned | Receipt

Date

Resubmitted

Date

Reloc Sent

Date

Reloc Rec'd

Date

Part 2. Application type. (See instructions for fee.)

1. I am applying for:(Check one.)
   a. ☒ An extension of stay in my current status
   b. ☐ A change of status. The new status I am requesting is: _____
   c. ☐ Other: (Describe grounds of eligibility.) _____

2. Number of people included in this application: (Check one.)
   a. ☒ I am the only applicant
   b. ☐ Members of my family are filing this application with me.
      The Total number of people included in this application is: _____
      (complete the supplement for each co-applicant)

☐ Applicant Interviewed on

Date

☐ Extension Granted to (Date): _____

Change of Status/Extension Granted
New Class: From(Date): _____
To(date): _____

Part 3. Processing Information.

1. I/We request that my/our current or requested status be extended until
   (MM/DD/YYYY): **06/25/2004**

2. Is this application based on an extension or change of status already granted to your spouse, child or parent?
   ☒ No ☐ Yes receipt # _____

3. Is this application based on a separate petition or application to give your spouse, child or parent an extension or change of status? ☒ No ☐ Yes, filed with this I-539.
   ☐ Yes, filed previously and pending with INS. INS receipt number: _____

4. If you answered "Yes" to Question 3, give the petitioner or applicant:
   N/A

   If the application is pending with INS, also give the following information.

   Office filed at **N/A**   Filed on (MM/DD/YYYY)

If denied:
☐ Still within period of stay

☐ S/D to: _____

☐ Place under docket control

Remarks:

Action Block

Part 4. Additional Information.

1. For applicant #1, provide passport information:
   Country of Issuance **Bolivia**   Valid to: (MM/DD/YYYY) **05/05/2004**

2. Foreign Address: Street Number and Name
   1510 - 14th Avenue South   Apt#

City or Town **Seattle**	State or Province **WA**
Country **U.S.A.**	Zip/Postal Code **98105**

To be completed by
Attorney or Representative, **if any**

☒ Fill in box if G-28 is attached to represent represent the applicant

ATTY State License #
WSBA # 170

Form I-539 (Rev. 09/04/01)N - Prior Versions May be Used Until 12/31/2001

Part 4. Additional Information.

3. Answer the following questions. If you answer "YES" to any question, explain on separate sheet of paper.

	Yes	No
a. Are you, or any other person included on the application, an applicant for an immigrant visa?		X
b. Has an immigrant petition ever been filed for you or for any other person included in this application?		X
c. Has a form I-485, Application to Register Permanent Residence or Adjust Status, ever been filed by you or by any other person included in this application?		X
d. Have you, or any other person included in this application, ever been arrested or convicted of any criminal offense since last entering the U.S.?		X
e. Have you, or any other person included in this application done anything that violated the terms of the nonimmigrant status you now hold?		X
f. Are you, or any other person included in this application, now in removal proceedings?		X
g. Have you, or any other person included in this application, been employed in the U.S. since last admitted or granted an extension or change of status?		X

- If you answered "YES" to Question 3f, give the following information concerning the removal proceedings on the attached page entitled **"Part 4. Additional information. Page for answers to 3f and 3g."** Include the name of the person in removal proceedings and information on jurisdiction, date proceedings began and status of proceedings.

- If you answered "No" to question 3g, fully describe how you are supporting yourself on the attached page entitled **"Part 4. Additional information. Page for answers to 3f and 3g."** Include the source, amount and basis for any income.

- If you answered "Yes" to Question 3g, fully describe the employment on the attached page entitled **"Part 4. Additional information. Page for answers to 3f and 3g."** Include the name of the person employed, name and address of the employer, weekly income and whether the employment was specifically authorized by INS.

Part 5. Signature *(Read the information on penalties in the instruction before completing this section. You must file this application while in the United States.)*

I certify, under penalty of perjury under the laws of the United States of America, that this application and the evidence submitted with it, is all true and correct. I authorize the release of any information from my record which the Immigration and Naturalization Service needs to determine eligibility for the benefit I am seeking.

Signature	Print your name			Date
Ernest A. Benedict	Ernest	A.	BENEDICT	8/10/2002

Please note: *If you do not completely fill out this form, or fail to submit required documents listed in the instructions, you may not be found eligible for the requested benefit and this application will have to be denied.*

Part 6. Signature of person preparing form if other than above. *(Sign below)*

I declare that I prepared this application at the request of the above person and it is based on all information of which I have knowledge.

Signature	Print your name	Date
Dan P. Danilov	Dan P. Danilov	8/10/2002

Firm Name and Address	Daytime Phone Number *(Area Code and Number)*	(206) 624-6868
Law Offices of Dan P. Danilov **Suite 2303 - One Union Square** **Seattle** WA 98101-3192	Fax Number *(Area Code and Number)*	(206) 624-0812

(Please remember to enclose the mailing label with your application)

Form I-539 (Rev. 09/04/01)N- Prior Versions May Be Used Until 12/31/2001:Page 2

Part 4. Additional information. Page for answers to 3f and 3g.

If you answered "Yes" to Question 3f in Part 4 on page 3 of this form, give the following information concerning the removal proceedings. Include the name of the person in removal proceedings and information on jurisdiction, date proceedings began and status of proceedings.

If you answered "No" to Question 3g in Part 4 on page 3 of this form, fully describe how you are supporting yourself. Include the source, amount and basis for any income.

If you answered "Yes" to Question 3g in Part 4 on page 3 of this form, fully describe the employment. Include the name of the person employed, name and address of the employer, weekly income and whether the employment was specifically authorized by INS.

Form I-539 (Rev. 09/04/01)N- Prior Versions May Be Used Until 12/31/2001: Page 3

SAMPLE 21 — Continued

Supplement-1
Attach to Form I-539 when more than one person is included in the petition or application.
(List each person separately. Do not include the person you named on the form).

Family Name	Given Name	Middle Name	Date of Birth (MM/DD/YYYY)
Country of Birth	Country of Citizenship	Social Security # (if any)	A# (if any)
Date of Arrival (MM/DD/YYYY)		I-94#	
Current Nonimmigrant Status		Expires on (MM/DD/YYYY)	
Country where passport issued		Expiration Date (MM/DD/YYYY)	

Family Name	Given Name	Middle Name	Date of Birth (MM/DD/YYYY)
Country of Birth	Country of Citizenship	Social Security # (if any)	A# (if any)
Date of Arrival (MM/DD/YYYY)		I-94#	
Current Nonimmigrant Status		Expires on (MM/DD/YYYY)	
Country where passport issued		Expiration Date (MM/DD/YYYY)	

Family Name	Given Name	Middle Name	Date of Birth (MM/DD/YYYY)
Country of Birth	Country of Citizenship	Social Security # (if any)	A# (if any)
Date of Arrival (MM/DD/YYYY)		I-94#	
Current Nonimmigrant Status		Expires on (MM/DD/YYYY)	
Country where passport issued		Expiration Date (MM/DD/YYYY)	

Family Name	Given Name	Middle Name	Date of Birth (MM/DD/YYYY)
Country of Birth	Country of Citizenship	Social Security # (if any)	A# (if any)
Date of Arrival (MM/DD/YYYY)		I-94#	
Current Nonimmigrant Status		Expires on (MM/DD/YYYY)	
Country where passport issued		Expiration Date (MM/DD/YYYY)	

Family Name	Given Name	Middle Name	Date of Birth (MM/DD/YYYY)
Country of Birth	Country of Citizenship	Social Security # (if any)	A# (if any)
Date of Arrival (MM/DD/YYYY)		I-94#	
Current Nonimmigrant Status		Expires on (MM/DD/YYYY)	
Country where passport issued		Expiration Date (MM/DD/YYYY)	

If you need additional space, attach a separate sheet(s) of paper.
Place your name, A # if any, date of birth, form number and application date at the top of the sheet(s) of paper.

Form I-539 (Rev. 09/04/01)Y Page 4

can extend a 120-day "grace period" in certain circumstances when the alien does not work without authorization from the INS.

A nonimmigrant must report to a US immigration officer at the port of entry for inspection and admission into the United States. At that time, the immigration officer will stamp the Arrival-Departure Record to show the permitted length of stay in the United States. A Notice to Nonimmigrants (see Sample 22) is attached to the original copy of the Arrival-Departure Record. This card informs the nonimmigrant that the length of time he or she is permitted to remain in the United States is written on the Arrival-Departure Record by the immigration inspector at the port of entry. It is not normally the same length of time the visa is valid.

The forms have been created to eliminate confusion of nonimmigrant aliens as to the length of time that they may lawfully remain in the United States and to maintain a record of the number of visitors who enter and leave the country.

5. AUTHORIZED PERIOD OF STAY

If the visitor overstays the authorized period of stay in the United States, even for one day, the visitor's visa is immediately and automatically canceled. The visitor may not be allowed to reenter the United States even though the passport may show a visa validity period of ten years, with multiple entries. The visitor shall be required to re-apply for a new visa in his or her country of nationality. The visitor cannot apply for a new visa from within any other country, without a showing of extraordinary circumstances.

6. VISA WAIVER PROGRAM

The Immigration Reform and Control Act of 1986 established a visa waiver program in which the nationals of certain countries would not need visas in order to visit the United States as tourists for periods of up to 90 days. These countries now include Andorra, Argentina, Australia, Austria, Belgium, Brunei, Denmark, Finland, France, Germany, Iceland, Ireland, Italy, Japan,

SAMPLE 22
NOTICE TO NONIMMIGRANTS

WELCOME TO THE UNITED STATES

The date in your visa, which states the period of validity, does not mean that you have permission to remain in the United States for such time.

You are authorized to stay in this country only until the date inscribed by the inspector on Form I-94 (attached).

☆ GPO: 1978-734-574
UNITED STATES DEPARTMENT OF JUSTICE
Immigration and Naturalization Service

STAPLE | M-211
(1-3-78)

Liechtenstein, Luxembourg, Monaco, Netherlands, New Zealand, Norway, San Marino, Spain, Sweden, Switzerland, and the United Kingdom.

If you are a citizen of any of these countries, your passport will be checked by your airline to ensure that you are, in fact, a citizen and that you are eligible for this program. You will receive Form I-94W Nonimmigrant Visa Waiver, which states that your stay has a 90-day limit from the time of entry.

The nationals of the countries included in this program are not bound by the visa waiver and are free to apply for tourist visas in the normal way. The advantage of having a visa is that you can apply for an extension of stay or a change of nonimmigrant status. Without a visa, neither of these two procedures is possible.

7. CANADIANS

Canadian citizens (native born or naturalized) residing in Canada can come into the United States as nonimmigrants without a visa, if their purpose is business or pleasure (i.e., if they would otherwise have had to get B-1 or B-2 nonimmigrant visas.) However, Canadian citizens who live in other countries must have US visas stamped in their passports in order to enter the United States.

The North American Free Trade Agreement extends the list of Canadian citizens resident in Canada who may enter the United States without obtaining a prior visa and without petitioning for a nonimmigrant work permit. However, all Canadians wishing to visit the United States as tourists, business visitors, or employees should carry proof of citizenship and proof of eligibility to enter the country without a visa. If the Canadian citizen is traveling to the United States to study, a visa is not required. However, the prospective student should present proof of Canadian citizenship and the Form I-20 Certificate of Eligibility for F-1 student or the Form IAP-66

Certificate of Eligibility for Exchange Visitor (J-1) Status illustrated in chapter 7. Evidence of means of support should also be provided.

8. NONIMMIGRANT VISAS FOR EMPLOYMENT IN THE UNITED STATES

All foreigners wishing to come to the United States as nonimmigrant workers have to submit a petition to the INS and obtain permission to work before they can be issued nonimmigrant visas to enter the country. Nonimmigrant visas issued for employment are listed in Table 6. They all require petitions to be granted by the INS before a visa can be issued.

See section **9.** below for a discussion of the treaty trader visa.

In all nonimmigrant visa applications based on employment in the United States, a Form I-129 Petition for a Nonimmigrant Worker must be filed by the prospective employer (or instructor in the case of H-3 trainees) (see Sample 23). It must be approved by the INS before a visa can be issued for travel.

If the applicant is an internationally recognized entertainer who will be performing at many venues throughout the country, each prospective employer may be required to file a separate petition. This cumbersome paperwork can be avoided if the temporary worker can appoint an agent to put all the various engagements and employers into one petition.

A trainee may come into the United States to receive instruction in any field from an individual, organization, or firm. These fields may include agriculture, communication, commerce, finance, government, transportation, and the professions, as well as purely industrial training.

Employees of a corporation who come to the United States to render specific or specialized services to a branch, subsidiary, or affiliate of their company may in some cases be granted intracompany transferee

TABLE 6
NONIMMIGRANT VISAS FOR EMPLOYMENT IN THE UNITED STATES

H-1A	Registered, professional nurses who are licensed to practice in the state where they will be working. (The H-1A visa program, created by the Immigration Nursing Relief Act of 1989, expired on September 30, 1997. While some members of the House of Representatives are trying to revive the category as "H-1C," currently it is no longer available.)
H-1B	People working in specialty occupations that require the minimum of a bachelor's degree or the equivalent of this degree (e.g. in 12 years of on-the-job experience in positions of increasing responsibility)
H-2A	Temporary agricultural workers coming to work in the United States to meet the need for temporary seasonal labor
H-2B	People coming to work in temporary jobs for which there is a shortage of skilled or unskilled US workers
H-3	People who are coming to the United States as trainees to participate in legitimate, existing training programs and who may be working as part of these programs
E-1	Treaty traders who come from eligible countries that have treaties of friendship and commerce with the United States and who carry out at least 50 percent of their trade between the United States and the treaty country
E-2	Treaty investors who will be investing in the United States and creating new employment for US workers (the investment must be substantial)
L-1	Intracompany transferees who will be coming to the United States to work at executive or managerial level or who are employees with specialized knowledge. The foreign entity must continue to exist and have an appropriate relationship to the US entity.
O-1	People of "extraordinary ability" in the sciences, arts, education, business, or sports
O-2	The support staff of O-1 visa holders
P-1	Internationally recognized entertainers who are part of a group and internationally recognized athletes who will be performing in the United States as an individual or as part of a team
P-2	Entertainers who will be performing in the United States as part of an exchange program
P-3	Artists and entertainers who will be performing culturally unique work in the United States as part of a group
Q-1	Cultural visitors who will be coming to the United States to participate in cultural programs
R-1	Religious workers and ministers of religion

visas. The US consulate can help you choose the correct classification if problems arise.

Spouses and children of temporary workers are not allowed to work when they accompany the principal applicant to the United States, but they may attend school. If necessary, the temporary worker will be required to show that he or she has sufficient money to support the family while the services or training are provided.

The application of these regulations to foreign medical graduates is discussed in detail in chapter 4.

9. TREATY TRADERS AND TREATY INVESTORS

An E nonimmigrant visa is issued to people who want to come to the United States in order to direct and develop the operations of a business in which they have invested substantial funds or where sizable trade exists. In order to qualify, the applicant must meet the following requirements:

(a) The application must come from a country with which the United States has an appropriate trade and navigational treaty. Treaty trader and treaty investor countries are listed in Table 7.

(b) The trading firm that the applicant represents must have the nationality of the treaty country (i.e., it should be incorporated under or registered as a business within the treaty country).

(c) The international trade must be substantial, in that there exists or will exist a sizable volume of trade.

(d) More than 50 percent of the trade involved must take place between the trader's country and the United States.

(e) The trader must be employed in a supervisory or executive capacity or have some specialized skills necessary to the operation of the firm.

Generally, treaty investors have to show that the investment is substantial and that they intend to invest it in a genuine business. The income from the investment must not be marginal. They must also be citizens of countries that have negotiated treaties with the United States.

The applicant can be involved in commercial trade, international banking, maritime insurance, transportation, communications, news-gathering activities, tourist agencies, or other business endeavors.

Citizens of Canada must apply for their E-1 Treaty Trader and/or E-2 Treaty Investor visas at US consulates in Canada. Other nationalities must apply for these visas or for change/extension/renewal of the E-1/E-2 Treaty visas in their home countries at US consulates.

10. ADJUSTMENT OF STATUS IN UNITED STATES TO PERMANENT RESIDENT

A person who has been inspected and admitted, or paroled (allowed in pending a decision in a deportation or exclusion hearing) into the United States may be eligible for adjustment of status to a permanent resident at the discretion of the INS.

In order to qualify for adjustment of status, an immigrant visa must be immediately available when the application for adjustment is filed, and the applicant must qualify under the existing laws and regulations, including having a medical examination.

People who are not eligible to apply for adjustment of status include the following:

(a) Those who entered the United States surreptitiously or without inspection

(b) Crew members of sea vessels and aircraft

(c) Exchange visitors who have to comply with the two-year foreign residence requirement

SAMPLE 23
FORM I-129 PETITION FOR A NONIMMIGRANT WORKER

U.S. Department of Justice
Immigration and Naturalization Service

OMB No. 1115-0168
Petition for a Nonimmigrant Worker

START HERE - Please Type or Print.

Part 1. Information about the employer filing this petition.
is an individual, use the top name line. Organizations should use the second line.

Family Name **N/A**	Given Name	Middle Initial

Company or Organization Name **Foundation for Feeding th Children**

Address - Attn: **Mrs. Janet McIntire**

Street Number and Name **1369 Marion Avenue**		Apt. # **15**
City **Seattle**	State or Province **WA**	
Country **U.S.A.**	Zip/Postal Code **98020**	

IRS Tax # **UBI 34-00000000000**

Part 2. Information about this Petition.
(See instructions to determine the fee)

1. **Requested Nonimmigrant classification:**
   (write classification symbol at right) **H1-B**

2. **Basis for Classification** *(check one)*
   a. ☒ New employment
   b. ☐ Continuation of previously approved employment without change
   c. ☐ Change in previously approved employment
   d. ☐ New concurrent employment

3. **Prior Petition.** If you checked other than "New Employment" in item 2 (above) give the most recent prior petition numbers for the worker(s): **N/A**

4. **Requested Action:** *(check one)*
   a. ☐ Notify the office in Part 4 so the person(s) can obtain a visa or be admitted (NOTE: a petition is not required for an E-1, E-2, or R visa)
   b. ☒ Change the person(s) status and extend their stay since they are all now in the U.S. in another status (see instructions for limitations). This is available only where you check "New Employment" in item 2, above.
   c. ☐ Extend or amend the stay of the person(s) since they now hold this status.

   Total number of workers in petition: **One**
   (See instructions for where more than one worker can be included.)

Part 3. Information about the person(s) you are filing for.
Complete the blocks below. Use the continuation sheet to name each person included in this petition.

If an entertainment group, give their group name.

Family Name **MOLINE**	Given Name **Jorge**	Middle Initial **A.**
Date of Birth *(Month/Day/Year)* **01/13/1966**	Country of Birth **Brazil**	
Social Security # **200-87-9999**	A # **None**	

If in the United States, complete the following:

Date of Arrival *(Month/Day/Year)* **05/01/2000**	I-94 # **000-000000 01**
Current Nonimmigrant Status **F-1**	Expires *(Month/Day/Year)* **08/04/2000**

Continued on back.

FOR INS USE ONLY

Returned	Receipt

Resubmitted

Reloc Sent

Reloc Rec'd

Interviewed
☐ Petitioner
☐ Beneficiary

Class: _____
# of Workers: _____
Priority Number: _____
Validity Dates: From _____
To _____

☐ **Classification Approved**
☐ Consulate/POE/PFI Notified

At: _____
☐ Extension Granted
☐ COS/Extension Granted

Partial Approval (explain)

Action Block

To be Completed by Attorney or Representative, if any
☒ Fill in box if G-28 is attached to represent the applicant

VOLAG# **SEA 0000 05**

ATTY State License # **WSBA # 170**

Form I-129 (Rev. 12/10/01)Y

Part 4. Processing Information

a. If the person named in Part 3 is outside the U.S. or a requested extension of stay or change of status cannot be granted, give the U.S. consulate or inspection facility you want to be notified if this petition is approved.

Type of Office *(check one)*: ☒ Consulate ☐ Pre-flight inspection ☐ Port of Entry

Office Address *(City)* **San Paulo** U.S. State or Foreign Country **Brazil**

Person's Foreign Address **123 Domisilio Conocido** **San Paulo** **Brazil**

b. Does each person in this petition have a valid passport?
☐ Not required to have passport ☐ No - explain on separate paper ☒ Yes

c. Are you filing any other petitions with this one? ☒ No ☐ Yes - How many? _____

d. Are applications for replacement/Initial I-94's being filed with this petition? ☒ No ☐ Yes - How many? _____

e. Are applications by dependents being filed with this petition? ☐ No ☒ Yes - How many? **2**

f. Is any person in this petition in exclusion or deportation proceedings? ☒ No ☐ Yes - explain on separate paper

g. Have you ever filed an immigrant petition for any person in this petition? ☒ No ☐ Yes - explain on separate paper

h. If you indicated you were filing a new petition in Part 2, within the past 7 years has any person in this petition:
1) ever been given the classification you are now requesting? ☒ No ☐ Yes - explain on separate paper
2) ever been denied the classification you are now requesting? ☒ No ☐ Yes - explain on separate paper

i. If you are filing for an entertainment group, has any person in this petition not been with the group for at least 1 year? ☒ No ☐ Yes - explain on separate paper

Part 5. Basic Information about the proposed employment and employer. *Attach the supplement relating to the classification you are requesting.*

Job Title **Certified Public Accountant**

Nontechnical Description of Job **Develp budget and overseas financial affairs for corporation.**

Address where the person(s) will work if different from the address in Part 1. **N/A**

Is this a full-time position? ☐ No - Hours per week ☒ Yes

Wages per week or per year **$580.00**

Other Compensation *(Explain)* **None**

Value per week or per year **N/A**

Dates of Intended employment From: **06/01/2002** To: **06/01/2006**

Type of Petitioner - *Check* ☐ U.S. citizen or permanent resident ☒ Organization ☐ Other - explain on separate paper

Type of business **Foundation which funds food for children internationally**

Year established **1981**

Current number of employees **500**

Gross Annual Income **$5,000,000.00**

Net Annual Income **Non-Profit**

Part 6. Signature. *Read the information on penalties in the instructions before completing this section.*

I certify, under penalty of perjury under the laws of the United States of America, that this petition, and the evidence submitted with it, is all true and correct. If filing this on behalf of an organization, I certify that I am empowered to do so by that organization. If this petition is to extend a prior petition, I certify that the proposed employment is under the same terms and conditions as in the prior approved petition. I authorize the release of any information from my records, or from the petitioning organization's records, which the Immigration and Naturalization Service needs to determine eligibility for the benefit being sought.

Signature and title *Janet McIntire* **Certified Public Accountant**

Print Name **Janet McIntire**

Date **May 1, 2002**

Please note: If you do not completely fill out this form and the required supplement, or fail to submit required documents listed in the instructions, then the person(s) filed for may not be found eligible for the requested benefit, and this petition may be denied.

Part 7. Signature of person preparing form if other than above.

I declare that I prepared this application at the request of the above person and it is based on all information of which I have knowledge.

Signature *Dan P. Danilov*

Print Name **Dan P. Danilov**

Date **May 1, 2002**

Firm Name and Address **Law Offices of Dan P. Danilov** **Suite 2303 - One Union Square, Seattle, WA 98101-3192**

Form I-129 (Rev. 12/10/01)Y Page 2

TABLE 7
TREATY TRADER AND TREATY INVESTOR COUNTRIES

Treaty trader countries

Argentina
Australia
Austria
Belgium
Bolivia
Bosnia-Herzegovina
Brunei
Canada
China (Taiwan)
Colombia
Costa Rica
Denmark
Estonia
Ethiopia
Finland
France
Georgia
Germany
Greece
Honduras
Iran (treaty inoperable)
Ireland
Israel
Italy
Japan
Korea
Latvia
Liberia
Luxembourg
Mexico
Netherlands
Norway
Oman
Pakistan
Paraguay
Philippines

Spain
Sri Lanka
Surinam
Sweden
Switzerland
Thailand
Togo
Turkey
United Kingdom
Yugoslavia

Treaty investor countries

Argentina
Armenia
Australia
Austria
Bangladesh
Belgium
Bosnia-Herzegovina
Bulgaria
Cameroon
Canada
China (Taiwan)
Columbia
Congo, Republic of
Costa Rica
Czech Republic
Ecuador
Egypt
Estonia
Ethiopia
Finland
France
Georgia
Germany
Grenada
Honduras

Iran (treaty inoperable)
Ireland
Italy
Japan
Kazakhstan
Korea
Kyragyzstan
Liberia
Luxembourg
Mexico
Moldova
Mongolia
Morocco
Netherlands
Norway
Oman
Pakistan
Panama
Paraguay
Philippines
Poland
Romania
Senegal
Slovak Republic
Spain
Surinam
Sweden
Switzerland
Thailand
Togo
Trinidad and Tobago
Tunisia
Turkey
Ukraine
United Kingdom (residence required)
Yugoslavia

(d) Transit visitors without a visa (people stopping to transfer in the United States while going to another destination)

(e) People who have been admitted into the United States but have accepted or continued unauthorized employment before filing a Form I-485 Application to Register Permanent Residence or Adjust Status, other than immediate relatives of US citizens

(f) People who are not admissible under any part of section 212(a) of the Immigration and Nationality Act, as amended

People who are not eligible for adjustment of status to a permanent resident within the United States must apply for immigrant visas at a US consulate abroad if they are otherwise eligible for permanent residence.

The granting of an adjustment of status from nonimmigrant to immigrant in the United States is regarded as a discretionary right exercised by the INS.

If there is any reason for the INS to believe that a nonimmigrant visitor has entered the United States with a preconceived intent to become a permanent resident (and thereby misled an interviewing consular officer or immigration inspector), the application may be denied or, if the facts warrant, an immigrant visa may be denied to a nonimmigrant on the basis of making false statements or misrepresentations to a US consul or immigration inspector.

People who have overstayed their permission to remain in the United States or have failed to comply with any of the conditions of their status are not eligible to apply for adjustment of status. They are required to return to their homelands to apply for immigrant visas at the US consulate in their home country.

Until recently, a special section of the law, section 245(i), allowed aliens who were not in legal immigration status to pay a fine of $1,000 to acquire lawful permanent resident status in the United States at an INS office. This special relief was very significant for aliens who had been unlawfully present in the United States. It allowed such aliens to adjust inside the United States without leaving. Now that this $1,000 fee has been eliminated, aliens who have been unlawfully present in the country for even one day must return to their countries of nationality to adjust their status in the United States.

What is worse is that now, since the passage of the 1996 Immigration Act (IIRIRA), an alien who remains out of status in the United States or unlawfully present for six months to one year, and who then leaves the country, is barred from returning to the United States in any status for three years. Those who have been out of status for over one year are barred from returning to the United States for ten years.

There are very few exceptions to this rule. The first exception that is still currently available is for those individuals who enter the country with inspection (i.e., with a visa) and who marry a US citizen. Such individuals, even after dropping out of status, are still allowed to adjust their status to that of a lawful permanent resident without having to leave the United States. Another frequently used exception is for individuals whose relatives filed an immigrant petition for them before January 14, 1998.

It has been mandatory until now for every adjustment of status applicant to attend an interview with an INS officer prior to this status being granted. However, in order to save government funds, the INS has amended its regulations to eliminate the interview requirement in certain cases. This will be at the discretion of the various INS offices, depending on the circumstances of each case.

For example, in cases where a nonimmigrant has been legally employed in the

United States for several years, the probability is high that he or she is eligible for adjustment, if all the requirements of the preference category in which he or she is applying have been met. In this case, the INS officer may waive the interview requirement and grant adjustment without it. Conversely, if the INS has information to indicate that the applicant worked illegally or is improperly qualified for the job in which he or she is employed, the interview will be eliminated as well and adjustment of status will be denied. The rule that will now apply is that, in most cases, an interview will not be required for —

(a) employment-based immigrant visa applicants,

(b) all children under the age of 14,

(c) parents of US citizens, and

(d) Cubans applying under the Cuban Adjustment Act of 1966.

11. EMPLOYMENT OF NONIMMIGRANTS

It is illegal for US employers to knowingly hire any person who is unauthorized to work in the United States. All employers are required to complete Form I-9 Employment Eligibility Verification for every employee at the time of hiring, and these records must be kept and maintained for designated periods of time, subject to inspection by special agents of the INS who may appear at places of work any time and without search warrants. The Employer Sanctions Law was passed in 1986 as part of the Immigration Reform and Control Act, which aimed at stemming the increasing flow of illegal immigrants who were being lured into the United States by the prospect of finding employment.

People in the United States on nonimmigrant visas may not adjust their status to immigrant if they have continued or accepted unauthorized employment, except for immediate relatives. If they have, they must return to their countries of birth or last residence and apply for an immigrant visa from there.

At one time, it was relatively easy for people living temporarily in the United States to obtain a social security card. However, because of the employer sanctions provision of the Immigration Reform and Control Act, all applicants for social security cards must now provide evidence of their right to be employed in the United States, or of their derivative status as the child or spouse of a nonimmigrant who has work authorization. Noncitizens must provide documentary evidence of legal immigrant status and nonimmigrants must provide evidence of their employment authorization. People born in the United States must also show satisfactory evidence. It is no longer possible to obtain a social security card "over the counter."

If you are admitted to the United States as an immigrant, you may apply for a social security card on the basis of documents that you will be given by the INS after you have been inspected and admitted for permanent residence. Other aliens who are admitted in various nonimmigrant classifications may apply for social security cards on the basis of evidence of their visas for authorized employment. Categories of nonimmigrant aliens in the United States who may pursue employment and, therefore, are eligible to apply for social security cards are listed in Table 8.

Special social security cards (with the words "Not Authorized for Employment") are available to investors who wish to open new bank accounts or deposit funds in any bank account in the United States.

TABLE 8
NONIMMIGRANTS WHO MAY BE LEGALLY EMPLOYED*

A-1   Ambassador, public minister, career diplomatic or consular officer, and members of their immediate families[1]

A-2   Other foreign government officials or employees, and members of their immediate families[1]

A-3   Attendants, servants or personal employees of A-1 and A-2 nonimmigrant aliens, and members of their immediate families[1]

B-1   Temporary visitor for business[2]

B-2   Temporary visitor for pleasure — employable only if Form I-94 (Arrival-Departure Record) is stamped "employment authorized."

D   Crewman (seaman or airman) — employable only on his vessel or plane while in a US port (and under certain conditions)

E-1   Treaty trader, spouse, and children[3]

E-2   Treaty investor, spouse, and children[3]

F-1   Student practical training and summer employment is permitted as is on-campus and off-campus employment during term time provided this does not exceed 20 hours a week. INS permission must be obtained.

G-2   Other representatives of recognized foreign member government to international organization and members of their immediate families[1]

G-3   Representatives of nonrecognized or nonmember foreign government to international organization, and members of their immediate families[1]

G-4   International organization officers or employees, and members of their immediate families[4]

G-5   Attendants, servants, or personal employees of G-1, G-2, G-3, and G-4 classes, and members of their immediate families[1]

H-1   Temporary worker of distinguished merit and ability — employable only with the petitioner (the company which filed for the H-1 visa for the employee)

H-2   Temporary worker performing temporary services unavailable in the United States — employable only with the petitioner

H-3   Trainee — employable only with the petitioner

I   Representatives of foreign information media, spouses, and children — employable only by the news media they represent in the United States[5]

J-1   Exchange visitor[6]

J-2   Spouse or child of exchange visitor — spouse may be employed with authorization from INS

K-1   Fiancé or fiancée of US citizen

K-2   Minor child of fiancé or fiancée of US citizen

TABLE 8 — Continued

L-1   Intracompany transferee (executive, managerial, and specialized personnel continuing employment with international firm or corporation) — employable only with the petitioning company

N-1   Parents or minor children of G-4 special immigrants

N-2   Unmarried minor children of N-1

O-1   People of extraordinary ability in the arts, sciences, education, business, and athletics

O-2   People working in support of O-1 — employable only by O-1 sponsor

P-1   Internationally recognized athletes and entertainers

P-2   Entertainers in cultural exchange programs — employable within these programs

P-3   Artists and entertainers in culturally unique performances

Q-1   International cultural visitors — employable as part of the exchange program

R-1   Ministers and religious workers — employable by religious organization with affiliations to own religious group abroad

---

*This list is for guidance only. It is suggested that, if there are any questions in individual cases, the situation be verified with the Immigration and Naturalization Service or with an attorney licensed to practice in a state of the United States, who has expertise in Immigration and Naturalization cases.

1. The principal is expected to work in the capacity in which employed by the foreign government or the international organization and the servant is expected to work as the principal's servant. The family members are not authorized to engage in any employment while in A-1, A-2, or A-3 status. However, if a family member works while in this status, the INS is not in a position to consider the work as a violation if the State Department continues to accept the alien as having official status. In some cases, the State Department may officially authorize employment for the family member.

2. Employable, within certain limitations, provided the alien continues to be an employee of a foreign company, continues to receive a salary from abroad, and is not paid a US salary (expense allowance permitted).

3. Principal alien employable only if working for certain foreign-owned companies and only if the employee is engaged in executive or supervisory duties or has special work. However, the INS does not consider that the family member has violated status by engaging in employment and will not require the family member's departure if the principal alien maintains E-1 and E-2 status.

4. Same as footnote 1. However, new regulations have been proposed which would establish formal regulations governing the employment of the alien spouses and unmarried dependent sons and daughters of the principal alien.

5. As in the case of spouses and children of "A," "E," and "G" aliens, the INS is not in a position to authorize the spouse and children of an "I" alien to accept employment. If the spouses or children should accept employment, they will not be deemed to have violated status and no action will be taken to require departure so long as the principal is maintaining status.

6. The J-1 alien can work only if permissible under the terms of the State Department approved exchange program. J-1 students may be permitted by the sponsor to accept summer employment (even if not specifically provided for in the program) and practical training. Permission to work rests with the sponsor, who is responsible for assuring compliance with the terms of the program approved by the Department of State, and not the INS.

9
ARRIVAL AT A US PORT OF ENTRY

1. THE ADMISSION PROCESS

The US immigration system is determined by Congress, which is responsible for the passage of the Immigration and Nationality Act and all other immigration legislation that has followed, and by the regulations passed pursuant to these new laws by the Immigration and Naturalization Service (INS), the Department of State, the Department of Labor, and other US governmental agencies.

1.1 Forms

Every non-US citizen who comes to the United States to live is presumed to be an intended immigrant and must have a valid and unexpired immigrant visa that has been issued to the applicant by a US consulate abroad, or a Form I-551 Alien Registration Receipt Card, or be exempt from these requirements.

All other people who seek to enter the United States on a temporary basis must have a valid nonimmigrant visa issued by a US consulate abroad in order to qualify for admission into the United States. Canadian citizens domiciled in Canada and the nationals of countries participating in the visa waiver program do not require nonimmigrant visas to enter the country, though there are restrictions. After the North American Free Trade Agreement (NAFTA) was passed, Mexicans became subject to the same conditions as Canadians in terms of their immigration rights in the United States.

1.2 Inspection

Possession of an immigrant or nonimmigrant visa that has been issued by a US consulate abroad is no guarantee that a foreigner will be admitted into the United States. Before being admitted into the United States, all foreigners first have to report for inspection and admission at a US port of entry.

If a secondary inspection reveals that a person does not meet a requirement established by law or regulation or if any documentation is incomplete or unsatisfactory, this person may be removed by the INS, in spite of having a valid visa issued by a US consulate abroad.

1.3 Physical examinations and background investigations

All applicants for immigrant visas are required to take complete physical examinations and are subject to background investigations. The medical and background checks determine whether or not there are health or legal barriers that prevent the applicant from being admitted into the United States as an immigrant, for example —

★ health,

★ economics,

★ criminal record,

★ moral issues, and

★ infringement of immigration laws.

1.4 Admission of aliens at US ports of entry

To be admitted into the United States, every foreigner arriving at a port of entry must have a valid visa, and a passport that is valid for six months beyond the visa expiry date, if these documents are required.

A returning lawful permanent resident may present a reentry permit, the result of an approved Form I-131 Application for Travel Document (see Sample 1 in chapter 1) or Form I-551 Alien Registration Receipt Card.

A person who is a lawful permanent resident returning from abroad after an absence from the United States of less than six months is admissible provided this person had no intention of abandoning permanent residence in the United States and that he or she is not excludable on grounds of health, mental illness, or criminal record. Even lawful permanent residents are subject to inspection each time they seek to enter the United States and can be found to be inadmissible and subject to removal.

A nonimmigrant visa may be revoked at any time for legal cause at the discretion of a consular officer, the secretary of state, or the INS. Revocation makes the visa invalid from the date of issuance.

2. EXPEDITED REMOVAL PROCEEDINGS

The presentation of a valid visa at a US port of entry does not mean that the foreigner will always be allowed to enter the United States. A US immigration officer is authorized to inspect the visa holder, and only after determining that the applicant is "clearly and beyond doubt entitled to land in the United States," admit him or her into the country.

If the applicant does not appear to be clearly and beyond doubt entitled to land in the United States, he or she may be placed on the same carrier that brought him or her to the United States, or detained

in the custody of the INS and held in an INS jail for expedited removal proceedings. Only under certain circumstances will arriving aliens be allowed the opportunity for a hearing in front of a US immigration judge.

There are basic differences between expedited removal proceedings, where the applicant "stands at the door" and a removal proceeding where the applicant is already in the United States. An applicant for admission has the responsibility of proving that he or she is someone who is clearly and beyond a reasonable doubt entitled to land in the United States. Therefore, constitutional guarantees and privileges do not apply to expedited removal proceedings.

The expedited removal process was produced by the Illegal Immigration Reform and Immigrant Responsibility Act of 1996 (IIRIRA), and took effect on April 1, 1997. Among those aliens that the statute states are subject to being removed from the United States without a hearing are:

(a) any foreign national arriving at a port of entry with improper documents or with no documents, and

(b) those aliens who have previously obtained an immigration benefit through misrepresentation.

Instead of a hearing before an immigration judge, the arriving foreign national is referred to "secondary inspection," where he or she is advised about expedited removal. If the foreign national expresses a credible fear of persecution or an intent to apply for asylum, the alien is then given a "credible fear interview" with an asylum officer. A foreign national who receives a favorable credible fear determination is then placed in full removal proceedings where the alien can apply for asylum. A foreign national who receives an unfavorable credible fear determination can "appeal" the decision to an immigration judge. In other words, if the asylum officer decides that the foreign national does not have a credible fear, the foreign national still has the right to request that an immigration judge review the asylum officer's negative credible fear determination. If the immigration judge agrees with the asylum officer that the alien does not have a credible fear, the alien cannot appeal that decision, and is removed through the expedited removal process. If, on the other hand, the immigration judge disagrees with an asylum officer's negative finding, the alien can apply for asylum through the removal proceeding process. Attorneys have complained about the new expedited removal proceedings because, during the initial asylum interviews, attorneys are not allowed to play an advocacy role, and are only allowed to consult with the client. Sample 24 shows an Application for Asylum and for Withholding of Removal.

The INS has the discretion to allow the foreign national to withdraw an application for admission rather than having an expedited removal order issued by the INS. For example, officers may permit withdrawal of the application for admission, or even allow deferred inspection, in cases where a lack of proper documents is the result of inadvertent error, misinformation, or where no fraud was intended (e.g., an expired nonimmigrant visa). About a third of those foreign nationals inadmissible under expedited removal are permitted to withdraw their applications for admission. This is important because withdrawing an application for admission allows a foreign national to avoid the drastic consequences associated with expedited removal, which include being inadmissible to the United States for five years.

Sometimes, applicants are returned to their native countries immediately on the same ship or airplane that brought them to the United States. The carrier must bear the expense of transportation. Only the attorney general may defer the removal of an excludable person. Admitting people from foreign countries to the United States has been viewed as a privilege granted by the US government, and it is granted only on the terms established by the United States.

OMB No. 1115-0086

U.S. Department of Justice
Immigration and Naturalization Service

Application for Asylum and for Withholding of Removal

Start Here- Please Type or Print. USE BLACK INK. SEE THE SEPARATE INSTRUCTION PAMPHLET FOR INFORMATION ABOUT ELIGIBILITY AND HOW TO COMPLETE AND FILE THIS APPLICATION. (Note: There is NO filing fee for this application.)

Please check the box if you also want to apply for withholding of removal under the Convention Against Torture. ☐

PART A.I. INFORMATION ABOUT YOU

1. Alien Registration Number(s)(A #'s) *(if any)* A00 000 000	2. Social Security No. *(if any)* None

3. Complete Last Name KULATORI	4. First Name Siroa	5. Middle Name

6. What other names have you used *(Include maiden name and aliases.)*
None

7. Residence in the U.S. C/O	Telephone Number **206/555-5555**
Street Number and Name **930 Turbot Street**	Apt. No.

City Seattle	State WA	ZIP Code 98000

8. Mailing Address in the U.S., if other than above **Same as above**	Telephone Number
Street Number and Name	Apt. No.

City	State	ZIP Code

9. Sex ☐ Male ☒ Female	10. Marital Status: ☒ Single ☐ Married ☐ Divorced ☐ Widowed

11. Date of Birth *(Mo/Day/Yr)* 06/06/1969	12. City and Country of Birth **Polduran Italy**

13. Present Nationality *(Citizenship)* Italy	14. Nationality at Birth Italy	15. Race, Ethnic or Tribal Group Italian	16. Religion Wicca

17. Check the box, a through c that applies: a. ☐ I have never been in immigration court proceedings.
b. ☐ I am now in immigration court proceedings. c. ☒ I am **not** now in immigration court proceedings, but I have been in the past.

18. Complete 18 a through c.
a. When did you last leave your country? *(Mo/Day/Yr)* 02/14/2001   b. What is your current I-94 Number, if any? **None**

c. Please list each entry to the U.S. beginning with your most recent entry.
List date (Mo/Day/Yr), and your status for each entry. *(Attach additional sheets as needed)*

Date **N/A**	Place **N/A**	Status **N/A**	Date Status Expires
Date	Place	Status	
Date	Place	Status	
Date	Place	Status	

19. What country issued your last passport or travel document **None**	20. Passport # **N/A** Travel Document # **N/A**	21. Expiration Date *(Mo/Day/Yr)*

22. What is your native language? **Italian**	23. Are you fluent in English? ☒ Yes ☐ No	24. What other languages do you speak fluently? **French**

FOR EOIR USE ONLY	**FOR INS USE ONLY**
	Action: Interview Date: _____ Decision: __ Approval Date _____ __ Denial Date: _____ __ Referral Date: _____ Asylum Officer ID# _____

Form I-589 (Rev. 10/18/01)N

OMB No. 1115-0086

PART A.II. INFORMATION ABOUT YOUR SPOUSE AND CHILDREN

Your Spouse ☒ I am not married. (Skip to *Your Children, below*)

1. Alien Registration Number (A#) *(If Any)*	2. Passport/ID Card No. *(if any)*	3. Date of Birth *(Mo/Day/Yr)*	4. Social Security No. *(If any)*
N/A	N/A	N/A	N/A

5. Complete Last Name	6. First Name	7. Middle Name	8. Maiden Name
N/A	N/A	N/A	N/A

9. Date of Marriage *(Mo/Day/Yr)*	10. Place of Marriage	11. City and Country of Birth
N/A	N/A	N/A

12. Nationality *(Citizenship)*	13. Race, Ethnic or Tribal Group	14. Sex ☐ Male ☐ Female
N/A	N/A	

15. Is this person in the U.S.? ☐ Yes *(Complete blocks 16 to 24)* ☐ No *(Specify location)*

N/A

16. Place of last entry in U.S.?	17. Date of last entry in the U.S. *(Mo/Day/Yr)*	18. I-94 No. *(If any)*	19. Status when last admitted *(Visa type, if any)*
N/A	N/A	N/A	N/A

20. What is your spouse's current status?	21. What is the expiration date of his/her authorized stay, if any? *(Mo/Day/Yr)*	22. Is your spouse in immigration court proceedings?	23. If previously in the U.S., date of previous arrival *(Mo/Day/Yr)*
N/A	N/A	☐ Yes ☐ No	N/A

24. If in the U.S., is your spouse to be included in this application? *(Check the appropriate box.)*

☐ Yes *(Attach one (1) photograph of your spouse in the upper right hand corner of page 9 on the extra copy of the application submitted for this person.)*

☐ No

Your Children. Please list **ALL** of your children, regardless of age, location, or marital status.

☒ I do not have any children *(Skip to Part A.III., Information about Your Background.)*

☐ I do have children. Total number of children _____

(Use Supplement A Form I-589 or attach additional pages and documentation if you have more than four (4) children.)

1. Alien Registration Number (A#) *(if any)*	2. Passport/ID Card No. *(If any)*	3. Marital Status *(Married Single, Divorced, Widowed)*	4. Social Security No. *(if any)*
N/A	N/A	N/A	N/A

5. Complete Last Name	6. First Name	7. Middle Name	8. Date of Birth *(Mo/Day/Yr)*
N/A	N/A	N/A	N/A

9. City and Country of Birth	10. Nationality *(Citizenship)*	11. Race, Ethnic or Tribal Group	12. Sex ☐ Male ☐ Female
N/A N/A	N/A	N/A	

13. Is this child in the U.S.? ☐ Yes *(Complete Blocks 14 to 21)* ☐ No *(Specify Location)*

N/A

14. Place of last entry in the U.S.?	15. Date of last entry in the U.S. *(Mo/Day/Yr)*	16. I-94 No. *(If any)*	17. Status when last admitted *(Visa type, if any)*
N/A	N/A	N/A	N/A

18. What is your child's current status?	19. What is the expiration date of his/her authorized stay, if any? *(Mo/Day/Yr)*	20. Is your child in immigration court proceedings?
N/A	N/A	☐ Yes ☐ No

21. If in the U.S., is this child to be included in this application? *(Check the appropriate box.)*

☐ Yes *(Attach one (1) photograph of your child in the upper right hand corner of page 9 on the extra copy of the application submitted for this person)*

☐ No

Form I-589 (Rev. 10/18/01)N Page 2

OMB No. 1115-0086

PART A.II. INFORMATION ABOUT YOUR SPOUSE AND CHILDREN Continued

1. Alien Registration Number (A#) *(if any)* N/A	2. Pass/ID Card No. *(if any)* N/A	3. Marital Status *(Married Single, Divorced, Widowed)* N/A	4. Social Security No. *(if any)* N/A
5. Complete Last Name N/A	6. First Name N/A	7. Middle Name	8. Date of Birth *(Mo/Day/Year)* N/A
9. City and Country of Birth N/A N/A	10. Nationality *(Citizenship)* N/A	11. Race, Ethnic or Tribal Group N/A	12. Sex ☐ Male ☐ Female

13. Is this child in the U.S.? ☐ Yes *(Complete blocks 14 to 21)* ☐ No *(Specify Location)*
N/A

14. Place of last entry in the U.S.? N/A	15. Date of last entry in the U.S.? *(Mo/Day/Yr)* N/A	16. I-94 No. *(If any)* N/A	17. Status when last admitted N/A
18. What is your child's current status? N/A	19. What is the expiration date of his/her authorized stay, *(if any)* *(Mo/Day/Yr)* N/A	20. Is your child in immigration court proceedings? ☐ Yes ☐ No	

21. If in the U.S., is this child to be included in this application? *(Check the appropriate box)*

☐ Yes *(Attach one (1) photograph of your child in the upper right hand corner of page 9 on the extra copy of the application submitted for this person.)*
☐ No

1. Alien Registration Number (A#)*(If any)* N/A	2. Passport/ID Card No. *(If any)* N/A	3. Marital Status *(Married, Single, Divorced, Widowed)* N/A	4. Social Security No. N/A
5. Complete Last Name N/A	6. First Name N/A	7. Middle Name N/A	8. Date of Birth *(Mo/Day/Yr)* N/A
9. City and Country of Birth N/A N/A	10. Nationality *(Citizenship)* N/A	11. Race, Ethnic or Tribal Group N/A	12. Sex ☐ Male ☐ Female

13. Is this Child in the U.S.? ☐ Yes *(Complete blocks 14 to 21)* ☐ No *(Specify Location)*
N/A

14. Place of last entry in the U.S.? N/A	15. Date of last entry in the U.S.? *(Mo/Day/Yr)* N/A	16. I-94 No. *(If any)* N/A	17. Status when last admitted *(Visa type, if any)* N/A
18. What is your child's current status? N/A	19. What is the expiration date of his/her authorized stay, if any? N/A	20. Is your child in immigration court proceedings? ☐ Yes ☐ No	

21. If in the U.S., is this child to be included in this application? *(Check the appropriate box)*

☐ Yes *(Attach one (1) photograph of your child in the upper right hand corner of page 9 on the extra copy of the application submitted for this person.)*
☐ No

1. Alien Registration Number (A#) *(If any)* N/A	2. Passport/ID Card No. *(If any)* N/A	3. Marital Status *(Married Single, Divorced, Widowed)* N/A	4. Social Security No. *(If any)* N/A
5. Complete Last Name N/A	6. First Name N/A	7. Middle Name N/A	8. Date of Birth *(Mo/Day/Yr)* N/A
9. City and Country of Birth N/A N/A	10. Nationality N/A	11. Race, Ethnic or Tribal Group N/A	12. Sex ☐ Male ☐ Female

13. Is the child in the U.S.? ☐ Yes *(Complete blocks 14 to 21)* ☐ No *(Specify Location)*
N/A

14. Place of last entry in the U.S.? N/A	15. Date of last entry in the U.S.? *(Mo/Day/Yr)* N/A	16. I-94 No. *(If any)* N/A	17. Status when last admitted *(Visa type, if any)* N/A
18. What is your child's current status? N/A	19. What is the expiration date of his/her authorized stay, if any? *(Mo/Day/Yr)* N/A	20. Is your child in immigration court proceedings ☐ Yes ☐ No	

21. If in the U.S., is this child to be included in this application? *(Check the appropriate box)*

☐ Yes *(Attach one (1) photograph of your child in the upper right hand corner of page 9 on the extra copy of the application submitted for this person.)*
☐ No

Form I-589 (Rev. 10/18/01)N Page 3

SAMPLE 24 — Continued

OMB No. 1115-0086

PART A.III. INFORMATION ABOUT YOUR BACKGROUND

1. Please list your last address where you lived before coming to the U.S. If this is not the country where your fear persecution, also list the last address in the country where you fear persecution. *(List Address, City/Town, Department, Province, or State, and Country.) (Use Supplement B Form I-589 or additional sheets of paper if necessary.)*

Number and Street *(Provide if available)*	City/Town	Department, Province or State	Country	Dates From (Mo/Yr)	To (Mo/Yr)
8622 Acme Street	Rome		Italy	11/1992	01/2001

2. Provide the following information about our residences during the last five years. List your present address first. *(Use Supplement Form B or additional sheets of paper if necessary.)*

Number and Street	City/Town	Department, Province or State	Country	Dates From (Mo/Yr)	To (Mo/Yr)
930 Turbot Street	Seattle	WA	USA	02/2001	
8622 Acme Street	Rome		Italy	11/1992	01/2001

3. Provide the following information about your education, beginning with the most recent. *(Use Supplement B Form I-589 or additional sheets of paper if necessary.)*

Name of School	Type of School	Location *(Address)*	Attended From (Mo/Yr)	To (Mo/Yr)
Silwa University	University	Rome, Italy	09/1988	06/1992
Oleg Elementary & High School	Elementary & High School	Venice, Italy	08/1975	06/1988

4. Provide the following information about your employment during the last five years. List your present employment first. *(Use Supplement Form B or additional sheets of paper if necessary.)*

Name and Address of Employer	Your Occupation	Dates From (Mo/Yr)	To (Mo/Yr)
None N/A	Unemployed	10 1998	Present
Association of Unions 335 Dixxoner Plaza, Silwa, Italy	Union President	08 1992	10 1998

5. Provide the following information about your parents and siblings (brother and sisters). Check box if the person is deceased *(Use Supplement B Form I-589 or additional sheets of paper if necessary.)*

Name	City/Town and Country of Birth	Current Location
Mother Kurtis L KULATORI	Polduran, Italy	☒ Deceased
Father Sema R KULATORI	Polduran, Italy	☐ Deceased Rome, Italy
Siblings		☐ Deceased
		☐ Deceased

Form I-589 (Rev. 10/18/01)N Page 4

OMB No. 1115-0086

PART B.   INFORMATION ABOUT YOUR APPLICATION

(Use Supplement B Form I-589 or attach additional sheets of paper as needed to complete your responses to the questions contained in PART B.)

When answering the following questions about your asylum or other protection claim (withholding of removal under 241(b)(3) of the Act or withholding of removal under the Convention Against Torture) you should provide a detailed and specific account of the basis of your claim to asylum or other protection. To the best of your ability, provide specific dates, places, and descriptions about each event or action described. You should attach documents evidencing the general conditions in the country from which you are seeking asylum or other protection and the specific facts on which you are relying to support your claim. If this documentation is unavailable or you are not providing this documentation with your application, please explain why in your responses to the following questions. Refer to Instructions, Part 1: Filing Instructions, Section II, "Basis of Eligibility," Parts A-D, Section V, "Completing the Form," Part B, and Section VII, "Additional Documents the You Should Submit" or more information on completing this section of the form.

1. Why are you applying for asylum or withholding of removal under section 241(b)(3) of the Act, or for withholding of removal under the Convention Against Torture? Check the appropriate box(es) below and then provide detailed answers to questions A and B below.

      I am seeking asylum or withholding of removal based on

            ☒ Race
            ☒ Religion
            ☐ Nationality
            ☒ Political opinion
            ☒ Membership in a particular social group
            ☐ Torture Convention

    A. Have you, your family, or close friends or colleagues ever experienced harm or mistreatment or threats in the past by anyone?

        ☐ No   ☒ Yes   If your answer is "Yes," explain in detail:

        1) What happened;
        2) When the harm or mistreatment or threats occurred;
        3) Who caused the harm or mistreatment or threats; and
        4) Why you believe the harm or mistreatment or threats occurred.

Please see my attached affidavit.

    B. Do you fear harm or mistreatment if you return to your home country?

        ☐ No   ☒ Yes   If your answer is "Yes," explain in detail:

        1) What harm or mistreatment you fear;
        2) Who you believe would harm or mistreat you; and
        3) Why you believe you would be harmed or mistreated.

Please see my attached affidavit.

Form I-589(Rev. 10/18/01)N Page 5

OMB No. 1115-0086

PART B. INFORMATION ABOUT YOUR APPLICATION Continued

2. Have you or your family members ever been charged, arrested, detained, interrogated, convicted and sentenced, or imprisoned in any country other than the United States?

☒ No   ☐ Yes If "Yes," explain the circumstances and reasons for action.

3.A. Have you or your family members ever belonged to or been associated with any organizations or groups in your home country, such as, but not limited to, a political party, student group, labor union, religious organization, military or paramilitary group, civil patrol, guerrilla organization, ethnic group, human rights group, or the press or media?

☒ No   ☐ Yes   If "Yes," describe for each person the level of participation, any leadership or other positions held, and the length of time you or your family members were involved in each organization or activity.

B. Do you or your family members continue to participate in any way in these organizations or groups?

☒ No   ☐ Yes   If "Yes," describe for each person, you or your family members' current level of participation, any leadership or other positions currently held, and the length of time you or your members have been involved in each organization or group.

4. Are you afraid of being subjected to torture in your home country or any other country to which you may be returned?

☐ No   ☒ Yes   If "Yes," explain why you are afraid and describe the nature of the torture you fear, by whom, and why it would be inflicted.

Please see my attached affidavit.

Form I-589(Rev. 10/18/01)N Page 6

OMB No. 1115-0086

PART C. ADDITIONAL INFORMATION ABOUT YOUR APPLICATION

(Use Supplement B Form I-589 or attach additional sheets of paper as needed to complete your responses to the questions contained in Part C.)

1. Have you, your spouse, your child(ren), your parents, or your siblings ever applied to the United States Government for refugee status, asylum, or withholding of removal? ☒ No ☐ Yes

    If "Yes" explain the decision and what happened to any status you, your spouse, your child(ren), your parents, or your siblings received as a result of that decision. Please indicate whether or not you were included in a parent or spouse's application. If so, please include your parent or spouse's A-number in your response. If you have been denied asylum by an Immigration Judge or the Board of Immigration Appeals, please describe any change(s) in conditions in your country or your own personal circumstances since the date of the denial that may affect your eligibility for asylum.

2. A. After leaving the country from which you are claiming asylum, did you or your spouse or child(ren), who are now in the United States, travel through or reside in any other country before entering the United States? ☒ No ☐ Yes

    B. Have you, your spouse, your child(ren), or other family members such as your parents or siblings ever applied for or received any lawful status in any country other than the one from which you are now claiming asylum? ☒ No ☐ Yes

    If "Yes" to either or both questions (2A and/or 2B), provide for each person the following: the name of each country and the length of stay; the person's status while there; the reasons for leaving; whether the person is entitled to return for lawful residence purposes; and whether the person applied for refugee status or for asylum while there, and, if not, why he or she did not do so.

3. Have you, your spouse, or child(ren) ever ordered, incited, assisted, or otherwise participated in causing harm or suffering to any person because of his or her race, religion, nationality, membership in a particular social group or belief in a particular political opinion?

    ☒ No ☐ Yes If "Yes," describe in detail each such incident and your own or your spouse's or child(ren)'s involvement.

Form I-589(Rev. 10/18/01)N Page 7

OMB No. 1115-0086

PART C.   ADDITIONAL INFORMATION ABOUT YOUR APPLICATION Continued

4.   After you left the country where you were harmed or feared harm, did you return to that country?

☒ No   ☐ Yes   If "Yes," describe in detail the circumstances of your visit (for example, the date(s) of the trip(s), the purpose(s) of the trip(s), and the length of time you remained in that country for the visit(s)).

5.   Are you filing the application more than one year after your last arrival in the United States?

☒ No   ☐ Yes   If "Yes," explain why you did not file within the first year after you arrived. You should be prepared to explain at your interview or hearing why you did not file your asylum application within the first year after you arrived. For guidance in answering this question, see Instructions, Part 1: Filing Instructions, Section V. "Completing the Form," Part C.

6.   Have you or any member of your family included in the application ever committed any crime and/or been arrested, charged, convicted and sentenced for any crimes in the United States?

☒ No   ☐ Yes   If "Yes," for each instance, specify in your response what occurred and the circumstances; dates; length of sentence received; location; the duration of the detention or imprisonment; the reason(s) for the detention or conviction; any formal charges that were lodged against you or your relatives included in your application; the reason(s) for release. Attach documents referring to these incidents, if they are available, or an explanation of why documents are not available.

Form I-589(Rev. 10/18/01)N Page 8

OMB No. 1115-0086

PART D.   YOUR SIGNATURE

After reading the information regarding penalties in the instructions, complete and sign below. If someone helped you prepare this application, he or she must complete Part E.

I certify, under penalty of perjury under the laws of the United States of America, that this application and the evidence submitted with it are all true and correct. Title 18, United States Code, Section 1546, provides in part; "Whoever knowingly makes under oath, or as permitted under penalty of perjury under section 1746 of Title 28, United States Code, knowingly subscribes as true, any false statement with respect to a material fact in any application, affidavit, or knowingly presents any such application, affidavit, or other document required by the immigration laws or regulations prescribed thereunder, or knowingly presents any such application, affidavit, or other document containing any such false statement or which fails to contain any reasonable basis in the law or fact - shall be fined in accordance with this title or imprisoned not more than five years, or both." I authorize the release of any information from my record which the Immigration and Naturalization Service needs to determine eligibility for the benefit I am seeking.

Staple your photograph here or the photograph of the family member to be included on the extra copy of the application submitted for that person.

WARNING: Applicants who are in the United States illegally are subject to removal if their asylum or withholding claims are not granted by an Asylum Officer or an Immigration Judge. Any information provided in completing this application may be used as a basis for the institution of, or as evidence in, removal proceedings even if the application is later withdrawn. Applicants determined to have knowingly made a frivolous application for asylum will be permanently ineligible for any benefits under the Immigration and Nationality Act. See 208(d)(6) of the Act and 8 CFR 208.20.

Print Complete Name	Write your name in your native alphabet
Siroa **KULATORI**	

Did your spouse, parent, or child(ren) assist you in completing this application?   ☒ No   ☐ Yes *(If "Yes," list the name and relationship.)*

(Name)	(Relationship)	(Name)	(Relationship)

Did someone other than your spouse, parent, or child(ren) prepare this application?   ☐ No   ☒ Yes *(If "Yes," complete Part E)*

Asylum applicants may be represented by counsel. Have you been provided with a list of persons who may be available to assist you, at little or no cost, with your asylum claim?   ☐ No   ☒ Yes

Signature of Applicant *(The person in Part A.I.)*

[_____]

Sign your name so it all appears within the brackets   Date *(Mo/Day/Yr)*

PART E.   DELCLARATION OF PERSON PREPARING FORM IF OTHER THAN APPLICANT, SPOUSE, PARENT OR CHILD

I declare that I have prepared this application at the request of the person named in Part D, that the responses provided are based on all information of which I have knowledge, or which was provided to me by the applicant and that the completed application was read to the applicant in his or her native language or a language he or she understands for verification before he or she signed the application in my presence. I am aware that the knowing placement of false information on the Form I-589 may also subject me to civil penalties under 8 U.S.C. 1324(c).

Signature of Preparer	Print Complete Name		
	Dan P. Danilov, Esquire		
Daytime Telephone Number **206/624-6868**	Address of Preparer: Street Number and Name **Law Offices of Dan Danilov, Suite 2303 - One Union Square**		
Apt. No.	City **Seattle**	State **WA**	ZIP Code **98101**

PART F.   TO BE COMPLETED AT INTERVIEW OR HEARING

You will be asked to complete this Part when you appear before an Asylum Officer of the Immigration and Naturalization Service (INS), or an Immigration Judge of the Executive Office for Immigration Review (EOIR) for examination.

I swear (affirm) that I know the contents of this application that I am signing, including the attached documents and supplements, that they are all true to the best of my knowledge taking into account correction(s) numbered _____ to _____ that were made by me or at my request

Signed and sworn to before me by the above named applicant on:

_____   _____
Signature of Applicant   Date *(Mo/Day/Yr)*

_____   _____
Write Your Name in Your Native Alphabet   Signature of Asylum Officer or Immigration Judge

Form I-589 (Rev. 10/18/01)N Page 9

10
REMOVAL PROCEEDINGS

Deportation and removal are words that strike fear into the hearts of most immigrants. It is a horrible thought that after all the efforts, time, and money you put into immigrating, you might be thrown out. Of course, your best defense against removal is to make sure that you do not do anything before or after entering the United States that might cause you to be removed, for example —

    (a) breaking any law, inside or outside the United States;

    (b) falsifying immigration papers;

    (c) lying to immigration officials;

    (d) smuggling illegal aliens;

    (e) participating in a sham marriage; or

    (f) failing to notify the INS about a change of address within ten days of changing residence.

All people who come to the United States either as immigrants or nonimmigrants should be aware that there are over 450 grounds for inadmissibility. Sections 212(a) of the Immigration and Nationality Act, as amended, contain some of them. The Statute of Limitations applies to only a few cases, so the passage of a lengthy period of time after the grounds for deportation arose does not provide a defense.

If you are convicted of a crime involving moral turpitude (a crime of "baseness, vileness, or depravity in the private and social duties" of a person), removal proceedings will be taken against you, even though you are a lawful permanent resident of the United States. The Immigration Act of 1996 (IIRIRA), also provides for the removal of permanent residents who have committed crimes long ago and lived exemplary lives for many years in the United States.

If you are convicted of a crime that might not be deemed a felony under US state or federal law, but which is still considered an aggravated felony under the Immigration and Nationality Act, you are generally not eligible for any immigration relief.

If, at any time after entering the United States, you are convicted for any crime involving moral turpitude, removal proceedings will be taken against you. The same is true for most crimes involving guns and/or drugs. These convictions need not have sentences imposed, nor do they need to be felonies.

At one time, anyone who divorced his or her US citizen or permanent resident spouse within two years of entering the country, was presumed to have fraudulently married in order to immigrate. The Immigration Marriage Fraud Amendments Act imposed a two-year conditional clause on permanent residence for the foreign spouses of US citizens in order to decrease the incidence of fraudulent marriages. Foreign spouses still stand the risk of removal if at their interview for permanent residence it is found that their marriage took place to evade immigration laws. A person who has been found to be removable on the ground of marriage fraud will not have another petition approved. On the other hand, the Board of Immigration Appeals case, Matter of Stockwell, does allow an alien to divorce his or her US citizen spouse and marry another US citizen, and apply for adjustment based on the new marriage, as long as the petition from the first marriage was simply denied or withdrawn, and not pursued to evade the immigration laws.

Nazi war criminals are also removable. This includes anyone who is revealed to have ordered, incited, assisted, or otherwise participated in the persecution of any person in the period between March 23, 1933, and May 8, 1945, at the direction of or in association with the Nazi government or one of its allies.

Many removal hearings involve students who have violated their status by failing to maintain full-time student status, failing to obtain an extension of stay, failing to obtain permission to transfer to another school, or by working without permission. If you come to the United States as a student, you should be careful to comply with regulations that apply to you.

If you are issued a Notice to Appear by the INS, you would be wise to see an immigration attorney promptly because of the complexities of the law.

1. THE REMOVAL HEARING

A removal hearing is a procedure to determine a person's right to be or remain in the United States after he or she has already entered the country. This is in contrast to former exclusion hearings, which determined whether the person had a right to enter the country. Both types of proceedings are now designated as "removal" proceedings.

1.1 Your rights

Removal proceedings are civil, not criminal, proceedings, so some constitutional prohibitions do not apply. For example, *ex post facto* laws (laws made after the fact or incident in question) are applicable to the person about to be removed.

If you are charged and detained by the INS, you are entitled to "due process" in the conduct of the removal hearing. This means that you —

(a) are entitled to receive notice of the charges,

(b) are to have the opportunity to examine the evidence against you and to cross-examine witnesses testifying against you, and

(c) have the right to present evidence on your own behalf.

Furthermore, you have all the constitutional rights and privileges, including the Fifth Amendment right against self-incrimination, that a citizen has.

1.2 The hearing process

At the removal proceeding, the INS is responsible for showing by clear, unequivocal, and convincing evidence that you are a removable alien.

The decision of the immigration judge must be based solely on the evidence presented at the hearing. The judge has to determine whether or not you are a person who is removable under the Immigration and Nationality Act. He or she must also decide whether you will be allowed to make a voluntary departure or whether you should be granted an adjustment of status to permanent residence. You may be granted or denied the privilege of a "creation of a record of lawful admission" if, for example, you are eligible for amnesty in terms of the existing laws. The judge also has the power to close or terminate the removal proceedings altogether.

You may be arrested and detained in custody, but can be released pending the hearing if you post a bond. This can be done at the discretion of the district director.

At the hearing, the INS will be represented by someone designated by the district director. This person will be an attorney. You can represent yourself or be represented by a friend or a lawyer. However, if you cannot afford to hire a lawyer, the INS is obligated to inform you that you may be entitled to the services of a legal aid lawyer at no expense to the government. You have the right to be represented by a lawyer at the hearing as long as it is without cost to the government.

After all the evidence has been heard, the judge may make an order indicating that one or more of the following steps are to be taken:

(a) You will be removed.

(b) The proceedings against you will be terminated.

(c) Your removal will be suspended.

(d) You will be allowed to adjust your status.

(e) You will be granted the right to depart voluntarily in lieu of removal.

At the discretion of the judge, other actions can be taken in order to dispose of the proceedings.

At a removal hearing, the judge must ask you where you want to be removed to. If the judge does not ask you where you want to go, depending upon the specific facts of your case, you may have grounds for an appeal to the Board of Immigration Appeals.

At any time during the removal hearings, you are entitled to make a motion to reopen or reconsider the proceedings. In order to do this, you have to file a written motion that either sets out new evidence that was not previously available, or states why you claim that an erroneous interpretation of the law or abuse of discretion was made. A filing fee of $110 is required.

2. RELIEF AVAILABLE

You may apply for Cancellation of Removal or you may request asylum in the United States on the basis that you fear you may be persecuted in your home country because of your race, religion, or political opinion. The Immigration Act of 1996 requires that aliens apply for asylum within one year of entering the United States

(unless there has been a change of their country's conditions or the alien can provide good cause why no asylum application was timely filed).

You can also apply to have your status adjusted from nonimmigrant to permanent resident. You make this application on Form I-485 Application to Register Permanent Residence or Adjust Status (see Sample 14). You must establish that you are eligible to be granted this status by showing that you had been inspected or paroled for admission into the United States on an immigrant visa or in one of the nonimmigrant categories available to you. Frequently, an application for a 212(h) waiver is also required.

You may not apply for an adjustment of status if you are a crew member, an exchange visitor who has not had the two-year foreign residence requirement waived, a person who entered while in transit to another country without a visa, or if you entered the country without inspection, or fraudulently.

2.1 Cancellation of removal

2.1.a Cancellation of removal for lawful permanent residents

To be statutorily eligible for cancellation of removal under section 240A(a) of the Immigration and Nationality Act, an alien must demonstrate not only that he or she has been lawfully admitted for permanent residence for not less than five years, but that he or she has resided in the United States continuously for seven years after having been admitted in any status, and has not been convicted of an aggravated felony. You may apply using form EOIR 42A Application for Cancellation of Removal for Certain Permanent Residents (see Sample 25). The filing fee is $100.

In addition to satisfying the three statutory eligibility requirements, an applicant for relief must also establish that he or she

SAMPLE 25
FORM EOIR-42A APPLICATION FOR CANCELLATION OF REMOVAL
FOR CERTAIN PERMANENT RESIDENTS

U.S. Department of Justice
Executive Office for Immigration Review

OMB #1125-0001
**Application for Cancellation of Removal
For Certain Permanent Residents**
(Under Section 240A of the Immigration and Nationality Act)

PLEASE READ ADVICE AND INSTRUCTIONS
BEFORE FILLING IN FORM

PLEASE TYPE OR PRINT

Fee Stamp

PART 1 - INFORMATION ABOUT YOURSELF

1) My present true name is: *(Last, First, Middle)*	2) Alien Registration Number:
OLEARY Jennifer Lynn	00 000 000

3) My name given at birth was: *(Last, First, Middle)*	4) Birth Place: *(City, Country)*
STANLEY, Jennifer	Queensbrough AUSTRALIA

5) Date of Birth: *(Month, Day, Year)*	6) Gender:	7) Height:	8) Hair Color:	9) Eye Color:
08/14/1968	☐ Male ☒ Female	5'6"	Red	Green

10) Current Nationality & Citizenship:	11) Social Security Number:	12) Home Phone Number:	13) Work Phone Number:
AUSTRALIA	000-00-0000	425/555-5555	206/555-5555

14) I currently reside at:	15) I have been known by these additional name(s):
Apt. number and/or in care of 246 - Dino Avenue North *Number and Street* Lynnwood WA 98000 *City or Town* *State* *ZIP Code*	N/A

16) I have resided in the following locations in the United States: (List PRESENT ADDRESS FIRST, and work back in time for at least 7
years.)

Street and Number - Apt. or Room# - City or Town - State - ZIP Code	Resided From: *(Month, Day, Year)*	Resided To: *(Month, Day, Year)*
246 - Dino Avenue North Lynnwood WA 98000	03/13/1993	PRESENT
31 Viale Triente Trieste Lynnwood WA 98000	07/04/1990	03/12/1993

PART 2.- INFORMATION ABOUT THIS APPLICATION

17) I, the undersigned, hereby request that my removal be cancelled under the provisions of section 240A(a) of the Immigration and
Nationality Act (INA). I believe that I am eligible for this relief because I have been a lawful permanent resident alien for 5 or more
years, have 7 years of continuous residence in the United States, and have not been convicted of an aggravated felony. I was
admitted as or adjusted to the status of an alien lawfully admitted for permanent residence on ___07/04/1990___
                                                                                                                        (date)

at ___Seattle, Washington___   .
          (place)

Please use a separate sheet for additional entries.
(1)

Form EOIR-42A
4.97

PART 3 - INFORMATION ABOUT YOUR PRESENCE IN THE UNITED STATES

18) My first arrival into the United States was under the name of: *(Last, First, Middle)* STANLEY   Jennifer   Lynn

19) My first arrival to the United States was on: *(Month, Day, Year)* 07/04/1990

20) Place or port of first Arrival: *(Place or Port, City, and State)* Seattle, WA

21) I:
- ☒ was admitted as a lawful permanent resident.
- ☐ was admitted as a nonimmigrant. Specify visa type: _____
- ☐ entered without inspection.
- ☐ other - specify _____

22) If admitted as a nonimmigrant, period for which admitted: *(Month, Day, Year)* / /   to N/A

23) My last extension of stay in the United States expired on: *(Month, Day, Year)* N/A

24) Since the date of my first arrival, I departed from and returned to the United States at the following places and on the following dates: *(Please list all departures regardless of how briefly you were absent from the United States)*
If you have never departed from the United States since your original date of arrival, please mark an X in the box: ☒

Port of Departure (Place or Port, City and State)	Departure Date (Month, Day, Year)	Purpose of Travel	Destination
N/A	N/A	N/A	N/A
Port of Return (Place or Port, City and State)	Return Date (Month, Day, Year)	Manner of Return	Inspected & Admitted?
N/A	N/A	N/A	☐ Yes ☐ No
Port of Departure (Place or Port, City and State)	Departure Date (Month, Day, Year)	Purpose of Travel	Destination
Port of Return (Place or Port, City and State)	Return Date (Month, Day, Year)	Manner of Return	Inspected & Admitted?
			☐ Yes ☐ No

25) Have you ever departed the United States:
a) under an order of deportation, exclusion or removal? ------- ☐ Yes ☒ No
b) pursuant to a grant of voluntary departure? ---------------- ☐ Yes ☒ No

PART 4 - INFORMATION ABOUT YOUR MARITAL STATUS AND SPOUSE   *(Continued on page 3)*

26) I am not married: ☐
    I am married: ☒

27) If married, the name of my spouse is: *(Last, First, Middle)* OLEARY   Roger   James

28) Date of marriage: *(Month, Day, Year)* 02/14/1990

29) The marriage took place in: *(City and Country)* Sydney, AUSTRALIA

30) Birth place of spouse: *(City and Country)* Phoenix,   AZ   USA

31) My spouse currently resides at:
Apt number and/or in care of 246 - Dino Avenue North
Number and Street Lynnwood   WA   98000
City or Town   *State/Country*   *ZIP Code*

32) Birth date of spouse: *(Month, Day, Year)* 01/22/1966

33) My spouse is a citizen of: *(Country)* USA

34) If your spouse is other than a native born United States citizen, answer the following:
He/she arrived in the United States at: *(City and State)* N/A
He/she arrived in the United States on: *(Month, Day, Year)* _____
His/her alien registration number is: A# _____
He/she was naturalized on: *(Month, Day, Year)* _____ at _____
(City and State)

35) My spouse ☒ - is ☐ - is not employed. If employed, please give salary and the name and address of the place(s) of employment:

Full Name and Address of Employer:	Earnings Per Week *(Approximate)*
First Pacific National Amalgamated Bank, Suite 288 GTO, Maranello Plaza, Seattle, WA 98000	$ 1500
	$
	$

Please use a separate sheet for additional entries.
(2)

Form EOIR-42-A
4 97

PART 4 - INFORMATION ABOUT YOUR MARITAL STATUS AND SPOUSE *(Continued)*

36) I ☐ -have ☒ -have not been previously married: *(If previously married, list the name of each prior spouse, the dates on which each marriage began and ended, the place where the marriage terminated, and describe how each marriage ended.)*

Name of prior spouse: *(Last, First, Middle)*	Date marriage began: Date marriage ended:	Place marriage ended: *(City and Country)*	Description or manner of how marriage was terminated or ended:
N/A	N/A N/A	N/A	N/A

Name of prior spouse: *(Last, First, Middle)*	Date marriage began: Date marriage ended:	Place marriage ended: *(City and Country)*	Description or manner of how marriage was termanated or ended:

37) Have you been ordered by any court, or are otherwise under any legal obligation, to provide child support and/or spousal maintenance as a result of a separation and/or divorce?   ☐ -Yes   ☒ -No

PART 5 - INFORMATION ABOUT YOUR EMPLOYMENT AND FINANCIAL STATUS

38) Since my arrival into the United States, I have been employed by the following - named persons or firms: *(Please begin with present employment and work back in time. Any periods of unemployment or school attendance should be specified.)*

Full Name and Address of Employer	Earnings Per Week *(Approximate)*	Type of Work Performed	Employed From: *(Month, Day, Year)*	Employed To: *(Month, Day, Year)*
Queen Anne Hospital 212 Inter-Cavallino Rampante, Seattle, WA 98000	$ 1200	R.N.	08/12/1990	PRESENT
	$			
	$			

39) If self-employed, describe the nature of the business, the name of the business, its address, and net income derived therefrom:

N/A

40) My assets (and if married, my spouse's assets) in the United States and other countries, not including clothing and household necessities, are:

Self		**Jointly Owned with Spouse**	
Cash, Stocks, and Bonds – – – – – $		Cash, Stocks, and Bonds – – – – – .	$ 100000
Real Estate – – – – – – – – – $		Real Estate – – – – – – – – –	$ 450000
Automobile (value minus amount owed)- $		Automobile (value minus amount owed)-	$ 20000
Other (describe on line below) – – – $		Other (describe on line below) – – – –	$
TOTAL $		TOTAL	$ 570000

41) I ☐ -have ☒ -have not received public or private relief or assistance(e.g. Welfare, Unemployment Benefits, Medicaid, ADC, etc.). If you have, please give full details including the type of relief or assistance received, date for which relief or assistance was received, place, and amount received during this time:

42) Please list each of the years in which you have filed an income tax return with the Internal Revenue Service:
1991, 1992, 1993, 1994, 1995, 1996, 1997, 1998

Please use a separate sheet for additional entries.
(3)

Form EOIR-42-A
4/97

PART 6 - INFORMATION ABOUT YOUR FAMILY *(Continued on page 5)*

43) I have __2__ _(Number of)_ children. Please list information for each child below, include assets and earnings information for children over the age of sixteen who have separate incomes:

Name of Child: *(Last, First, Middle)* Child's Alien Registration Number:	Citizen of What Country: Birth Date: *(Month, Day, Year)*	Now Residing At: *(City and Country)* Birth Place: *(City and Country)*	Immigration Status of Child?
OLEARY Mary A#: N/A Estimated Total of Assets: $ N/A	USA 12/26/1997 Estimated Average Weekly Earnings: $ N/A	Lynnwood, WA USA Seattle, WA USA	Citizen
OLEARY Enzo A#: N/A Estimated Total of Assets: $ N/A	USA 02/18/1992 Estimated Average Weekly Earnings: $ N/A	Lynnwood, WA USA Seattle, WA USA	Citizen
A#: Estimated Total of Assets: $		Estimated Average Weekly Earnings: $	

44) If your application is denied, would your spouse and all of your children accompany you to your:

Country of Birth -   ☐ Yes ☒ No

Country of Nationality -   ☐ Yes ☒ No

Country of Last Residence -   ☐ Yes ☒ No

If you answered "NO" to any of the responses, please explain: _____
Children are U.S. Citizens. Son Enzo has undergone a
liver transplant and is under mandatory continuing care
and treatment. My parents are deceased, no family in
Australia. My only living relative resides in Poulsbo, WA.

45) Members of my family, including my spouse and/or child(ren) ☐ - have ☒ - have not received public or private relief or assistance (e.g., Unemployment Benefits, Welfare, Medicaid, ADC, etc.). If any member of your immediate family has received such relief or assistance, please give full details including identity of person(s) receiving relief or assistance, dates for which relief or assistance was received, place, and amount received during this time: _____

46) Please give the requested information about your parents, brothers, sisters, aunts, uncles. and grandparents. As to residence, show street address, city, and state, if in the United States; otherwise show only country:

Name: *(Last, First, Middle)* Alien Registration Number:	Citizen of What Country: Birth Date: *(Month, Day, Year)*	Relationship to Me: Birth Place: *(Place and Country)*	Immigration Status of Listed Relative
STANLEY, Hazel A#: 00 000 000 Complete Address of Current Residence: 456 Mondial Road Poulsbo, WA 98000	AUSTRALIA 03/06/1970	Sister Melbourne, AUSTRALIA	Perm. Res.
PARENTS - Both are deceased A#: N/A Complete Address of Current Residence: N/A	Deceased N/A	Deceased N/A N/A	Deceased

Please use a separate sheet for additional entries.
(4)

Form EOIR-42A
4 97

PART 7 - MISCELLANEOUS INFORMATION	*(Continued on page 6)*

47) I ☐ - have ☒ - have not entered the United States as a crewman after June 30, 1964.

48) I ☐ - have ☒ - have not been admitted as, or after arrival in the United States acquired the status of, an exchange alien.

49) I ☒ - have ☐ - have not submitted address reports as required by section 265 of the Immigration and Nationality Act.

50) I ☒ -have ☐ -have never(either in the United Stated or in any foreign country)been arrested, summoned into court as a defendant, convicted, fined, imprisoned, placed on probation, or forfeited collateral for an act involving a felony, misdemeanor, or breach of any public law or ordinance(including, but not limited to, traffic violations or driving incidents involving alcohol). *(If answer is in the affirmative, please give a brief description of each offense including the name and location of the offense, date of conviction, any penalty imposed, any sentence imposed, and the time actually served).*

I was arrested for shoplifting $25.00 worth of socks at a department store in Seattle on August 1, 1998, and I was sentenced to 30 days, suspended 30 days, and given 3 months probation. Copies of my complete criminal record are attached.

51) Have you ever served in the Armed Forces of the United States? ☐ - Yes ☒ - No. If "Yes" please state branch *(Army, Navy, etc.)* and service number. N/A

Place of entry on duty: *(City, and State)* N/A

Date of entry on duty: *(Month, Day, Year)* N/A Date of discharge: *(Month, Day, Year)* N/A

Type of discharge *(Honorable, Dishonorable, etc.):* N/A

I served in active duty status from: *(Month, Day, Year)* N/A to *(Month, Day, Year)* N/A

52) Have you ever left the United States or the jurisdiction of the district where you registered for the draft to avoid being drafted into the military or naval forces of the United States? ☐ Yes ☒ No

53) Have you ever deserted from the military or naval forces of the United Stated while the United Stated was at war? ☐ Yes ☒ No

54) If male, did you register under the Selective Service (Draft) Law of 1917, 1918, 1948, 1951, or later Draft Laws? ☐ Yes ☐ No
If "Yes," please give date, Selective Service number, local draft board number, and your last draft classification: _____
N/A

55) Were you ever exempted from service because of conscientious objection, alienage, or any other reason? ☐ Yes ☒ No

56) Please list your present or past membership in or affiliation with every political organization, association, fund, foundation, party, club, society, or similar group in the United States or any other place since your 16th birthday. Include any foreign military service in this part. If none, write "NONE". Include the name of the organization, location, nature of the organization, and the dates of membership.

Name of Organization	Location of Organization	Nature of Organization	Member From: *(Month, Day, Year)*	Member To: *(Month, Day, Year)*
RN Society of Wash.	Bellevue, WA	Registered Nurses	04/01/1991	Present

Please a separate sheet for additional entries.

(5)

Form EOIR-42A
4 97

PART 7 - MISCELLANEOUS INFORMATION *(Continued)*

57) Have you ever:

☐ Yes ☒ No been ordered deported or removed?

☐ Yes ☒ No overstayed a grant of voluntary departure from an Immigration Judge or the Immigration and Naturalization Service (INS)?

☐ Yes ☒ No failed to appear for deportation or removal?

58) Have you ever been:

☐ Yes ☒ No a habitual drinker?

☐ Yes ☒ No one whose income is derived principally from illegal gambling?

☐ Yes ☒ No one who has given false testimony for the purpose of obtaining immigration benefits?

☐ Yes ☒ No engaged in prostitution or unlawful commercialized vice?

☐ Yes ☒ No involved in a serious criminal offense and asserted immunity from prosecution?

☐ Yes ☒ No a polygamist?

☐ Yes ☒ No one who aided and/or abetted another to enter the United States Illegally?

☐ Yes ☒ No a trafficker of a controlled substance, or a knowing assister, abettor, conspirator, or colluder with others in any such controlled substance offense (not including a single offense of simple possession of 30 grams or less of marijuana)?

☐ Yes ☒ No inadmissible or deportable on security-related grounds under sections 212(a)(3) or 237(a)(4) of the INA?

☐ Yes ☒ No one who has ordered, incited, assisted, or otherwise participated in the persecution of an individual on account of his or her race, religion, nationality, membership in a particular social group, or political opinion?

☐ Yes ☒ No a person previously granted relief under sections 212(c) or 244(a) of the INA or whose removal has perviously been cancelled under section 240A of the INA?

59) The following certificates or other supporting documents are attached hereto as a part of this application; *(Refer to the Instruction Sheet for documents which should be Attached).*

INDEX to all required supporting documents, including:

Marriage Certificate

Birth Certificates

Medical records of son, letters/evaluations from doctors

Death Certificates of Parents

Complete criminal records

Affidavit from Employer

Affidavits from friends, pastor, co-workers

Mortgage documents

Tax Returns

Bank Statements

Family Impact Study

Please use a separate sheet for additional entries.
(6)

Form EOIR-42A
4 97

PART 7 - MISCELLANEOUS INFORMATION *(Continued)*

APPLICATION NOT TO BE SIGNED BELOW UNTIL APPLICANT APPEARS BEFORE AN IMMIGRATION JUDGE

I do swear (affirm) that the contents of the above application, including the documents attached hereto, are true to the best of my knowledge and that this application is now signed by me with my full, true name.

_____
(Complete and true signature of applicant or parent or guardian)

Subscribed and sworn to before me by the above-named applicant at

_____

_____
Immigration Judge

_____
Date: (Month, Day, Year)

CERTIFICATE OF SERVICE

I hereby certify that a copy of the foregoing was: ☒ - <u>delivered in person,</u>　　☐ - <u>mailed first class, postage prepaid</u>

on _____02/16/1999_____ *(Month, Day, Year)* to _____

Office of the INS District Counsel, 1000 Second Avenue, Suite 2900, Seattle, WA 98104

_____
Signature of Applicant (or attorney or representative)

warrants such relief as a matter of the immigration judge's discretion. Factors that the immigration judge may consider in determining whether the alien deserves a discretionary grant of relief include:

★ family ties within the United States,

★ residence of long duration in this country (particularly when the inception of residence occurred at a young age),

★ evidence of hardship to the respondent and his or her family if removal occurs,

★ service in the US armed forces,

★ a history of employment,

★ the existence of property or business ties,

★ evidence of value and service to the community,

★ proof of genuine rehabilitation, and

★ other evidence attesting to a respondent's good character.

2.1.b Cancellation of removal for nonpermanent residents

A nonpermanent resident can apply for Cancellation of Removal on Form EOIR-42B (see Sample 26). The filing fee is $100. You must show that you were continuously and physically present in the United States for the previous ten years, that you have been of good moral character, and that the removal would result in exceptional and extremely unusual hardship to your US citizen or lawful permanent resident spouse, parent, or child.

Form EOIR-42B itself comes with fairly explicit instructions which should be followed.

To support your Form EOIR-42B, you must prepare numerous supporting documents and have them ready to present to the judge at your hearing. Bring copies of all the documents to the deportation hearing so that you can keep the originals. All documents should be translated if not already in English. Submit a copy of any temporary entry permit that you were given when you first came into the United States.

Remember, that in order to obtain this second type of Cancellation of Removal relief, you must show that your removal would result in exceptional and extremely unusual hardship to a US citizen or permanent resident to whom you are closely related by blood or marriage — a tough standard to meet. Documents such as a birth or marriage certificate are used to establish a relationship to the people who would suffer such hardship if you were removed. A divorce decree or death certificate may also be needed to establish the validity of a marriage or the existence of a close relationship to a US citizen or lawful permanent resident.

In order to establish that you have continuously resided in the United States for ten years, you should produce documents such as —

★ bank books,

★ leases,

★ deeds,

★ licenses,

★ accident reports,

★ medical/hospital records,

★ driver's licenses or old photo IDs,

★ letters,

★ church records,

★ school records,

★ employment records, and

★ tax receipts.

You also have to show the immigration judge that during your stay in the United States you were a person of good moral character. In order to do this, you must show police records from all the areas where you lived for more than six months during the past ten or more years.

Two US citizens should sign affidavits in which they say under oath that they knew you for a specified period of time and during that time they formed a good opinion of your character (see Sample 27). You should also produce an affidavit from an employer attesting to your good character during the period of employment. The employer's affidavit should set out what kind of work you performed, how long you were employed, and what you earned (see Sample 28).

2.2 Record of lawful admission

If you entered the United States before June 30, 1972, and have no record of admission, you can ask for registry during the removal proceedings by filing Form I-485 Application to Register Permanent Residence or Adjust Status (see Sample 14 in chapter 3). You must show that you have resided continuously in the United States since that entry and that you have been a person of good moral character and are otherwise eligible for registry.

If your application is granted, you will be given a record of lawful admission.

3. VOLUNTARY DEPARTURE AT OWN EXPENSE

You may ask for permission to leave the United States at your own expense and avoid having an Order of Removal filed against you. Pursuant to IIRIRA, voluntary departure is now available for all persons at a removal hearing, whether or not they are inadmissible (or formerly excludable) persons. However, to qualify for voluntary departure at the end of removal proceedings, each alien may have to post a $500 voluntary departure bond with the Immigration Service within five days of the judge's order. The five-days rule is absolute.

Voluntary departure saves the US government resources by allowing aliens to depart at their own expense rather than at the expense of the government. Secondly, voluntary departure benefits the aliens involved by allowing them to avoid the harsh consequences of a formal order of removal.

Prior to IIRIRA, the authority for voluntary departure was found in section 244(e) of the act, which contained no time limitation. Now, for the first time, there are statutory restrictions limiting the time for which voluntary departure may be authorized.

The new maximum time limits for voluntary departure are harsh: 120 days maximum prior to completion of removal proceedings; and 60 days at the completion of removal proceedings. In order to obtain voluntary departure from an immigration judge under section 240B(a) of the act, an alien must request it prior to or at the master calendar hearing at which the case is initially scheduled for a merits hearing, which is not necessarily the first master calendar hearing. This ensures that the alien is not obligated to request voluntary departure at preliminary stages of the process, before the case is ready to be scheduled for a merits hearing. The total period of voluntary departure, including all extensions, may not exceed 120 days for voluntary departure granted before the end of removal proceedings, or 60 days granted at the end of removal proceedings.

If you have been granted voluntary departure, an Order of Removal automatically becomes final. If you do not voluntarily depart, you will be required to surrender to the INS within 30 days of receiving your Notice to Surrender. If you fail to surrender, you could be denied discretionary relief from removal, such as the following:

★ Asylum

★ Waiver of Inadmissibility for Fraud

★ Cancellation of Removal (Suspension of Deportation)

★ Voluntary Departure

SAMPLE 26
FORM EOIR-42B APPLICATION FOR CANCELLATION OF REMOVAL
AND ADJUSTMENT OF STATUS OF CERTAIN NONPERMANENT RESIDENTS

U.S. Department of Justice
Executive Office for Immigration Review

OMB #1125-0001

**Application for Cancellation of Removal and
Adjustment of Status Certain Nonpermanent Residents**

**PLEASE READ ADVICE AND INSTRUCTIONS
BEFORE FILLING IN FORM**

PLEASE TYPE OR PRINT

Fee Stamp

PART 1 - INFORMATION ABOUT YOURSELF

1) My present true name is: *(Last, First, Middle)* MARTINEZ, Salvador Juan	2) Alien Registration Number: None
3) My name given at birth was: *(Last, First, Middle)* Same as in Item 1 above	4) Birth Place: *(City, Country)* Jalisco, MEXICO

5) Date of Birth: *(Month, Day, Year)* 06/13/1965	6) Gender: ☒ Male ☐ Female	7) Height: 5'10"	8) Hair Color: Brown	9) Eye Color: Brown

10) Current Nationality & Citizenship: MEXICO	11) Social Security Number: None	12) Home Phone Number: 509/555-5555	13) Work Phone Number: 509/555-1212

14) I currently reside at: B-3 *Apt. number and/or in care of* 4596 Tornado Way *Number and Street* Yakima WA 98000 *City or Town State ZIP Code*	15) I have been known by the additional name(s): None

16) During the last 10 years, I resided in the following locations in the United States: (If less than 10 years, set forth the information for the period you have been in the United States) List PRESENT ADDRESS FIRST and work back in time

Street and Number - Apt. or Room# - City or Town - State - ZIP Code				Resided From: *(Month, Day, Year)*	Resided To: *(Month, Day, Year)*
4596 Tornado Way	Yakima	WA	98000	05/1992	PRESENT
3961 Chason Street	Brewster	WA	98000	12/1990	5/1992
817 Zero Avenue	Los Angeles	CA	93000	09/1987	12/1990

PART 2 - INFORMATION ABOUT THIS APPLICATION

17) I, the undersigned, hereby request that my removal be cancelled under the provisions of section 244A(b) of the Immigration and Nationality Act (INA). I believe that I am eligible for cancellation of removal because: (check all apply)

☒ My removal would result in exceptional and extremely unusual hardship to my: *(Place a **USC** in the space if the family member is a citizen of the United States, an **L** if the family member is a lawful permanent resident of the United States, an **X** if the family member is neither and leave **BLANK** if not applicable.)*

_____ Husband   __X__ Wife   _____ Father   _____ Mother   __USC__ Child or Children

With the exception of absences described in question #25, I have resided in the United States since:
(Month, Day, Year) ___09/14/1987_____

☐ I, or my child, have been battered or subjected to extreme cruelty by a United States citizen or lawful permanent resident spouse or parent.

With the exception of the absences described in question #25, I have been physically present in the United States since:
(Month, Day, Year) _____

Please use a separate sheet for additional entries.
(1)

Form EOIR-42B
4-97

PART 3 - INFORMATION ABOUT YOUR PRESENCE IN THE UNITED STATES

18) I first entered the United States under the name of: *(Last, First, Middle)*
MARTINEZ,   Salvador   Juan

19) I first entered the United States on: *(Month, Day, Year)*
09/14/1987

20) Place or port of first arrival: *(Place or Port, City, and State)*
San Ysidro, CA

21) I arrived: ☐ as a lawful permanent resident, ☐ as a Visitor, ☐ as a Student, ☒ without inspection, or ☐ Other *(Place an X in the correct box, if Other is selected please explain):*

22) If admitted as a nonimmigrant, period for which admitted: *(Month, Day, Year)* / /   to N/A

23) My last extension of stay in the United States expired on: *(Month, Day, Year)*
N/A

24) If not inspected or if arrival occurred at other than a regular port, describe the circumstances as accurately as possible:

Walked across the border.

25) Since the date of my first arrival I departed from and returned to the United States at the following places and on the following dates:
(Please list all departures regardless of how briefly you were absent from the United States)
If you have never departed from the United States since your original date of arrival, please mark an X in the box: ☒

Port of Departure *(Place or Port, City and State)*	Departure Date *(Month, Day, Year)*	Purpose of Travel	Destination
N/A	N/A	N/A	N/A
Port of Return *(Place or Port, City and State)*	Return Date *(Month, Day, Year)*	Manner of Return	Inspected & Admitted?
N/A	N/A	N/A	☐ Yes ☐ No
Port of Departure *(Place or Port, City and State)*	Departure Date *(Month, Day, Year)*	Purpose of Travel	Destination
Port of Return *(Place or Port, City and State)*	Return Date *(Month, Day, Year)*	Manner of Return	Inspected & Admitted?
			☐ Yes ☐ No

26) Have you ever departed the United States:
a) under an order of deportation, exclusion or removal? ------- ☐ Yes ☒ No
b) pursuant to a grant of voluntary departure? ----------------- ☐ Yes ☒ No

PART 4 - INFORMATION ABOUT YOUR MARITAL STATUS AND SPOUSE *(Continued on page 3)*

27) I am not married: ☐
I am married: ☒

28) If married, the name of my spouse is: *(Last, First, Middle)*
MARTINEZ,   Maria   Anna

29) Date of marriage: *(Month, Day, Year)*
07/01/1987

30) The marriage took place in: *(City and Country)*
Jalisco, MEXICO

31) Birth place of spouse: *(City and Country)*
Jalisco,   MEXICO

32) My spouse currently resides at:
B-3
Apt number and/or in care of 4596 Tornado Way
Number and Street Yakima,   WA   98000
City or Town   *State/Country*   *ZIP Code*

33) Birth date of spouse: *(Month, Day, Year)*
03/19/1966

34) My spouse is a citizen of: *(Country)*
MEXICO

35) If your spouse is other than a native born United States citizen, answer the following:
He/she arrived in the United States at: *(City and State)*   San Ysidro, CA
He/she arrived in the United States on: *(Month, Day, Year)* 09/14/1997
His/her alien registration number is: A#   None
He/she was naturalized on: *(Month, Day, Year)* N/A   at   N/A
(City and State)

36) My spouse ☐ - is ☒ - is not employed. If employed, please give salary and the name and address of the place(s) of employment:

Full Name and Address of Employer:	Earnings Per Week *(Approximate)*
	$
	$
	$

Form EOIR-42B
4 97

PART 4 - INFORMATION ABOUT YOUR MARITAL STATUS AND SPOUSE *(CONTINUED)*

37) I ☐ -have ☒ -have not been previously married: *(If previously married, list the name of each prior spouse, the dates on which each marriage began and ended, the place where the marriage terminated, and describe how each marriage ended.)*

Name of prior spouse: *(Last, First, Middle)*	Date marriage began: Date marriage ended:	Place marriage ended: *(City and Country)*	Description or manner of how marriage was terminated or ended:
N/A	N/A N/A	N/A	N/A

38) My present spouse ☐ -has ☒ -has not been previously married: *(If previously married, list the name of each prior spouse, the dates on which the marriage began and ended, the place where the marriage terminated, and describe how each marriage ended.)*

Name of prior spouse: *(Last, First, Middle)*	Date marriage began: Date marriage ended:	Place marriage ended: *(City and Country)*	Description or manner of how marriage was termanated or ended:
N/A	N/A N/A	N/A	N/A

39) Have you been ordered by any court, or are otherwise under any legal obligation, to provide child support and/or spousal maintenance as a result of a separation and/or divorce? ☐ -Yes ☒ -No

PART 5 - INFORMATION ABOUT YOUR EMPLOYMENT AND FINANCIAL STATUS

40) Since my arrival into the United States, I have been employed by the following - named persons or firms: *(Please begin with present employment and work back in time. Any periods of unemployment or school attendance should be specified.)*

Full Name and Address of Employer	Earnings Per Week *(Approximate)*	Type of Work Performed	Employed From: *(Month, Day, Year)*	Employed To: *(Month, Day, Year)*
Green Tree Farms 1234 Horsehead Road, Yakima, WA 98000	$ 500	Labor	06/1992	PRESENT
Brewster Pine Farms 9876 Pine Tree Way SE, Brewster, WA 98000	$ 400	Labor	10/1987	06/1992
	$			

41) If self-employed, describe the nature of the business, the name of the business, its address, and net income derived therefrom:

N/A

42) My assets (and if married, my spouse's assets) in the United States and other countries, not including clothing and household necessities, are:

Self		**Jointly Owned with Spouse**	
Cash, Stocks, and Bonds – – – – –	$ _____	Cash, Stocks, and Bonds – – – – – ·	$ 8000
Real Estate – – – – – – – – ·	$ _____	Real Estate – – – – – – – – – ·	$ 70000
Automobile (dollar value-amount owed)-	$ _____	Automobile (dollar value-amount owed)-	$ 5000
Other (describe on line below) – – –	$ _____	Other (describe on line below) – – – –	$ _____
TOTAL	$ _____	TOTAL	$ 83000

43) I ☐ -have ☒ -have not received public or private relief or assistance(e.g. Welfare, Unemployment Benefits, Medicaid, ADC, etc.). If you have, please give full details including the type of relief or assistance received, date for which relief or assistance was received, place, and amount received during this time: _____

44) Please list each of the years in which you have filed an income tax return with the Internal Revenue Service: _____
1988, 1989, 1990, 1991, 1992, 1993, 1994, 1995, 1996, 1997

Please use a separate sheet for additional entries.
(3)

Form EOIR-42B
4 97

PART 6 - INFORMATION ABOUT YOUR FAMILY *(Continued on page 5)*

45) I have __2__ *(Number of)* children. Please list information for each child below, include assets and earnings information for children over the age of sixteen who have separate incomes:

Name of Child: *(Last, First, Middle)* / Child's Alien Registration Number:	Citizen of What Country: / Birth Date: *(Month, Day, Year)*	Now Residing At: *(City and Country)* / Birth Place: *(City and Country)*	Immigration Status of Child?
MARTINEZ, Julia Angelina / A#: N/A / Estimated Total of Assets: $ N/A	USA / 02/04/1988	Yakima, WA USA / Los Angeles, CA USA / Estimated Average Weekly Earnings: $ N/A	Citizen
MARTINEZ, Jose Miguel / A#: N/A / Estimated Total of Assets: $ N/A	USA / 03/07/1993	Yakima, WA USA / Los Angeles, CA USA / Estimated Average Weekly Earnings: $ N/A	Citizen
A#: / Estimated Total of Assets: $		Estimated Average Weekly Earnings: $	

46) If your application is denied, would your spouse and all of your children accompany you to your:

Country of Birth - ☐ Yes ☒ No

Country of Nationality - ☐ Yes ☒ No

Country of Last Residence - ☐ Yes ☒ No

If you answered "NO" to any of the responses, please explain: _____
My children are citizens. My daughter speaks very little Spanish, and is at the top of her class in school. My son has been diagnosed with a rare auto-immune disease that he cannot receive treatment for in Mexico.

47) Members of my family, including my spouse and/or child(ren) ☐ - have ☒ - have not received public or private relief or assistance (e.g., Unemployment Benefits, Welfare, Medicaid, ADC, etc.). If any member of your immediate family has received such relief or assistance, please give full details including identity of person(s) receiving relief or assistance, dates for which relief or assistance was received, place, and amount received during this time: _____
N/A

48) Please give the requested information about your parents, brothers, sisters, aunts, uncles, and grandparents. As to residence, show street address, city, and state, if in the United States; otherwise show only country:

Name: *(Last, First, Middle)* / Alien Registration Number:	Citizen of What Country: / Birth Date: *(Month, Day, Year)*	Relationship to Me: / Birth Place: *(Place and Country)*	Immigration Status of Listed Relative
MARTINEZ, Jose / A#: None / Complete Address of Current Residence: MEXICO	MEXICO / 07/09/1943	Father / Tijuana, MEXICO	None
MARTINEZ, Maria / A#: None / Complete Address of Current Residence: MEXICO	MEXICO / 09/09/1945	Mother / Cabo, MEXICO	None

Please use a separate sheet for additional entries.
(4)

Form EOIR-42B
4/97

PART 6 - INFORMATION ABOUT YOUR FAMILY   *(Continued)*

IF THIS APPICATION IS BASED ON HARDSHIP TO A PARENT OR PARENTS, QUESTIONS 49 TO 52 MUST BE ANSWERED.

49) As such parent who is not a citizen of the United States, give the date and place of arrival in the United States including full
details as to the manner and terms of admission into the United States: _____

N/A _____

_____

50) My father ☐ - is ☐ -is not employed. If employed, please give salary and the name and address of the place(s) of employment.

Full Name and Address of Employer	Earnings Per Week *(Approximate)*
N/A	$ N/A

51) My mother ☐ - is ☐ - is not employed. If employed, please give salary and the name and address of the place(s) of employment.

Full Name and Address of Employer	Earnings Per Week *(Approximate)*
N/A	$ N/A

52) My parent's assets in the United States and other countries not including clothing and household necessities are:

Assets of Father consist of the following:
Cash, Stocks, and Bonds – – – – – – – $ _____
Real Estate – – – – – – – – – – – $ _____
Automobile (dollar value - amount owed) - $ _____
Other (describe on line below) – – – – $ _____
_____   TOTAL $ N/A

Assets of mother consist of the following:
Cash, Stocks, and Bonds – – – – – – $ _____
Real Estate – – – – – – – – – – – $ _____
Automobile (dollar value - amount owed) - $ _____
Other (describe on line below) – – – – $ _____
_____   TOTAL $ N/A

PART 7 - MISCELLANEOUS INFORMATION   *(Continued on page 6)*

53) I ☐ - have ☒ - have not entred the United States as a crewman after June 30, 1964.

54) I ☐ - have ☒ - have not been admitted as, or after arrival in the United States acquired the status of, an exchange alien.

55) I ☐ - have ☒ - have not submitted address reports as required by section 265 of the Immigration and Nationality Act.

56) I ☐ -have ☒ -have never(either in the United Stated or in any foreign country)been arrested, summoned into court as a defendant
convicted, fined, imprisoned, placed on probation, or forfeited collateral for an act involving a felony, misdemeanor, or breach of
any public law or ordinance(including, but not limited to, traffic violations or driving incidents involving alcohol).   *(If answer is in
the affirmative, please give a brief description of each offense including the name and location of the offense, any penalty imposed,
any sentence imposed, and the time actually served).* _____

_____

_____

_____

57) Have you ever served in the Armed Forces of the United States?   ☐ - Yes ☒ - No. If "Yes" please state branch   *(Army, Navy,*
etc.) and service number. _____ N/A _____
Place of entry on duty: *(Place, City, and State)* _____ N/A _____
Date of entry on duty: *(Month, Day, Year)* _____ N/A _____   Date of discharge: *(Month, Day, Year)* _____ N/A _____
Type of discharge *(Honorable, Dishonorable, etc.):* _____ N/A _____
I served in active duty status from: *(Month, Day, Year)* _____ N/A _____   to *(Month, Day, Year)* _____ N/A _____

58) Have you ever left the United States or the jurisdiction of the district where you registered for the draft to avoid being drafted into
the military or naval forces of the United States?   ☐ Yes ☒ No

Please a separate sheet for additional entries.
(5)

Form EOIR-42B
4 97

PART 7 - MISCELLANEOUS INFORMATION *(Continued)*

59) Have you ever deserted from the military or naval forces of the United Stated while the United Stated was at war? ☐ Yes ☒ No

60) If male, did you register under the Selective Service (Draft) Law of 1917, 1918, 1948, 1951, or later Draft Laws? ☐ Yes ☒ No
If "Yes," please give date, Selective Service number, local draft board number, and your last draft classification: _____

61) Were you ever exempted from service because of conscientious objection, alienage, or any other reason? ☐ Yes ☒ No

62) Please list your present or past membership in or affiliation with every political organization, association, fund, foundation, party, club, society, or similar group in the United States or any other place since your 16th birthday. Include any foreign military service in this part. If none, write "NONE". Include the name of the organization, location, nature of the organization, and the dates of membership.

Name of Organization	Location of Organization	Nature of Organization	Member From: *(Month, Day, Year)*	Member To: *(Month, Day, Year)*
None	N/A	N/A	N/A	N/A

63) Have you ever:
☐ Yes ☒ No been ordered deported or removed?
☐ Yes ☒ No overstayed a grant of voluntary departure from an Immigration Judge or the Immigration and Naturalization Service (INS)?
☐ Yes ☒ No failed to appear for removal or deportation?

64) Have you ever been:
☐ Yes ☒ No a habitual drinker?
☐ Yes ☒ No one whose income is derived principally from illegal gambling?
☐ Yes ☒ No one who has given false testimony for the purpose of obtaining immigration benefits?
☐ Yes ☒ No engaged in prostitution or unlawful commercialized vice?
☐ Yes ☒ No involved in a serious criminal offense and asserted immunity from prosecution?
☐ yes ☒ No a polygamist?
☐ Yes ☒ No one who aided and/or abetted another to enter the United States Illegally?
☐ Yes ☒ No a trafficker of a controlled substance, or a knowing assister, abettor, conspirator, or colluder with others in any such controlled substance offense (not including a single offense of simple possession of 30 grams or less of marijuana)?
☐ Yes ☒ No inadmissible or deportable on security-related grounds under sections 212(a)(3) or 237(a)(4) of the INA?
☐ Yes ☒ No one who has ordered, incited, assisted, or otherwise participated in the persecution of an individual on account of his or her race, religion, nationality, membership in a particular social group,or political opinion?
☐ Yes ☒ No a person previously granted relief under sections 212(c) or 244(a) of the INA or whose removal has previously been cancelled under section 240A of the INA?

64) Are you: ☐ Yes ☒ No the beneficiary of an approved visa petition?
If yes, can you: ☐ Yes ☐ No arrange a trip outside the United States to obtain an immigrant visa. If no, please explain:
_____
_____
_____
_____

Please use a separate sheet for additional entries.
(6)

Form EOIR-42B
4 97

SAMPLE 26 — Continued

PART 7 - MISCELLANEOUS INFORMATION *(Continued)*

65) The following certificates or other supporting documents are attached hereto as a part of this application: *(Refer to the Instruction Sheet for documents which should be attached).*

INDEX to all required supporting documents, including:

Marriage Certificate

Birth Certificate

Medical records of son, letters/evaluations from doctors

School records of daughter, letters from teachers

Affidavit from employer

Affidavits from friends, pastor, co-workers

Mortgage documents

Bills, accounts, payment records

Vehicle purchase agreement

Rent receipts

Tax returns

Bank statements

Family Impact Study

APPLICATION NOT TO BE SIGNED BELOW UNTIL APPLICANT APPEARS BEFORE AN IMMIGRATION JUDGE

I do swear (affirm) that the contents of the above application, including the documents attached hereto, are true to the best of my knowledge, and that this application is now signed by me with my full, true name.

_____
(Complete and true signature of applicant or parent or guardian)

Subscribed and sworn to before me by the above-named applicant at

_____

_____
Immigration Judge

_____
Date: (Month, Day, Year)

CERTIFICATE OF SERVICE

I hereby certify that a copy of the foregoing was: ☐ - delivered in person,   ☒ - mailed first class, postage prepaid   on
02/17/1999   *(Month, Day, Year)* to _____
(INS District Counsel and Address)

Office of the INS District Counsel, 1000 Second Avenue, Suite 2900, Seattle, WA 98104

_____
Signature of Applicant (or attorney or representative)

Please use a separate sheet for additional entries.
(7)

Form EOIR-42B
4 97

★ Adjustment of Status

★ Change of Status

★ Registry (Amnesty)

It is a criminal felony and a violation of the immigration laws to return to the United States after deportation without permission from the attorney general.

4. RIGHTS OF APPEAL

4.1 Board of Immigration Appeals

In most cases, you can appeal a decision by a US immigration judge in a removal proceeding to the Board of Immigration Appeals. You must always be notified of your right to appeal when a decision is made against you. Usually, when you are notified of your right to appeal, you will be given instructions on how to do so. To lodge your appeal, you will need to file a Form EOIR 26 Notice of Appeal to the Board of Immigration Appeals (see Sample 29). The filing fee is $110 and should be made payable to the United States Department of Justice, an exception to the usual practice of making filing fee checks payable to the Immigration and Naturalization Service. If you are represented by an attorney for the appeal, the attorney must sign and file Form EOIR-27 Notice of Appearance as Attorney or Representative Before the Board of Immigration Appeals (Sample 30).

4.2 No judicial review of discretionary decisions

While the new immigration law did away with most federal court review of discretionary decisions, with the exception of asylum decisions, an alien can still apply for review of an order of removal if the alien can present a colorable claim of a violation of the alien's constitutional rights. The alien should file a Petition for Writ of Habeas Corpus in the Federal District Court that had geographic jurisdiction over the immigration judge's removal proceedings, and, until the US Supreme Court settles all the jurisdictional questions, the alien should consider filing a concurrent appeal in the US Circuit Court of Appeals within 30 days of an adverse decision by the Board of Immigration Appeals.

SAMPLE 27
AFFIDAVIT TESTIFYING TO GOOD CHARACTER

UNITED STATES OF AMERICA

STATE OF __Washington__   )
)ss
COUNTY OF ____Yakima____   )

_____Laura Gomez_____, being first duly sworn
on oath, deposes and says:

That I am over the age of twenty-one years and competent
to be a witness.

That I am making the within Affidavit in behalf of
__Longina MENDOZA-Castillo__ to submit with __her__
Application for Suspension of Deportation on the ground that
__she__ has resided continuously for more than seven years in the
United States.

That I have personal knowledge and information that
__Longina MENDOZA-Castillo__ has resided continuously in the
United States since __1992__ for the following reasons:

1. That I had met __Longina MENDOZA-Castillo__ on or about
__January 1992__ in __Chehalis, Washington__.

2. That __we lived next door to each other.__

3. That __Ms. Mendoza does not speak English and I
could converse with her in Spanish.__

That I have personal knowledge and information that
__Longina MENDOZA-Castillo__ has been a person of good
moral character during the past seven years because of my
personal friendship with _____her_____;during said time
I have not received any information to the contrary which
would refect adversely upon __Longina MENDOZA-Castillo__.

That I am a citizen of the United States and

That I recommend that the Immigration and Naturalization
Service approve the Application for Suspension of Deportation
of __Longina MENDOZA-Castillo__.

_____Laura Gomez_____

Subscribed and sworn to before me this __3rd__ day of
___June___, 200-.

_____Dan P. Danilov_____
Notary Public in and for the
State of __Washington__, residing
at __Bellevue.__

AFFIDAVIT

STATE OF __California__)
) ss
COUNTY OF __Los Angeles__)

____Margarita Rocha____, being first duly sworn on
oath, deposes and says:

   That I am over the age of twenty-one years and competent
to be a witness. That I am a citizen of the United States and/or
Alien Permanent Resident with Alien Registration Receipt No. A____.

   That I make this Affidavit in behalf of Longina MENDOZA-Castillo
to submit with __her__ Application for Suspension of Deportation
on the ground that __she__ has resided continuously for more
than seven years in the United States.

   That __Longina MENDOZA-Castillo__ was employed by me in
__my home from 12/20- to 12/20-__ as a __domestic servant__
and his/her wages amount to the sum of $200.00 per week, plus room
and board.

   That Longina MENDOZA-Castillo is a good and conscientious
employee, and I have no knowledge or information that he/she
is not a person of good moral character for the reason that during
the course of __her__ employment with me, he/she has
demonstrated to be a person of good moral character.

   That I recommend that the Immigration and Naturalization
Service approve the Application for Suspension of Deportation of
Longina MENDOZA-Castillo.

                              Margarita Rocha

   Subscribed and sworn to before me this __28th__ day of
__June__, 200-.

                              John Daniels
                              Notary Public in and for the
                              State of __California__,
                              residing at __Los Angeles__

U.S. Department of Justice
Executive Office for Immigration Review
Board of Immigration Appeals

Notice of Appeal from a Decision of an
Immigration Judge

Staple Check or Money Order Here. Include Name(s) and "A" number(s) on the face of the check or money order.

1. List Name(s) and "A" Number(s) of all Respondent(s)/Applicant(s):

   THUMB, Thomas   #A 45 691 346

   For Official Use Only

   ! **WARNING:** Names and "A" Numbers of **everyone** appealing the Immigration Judge's decision must be written in item #1.

2. I am the ☑ Respondent/Applicant ☐ INS *(Mark only one box.)*

3. I am ☐ DETAINED ☑ NOT DETAINED *(Mark only one box.)*

4. My last hearing was at ___Office of Immigration Court, Seattle, WA___ *(Location, City, State)*

5. **What decision are you appealing?**

   Mark only one box below. If you want to appeal more than one decision, you must use more than one Notice of Appeal (Form EOIR-26).

   ☑ I am filing an appeal from the Immigration Judge's decision *in **merits** proceedings* (example: removal, deportation, exclusion, asylum, etc.) dated ___01/25/1999___ .

   ☐ I am filing an appeal from the Immigration Judge's decision *in **bond** proceedings* dated

   _____ .

   ☐ I am filing an appeal from the Immigration Judge's decision ***denying a motion to reopen or a motion to reconsider*** dated _____ .

   (Please attach a copy of the Immigration Judge's decision you are appealing.)

OMB# 1125-0002; Expires 12/31/02

Form EOIR-26
Revised Sept. 2002

Page 1 of 3

THUMB, Thomas   #A 45 691 346

6. State in detail the reason(s) for this appeal. Please refer to the Instructions at part F for further guidance. You are not limited to the space provided below; use more sheets of paper if necessary. Write your name(s) and "A" number(s) on every sheet.

1. Immigration Judge erred as a matter of law and abused his discretion when he concluded that respondent was statutorily ineligible for asylum and/or withholding of removal when the respondent's testimony was internally consistent, not exaggerated, uncontradicted, and when the respondent provided specific details regarding persecution directed against himself, including his arrest and torture at the hands of the Republic of Rutland's police, such persecution and torture based upon his religion, membership in a particular social group, and the political opinion imputed to him.

2. The respondent was denied due process and a fair hearing when the Immigration Judge refused to allow the respondent the opportunity to present evidence and witnesses on his behalf.

3. The respondent reserves the right to raise additional arguments following receipt and review of the transcript of proceedings.

(Attach additional sheets if necessary)

WARNING: You must clearly explain the specific facts and law on which you based your appeal of the Immigration Judge's decision. The Board may summarily dismiss your appeal if it cannot tell from this Notice of Appeal, or any statements attached to this Notice of Appeal, why you are appealing.

7. Do you desire oral argument before the Board of Immigration Appeals?   ☒ Yes   ☐ No

8. Do you intend to file a separate written brief or statement after filing this Notice of Appeal?   ☒ Yes   ☐ No

WARNING: If you mark "Yes" in item #8, you will be expected to file a written brief or statement after you receive a briefing schedule from the Board. The Board may summarily dismiss your appeal if you do not file a brief or statement within the time set in the briefing schedule.

9. **SIGN HERE** →   X _____   _____
Signature of Person Appealing   Date
(or attorney or representative)

Form EOIR-26
Revised Sept. 2002

Page 2 of 3

10.	Mailing Address of Respondent(s)/Applicant(s)	11.	Mailing Address of Attorney or Representative for the Respondent(s)/Applicant(s)
	Thomas THUMB		**LAW OFFICES OF DAN P. DANILOV**
	(Name)		(Name)
	999 Littleguy Place		**Suite 2303 One Union Square**
	(Street Address)		(Street Address)
	(Apartment or Room Number)		(Suite or Room Number)
	Seattle WA 98125		**Seattle WA 98101**
	(City, State, Zip Code)		(City, State, Zip Code)
	(Telephone Number)		(Telephone Number)

NOTE: You must notify the Board within five (5) working days if you move to a new address. You must use an alien's Change of Address Form (Form EOIR-33/BIA).

NOTE: If an attorney or representative signs this appeal for you, he or she must file *with this appeal*, a Notice of Entry of Appearance as Attorney or Representative Before the Board of Immigration Appeals (Form EOIR-27).

12.

PROOF OF SERVICE
(You Must Complete This)

I _____ **DAN P. DANILOV** _____ mailed or delivered a copy of this Notice of Appeal
           (Name)

on _____ **10/2002** _____ to _____ **INS Office of District Counsel** _____
        (Date)   (Opposing Party)

at _____ **1000 - Second Avenue,   Ste #2900,   Seattle,   WA   98104** _____
                    (Address of Opposing Party)

[SIGN HERE →] X _____
                                    Signature

NOTE: If you are the Respondent or Applicant, the "Opposing Party" is the District Counsel for the INS.

WARNING: If you do not complete this section properly, your appeal will be rejected or dismissed.

WARNING: If you do not attach the fee or a completed Fee Waiver Request (Form EOIR-26A) to this appeal, your appeal will be rejected or dismissed.

☒ Read all of the General Instructions   **HAVE**   ☒ Signed the form
☒ Provided all of the requested information   **YOU?**   ☒ Served a copy of this form and all attachments
☒ Completed this form in English   on the opposing party
☒ Provided a certified English translation   ☒ Completed and signed the Proof of Service
   for all non-English attachments   ☒ Attached the required fee or Fee Waiver Request

Page 3 of 3

Form EOIR-26
Revised Sept. 2002

SAMPLE 30
FORM EOIR-27 NOTICE OF ENTRY OF APPEARANCE AS ATTORNEY OR REPRESENTATIVE BEFORE THE BOARD OF IMMIGRATION APPEALS EXECUTIVE OFFICE FOR IMMIGRATION REVIEW

NOTICE OF ENTRY OF APPEARANCE AS ATTORNEY OR REPRESENTATIVE
BEFORE THE BOARD OF IMMIGRATION APPEALS
EXECUTIVE OFFICE FOR IMMIGRATION REVIEW

TYPE OF PROCEEDING:

☒ Deportation	☐ Bond Redetermination	☐ Disciplinary
☐ Removal	☐ Motion to Reopen/Reconsider	
☐ Exclusion	☐ Rescission	

DATE **8/10/2002**
ALIEN NUMBER(S) (list lead alien number and all family member alien numbers if applicable)

A00 000 000

I hereby enter my appearance as attorney or representative for, and at the request of, the following named person(s):

NAME (First)	(Middle Initial)	(Last)
Thomas	**A.**	**THUMB**

ADDRESS (Number & Street)	(Apt. No.)	(City)	(State)	(Zip Code)
999 Littleguy Avenue		**Anywhere**	**WA**	**98000**

Please check one of the following:

☒ 1. I am a member in <u>good standing</u> of the bar of the highest court(s) of the following State(s), possession(s), Territory(ies), Commonwealth(s), or the District of Columbia:

Name(s) of Court(s)   *State Bar No. (if applicable)*

Washington State

Supreme Court

(Please use space on reverse side to list additional jurisdictions.)

I ☒ am not (or ☐ am - explain fully on reverse side) subject to any order of any court or administrative agency disbarring, suspending, enjoining, restraining, or otherwise restricting me in the practice of law and <u>the</u> courts listed above comprise <u>all</u> of the jurisdictions other than federal courts where I am licensed to practice law.

☐ 2. I am an accredited representative of the following qualified non-profit religious, charitable, social service, or similar organization established in the United States, so recognized by the Executive Office for Immigration Review (provide name of organization): _____

☐ 3. I am a law student or law graduate, reputable individual, accredited official, or other person authorized to represent individuals pursuant to 8 C.F.R. § 292. (Explain fully on reverse side.)

I have read and understand the statements provided on the reverse side of this form that set forth the regulations and conditions governing appearances and representation before the Board of Immigration Appeals. I declare under penalty of perjury under the laws of the United States of America that the foregoing is true and correct.

SIGNATURE OF ATTORNEY OR REPRESENTATIVE	EOIR ID#	TELEPHONE NUMBER (Include Area Code)	DATE
Dan P. Danilov		**206/624-6868**	

NAME OF ATTORNEY OR REPRESENTATIVE (TYPE OR PRINT)	ADDRESS	☐ Check here if this is a new address.
Law Offices of Dan P. Danilov	**Suite 2303 - One Union Square**	
	Seattle	**WA**	**98101**

Certificate of Service

I **Law Offices of Dan P. Danilov** mailed or delivered a copy of the foregoing on **8/10/2002** to the Immigration
(Name)   (Date)

and Naturalization Service at **815 Airport Way South, Seattle, WA 98134**
(Address)

X _____ *Dan P. Danilov* _____
Signature of Attorney or Representative

OMB#1125-0005

FORM EOIR-27
August 99

(Note: Alien may be required to sign Acknowledgement and Consent on reverse side of this form.)

I HEREBY ACKNOWLEDGE THAT THE ABOVE-NAMED ATTORNEY OR REPRESENTATIVE REPRESENTS ME IN THESE PROCEEDINGS AND I CONSENT TO DISCLOSURE TO HIM/HER OF ANY RECORDS PERTAINING TO ME WHICH APPEAR IN ANY EOIR SYSTEM OF RECORDS.

NAME OF PERSON CONSENTING	SIGNATURE OF PERSON CONSENTING	DATE
Thomas A. THUMB	*Thomas Thumb*	8/10/02

(NOTE: *The Privacy Act of 1974 requires that if the person being represented is or claims to be a citizen of the United States or an alien lawfully admitted for permanent residence, he/she must sign this form.*)

APPEARANCES - An appearance shall be filed on EOIR Form-27 by the attorney or representative appearing in each case before the Board of Immigration Appeals (see 8 C.F.R. § 3.38((g)), even though the attorney or representative may have appeared in the case before the Immigration Judge or the Immigration and Naturalization Service. When an appeerence is made by a person acting in a representative capacity, his/her personal appearance or signature shall constitute a representation that, under the provisions of 8 C.F.R. Chapter 3, he/she is authorized and qualified to represent individuals. Thereafter, substitution or withdrawal may be permitted upon the approval of the Board of a request by the attorney or representative of record in accordance with Matter of Resales, 19 I&N Dec. 655 (1988). Further proof of authority to act in a representative capacity may be required.

REPRESENTATION - A person entitled to representation may be represented by any of the following:

(1) Attorneys in the United States as defined in 8 C.F.R. § 1.1(f).

(2) Law students and law graduates not yet admitted to the bar as defined in 8 C.F.R. § 292.1(a)(2).

(3) Reputable individuals as defined in 8 C.F.R. § 292.1(a)(3).

(4) Accredited representative as defined in 8 C.F.R. § 292.1(a)(4).

(5) Accredited officials as defined in 8 C.F.R. § 292.1(a)(5).

THIS FORM MAY NOT BE USED TO REQUEST RECORDS UNDER THE FREEDOM OF INFORMATION ACT OR THE PRIVACY ACT. THE MANNER OF REQUESTING SUCH RECORDS IS CONTAINED IN 28 C.F.R. §§ 16.1-16.11 AND APPENDICES.

Public reporting burden for the collection of information is estimated to average 6 minutes per response, including the time for reviewing the data needed, completing and reviewing the collection of information, and record-keeping. Send comments regarding this burden estimate or any other aspect of this information collection including suggestions for reviewing this burden to the Executive Office for Immigration Review, 5107 Leesburg Pike, Suite 2400, Falls Church, VA 22041.

(Please attach additional sheets of paper as necessary.)

*U.S. GPO: 2000-461-076/21608

11

ADJUSTMENT OF STATUS TO PERMANENT RESIDENCE IN THE UNITED STATES

1. WHO CAN APPLY?

Adjustment of status is the most important form of relief available to nonimmigrants who wish to remain in the United States.

Whether an individual's status is adjusted to that of a permanent resident is at the discretion of the Immigration and Naturalization Service (INS). Temporary visitors, people who are engaged to US citizens, people who have married US citizens after coming here on a temporary visa, and people who have changed their intentions after being admitted to the country all seek this kind of relief.

Other applicants who qualify are brothers and sisters of US citizens or permanent residents, businesspeople who come on B-1 visas for business purposes, and executives and managers who are admitted either as treaty traders, treaty investors, or intracompany transferees of foreign corporations with subsidiaries in the United States.

The Nicaraguan Adjustment and Central American Relief Act (NARCARA), passed in November 1997, provides an amnesty for certain Nicaraguans and Cubans who have continuously resided in the United States since on or before December 1, 1995.

For most other aliens to qualify for adjustment of status, an immigrant visa must be immediately available at the time of applying and they must satisfy the following conditions:

(a) Qualify under all the immigration laws and regulations, including the requirement that they have a medical examination that finds them free of contagious disease

(b) Have been properly admitted into the United States. They could have been admitted after an inspection by an immigration officer at a port of entry.

(c) Otherwise be eligible for a visa in that there are no grounds on which they can be removed from the United States under section 212

(d) Establish that they will not become a public charge. They do this by having a sponsor file a Form I-864 Affidavit of Support in the United States (see Sample 7 in chapter 2) along with the other supporting evidence discussed in chapter 2.

2. WHO CANNOT APPLY?

You are not eligible to apply for adjustment of status to permanent residence if you came into the United States surreptitiously (without inspection) if you are a crew member, or if you are an exchange visitor who has not complied with the two-year foreign residency requirement or had it waived. Neither are you eligible for adjustment of status if you are in the United States while in transit to another country.

Adjustment of status is not available to aliens who accept or continue in unauthorized employment prior to filing Form I-485 Application to Register Permanent Residence or Adjust Status, unless they are immediate relatives of US citizens (see Sample 14 in chapter 3). Nor is it available to those who would be excluded for health reasons, unless waived via Form I-601 (see Sample 9), or those foreign medical graduates who have not passed the visa qualifying examinations.

People who are not eligible for adjustment of status to permanent residence within the United States must apply for immigrant visas at a US consulate abroad.

The formerly available privilege/penalty adjustment fee of $1,000 for those who have gone out of status in the United States, which allowed out-of-status individuals to adjust without leaving the United States expired, for most uses, on January 14, 1998. It is now only available for those beneficiaries whose sponsors filed visa petitions before January 14, 1998.

3. WHY ADJUST YOUR STATUS IN THE UNITED STATES?

There are advantages to seeking adjustment of status while in the United States. For one thing, you are given all of the privileges and immunities of the Constitution of the United States like any US citizen.

In the United States, the attitude taken is likely to be more liberal than that taken by a US consul abroad. One of the purposes of the immigration laws is to allow families to be reunited in the United States and that may be beyond the powers of a US consul as his or her duties are only ministerial (i.e., carrying out orders) and not discretionary.

In addition, once you have been inspected and admitted to the United States by an INS officer at a port of entry, it is up to the immigration service to show that you are a person who should be removed. You do not have to show, as in a removal proceeding, that you are a person who is clearly and beyond a reasonable doubt entitled to remain in the United States. However, the 1996 Immigration Act (IIRIRA) has placed the burden on the alien to prove admissibility.

Furthermore, if you are already in the United States, you will have the support of family or friends and will be able to hire an experienced immigration attorney to present your case.

If the district director refuses your application for adjustment of status, you can appeal to a US immigration judge. If the judge refuses your application, you may appeal to the Board of Immigration Appeals and from there to Federal Court if you are alleging a colorable claim that your constitutional rights have been violated (e.g., due process or equal protection violations).

In contrast, if you are applying for an immigrant visa at a US consulate abroad, the decision of the US consul is regarded as final in most cases, although the decision can be reviewed by the Department of State in Washington, DC. While the Department of State has no authority to order a US consul to approve an immigration application; it can issue what is called an Advisory Opinion to curb consular abuses.

The rules and regulations governing the approval of immigration visas by US consuls are very technical and they are generally not subject to review by the courts.

4. HOW TO APPLY

The INS investigates all applications for adjustment of status to a permanent resident; if there is any evidence of fraud or misrepresentation to either the US consul abroad or to the INS officer at the port of entry, the application will be denied. As the right to have your status changed is discretionary, the INS can refuse your application if it feels, for instance, that you entered the country with the intent to become a permanent resident and so made false statements or misrepresentations when being interviewed for your visitor visa or entry into the United States.

The application for permanent resident status is made before the district director of the INS. Your application may be granted, but if it is denied, it can be resubmitted at a removal hearing. Depending upon the specific facts of the case, if substantial ties exist between yourself and a US citizen or lawful permanent resident and hardship would result if you were removed, the adjustment of status may be granted. If this course is taken, you need not leave the United States to apply for an immigrant visa at a US consulate in your native country. Even if you are prevented from adjusting in the United States, if you can show exceptional and extremely unusual hardship to your immediate relative in the United States, you may qualify for a waiver for your expeditious return to the United States.

In order to apply for adjustment of status from nonimmigrant to lawful permanent resident, you first have to file Form I-485 Application to Register Permanent Residence or Adjust Status (see Sample 14). As with all immigration forms, read it carefully before filling it out with a typewriter or ball-point pen.

If a lawyer is acting for you, you must file a G-28 Notice of Entry of Appearance as Attorney or Representative (see Sample 5 in chapter 2).

You must also provide the following:

(a) Birth certificate

(b) Three color photographs of yourself (1" x 1") with the right ear showing

(c) Form G-325 Biographic Information sheet (see Sample 31)

(d) Form I-864 Affidavit of Support (see Sample 7 in chapter 2) along with the supporting material discussed in section **3.** of chapter 2

(e) Medical Examination form I-693, which must be completed by an Immigration Service approved physician

(f) A filing fee of $255, plus a $50 filing fee for subsequent fingerprinting

Other supporting documents that you could or would file if your particular circumstances required it include

(a) Form I-130 Petition for Alien Relative (see Sample 3 in chapter 2) (filing fee $130),

(b) Form I-129F Petition for Alien Fiancé(e) (see Sample 11 in chapter 2),

(c) Form I-601 Application for Waiver of Grounds of Excludability (see Sample 9 in chapter 2) (filing fee $195), and

(d) Form I-212 Application for Permission to Reapply for Admission After Deportation (filing fee $195).

4.1 One-step filing system for relatives of US citizens or permanent residents

Applicants for adjustment of status who are the immediate relatives of US citizens who are entitled to petition for them, may follow a procedure called a one-step filing system, as follows:

(a) The petitioner (US citizen) files a Form I-130 Immigrant Petition for Relative, Fiancé(e) or Orphan with the district director of the INS in the jurisdiction of the residence of the petitioner. At the same time, the beneficiary (alien spouse or immediate relative) files Form I-485 Application to Register Permanent Residence or Adjust Status and all other accompanying forms/applications as per the instruction sheet. The beneficiary must pay the combined filing fee of $385 ($255 for Form I-485 and $130 for Form I-130) and file the necessary documents as outlined on the instruction sheets. At the same time, the beneficiary may apply for and receive employment authorization by filing Form I-765 Application for Employment Authorization (see Sample 32). A work permit may be issued to the applicant within 30 days of the day the application is filed.

(b) An appointment date for a personal interview with an immigration official at the same location will be provided for the petitioner and beneficiary normally within five months.

(c) If all goes well at the interview and the applications are approved, the beneficiary will be granted adjustment of status to a conditional resident and a confirming notice will be provided together with an appropriate stamp placed in the passport of the beneficiary.

(d) Thereafter, the beneficiary will receive Form I-551 Alien Registration Receipt Card in the mail within four to six months, designating the applicant as a conditional permanent resident.

Note: This procedure is only available to individuals who are in a preference category that is currently available or has no backlog. Beneficiary applicants should not depart from the United States within the waiting period for the interview or they will be required to apply for their immigrant visas at US consulates overseas. Any departure can be deemed to be abandonment of the adjustment application. An application for Form I-131 Advance Parole (filing fee $110), filed and approved by INS before the alien's departure, may preserve the alien's status of "pending adjustment of status" in the United States.

4.2 Spouses of citizens or permanent residents

To change conditional resident status to permanent resident for a person who obtained such status through marriage to a citizen of the United States or through marriage to another legal permanent resident and who was admitted or adjusted as conditional resident, you must file Form I-751 Petition to Remove the Conditions on Residence (see Sample 10 in chapter 2). This form has a filing fee of $145. You must file this petition jointly with the spouse through whom your status was obtained (the petitioning spouse).

If you are no longer married to the spouse through whom residence was obtained, or are otherwise unable to file this petition jointly with the spouse, you may be eligible for a waiver of the joint filing requirement and must specify the conditions for this situation in the Form I-751. Two related forms used by an abused alien spouse are the Form I-360 (filing fee $130), and the Form EOIR-42B (filing fee $100). The latter form is used when the alien is already in removal proceedings.

U.S. Department of Justice
Immigration and Naturalization Service

OMB No. 1115-0066
BIOGRAPHIC INFORMATION

(Family name)	(First name)	(Middle name)	☒ MALE ☐ FEMALE	BIRTHDATE (Mo.-Day-Yr.)	NATIONALITY	FILE NUMBER
GOMEZ–Salas	Jose	NMN		11/16/1951	Mexican	A19 624 158

ALL OTHER NAMES USED (Including names by previous marriages)	CITY AND COUNTRY OF BIRTH	SOCIAL SECURITY NO. (If any)
none	Nogales Sonora MEXICO	434 58 5440

	FAMILY NAME	FIRST NAME	DATE, CITY AND COUNTRY OF BIRTH (If known)	CITY AND COUNTRY OF RESIDENCE.
FATHER	GOMEZ	Manuel	10/01/1925 Colima, MEXICO	Tepalmes, MEXICO
MOTHER (Maiden name)	SALAS	Estell	08/16/1930 Tepalmes, MEXICO	Tepalmes, MEXICO

HUSBAND (If none, so state) OR WIFE FAMILY NAME (For wife, give maiden name)	FIRST NAME	BIRTHDATE	CITY & COUNTRY OF BIRTH	DATE OF MARRIAGE	PLACE OF MARRIAGE
FUENTES	Maria	08/14/54	San Angelo TX USA	07/15/1986	Seattle, WA

FORMER HUSBANDS OR WIVES (If none, so state) FAMILY NAME (For wife, give maiden name)	FIRST NAME	BIRTHDATE	DATE & PLACE OF MARRIAGE	DATE AND PLACE OF TERMINATION OF MARRIAGE
none				

APPLICANT'S RESIDENCE LAST FIVE YEARS. LIST PRESENT ADDRESS FIRST.

STREET AND NUMBER	CITY	PROVINCE OR STATE	COUNTRY	FROM MONTH	FROM YEAR	TO MONTH	TO YEAR
814 – 54th Avenue NE	Seattle	WA	USA	08	1977	PRESENT TIME	
Rt. 2, Box 10	Yakima	WA	USA	01	1977	07	1977

APPLICANT'S LAST ADDRESS OUTSIDE THE UNITED STATES OF MORE THAN ONE YEAR

STREET AND NUMBER	CITY	PROVINCE OR STATE	COUNTRY	FROM MONTH	FROM YEAR	TO MONTH	TO YEAR
Domisilio Conocido	Tepalmes	Colima	MEXICO	11	1951	01	1977

APPLICANT'S EMPLOYMENT LAST FIVE YEARS. (IF NONE, SO STATE) LIST PRESENT EMPLOYMENT FIRST

FULL NAME AND ADDRESS OF EMPLOYER	OCCUPATION (SPECIFY)	FROM MONTH	FROM YEAR	TO MONTH	TO YEAR
Tasty Food Products, Seattle, WA	Mach. Operator	08	1978	PRESENT TIME	
Shipping Lines, Inc. Yakima, WA	Truck Driver	01	1978	07	1977

Show below last occupation abroad if not shown above. (Include all information requested above.)

Construction de Maldonado, Tempalmes, MEXICO	worker	11	1971	01	1978

THIS FORM IS SUBMITTED IN CONNECTION WITH APPLICATION FOR	SIGNATURE OF APPLICANT	DATE
☐ NATURALIZATION ☐ OTHER (SPECIFY): ☒ STATUS AS PERMANENT RESIDENT	*Jose Gomez Salas.*	11/2002

Submit both copies of this form.

IF YOUR NATIVE ALPHABET IS IN OTHER THAN ROMAN LETTERS, WRITE YOUR NAME IN YOUR NATIVE ALPHABET IN THIS SPACE:

PENALTIES: SEVERE PENALTIES ARE PROVIDED BY LAW FOR KNOWINGLY AND WILLFULLY FALSIFYING OR CONCEALING A MATERIAL FACT.

APPLICANT BE SURE TO PUT YOUR NAME AND ALIEN REGISTRATION NUMBER IN THE BOX OUTLINED BY HEAVY BORDER BELOW.

COMPLETE THIS BOX (Family name)	(Given name)	(Middle name)	(Alien registration number)
GOMEZ–Salas	Jose	NMN	#A 19 624 158

Form G-325 (Rev. 09/11/00)Y

(1) Ident.

SAMPLE 32
FORM I-765 APPLICATION FOR EMPLOYMENT AUTHORIZATION

U.S. Department of Justice
Immigration and Naturalization Service

OMB No. 1115-0163; Expires 04/30/05

Application for Employment Authorization

Do Not Write in This Block.

Remarks	Action Stamp	Fee Stamp
A#		

Applicant is filing under §274a.12 _____

☐ Application Approved. Employment Authorized / Extended *(Circle One)* until _____ (Date).
_____ (Date).

Subject to the following conditions: _____

☐ Application Denied.
☐ Failed to establish eligibility under 8 CFR 274a.12 (a) or (c).
☐ Failed to establish economic necessity as required in 8 CFR 274a.12(c)(14), (18) and 8 CFR 214.2(f)

I am applying for:
☒ Permission to accept employment.
☐ Replacement *(of lost employment authorization document)*.
☐ Renewal of my permission to accept employment *(attach previous employment authorization document)*.

1. Name (Family Name in CAPS) (First) (Middle)
GOMEZ–Salas   Jose   NMN

2. Other Names Used (Include Maiden Name)
none

3. Address in the United States (Number and Street) (Apt. Number)
14301 State Street

(Town or City) (State/Country) (ZIP Code)
Seattle   WA   USA   98104

4. Country of Citizenship/Nationality
Mexico / Mexican

5. Place of Birth (Town or City) (State/Province) (Country)
Temaples   Colima   MEXICO

6. Date of Birth   7. Sex
11/15/1951   ☒ Male ☐ Female

8. Marital Status ☒ Married ☐ Single ☐ Widowed ☐ Divorced

9. Social Security Number (Include all Numbers you have ever used) (if any)
000 00 0003

10. Alien Registration Number (A-Number) or I-94 Number (if any)
#A 12 453 149

11. Have you ever before applied for employment authorization from INS?
☐ Yes (If yes, complete below)   ☒ No
Which INS Office?   Date(s)

Results (Granted or Denied - attach all documentation)

12. Date of Last Entry into the U.S. (Month/Day/Year)
05/12/2001

13. Place of Last Entry into the U.S.
Seattle,   WA

14. Manner of Last Entry (Visitor, Student, etc.)
B–2

15. Current Immigration Status (Visitor, Student, etc.)
B–2

16. Go to Part 2 of the Instructions, Eligibility Categories. In the space below, place the letter and number of the category you selected from the instructions (For example, (a)(8), (c)(17)(iii), etc.).

Eligibility under 8 CFR 274a.12

(C) (0) (9)

Certification.

Your Certification: I certify, under penalty of perjury under the laws of the United States of America, that the foregoing is true and correct. Furthermore, I authorize the release of any information which the Immigration and Naturalization Service needs to determine eligibility for the benefit I am seeking. I have read the Instructions in Part 2 and have identified the appropriate eligibility category in Block 16.

Signature *Jose Gomez-Salas*   Telephone Number **212/5551212**   Date **11/2002**

Signature of Person Preparing Form, If Other Than Above: I declare that this document was prepared by me at the request of the applicant and is based on all information of which I have any knowledge.

Print Name   Address   Signature   Date
DAN P. DANILOV   Suite 2303 One Union Sq.
Seattle, WA   98101   *Dan P. Danilov*   **10/2002**

	Initial Receipt	Resubmitted	Relocated		Completed		
			Rec'd	Sent	Approved	Denied	Returned

Form I-765 (Rev. 5/09/02)Y

(a)(3)--Refugee. File your EAD application with either a copy of your Form I-590, Registration for Classification as Refugee, approval letter or a copy of a Form I-730, Refugee/Asylee Relative Petition, approval notice.

(a)(4)--Paroled as a Refugee. File your EAD application with a copy of your Form I-94, Departure Record.

(a)(5)--Asylee, (granted asylum). File your EAD application with a copy of the INS letter granting you asylum. It is not necessary to apply for an EAD as an asylee until 90 days before the expiration of your current EAD.

(a)(6)--K-I Nonimmigrant Fiancé(e) of U.S. Citizen or K-2 Dependent. File your EAD application if you are filing within 90 days from the date of entry. This EAD cannot be renewed. Any EAD application other than for a replacement must be based on your pending application for adjustment under (c)(9). FEE REQUIRED.

(a)(7)--N-8 or N-9 Nonimmigrant. File your EAD application with the required evidence listed in Part 3.

(a)(8)--Citizen of Micronesia or the Marshall Islands or Palau. File your EAD application if you were admitted to the United States as a citizen of the Federated States of Micronesia (CFA/FSM) or of the Marshall Islands (CFA/MIS) pursuant to agreements between the United States and the former trust territories.

(a)(10)--Granted Withholding of Deportation. File your EAD application with a copy of the Immigration Judge's order. It is not necessary to apply for a new EAD until 90 days before the expiration of your current EAD.

(a)(11)--Deferred Enforced Departure (DED)/Extended Voluntary Departure. File your EAD application with evidence of your identity and nationality.

(a)(12)--Temporary Protected Status (TPS). File your EAD application with Form I-821, Application for Temporary Protected Status. FEE REQUIRED.

(a)(13)--Family Unity Program. File your EAD application with a copy of the approval notice, if you have been granted status under this program. You may choose to file your EAD application concurrently with your Form I-817, Application for Voluntary Departure under the Family Unity Program. The INS may take up to 90 days from the date upon which you are granted status under the Family Unity Program to adjudicate your EAD application. If you were denied Family Unity status solely because your legalized spouse or parent first applied under the Legalization/SAW programs after May 5, 1988, file your EAD application with a new Form I-817 application and a copy of the original denial. However, if your EAD application is based on continuing eligibility under (c)(12), please refer to Deportable Alien Granted Voluntary Departure. FEE REQUIRED.

(c)(I)--Dependent of A-I or A-2 Foreign Government Officials. File your EAD application with a Form I-566, Application for Employment by Spouse or Unmarried Dependent Son or Daughter of A-I or A-2 Official or Employee of Diplomatic or Consular Establishment or G-4 Officer or Employee of International Organization, with the Department of State endorsement.

(c)(2)--Dependent of CCNAA E-I Nonimmigrant. File your EAD application with the required certification from the American Institute in Taiwan if you are the spouse, or unmarried child, of an E-I employee of the Coordination Council for North American Affairs. FEE REQUIRED.

(c)(3)(i)--F-I Student Seeking Optional Practical Training in an Occupation Directly Related to Studies. File your EAD application with a Certificate of Eligibility of Nonimmigrant (F-I) Student Status (Form I-20 A-B/I-20 ID) endorsed by a designated school official within the past 30 days. FEE REQUIRED.

(c)(3)(ii)--F-I Student Offered Off-Campus Employment under the Sponsorship of a Qualifying International Organization. File your EAD application with the international organization's letter of certification that the proposed employment is within the scope of its sponsorship and a Certificate of Eligibility of Nonimmigrant (F-I) Student Status--For Academic and Language Students (Form I-20 A-B/I-20 ID) endorsed by the designated school official within the past 30 days. FEE REQUIRED.

(c)(3)(iii)--F-I Student Seeking Off-Campus Employment Due to Severe Economic Hardship. File your EAD application with Form I-20 A-B/I-20 ID, Certificate of Eligibility of Nonimmigrant (F-I) Student Status--For Academic and Language Students; Form I-538, Certification by Designated School Official, and any evidence you wish to submit, such as affidavits, which detail the unforeseen economic circumstances that cause your request, and evidence you have tried to find off-campus employment with an employer who has filed a labor and wage attestation. FEE REQUIRED.

(c)(4)--Dependent of G-I, G-3 or G-4 Nonimmigrant. File your EAD application with a Form I-566, Application for Employment by Spouse or Unmarried Dependent Son or Daughter of A-I or A-2 Official or Employee of Diplomatic or Consular Establishment or G-4 Officer or Employee of International Organization, with the Department of State endorsement if you are the dependent of a qualifying G-I, G-3 or G-4 officer of, representative to, or employee of an international organization and you hold a valid nonimmigrant status.

(c)(5)--J-2 Spouse or Minor Child of an Exchange Visitor. File your EAD application with a copy of your J-I's (principal alien's) Certificate of Eligibility for Exchange Visitor (J-I) Status (Form IAP-66). You must submit a written statement, with any supporting evidence showing, that your employment is not necessary to support the J-I but is for other purposes. FEE REQUIRED.

(c)(6)--M-I Student Seeking Practical Training after Completing Studies. File your EAD application with a completed Form I-538, Application by Nonimmigrant Student for Extension of Stay, School Transfer, or Permission to Accept or Continue Employment, Form I-20 M-N, Certificate of Eligibility for Nonimmigrant (M-I) Student Status--For Vocational Students endorsed by the designated school official within the past 30 days. FEE REQUIRED.

(c)(7)--Dependent of NATO Personnel. File your EAD application with a letter from the Department of Defense or NATO/SACLANT verifying your principal alien's status, your status, and your relationship to your principal alien. FEE REQUIRED.

(c)(8)--Asylum Applicant under the ABC Settlement Agreement. If you are an El Salvadoran or Guatemalan national eligible for benefits under the ABC settlement agreement, American Baptist Churches v. Thornburgh, 760 F. Supp. 796 (N.D. Cal. 1991), there are special instructions applicable to filing your Form I-765 which supplement these instructions. These instructions and the application can be obtained by asking for an "ABC packet at your local INS office or by calling 1-800-755-0777.

(c)(9)--Adjustment Applicant. File your EAD application with a copy of the receipt notice or other evidence that your Form I-485, Application for Permanent Residence, is pending. You may file Form I-765 together with your Form I-485. FEE REQUIRED.

(c)(10)--Applicant for Suspension of Deportation. File your EAD application with evidence that your Form I-256A, Application for Suspension of Deportation, is pending. FEE REQUIRED.

(c)(II)--Paroled in the Public Interest. File your EAD application if you were paroled into the United States for emergent reasons or reasons strictly in the public interest. FEE REQUIRED.

(c)(12)--Deportable Alien Granted Voluntary Departure. File your EAD application with a copy of the order or notice granting voluntary departure, and evidence establishing your economic need to work. FEE REQUIRED.

(c)(14)--Deferred Action. File your EAD application with a copy of the order, notice or document placing you in deferred action and evidence establishing economic necessity for an EAD. FEE REQUIRED.

(c)(16)--Adjustment Applicant Based on Continuous Residence Since January 1, 1972. File your EAD application with your Form I-485, Application for Permanent Residence; a copy of your receipt notice; or other evidence that the Form I-485 is pending.

(c)(17)(i)--B-I Nonimmigrant who is the personal or domestic servant of a nonimmigrant employer. File your EAD application with:
· Evidence from your employer that he or she is a B, E, F, H, I, J, L, M, O, P, R or TN nonimmigrant and you were employed for at least one year by the employer before the employer entered the United States or your employer regularly employs personal and domestic servants and has done so for a period of years before coming to the United States; and
· Evidence that you have either worked for this employer as a personal or domestic servant for at least one year or, evidence that you have at least one year's experience as a personal or domestic servant; and
· Evidence establishing that you have a residence abroad which you have no intention of abandoning. FEE REQUIRED.

(c)(17)(ii)--B-I Nonimmigrant Domestic Servant of a U.S. Citizen. File your EAD application with:
· Evidence from your employer that he or she is a U.S. Citizen; and
· Evidence that your employer has a permanent home abroad or is stationed outside the United States and is temporarily visiting the United States or the citizen's current assignment in the United States will not be longer than four (4) years; and
· Evidence that he or she has employed you as a domestic servant abroad for at least six (6) months prior to your admission to the United States. FEE REQUIRED.

(c)(17)(iii)--B-I Nonimmigrant Employed by a Foreign Airline. File your EAD application with a letter, from the airline, fully describing your duties and indicating that your position would entitle you to E nonimmigrant status except for the fact that you are not a national of the same country as the airline or because there is no treaty of commerce and navigation in effect between the United States and that country. FEE REQUIRED.

(c)(18)--Final Order of Deportation. File your EAD application with a copy of the order of supervision and a request for employment authorization which may be based on, but not limited to the following:
· Existence of economic necessity to be employed;
· Existence of a dependent spouse and/or children in the United States who rely on you for support; and
· Anticipated length of time before you can be removed from the United States. FEE REQUIRED.

(c)(19)--Applying for Temporary Protected Status (TPS)/Temporary Treatment Benefits. File your EAD application with your TPS application, Form I-821. If you are using this application to register for TPS and do not want to work in the United States, you must submit a letter indicating this application is for registration purposes only. No fee is required to register. FEE REQUIRED.

12
NATURALIZATION FOR US CITIZENSHIP

Admission into the United States as a permanent resident does not mean that you will automatically get US citizenship. US citizenship is obtained in one of two ways: by birth or by naturalization. Anyone born in the United States and subject to its jurisdiction, even though the parents are not citizens, is a US citizen by birth. Also, children who were born abroad to parents who are US citizens are citizens of the United States.

Anyone not born in the United States who wishes to become a US citizen must apply for naturalization.

1. STATUTORY REQUIREMENTS

To apply for naturalization, you must be 18 years or older, a lawful permanent resident of the United States, and must have lived in the United States "continuously" for at least five years, or three years if you are the spouse of a US citizen. You should have held a Form I-551 Alien Registration Receipt Card during this period. You must not have been arrested or convicted of a crime involving moral turpitude in the last five years. You must be able to read, write, and speak English and have a knowledge of the history and government of the United States. At the examination, you will be required to understand and answer questions on these subjects. You will also be required to write in English a sentence like "The flag is red, white, and blue," and you will have to say you believe in and value the principles of the US Constitution.

In 1978, Congress changed the regulations to allow people who have been legal permanent residents in the United States for 20 years and who are at least 50 years

old to qualify for US citizenship without having to demonstrate proficiency in English. This also applies to people over the age of 55 who have been legal permanent residents for at least 15 years. However, they still need to know the basics of US government and history and must take a test in their native language with the assistance of an interpreter.

To apply for naturalization, file a Form N-400 Application for Naturalization along with the filing fee of $260 (see Sample 33). An additional filing fee of $50 must be simultaneously submitted to cover the Immigration Service's costs in fingerprinting you at one of the new Application Service Centers established by a law passed in November 1997. The Immigration Service will contact the naturalization applicant by mail after receiving the N-400 application to specify a period of time for applicants to have their fingerprints taken.

2. SERVICE IN US ARMED FORCES

Both a person who performed honorable wartime service in the US armed forces before October 15, 1978, and someone who is the surviving spouse of a citizen who died while on active duty with the US armed forces are eligible to apply for naturalization.

In order to set the process in motion, you must submit your Form N-400 Application for Naturalization. You will be notified to appear at a preliminary examination at the INS office to make sure that your application and supporting documents are correct. Witnesses are no longer required.

SAMPLE 33
FORM N-400 APPLICATION FOR NATURALIZATION

U.S. Department of Justice
Immigration and Naturalization Service

OMB No. 1115-0009
Application for Naturalization

Print clearly or type your answers using CAPITAL letters. Failure to print clearly may delay your application. Use black or blue ink.

Part I: Your Name *(The Person Applying for Naturalization)*

Write your INS "A"- number here:

A ___ ___ **A00 000 000** ___ ___ ___

A. Your current legal name.

Family Name *(Last Name)*

GOMEZ-SALAZ

Given Name *(First Name)*	Full Middle Name *(If applicable)*
Jose	

FOR INS USE ONLY

Bar Code	Date Stamp

Remarks

B. Your name <u>exactly</u> as it appears on your Permanent Resident Card.

Family Name *(Last Name)*

GOMEZ-SALAZ

Given Name *(First Name)*	Full Middle Name *(If applicable)*
Jose	

C. If you have ever used other names, provide them below.

Family Name *(Last Name)*	Given Name *(First Name)*	Middle Name
None		

D. Name change *(optional)*

Please read the Instructions before you decide whether to change your name.

1. Would you like to legally change your name? ☐ Yes ☒ No
2. If "Yes," print the new name you would like to use. Do not use initials or abbreviation when writing your new name.

Family Name *(Last Name)*

Given Name *(First Name)*	Full Middle Name

Action

Part 2. Information About Your Eligibility   *(Check Only One)*

I am at least 18 years old **AND**

A. ☒ I have been a Lawful Permanent Resident of the United States for at least 5 years.

B. ☐ I have been a Lawful Permanent Resident of the United States for at least 3 years, AND
I have been married to and living with the same U.S. citizen for the last 3 years AND
my spouse has been a U.S. citizen for the last 3 years.

C. ☐ I am applying on the basis of qualifying military service.

D. ☐ Other *(Please explain)* _____

Form N-400 (Rev. 05/31/01)N

SAMPLE 33 — Continued

Part 3. Information About You

Write your INS "A"- number here:

A ___ __ __ __ __ __ __ __ A00 000 000

A. Social Security Number

000 00 0000

B. Date of Birth *(Month/Day/Year)*

11/16/1953

C. Date You Became a Permanent Resident *(Month/Day/Year)*

10/08/1996

D. Country of Birth

MEXICO

E. Country of Nationality

Mexico

F. Are either of your parents U.S. citizens? *(if yes, see Instructions)* ☐ Yes ☒ No

G. What is your current marital status? ☐ Single, Never Married ☒ Married ☐ Divorced ☐ Widowed

☐ Marriage Annulled or Other *(Explain)* _____

H. Are you requesting a waiver of the English and/or U.S. History and Government requirements based on a disability or impairment and attaching a Form N-648 with your application? ☐ Yes ☒ No

I. Are you requesting an accommodation to the naturalization process because of a disability or impairment? *(See Instructions for some examples of accommodations.)* ☐ Yes ☒ No

If you answered "Yes", check the box below that applies:

☐ I am deaf or hearing impaired and need a sign language interpreter who users the following language: _____

☐ I use a wheelchair.

☐ I am blind or sight impaired.

☐ I will need another type of accommodation. Please explain: _____

Part 4. Addresses and Telephone Numbers

A. Home Address - Street Number and Name *(Do NOT write a P.O. Box in this space)*

14301 State Street

Apartment Number

City	County	State	ZIP Code	Country
Seattle	King	WA	98104	U.S.A

B. Care of

Mail Address - Street Number and Name *(If different from home address)*

Apartment Number

City	State	ZIP Code	Country

C. Daytime Phone Number *(If any)*

206/555-5555

Evening Phone Number *(If any)*

E-mail Address *(If any)*

Form N-400 (Rev. 05/31/01)N Page 2

Part 5. Information for Criminal Records Search	Write your INS "A"- number here: A _____ A00 000 000 ____ ____ ____ ____

Note: The categories below are those required by the FBI. See Instructions for more information.

A. Gender
☒ Male ☐ Female

B. Height
6   0
Feet   Inches

C. Weight
175
Pounds

D. Race
☒ White ☐ Asian or Pacific Islander ☐ Black ☐ American Indian or Alaskan Native ☐ Unknown

E. Hair color
☒ Black ☐ Brown ☐ Blonde ☐ Gray ☐ White ☐ Red ☐ Sandy ☐ Bald (No Hair)

F. Eye color
☒ Brown ☐ Blue ☐ Green ☐ Hazel ☐ Gray ☐ Black ☐ Pink ☐ Maroon ☐ Other

Part 6. Information About Your Residence and Employment

A. Where have you lived during the last 5 years? Begin with where you live now and then list every place you lived for the last 5 years. If you need more space, use a separate sheet of paper.

Street Number and Name, Apartment Number, City, State, Zip Code and Country	Dates (Month/Year) From	To
Current Home Address - Same as Part 4.A	05/10/1996 __	Present
	__ __ __ __ __ __	__ __ __ __ __ __
	__ __ __ __ __ __	__ __ __ __ __ __
	__ __ __ __ __ __	__ __ __ __ __ __
	__ __ __ __ __ __	__ __ __ __ __ __

B. Where have you worked (or, if you were a student, what schools did you attend) during the last 5 years? Include military service. Begin with your current or latest employer and then list every place you have worked or studied for the last 5 years. If you need more space, use a separate sheet of paper.

Employer or School Name	Employer or School Address (Street, City and State)	Dates (Month/Year) From	To	Your Occupation
Veggie-Bite	986 Australlian Road	6/19/1996	__ __ __ __ __	Sales
		__ __ __ __ __	__ __ __ __ __	
		__ __ __ __ __	__ __ __ __ __	
		__ __ __ __ __	__ __ __ __ __	
		__ __ __ __ __	__ __ __ __ __	

Form N-400 (Rev. 05/31/01)N Page 3

Part 7. Time Outside the United States	Write your INS "A"- number here:
(Including Trips to Canada, Mexico, and the Caribbean Islands)	A __ __ __ __ __ __ __ __ __ A00 000 000

A. How many total days did you spend outside of the United States during the past 5 years? | 0 | days

B. How many trips of 24 hours or more have you taken outside of the United States during the past 5 years? | 0 | trips

C. List below all the trips of 24 hours or more that you have taken outside of the United States since becoming a Lawful Permanent Resident. Begin with your most recent trip. If you need more space, use a separate sheet of paper.

Date You Left the United States (Month/Day/Year)	Date You Returned to the United States (Month/Day/Year)	Did Trip Last 6 Months or More?	Countries to Which You Traveled	Total Days Out of the United States
__ __ __ __ __ __	__ __ __ __ __ __	☐ Yes ☐ No		
__ __ __ __ __ __	__ __ __ __ __ __	☐ Yes ☐ No		
__ __ __ __ __ __	__ __ __ __ __ __	☐ Yes ☐ No		
__ __ __ __ __ __	__ __ __ __ __ __	☐ Yes ☐ No		
__ __ __ __ __ __	__ __ __ __ __ __	☐ Yes ☐ No		
__ __ __ __ __ __	__ __ __ __ __ __	☐ Yes ☐ No		
__ __ __ __ __ __	__ __ __ __ __ __	☐ Yes ☐ No		
__ __ __ __ __ __	__ __ __ __ __ __	☐ Yes ☐ No		
__ __ __ __ __ __	__ __ __ __ __ __	☐ Yes ☐ No		
__ __ __ __ __ __	__ __ __ __ __ __	☐ Yes ☐ No		

Part 8. Information About Your Marital History

A. How many times have you been married (including annulled marriages)? | 0 | If you have NEVER been married, go to Part 9.

B. If you are married, give the following information about your spouse:

1. Spouse's Family Name *(Last Name)*   Given Name *(First Name)*   Full Middle Name *(If applicable)*

2. Date of Birth*(Month/Day/Year)*   3. Date of Marriage *(Month/Day/Year)*   4. Spouse's Social Security Number

__ __ __ __ __ __   __ __ __ __ __ __   __ __ __ __ __ __

5 Home Address - Street Number and Name   Apartment Number

City   State   ZIP Code

Part 8. Information About Your Marital History *(Continued)*

Write your INS "A"- number here:

A __ __ __ __ __ __ __ __   A00 000 000

C. Is your spouse a U.S. citizen? ☐ Yes ☐ No

D. If your spouse is a U.S. citizen, give the following information:

1. When did your spouse become a U.S. citizen? ☐ At Birth ☐ Other

If "Other," give the following information:

2. Date your spouse became a U.S. citizen

__ __ __ __ __ __ __ __

3. Place your spouse became a U.S. citizen *(Please see Instructions)*

City and State

E. If your spouse is NOT a U.S. citizen, give the following information:

1. Spouse's Country of Citizenship

2. Spouse's INS "A"- Number *(If applicable)*

A __ __ __ __ __ __ __ __

3. Spouse's Immigration Status

☐ Lawful Permanent Resident   ☐ Other _____

F. If you were married before, provide the following information about your prior spouse. If you have more than one previous marriage, use a separate sheet of paper to provide the information requested in questions 1-5 below.

1. Prior Spouse's Family Name *(Last Name)* | Given Name *(First Name)* | Full Middle Name *(If applicable)*

2. Prior Spouse's Immigration Status

☐ U.S. Citizen

☐ Lawful Permanent Resident

☐ Other _____

3. Date of Marriage *(Month/Day/Year)*

__ __ __ __ __ __ __ __

4. Date Marriage Ended *(Month/Day/Year)*

__ __ __ __ __ __ __ __

5. How Marriage Ended

☐ Divorce ☐ Spouse Died ☐ Other _____

G. How many times has your current spouse been married (including annulled marriages)? ☐

If your spouse has EVER been married before, give the following information about your spouse's prior marriage.
If your spouse has more than one previous marriage, use a separate sheet of paper to provide the information requested in questions 1 - 5 below.

1. Prior Spouse's Family Name *(Last Name)* | Given Name *(First Name)* | Full Middle Name *(If applicable)*

2. Prior Spouse's Immigration Status

☐ U.S. Citizen

☐ Lawful Permanent Resident

☐ Other _____

3. Date of Marriage *(Month/Day/Year)*

__ __ __ __ __ __ __ __

4. Date Marriage Ended *(Month/Day/Year)*

__ __ __ __ __ __ __ __

5. How Marriage End

☐ Divorce ☐ Spouse Died ☐ Other _____

Form N-400 (Rev. 05/31/01)N Page 5

SAMPLE 33 — Continued

Part 9. Information About Your Children	Write your INS "A"- number here:
	A00 000 000
	A __ __ __ __ __ __ __ __ __

A. How many sons and daughters have you had? For more information on which sons and daughters you should include and how to complete this section, see the Instructions.

`0`

B. Provide the following information about all of your sons and daughters. If you need more space, use a separate sheet of paper.

Full name of Son or Daughter	Date of Birth *(Month/Day/Year)*	INS "A"- number *(if child has one)*	Country of Birth	Current Address *(Street, City, State & Country)*
None				
	__ __ __ __ __ __	A __ __ __ __ __ __ __		
	__ __ __ __ __ __	A __ __ __ __ __ __ __		
	__ __ __ __ __ __	A __ __ __ __ __ __ __		
	__ __ __ __ __ __	A __ __ __ __ __ __ __		
	__ __ __ __ __ __	A __ __ __ __ __ __ __		
	__ __ __ __ __ __	A __ __ __ __ __ __ __		
	__ __ __ __ __ __	A __ __ __ __ __ __ __		
	__ __ __ __ __ __	A __ __ __ __ __ __ __		

Part 10. Additional Questions

Please answer questions 1 through 14. If you answer "Yes" to any of these questions, include a written explanation with this form. Your written explanation should (1) explain why your answer was "Yes," and (2) provide any additional information that helps to explain your answer.

A. General Questions

1. Have you **EVER** claimed to be a U.S. citizen *(in writing or any other way)?* ☐ Yes ☒ No

2. Have you **EVER** registered to vote in any Federal, state, or local election in the United States? ☐ Yes ☒ No

3. Have you **EVER** voted in any Federal, state, or local election in the United States? ☐ Yes ☒ No

4. Since becoming a Lawful Permanent Resident, have you **EVER** failed to file a required Federal, state, or local tax return? ☐ Yes ☒ No

5. Do you owe any Federal, state, or local taxes that are overdue? ☐ Yes ☒ No

6. Do you have any title of nobility in any foreign country? ☐ Yes ☒ No

7. Have you ever been declared legally incompetent or been confined to a mental institution within the last 5 years? ☐ Yes ☒ No

Form N-400 (Rev. 05/31/01)N Page 6

SAMPLE 33 — Continued

<table>
<tr><td>**Part 10. Additional Questions** *(Continued)*</td><td>Write your INS "A"- number here:
A00 000 000
A __ __ __ __ __ __ __ __ __</td></tr>
</table>

B. Affiliations

8. a. Have you **EVER** been a member of or associated with any organization, association, fund, foundation, party, club, society, or similar group in the United States or in any other place? ☐ Yes ☒ No

b. If you answered "Yes," list the name of each group below. If you need more space, attach the names of the other group(s) on a separate sheet of paper.

Name of Group	Name of Group
1.	6.
2.	7.
3.	8.
4.	9.
5.	10.

9. Have you **EVER** been a member of or in any way associated *(either directly or indirectly)* with:

  a. The Communist Party? ☐ Yes ☒ No

  b. Any other totalitarian party? ☐ Yes ☒ No

  c. A terrorist organization? ☐ Yes ☒ No

10. Have you **EVER** advocated *(either directly or indirectly)* the overthrow of any government by force or violence? ☐ Yes ☒ No

11. Have you **EVER** persecuted *(either directly or indirectly)* any person because of race, religion, national origin, membership in a particular social group, or political opinion? ☐ Yes ☒ No

12. Between March 23, 1933, and May 8, 1945, did you work for or associate in any way *(either directly or indirectly)* with:

  a. The Nazi government of Germany? ☐ Yes ☒ No

  b. Any government in any area (1) occupied by, (2) allied with, or (3) established with the help of the Nazi government of Germany? ☐ Yes ☒ No

  c. Any German, Nazi, or S.S. military unit, paramilitary unit, self-defense unit, vigilante unit, citizen unit, police unit, government agency or office, extermination camp, concentration camp, prisoner of war camp, prison, labor camp, or transit camp? ☐ Yes ☒ No

C. Continuous Residence

Since becoming a Lawful Permanent Resident of the United States:

13. Have you **EVER** called yourself a "nonresident" on a Federal, state, or local tax return? ☐ Yes ☒ No

14. Have you **EVER** failed to file a Federal, state, or local tax return because you considered yourself to be a "nonresident"? ☐ Yes ☒ No

Form N-400 (Rev. 05/31/01)N Page 7

Part 10. Additional Questions *(Continued)*	Write your INS "A"- number here: A __ __ __ **A00 000 000** __ __ __ __

D. Good Moral Character

For the purposes of this application , you must answer "Yes" to the following questions, if applicable, even if your records were sealed or otherwise cleared or if anyone, including a judge, law enforcement officer, or attorney, told you that you no longer have a record.

15. Have you **EVER** committed a crime or offense for which you were NOT arrested? ☐ Yes ☒ No

16. Have you **EVER** been arrested, cited, or detained by any law enforcement officer (including INS and military officers) for any reason? ☐ Yes ☒ No

17. Have you **EVER** been charged with committing any crime or offense? ☐ Yes ☒ No

18. Have you **EVER** been convicted of a crime or offense? ☐ Yes ☒ No

19. Have you **EVER** been placed in an alternative sentencing or a rehabilitative program (for example: diversion, deferred prosecution, withheld adjudication, deferred adjudication)? ☐ Yes ☒ No

20. Have you **EVER** received a suspended sentence, been placed on probation, or been paroled? ☐ Yes ☒ No

21 Have you **EVER** been in jail or prison? ☐ Yes ☒ No

If you answered "Yes" to any of questions 15 through 21, complete the following table. If you need more space, use a separate sheet of paper to give the same information.

Why were you arrested, cited, detained, or charged?	Date arrested, cited, detained, or charged *(Month/Day/Year)*	Where were you arrested, cited, detained or charged? *(City, State, Country)*	Outcome or disposition of the arrest, citation, detention or charge *(No charges filed, charges dismissed, jail, probation, etc.)*

Answer questions 22 through 33. If you answer "Yes" to any of these questions, attach (1) your written explanation why your answer was "Yes," and (2) any additional information or documentation that helps explain your answer.

22. Have you **EVER**:

    a. been a habitual drunkard? ☐ Yes ☒ No

    b. been a prostitute, or procured anyone for prostitution? ☐ Yes ☒ No

    c. sold or smuggled controlled substances, illegal drugs or narcotics? ☐ Yes ☒ No

    d. been married to more than one person at the same time? ☐ Yes ☒ No

    e. helped anyone enter or try to enter the United States illegally? ☐ Yes ☒ No

    f. gambled illegally or received income from illegal gambling? ☐ Yes ☒ No

    g. failed to support your dependents or to pay alimony? ☐ Yes ☒ No

23. Have you **EVER** given false or misleading information to any U.S. government official while applying for any immigration benefit or to prevent deportation, exclusion, or removal? ☐ Yes ☒ No

24. Have you **EVER** lied to any U.S. government official to gain entry or admission into the United States? ☐ Yes ☒ No

Form N-400 (Rev. 05/31/01)N Page 8

Part 10. Additional Questions *(Continued)*	Write your INS "A"- number here: A __ __ __ A00 000 000 __ __ __

E. Removal, Exclusion, and Deportation Proceedings

25. Are removal, exclusion, rescission or deportation proceedings pending against you? ☐ Yes ☒ No

26. Have you **EVER** been removed, excluded, or deported from the United States? ☐ Yes ☒ No

27. Have you **EVER** been ordered to be removed, excluded, or deported from the United States? ☐ Yes ☒ No

28. Have you **EVER** applied for any kind of relief from removal, exclusion, or deportation? ☐ Yes ☒ No

F. Military service

29. Have you **EVER** served in the U.S. Armed Forces? ☐ Yes ☒ No

30. Have you **EVER** left the United States to avoid being drafted into the U.S. Armed Forces? ☐ Yes ☒ No

31. Have you **EVER** applied for any kind of exemption from military service in the U.S. Armed Forces? ☐ Yes ☒ No

32. Have you **EVER** deserted from the U.S. Armed Forces? ☐ Yes ☒ No

G. Selective Service Registration

33. Are you a male who lived in the United States at any time between your 18th and 26th birthdays in any status except as a lawful nonimmigrant? ☐ Yes ☒ No

If you answered "NO", go on to question 34.

If you answered "YES", provide the information below.

If you answered "YES", but you did NOT register with the Selective Service System and are still under 26 years of age, you must register before you apply for naturalization, so that you can complete the information below:

Date Registered (Month/Day/Year) [ ]   Selective Service Number [__ __ __ __ __ __ __ __]

If you answered "YES", but you did NOT register with the Selective Service and you are now 26 years old or older, attach a statement explaining why you did not register.

H. Oath Requirements   *(See Part 14 for the text of the oath)*

Answer questions 34 through 39. If you answer "No" to any of these questions, attach (1) your written explanation why the answer was "No" and (2) any additional information or documentation that helps to explain your answer.

34. Do you support the Constitution and form of government of the United States? ☒ Yes ☐ No

35. Do you understand the full Oath of Allegiance to the United States? ☒ Yes ☐ No

36. Are you willing to take the full Oath of Allegiance to the United States? ☒ Yes ☐ No

37. If the law requires it, are you willing to bear arms on behalf of the United States? ☒ Yes ☐ No

38. If the law requires it, are you willing to perform noncombatant services in the U.S. Armed Forces? ☒ Yes ☐ No

39. If the law requires it, are you willing to perform work of national importance under civilian direction? ☒ Yes ☐ No

Form N-400 (Rev. 05/31/01)N Page 9

Part 11. Your Signature

Write your INS "A"- number here:

A   **A00 000 000** __ __ __ __ __

I certify, under penalty of perjury under the laws of the United States of America, that this application, and the evidence submitted with it, are all true and correct. I authorize the release of any information which INS needs to determine my eligibility for naturalization.

Your Signature

Date *(Month/Day/Year)*

08/10/2002 __ __ __ __ __

Part 12. Signature of Person Who Prepared This Application for You *(if applicable)*

I declare under penalty of perjury that I prepared this application at the request of the above person. The answers provided are based on information of which I have personal knowledge and/or were provided to me by the above named person in response to the *exact questions* contained on this form.

Preparer's Printed Name

Law Offices of Dan P. Danilov

Preparer's Signature

Date *(Month/Day/Year)*

8/10/2002 __ __ __ __

Preparer's Firm or Organization Name *(If applicable)*

Law Offices of Dan P. Danilov

Preparer's Daytime Phone Number

206/624-6868

Preparer's Address - Street Number and Name

Suite 2303 - One Union Square

City

Seattle

State

WA

ZIP Code

98101

Do Not Complete Part 13 and 14 Until an INS Officer Instructs You To Do So

Part 13. Signature at Interview

I swear (affirm) and certify under penalty of perjury under the laws of the United States of America that I know that the contents of this application for naturalization subscribed by me, including corrections numbered 1 through _____ and the evidence submitted by me numbered pages 1 through _____, are true and correct to the best of my knowledge and belief.

Subscribed to and sworn to (affirmed) before me _____

Officer's Printed Name or Stamp

Date *(Month/Day/Year)*

Complete Signature of Applicant

Officer's Signature

Part 14. Oath of Allegiance

If your application is approved, you will be scheduled for a public oath ceremony at which time you will be required to take the following oath of allegiance immediately prior to becoming a naturalized citizen. By signing below, you acknowledge your willingness and ability to take this oath:

I hereby declare, on oath, that I absolutely and entirely renounce and abjure all allegiance and fidelity to any foreign prince, potentate, state, or sovereignty, of whom or which I have heretofore been a subject or citizen;

that I will support and defend the Constitution and laws of the United States of America against all enemies, foreign and domestic;
that I will bear true faith and allegiance to the same;
that I will bear arms on behalf of the United States when required by the law;
that I will perform noncombatant service in the Armed Forces of the United States when required by the law;
that I will perform work of national importance under civilian direction when required by the law; and
that I take this obligation freely, without any mental reservation or purpose of evasion; so help me God.

Printed Name of Applicant

Complete Signature of Applicant

Form N-400 (Rev. 05/31/01)N Page 10

You will be required to take an oath and a simple test about US history and government. The test usually involves answering a series of questions by a naturalization examiner as well as an English reading and writing test.

After the preliminary hearing is completed at your local INS office, you will be sworn in and granted citizenship. If you wish, you may be sworn in the US District Court, but you must wait for a later hearing date.

3. OATH OF ALLEGIANCE TO THE UNITED STATES

The final hearing to become a US citizen takes place in the office of the local INS office where the formal ceremony is completed and you take the Oath of Allegiance to the United States of America. Your relatives and friends are welcome to attend the court hearing. At the close of the ceremony you will receive a Certificate of Naturalization.

4. WHO CAN APPLY FOR A CERTIFICATE OF US CITIZENSHIP?

There are certain groups of people who do not have to apply for naturalization because they already hold a special right to citizenship. These groups include children of US citizens or permanent residents born outside of the United States and women who lost their citizenship through marriage to a noncitizen. Those who qualify in these groups can apply for citizenship by filing a Form N-600 Application for Certificate of Citizenship (see Sample 34). The fee is $185.

4.1 Legitimate children of US parents

If you were born before May 24, 1934, and your father was a citizen who had lived in the United States before you were born, you can apply for a Certificate of Citizenship. The citizenship of your mother is not material.

If you were born on or after May 24, 1934, and before January 13, 1941, both your parents were citizens, and one parent resided in the United States before you were born, you are eligible to apply for a Certificate of Citizenship. If only one of your parents was a US citizen, then that parent must have lived in the United States for some period of time before you were born.

In addition, you must have lived in the United States for a minimum of five years between the ages of 13 and 21 before you can apply. If your US parent was employed by a US organization abroad, you may retain your citizenship if you took up US residence in the United States before you were 16 years old and before December 24, 1952.

If you cannot meet these requirements, you can retain your citizenship by showing that you were physically present in the United States for at least two years when you were between 14 and 18 years old. The two years' physical presence requirement applies to anyone born on or after May 24, 1934.

If you were born on or after January 13, 1941, and before December 24, 1952, and both of your parents were US citizens, then you have no problem. If only one of your parents was a US citizen, that parent must have lived in the United States or its possessions for at least ten years, at least five of which were after reaching 16 years of age. If your US parent served honorably in the US armed forces between December 7, 1941, and December 24, 1952, five years of the ten years' US residence period may be calculated after the parent reached 12 years of age.

You must have lived in the United States or any of its outlying possessions between the ages of 13 and 21 years for a period of not less than five years. If you lived in the United States before reaching 16 and you show that you were physically present in the United States for at least two years before December 24, 1952, your citizenship

SAMPLE 34
FORM N-600 APPLICATION FOR CERTIFICATE OF CITIZENSHIP

OMB NO. 1115-0018

Application for
Certificate of Citizenship

U.S. Department of Justice
Immigration and Naturalization Service

FEE STAMP

Take or mail this application to:
IMMIGRATION AND NATURALIZATION SERVICE

Date __08/10/2002__

(Print or type) **Maria**   **GOMEZ-SALAZ**   *nee* _____
(Full, True Name, without Abbreviations)   (Maiden name, if any)

14301 State Street
(Apartment number, Street address, and, if appropriate, "in care of")

Seattle		**WA**	**98104**
(City)	(County)	(State)	(ZIP Code)

ALIEN REGISTRATION

NO. __A00 000 000__

206/555-5555
(Telephone Number)

(SEE INSTRUCTIONS. BE SURE YOU UNDERSTAND EACH QUESTION BEFORE YOU ANSWER IT.)

I hereby apply to the Commissioner of Immigration and Naturalization for a certificate showing that I am a citizen of the United States of America.

(1) I was born in __Tepalmes__   __Colima__   on ____11/16/1953____
                    (City) (State or country)   (Month) (Day) (Year)

(2) My personal description is: Gender; **130** ; height **6** feet **0** inches;

Marital status: ☐ Single; ☒ Married; ☐ Divorced; ☐ Widow(er).

(3) I arrived in the United States at __New York, New York__   on ___06/08/1996___
                                        (City and State)   (Month) (Day) (Year)

under the name **Maria GOMEZ-SALAS**   by means of   **Ship**
                                                                        (Name of ship or other means of arrival)

☐ on U.S. Passport No. _____ issued to me at _____ on __/ /__
                                                                              (Month) (Day) (Year)

☒ on an Immigrant Visa ☐ Other (specify) _____

(4) FILL IN THIS BLOCK ONLY IF YOU ARRIVED IN THE UNITED STATES BEFORE JULY 1, 1924.
(a) My last permanent foreign residence was _____ (City) _____ (Country)
(b) I took the ship or other conveyance to the United States at _____ (City) _____ (Country)
(c) I was coming to _____ at _____ (Name of person in the United States) (City and State where this person was living)
(d) I traveled to the United States with _____ (Name of passengers or relatives with whom you traveled, and their relationship to you, if any)

(5) Have you been out of the United States since you first arrived? ☐ Yes ☒ No; If "Yes" fill in the following information for every absence.

DATE DEPARTED	DATE RETURNED	Name of airlines or other means used to return to the United States	Port of return to the United States

(6) I __have not__ filed a petition for naturalization.(*If "have", attach full explanation.*)
     (have) (have not)

TO THE APPLICANT. - Do not write between the double lines below. Continue on next page.

ARRIVAL RECORDS EXAMINED	**ARRIVAL RECORD FOUND**
Card index _____	Place _____ Date _____
Index books _____	Name _____
Manifests _____	Manner _____
_____	Marital status _____ Age _____
	(Signature of person making search)

Form N-600 (Rev.10/11/00) Y

(CONTINUE HERE)

(7) **I claim United States citizenship through my** *(check whichever applicable)* ☒ father; ☐ mother; ☐ both parents;

☐ adoptive parent(s); ☐ husband

(8) **My father's name is** Oleo   SALAS   ; he was born on   05/8/1935
                                                                                      (Month)   (Day)   (Year)

at   Kansas   ; and resides at 459 Rochester Avenue   Seattle, WA
          (City)   (State or Country)   (Street address, city, and State or country. If dead, write

  98105   He became a citizen of the United States by ☒ birth; ☐ naturalization on _____
"dead" and date of death.)   (Month)   (Day)   (Year)

in the _____ Certificate of Naturalization No. _____
        (Name of court, city, and State)

☐ through his parent(s), and _____ issued Certificate of Citizenship No. A or AA _____
                                (was)   (was not)

(If known) His former Alien Registration No. was _____

He   **has not**   lost United States citizenship. *(If citizenship lost, attach full explanation)*
    (has) (has not)

He resided in the United States from   **1935**   to   **2002**   ; from _____ to _____ ; from _____ to _____
                                        (Year)   (Year)   (Year)   (Year)   (Year)   (Year)

from _____ to _____ ; from _____ to _____ ; I am the child of his   **1st**   marriage.
     (Year)   (Year)   (Year)   (Year)   (1st, 2d, 3d, etc.)

(9) **My mother's present name is** Maria   SALAS   ; her maiden name was   GONZALEZ   ;

she was born on   05/18/1940   ; at   Juarez MEXICO   ; she resides
                  (Month)   (Day)   (Year)   (City)   (State or country)

at 459 Rochester Avenue   Seattle   WA   98105   She became a citizen of the
                        (Street address, city, and State or country. If dead, write "dead" and date of death.)

United States by ☒ birth; ☐ naturalization under the name of _____

on _____ in the _____
    (Month) (Day) (Year)   (Name of court, city, and State)

Certificate of Naturalization No. _____ ☐ through her parent(s), and _____ issued Certificate
                                                                                   (was)(was not)

of Citizenship No. A or AA _____ (If known) Her former Alien Registration No. was _____

She   **has not**   lost United States citizenship. *(If citizenship lost, attach full explanation)*
     (has) (has not)

She resided in the United States from   **1940**   to   **2002**   ; from _____ to _____ ; from _____ to _____ ;
                                          (Year)   (Year)   (Year)   (Year)   (Year)   (Year)

from _____ to _____ ; from _____ to _____ ; I am the child of her   **1st**   marriage.
     (Year)   (Year)   (Year)   (Year)   (1st, 2d, 3d, etc.)

(10) My mother and my father were married to each other on   **05/05/1981**   at **Seattle WA**
                                                              (Month)(Day)(Year)   (City)   (State or country)

(11) If claim is through adoptive parent(s):
I was adopted on _____ in the _____
                  (Month)(Day)(Year)   (Name of Court)

at _____ by my _____ who were not United States citizens at that time.
    (City or town)(State)(Country)   (mother, father, parents)

(12) My _____ served in the Armed Forces of the United States from _____ to _____ and _____
        (father) (mother)   (Date)   (Date)   (was) (was not)

honorably discharged.

(13) I   **have not**   lost my United States citizenship. *(If citizenship lost, attach full explanation.)*
        (have) (have not)

(14) I submit the following documents with this application:

      Nature of Document   *Names of Persons Concerned*

_____   _____

_____   _____

_____   _____

_____   _____

_____   _____

Form N-600 (Rev. 10/11/00) Y Page 2

(15) Fill in this block if your brother, sister, mother or father ever applied to the INS for a certificate of citizenship.

NAME OF RELATIVE	RELATIONSHIP	DATE OF BIRTH	WHEN APPLICATION SUBMITTED	CERTIFICATE NO. AND FILE NO., IF KNOWN, AND LOCATION OF OFFICE
None				

(16) Fill in this block only if your are now or ever have been a married woman. I have been married __1__ time(s), as follows:
(1, 2, 3, etc.)

DATE MARRIED	NAME OF HUSBAND		CITIZENSHIP OF HUSBAND	IF MARRIAGE HAS BEEN TERMINATED:	
				Date Marriage Ended	How Marriage Ended *(Death or divorce)*
05/05/1981	Jose	GOMEZ-Salas	United States		

(17) Fill in this block only if you claim citizenship through a husband. *(Marriage must have occurred prior to September 22, 1922.)*
Name of citizen husband _____ ;he was born on _____
(Give full and complete name) *(Month) (Day) (Year)*
at _____ ;and resides at _____ He became a citizen of the
(City) (State or country) *(Street address, city, and State or country. If dead, write "dead" and date of death.)*
United States by ☐ birth; ☐naturalization on _____ in the _____ Certificate of
(Month)(Day)(Year) *(Name of court, city, and State)*
Naturalization No. _____ ; ☐ through his parent(s), and _____ issued Certificate of Citizenship No. A or AA
(was)(was not)
_____ . He _____ since lost United States citizenship.*(If citizenship lost, attach full explanation.)*
(has)(has not)
I am of the _____ race. Before my marriage to him, he was married _____ time(s), as follows:
(1, 2, 3, etc.)

DATE MARRIED	NAME OF WIFE	IF MARRIAGE HAS BEEN TERMINATED:	
		Date Marriage Ended	How Marriage Ended *(Death or divorce)*

(18) Fill in this block only if you claim citizenship through your stepfather. *(Applicable only if mother married U.S. Citizen prior to September 22, 1922.)*
The full name of my stepfather is _____ ; he was born on _____ at _____ ;
(Month)(Day)(Year) *(City)(State or country)*
and resides at _____ He became a citizen of the United States by ☐birth;
(Street address, city, and State or country. If dead, write "dead" and date of death.)
☐ naturalization on _____ in the _____ Certificate of Naturalization No. _____ ;
(Month)(Day)(Year) *(Name of court, city, and State)*
☐ through his parent(s), and _____ issued Certificate of Citizenship No. A or AA _____ He _____ since lost United
(was)(was not) *(has)(has not)*
States citizenship. *(If citizenship lost, attach full explanation.)* He and my mother were married to each other on _____ at _____
(Month)(Day)(Year) *(City and State or country)*
My mother is of the _____ race. She _____ issued Certificate of Citizenship No. A _____
(was) (was not)
Before marrying my mother, my stepfather was married _____ time(s), as follows:
(1, 2, 3, etc.)

DATE MARRIED	NAME OF WIFE	IF MARRIAGE HAS BEEN TERMINATED:	
		Date Marriage Ended	How Marriage Ended *(Death or divorce)*

(19) I **have not** previously applied for a certificate of citizenship on _____ , at _____
(have) (have not) *(Date)* *(Office)*

(20) Signature of person preparing form, if other than applicant. I declare that this document was prepared by me at the request of the applicant and is based on all information of which I have any knowledge. SIGNATURE: *Law Offices of Don P. Danilov*	
ADDRESS: **Seattle, WA 98101**	DATE: 8/10/02

(SIGN HERE) *Maria Gomez-Salas*
(Signature of applicant or parent or guardian)

Form N-600 (Rev. 10/11/00)Y page 3

SAMPLE 34 — Continued

APPLICANT · Do not fill in or sign anything on this page

AFFIDAVIT

I, the _____ , do swear
(Applicant, parent, guardian)
that I know and understand the contents of this application, signed by me, and
of attached supplementary pages numbered (   ) to (   ), inclusive
that the same are true to the best of my knowledge and belief: and that
corrections numbered (   )to (   ) were made by me or at my request.

Subscribed and sworn to before me upon applicant examination of the applicant
(parent, guardian) at _____
this _____ day of _____ , _____
and continued solely for:

_____
(Signature of applicant, parent, guardian)

_____
(Officer's Signature and Title)

REPORT AND RECOMMENDATION ON APPLICATION

On the basis of the documents, records, and persons examined, and the identification upon personal appearance of the underage beneficiary, I find that
all the facts and conclusions set forth under oath in this application are _____ true and correct; that the applicant did _____ derive or acquire United
States citizenship on _____ , through
(month) (Day)(Year)

and that (s)he_____been expatriated since that time. I recommend that this application be_____ and that
(has) (has not)   (granted) (denied)
_____Certificate of citizenship be _____ issued in the name of _____
(A) (AA)
In addition to the documents listed in Item 14, the following documents and records have been examined:

Person Examined	Address	Relationship to Applicant	Date Testimony Heard
_____	_____	_____	_____
	_____		
_____	_____	_____	_____
	_____		

Supplementary Report(s) No.(s)_____ Attached.
Date _____ , _____

_____
(Officer's Signature and Title)

I do_____ concur in the recommendation.
Date _____ , _____

_____
(Signature of District Director or Officer in Charge)

Form N-600 (Rev. 10/11/00)Y Page 4

will be retained. If you came to the United States before reaching 16 years of age but after the December 24, 1952, deadline, you must show two years' continuous physical presence in the United States between the ages of 14 and 28.

If you are the legitimate child of US citizen parents and were born after December 24, 1952, you need not comply with any residency requirements yourself. If, however, only one of your parents was a US citizen, that parent must have lived in the United States for ten years and five of those years must have passed after your parent turned 14. If you were born between December 24, 1952, and October 10, 1978, you have to show that you lived in the United States for at least two years when you were between the ages of 14 and 28.

Children born after October 10, 1978, can retain US citizenship without living in the United States.

The law is not retroactive and anyone who had lost US citizenship under previous laws would not have it restored to him or her. Table 9 displays the citizenship requirements for legitimate children born outside the United States.

4.2 Illegitimate children

If you are the illegitimate child of a US citizen, your right to apply for a Certificate of Citizenship depends on the status of your mother and on whether or not your father legitimated your birth.

If you were born before May 24, 1934, and your mother was a US citizen who lived in the United States before your birth, you acquired US citizenship at birth. If your father was a US citizen who legitimated your birth to someone who was not a citizen (i.e., married your mother or adopted you legally), you acquired citizenship as of the date of birth as long as your father was a US citizen who had previously lived in the United States or outlying possessions.

If you were born on or after May 24, 1934, and your mother was a US citizen who had lived in the United States before you were born, you acquired citizenship on the date of birth. If your father was a US citizen who later legitimated your birth, you acquired citizenship as of your date of birth as long as he had resided in the United States or outlying possessions before you were born.

If you were born on or after January 13, 1941, and before December 24, 1952, and your mother was a citizen who had lived in the United States before you were born, you acquired citizenship at birth. If your paternity was established when you were underage and your father was a citizen when you were born who had ten years' residence in the United States with five of those years spent in the United States after turning 16, you acquired citizenship as of your date of birth.

If you were born on or after December 14, 1952, and your mother was a US citizen who had lived in the United States for one year continuously before your birth, you acquired citizenship at birth.

If you were legitimated while under 21 years of age and both your parents were citizens and at least one of your parents had lived in the United States prior to your birth, you acquired citizenship as of birth.

If you were legitimated while under 21 and only one parent was a US citizen, your citizen parent must have been physically present in the United States or one of its outlying possessions for at least ten years, five of which passed after he or she turned 14 and before you were born. You must have resided continuously in the United States for at least five years between 14 and 28 years old. Table 10 displays the citizenship requirements for illegitimate children born outside the United States.

TABLE 9
CITIZENSHIP REQUIREMENTS FOR LEGITIMATE CHILDREN BORN OUTSIDE THE UNITED STATES TO US CITIZENS

Date of birth	Citizenship status and residence required of parent or parents	Residence required of child in order to retain citizenship
Prior to 5/24/34	*Father* must have been a citizen who had resided in the United States prior to birth of child. Citizenship of mother is immaterial.	None
On or after 5/24/34 and before 1/13/41	*Both parents* citizens, one of whom had resided in the United States prior to birth of the child.	None
	Either parent a citizen, the other an alien. Citizen parent must have resided in the United States prior to birth of child.	Five years in the United States between ages of 13 and 21 unless parent is employed abroad by an American organization*
On or after 1/13/41 and before 12/24/52	*Both parents* citizens, one of whom had resided in the United States or outlying possessions prior to birth of the child.	None
	Either parent a citizen, the other an alien. Citizen parent must have resided in United States or outlying possessions ten years, five of which were after attaining age of 16 years. If citizen parents served honorably in US armed forces between 12/7/41 and 12/31/46, five of ten years' residence may be after age of 12.	
On or after 12/24/52	*Both parents* citizens, one of whom had resided in the United States or outlying possessions prior to birth of the child.	None

TABLE 9 — Continued

Date of birth	Citizenship status and residence required of parent or parents	Residence required of child in order to retain citizenship
	Either parent a citizen, the other an alien. Citizen parent must have been physically present in United States or possession ten years, five of which were after the age of 14 years.Honorable service in US armed forces counts as physical presence.	Two years continuous physical presence in the United States between the ages of 14 and 28

The two years' continuous physical presence requirement is retroactive and applicable to anyone born on or after May 24, 1934 |
| On or after 10/10/78 | | Children can retain citizenship without residing in the United States. This law is not retroactive. |

*Citizenship may be retained by complying with either of these provisions or the retention provisions applicable on or after 12/24/52 if the person had taken up residence in the United States before attaining age of 16 years and before 12/24/52.

A person who had not attained the age of 16 years and had not taken up residence in the United States before 12/24/52 must comply with the citizenship requirements applicable.

4.3 Women who lost their citizenship on marriage

For women who lost their US citizenship by marrying an alien, there are several provisions for regaining citizenship.

Women who marry aliens today may retain citizenship simply by taking the Oath of Allegiance. Since December 24, 1952, a woman who lost citizenship by marriage to an alien after September 22, 1922, has been able to resume citizenship by taking the oath.

For marriages that were terminated, the resumption of citizenship depends on when and where the marriage was terminated.

If you lived in the United States at the time the marriage was terminated, special factors apply for citizenship to be regained promptly. If you lived outside the United States, you are subject to certain residence or registration requirements.

If your marriage was terminated on or after September 22, 1922, and before June 6, 1936, and you had resided in the United States continuously from the date of marriage, your citizenship was resumed on July 2, 1940. This provision applies to native-born women and includes those women who were born abroad and who acquired citizenship at birth and lost their citizenship because they married an alien before September 22, 1922.

If you were residing outside of the United States when your marriage was terminated, your citizenship was resumed on July 25, 1936 (if not previously resumed). All women whose marriages terminated in this time period have to take the Oath of Allegiance before they exercise the rights of a US citizen.

Those whose marriages terminated before January 13, 1941, and after July 25, 1936, had their citizenship restored immediately whether they lived abroad or in the United States. In either case, they had to take the Oath of Allegiance before exercising their rights of citizenship.

If your marriage to an alien was terminated on or after January 13, 1941, you can resume your citizenship by taking the Oath of Allegiance before a clerk of the naturalization court. If you live abroad, you can take the Oath of Allegiance before a US consular office.

In all cases where the marriage was terminated after September 22, 1922, the applicant must have been a native-born citizen or have acquired citizenship at birth if born abroad. Furthermore, the applicant must take the Oath of Allegiance before exercising the rights of a citizen. See Table 11 for a summary of the above requirements.

4.4 Children born to lawful permanent residents

If one of your parents was naturalized before May 24, 1934, you can claim US citizenship if the naturalization took place before your 21st birthday. You must have been registered as a lawful permanent resident before May 24, 1934, and before your 21st birthday. Your citizenship begins five years after acquiring lawful permanent resident status.

If one of your parents was naturalized on or after May 24, 1934, and before January 13, 1941, if the naturalization took place before your 21st birthday, and if you were lawfully admitted to the United States as a permanent resident before your 21st birthday, you can claim citizenship. In addition, you must have lived for five years as a lawful permanent resident in the United States. The five years must have begun before your 21st birthday and before January 13, 1941. Note that in the case of people whose parents were naturalized before May 24, 1934, but who were not admitted

to the United States until after that date, all of the above requirements applicable to the residence of the child apply.

The five-year residence requirement of the child can be waived if both parents are naturalized or the surviving parent or divorced parent with legal custody is naturalized.

If your parents were naturalized on or after January 13, 1941, and before December 24, 1952, you are subject to the following conditions. Both parents (one, if you had only one parent as a result of death or divorce) must have become naturalized. If one of your parents was an alien and the other a citizen, then the alien must have become naturalized within that period. In addition, your parent or parents must have become naturalized before your 18th birthday and you must have been lawfully admitted as a permanent resident before your 18th birthday.

If you were born to an unmarried woman during this period, you cannot claim US citizenship unless you were legitimated by a US citizen before you turned 16, in accordance with the law of your residence or domicile at that time.

If your parents were naturalized on or after December 24, 1952, both of them or your noncitizen parent must have become naturalized within this period. If you have only one parent as a result of death or divorce, he or she must have become naturalized within that period. Your parents' naturalization must have taken place before your 18th birthday and you must have been admitted as a lawful permanent resident before your 18th birthday. The residence requirements for a child also apply if you were born out of wedlock, legitimated before you were 16 years old, and in the custody of the legitimating parent. You must also meet these residence requirements if no paternity was established yet your parent remained a resident of the United States. See Table 12 for a summary of the above.

TABLE 10
CITIZENSHIP REQUIREMENTS FOR ILLEGITIMATE CHILDREN
BORN OUTSIDE THE UNITED STATES

Date of birth	Citizenship status and residence requirement of parent
Before 5/24/34	Acquired US citizenship at birth if the mother was a citizen of the United States who had resided in the United States or outlying possessions prior to birth of the child, provided paternity by legitimation not established before 1/13/41 and during minority of the child.*
On or after 5/24/34 and before 1/13/41	Acquired US citizenship at birth if the mother was a citizen who had previously resided in the United States or outlying possessions prior to birth of the child.*
On or after 1/13/41 and before 12/24/52	Acquired US citizenship at birth if mother was a citizen who had previously resided in the United States or outlying possessions prior to birth of the child.* **OR** If paternity established during the child's minority, father must have been a citizen at time of birth of the child and must have had ten years' residence in United States or outlying possessions, five of which were after age of 16 years.
On or after 12/24/52	Acquired US citizenship at birth if mother was a citizen of the United States at time of birth of child and had been physically present in the United States or one of its outlying possessions for at least one year continuously prior to birth of the child. **OR** If child legitimated while under age of 21 years and both parents were citizens, one of whom had resided in United States or one of its outlying possessions prior to birth of child, then child acquired US citizenship at birth. **OR** If child legitimated while under age of 21 years and either parent was a citizen and the other an alien, then citizen parent must have been physically present in the United States or one of its outlying possessions at least ten years, at least five of which must have been after attaining age of 14 and prior to birth of the child, then child must have five years continuous physical presence in the United States between ages of 14 and 28.

*If the child did not acquire US citizenship through mother, citizenship was acquired as of date of birth if legitimated and the father was a US citizen who had previously resided in the United States, or outlying possessions.

TABLE 11
RESUMPTION OF CITIZENSHIP FOR WOMEN WHO LOST CITIZENSHIP ON MARRIAGE

Date marriage terminated	Date of resumption of citizenship if residence was: In the United States	Abroad
Before 3/2/07	Resumed upon date marriage terminated	Resumed upon returning to United States to reside before 9/22/22 **OR** Resumed upon registering with US consul after 3/01/07 and before 3/02/08
On or after 3/2/07 and before 9/22/22	Resumed by continuing to reside in the United States	Resumed upon returning to United States before 9/22/22 **OR** By registering with US consul within one year after termination of marriage
On or after 9/22/22 and before 6/25/36	Resumed on 6/25/36 if not previously resumed[1,2]	Resumed on 6/25/36 if not previously resumed[1,2]
On or after 6/25/36 and before 1/13/41	Resumed on date marriage terminated[1,2]	Resumed on date marriage terminated[1,2]
On or after 1/13/41	Resumed on taking oath of allegiance before clerk of naturalization court[1,2,3]	Resumed upon taking oath of allegiance before US consular officer[1,2,3]

Note: If the woman resided in the United States continuously from date of her marriage until July 2, 1940, and the marriage had not terminated, citizenship was resumed on July 2, 1940. [1,2]

1. Applied to native-born citizens, including those born abroad and who acquired US citizenship at birth, who lost citizenship solely by reason of marriage before 9/22/22.

2. Required to take oath of allegiance before exercising the rights of citizenship.

3. On or after 12/24/52, a woman who lost citizenship solely by marriage to an alien ineligible to citizenship on or after 9/22/22 may resume US citizenship in this manner.

Children who are born outside the United States and who are under 16 when adopted by US citizens may now apply for permanent residence immediately after entering the United States. In the past, a two-year residence period was required.

If you think that you might qualify to recover lost citizenship or acquire it by birth, check with your nearest INS office or US consulate. They will be able to assist you in determining whether or not you should apply for Citizenship Certificate.

5. THE CHILD CITIZENSHIP ACT OF 2000

The Child Citizen Act of 2000 came into effect on February 27, 2001. The new law permits foreign-born children and adopted children to acquire citizenship automatically.

To be eligible, a child must meet the following requirements:

★ The child has at least one US citizen parent (by birth or naturalization).

★ The US citizen parent has been physically present in the United States for at least five years (at least two of which were after the age of 14).

★ The child us younger than 18 years of age.

★ The child is living outside the United States in the legal and physical custody of the US citizen parent.

★ The child is temporarily present in the United States. The child must have entered the United States legally and have maintained lawful status during his or her stay.

★ The adopted child meets the requirements applicable to adopted children under immigration law.

6. FILIPINO WAR VETERANS

In the past few years, several US District Courts have held that the Filipino veterans of US armed forces in World War II are eligible for naturalization under expired World War II naturalization legislation. However, the Supreme Court declared that Filipino War Veterans of World War II are not eligible for US citizenship unless they can show that they took some action after the war to seek naturalization.

After numerous court actions were filed to challenge the findings of the Supreme Court, the Immigration Act of 1990 cleared the confusion surrounding this issue by granting naturalization rights to all Filipino members of the US armed services who served with the US armed forces between September 1, 1939, and December 31, 1946. The deadline for applying for naturalization under this program was November 28, 1993.

7. FOREIGN SPOUSE OF A US CITIZEN WORKING OVERSEAS

A foreign spouse who is married and resides with a US citizen spouse whose employment is overseas, may qualify for speedy naturalization. The foreign spouse who files Form N-400 Application for Naturalization (see Sample 33), may be naturalized without the usual requirement of three to five years of continuous residence in the United States.

The form must be filed with the INS in the District of the last residence of the foreign spouse in the United States. The foreign spouse can then ask for an interview appointment without waiting the usual eight to ten months.

In order to qualify for the speedy naturalization, the foreign spouse must be married to a US citizen who is in one of the following categories:

★ Employed by the US Government

★ Employed by an American institution of research recognized by the attorney general

★ Employed by an American firm or corporation engaged in whole or in part in the development of foreign trade and commerce of the United States or a subsidiary thereof

★ Employed by a public international organization in which the United States participates by treaty or statute

★ Authorized to perform the ministerial or priestly functions of a religious denomination that has a bona fide organization within the United States

★ Engaged solely as a missionary by a religious denomination or by an inter-denominational mission organization that has a bona fide organization within the United States

The foreign spouse must be in the United States at the time of naturalization, and at that time, the immigrant will declare before the attorney general, his or her intention to take up residence in the United States as soon as the US citizen spouse's employment overseas ends.

8. MILITARY IMMIGRANTS POST SEPTEMBER 11, 2001

In 2002, Executive Order 13269 was implemented. This order speeds up the process for naturalization of immigrants and non-citizen nationals who were on active duty in the Armed Forces when the United States went to war on terrorism on September 11, 2001. The people who were serving honorably or who were honorably discharged at any time on or after September 11, 2001, can apply for naturalization and be eligible under Section 329 of the Immigration and Nationality Act.

Along with their application, military immigrants need to include the following documents:

★ Form N-400 (Application for Naturalization)

★ Fingerprints

★ Form G-325 B (Biographic form)

★ Form N-426 (Certificate of Military or Naval Service)

Military immigrants can submit their applications through their army base or they can file the forms directly with the INS of last residence.

TABLE 12
CITIZENSHIP REQUIREMENTS FOR CHILDREN
BORN TO LAWFUL PERMANENT RESIDENTS

Date of naturalization	Parent naturalized	Prerequisites for acquisition
Before 5/24/34	Either parent	Parent must have been naturalized before child's 21st birthday. **AND** Child must be lawful permanent residents before 5/24/34 and before 21st birthday and citizenship begins five years after lawful permanent resident.
On or after 5/24/34	Either parent	Parent must have been naturalized before child's 21st birthday. **AND** Child must have been lawfully admitted for permanent residence prior to 21st birthday. **AND** Child must have five years' lawful permanent residence in the United States commencing during minority and beginning before January 13, 1941.[1]
On or after 1/13/41 and before 12/24/52	Both parents, surviving parent or legally separated parent having legal custody, **OR** Alien parent if one parent is a citizen of United States.[2]	Parent or parents must have been naturalized before child's 18th birthday. **AND** Child must have been lawfully admitted for permanent residence before 18th birthday.
On or after 12/24/52	Both parents, surviving parent, parent having legal custody of alien parent if one parent is a citizen of United States.[3,4,5]	Parent or parents must have been naturalized before child's 18th birthday (section 3208.321). **AND** Child must have been lawfully admitted for permanent residence before 18th birthday.

(for footnotes, see next page)

TABLE 12 — Continued

1. If parent naturalized before 5/24/34 and child was admitted on or after 5/24/34, then child must meet requirement applicable after 5/24/34. Five years' residence not required in case of naturalization of both parents, surviving parent or divorced parent having legal custody.

2. Citizenship not derived by a child born out of wedlock unless it has been legitimated before age of 16 years under law of child's residence or domicile or is in legal custody of legitimating parent.

3. If child born out of wedlock is legitimated before age of 16 years and in custody of legitimating parent, prerequisite in column 3 must be met.

4. If child is born out of wedlock and paternity not established.

5. Now applies to children adopted while under 16 residing as lawful permanent residents and in the custody of adoptive parents at the time of the parents' naturalization.

APPENDIX 1
FREE INFORMATION SOURCES ON
US IMMIGRATION LAWS

For free information on the latest US immigration laws, regulations, and policies; the following sources are available:

1. Immigration and Naturalization Service (INS)
    <www.ins.gov>

2. Availability of immigrant visa numbers — US Department of State
    <www.travel.state.gov/visa_bulletin.html>

3. US Immigration Service: general information
    1-800-375-5283

4. Status of deportation and removal cases at US Immigration Courts: 1-800-898-7180

5. Weekly reports on US immigration laws, *Siskind's Immigration Bulletin*
    Web site address <www.visalaw.com>
    E-mail <gsiskind@visalaw.com>

6. Information about latest INS applications and forms
    <www.ins.usdoj.gov/graphics/formsfee/forms>

7. INS application and petition fee increases
    www.ins.usdoj.gov/graphics/formsfee/feechart.htm>

8. Daily reports on US immigration laws prepared by American Immigration LLC

APPENDIX 2
ADDRESSES OF IMMIGRATION AND
NATURALIZATION SERVICE OFFICES

WITHIN THE UNITED STATES

Alaska
Anchorage INS
620 East 10th Avenue, Suite 102
Anchorage, AK 95501

Arizona
Phoenix INS
Federal Building
2035 North Central Avenue
Phoenix, AZ 85004

Tucson INS
6431 South Country Club Road
Tucson, AZ 85706-5907

California
Fresno INS
865 Fulton Mall
Fresno, CA 93721

Los Angeles INS
300 North Los Angeles Street, Room 1001
Los Angeles, CA 90012

Sacramento INS Sub office
650 Capitol Mall
Sacramento, CA 95814

San Diego INS
880 Front Street, Suite 1234
San Diego, CA 92101-8834

San Francisco INS
Appraisers Bldg.
630 Sansome Street
San Francisco, CA 94111-2280

San Jose INS
1887 Monterey Road
San Jose, CA 95112

Colorado
Denver INS
Albrook Center
4730 Paris Street
Denver, CO 80239

Connecticut
Hartford INS
450 Main Street, 4th Floor
Hartford, CT 06103-3060

Florida
Jacksonville INS Sub office
4121 Southpoint Boulevard
Jacksonville, FL 32216

Miami INS
7880 Biscayne Blvd., 11th Floor
Miami, FL 33138-4727

West Palm Beach INS
301 Broadway
Riviera Beach, FL 33401

Tampa INS
5524 West Cypress Street
Tampa, FL 33607-1708

Georgia
Atlanta INS
77 Forsyth Street SW, Room 385
Atlanta, GA 30303

Hawaii
Honolulu INS
595 Ala Moana Boulevard
Honolulu, HI 96813-4999

Idaho
Boise INS Sub office
1185 South Vinnell Way
Boise, ID 83709

Illinois
Chicago INS
10 West Jackson Blvd., Suite 600
Chicago, IL 60604

Indianapolis
Indianapolis INS
Gateway Plaza, Room 400
950 North Meridian Street
Indianapolis, IN 46204

Kentucky
Louisville INS
US Courthouse Bldg.
601 West Broadway, Room 390
Louisville, KY 40202

Louisana
New Orleans INS
701 Loyola Avenue, Room T-8011
New Orleans, LA 70113

Maine
Portland, Maine District
176 Gannett Drive
Portland, ME 04106

Maryland
Baltimore INS
Fallon Federal Building
31 Hopkins Plaza
Baltimore, MD 21201

Massachussetts
Boston INS
JFK Federal Bldg., Room E-123
Government Center
Boston, MA 02203

Michigan
Detroit INS
Federal Building, INS
333 Mount Elliott Street, 2nd Floor
Detroit, MI 48207-4381

Minnesota
St. Paul INS
2901 Metro Drive, Suite 100
Bloomington, MN 55425

Missouri
Kansas City INS
9747 North Conant Avenue
Kansas City, MO 64153

St. Louis INS
1222 Spruce Street, Room 1.100
St. Louis, MO 63103-2815

Montana
Helena INS
2800 Skyway Drive
Helena, MT 59602

Nebraska
Omaha INS
3736 South 132nd Street
Omaha, NE 68144

Nevada
Las Vegas INS
3373 Pepper Lane
Las Vegas, NV 89120-2739

Reno INS
1351 Corporate Boulevard
Reno, NV 89502

New Jersey
Newark INS
Peter Rodino Federal Bldg.
970 Broad Street
Newark, NJ 07102

New Mexico
Albuquerque INS Sub office
1720 Randolph Road SE
Albuquerque, NM 87106

New York
Albany INS Sub office
1086 Troy-Schenectady Road
Latham, NY 12110

Buffalo INS
Federal Center
130 Delaware Avenue, Room 203
Buffalo, NY 14202

New York INS
26 Federal Plaza, Room 14-102
New York, NY 10278

North Carolina
Charlotte INS Sub office
210 East Woodlawn Road
Building 6, Suite 138
Charlotte, NC 28217

Ohio
Cincinnati INS Sub office
JW Peck Federal Bldg.
550 Main Street, Room 4001
Cincinnati, OH 45202

Cleveland INS
AJC Federal Bldg.
1240 East 9th Street, Room 1917
Cleveland, OH 44199

Oklahoma
Oklahoma City INS
4149 Highline Blvd., Suite 300
Oklahoma City, OK 73108-2081

Oregon
Portland INS
Federal Office Bldg.
511 NW Broadway
Portland, OR 97209

Pennsylvania
Pittsburgh INS Sub office
Federal Building, Room 314
1000 Liberty Avenue
Pittsburgh, PA 15222-4181

Philadelphia INS
1600 Callowhill Street, 4th Floor
Philadelphia, PA 19130

Rhode Island
Providence INS Sub office
200 Dyer Street
Providence, RI 02903

South Carolina
Charleston INS
170 Meeting Street, 5th Floor
Charleston, SC 29401

Tennessee
Memphis INS Sub office
1341 Sycamore View Road, Suite 100
Memphis, TN 38134

Texas
Dallas INS
8101 North Stemmons Freeway
Dallas, TX 75247

El Paso INS
1535 Hawkins Boulevard, Suite 167
El Paso, TX 79925

Harlingen INS
2102 Teege Avenue
Harlingen, TX 78550-4667

Houston INS
126 North Point
Houston, TX 77060

San Antonio INS
8940 Fourwinds Drive
San Antonio, TX 78239

Utah
Salt Lake City INS Sub office
5272 South College Drive, #100
Murray, UT 84123

Vermont
St. Albans INS
64 Gricebrook Road
St. Albans, VT 05478

Virginia
Washington INS
4420 North Fairfax Drive, Room 500
Arlington, VA 22203

Norfolk INS Sub office
5280 Henneman Drive
Norfolk, VA 23513

Washington
Seattle INS
815 Airport Way South
Seattle, WA 98134

Spokane INS Sub office
US Federal Courthouse Bldg., Room 691
West 920 Riverside Avenue
Spokane, WA 99201

Washington, DC
Washington, DC Headquarters
4420 North Fairfax Drive
Arlington, VA 22203

Wisconsin
Milwaukee INS Sub office
310 East Knapp Street
Milwaukee, WI 53202

OUTSIDE THE UNITED STATES

Germany
Frankfurt INS
c/o American Consulate General
PSC 115, APO AE 09213-0015

Greece
Athens INS
c/o PSC 108, Box 32
APO AE 09842

Hong Kong
Hong Kong INS
c/o PSC 461, Box 5
FPO AP 96521

Italy
Rome INS
c/o Visa Section
PSC 59, Box 100
APO AE 09624

Korea
Seoul INS
c/o Unit 15550
APO AP 96205-0001

Mexico
Ciudad Juarez INS
c/o P.O. Box 10545
El Paso, TX 7995-0545

Guadalajara INS
c/o American Consulate General
Guadalajara
P.O. Box 3088
Laredo, TX 78044-3088

Monterrey INS
c/o US Consulate General
PO Box 3098
Laredo, TX 78044

Panama
Panama City INS
c/o American Embassy—Panama
Unit 0945
APO AA 34002

Philippine Islands
Manila INS
c/o PSC 500, Box 26
FPO AP 96515-1000

Puerto Rico
San Juan INS
San Patricio Office Center
7 Tabonuco Street, Suite 100
Guaynabo, Puerto Rico 00968

Singapore
Singapore INS
c/o US Embassy
FPO San Francisco, CA 96699

Thailand
Bangkok INS
c/o US Embassy
APO San Francisco, CA 96346

Virgin Islands
St. Thomas INS Sub office
Nisky Center, Suite 1A, First Floor South
Charlotte Amalie, St. Thomas
Virgin Islands 00802

St. Croix INS
PO Box 1468, Kingshill
Christiansted, St. Croix
Virgin Islands 00820

APPENDIX 3
COMMONLY ASKED QUESTIONS BY EXAMINERS FOR UNITED STATES CITIZENSHIP AND SUGGESTED ANSWERS

1. **What form of government do we have in this country?**

   Republican.

2. **What do you understand by a republican form of government?**

   The people elect their governing officers and give them the power to make and enforce the laws. The head of state is also elected.

3. **What is the Constitution?**

   The Constitution is the fundamental law of the land, the supreme law of the United States upon which all other laws are based and with which all other laws must agree.

4. **Upon what principles is the US Constitution based?**

   The US Constitution is based on the principles of liberty, equality, and justice for everyone.

5. **What is an amendment?**

   An amendment is a change or addition to the Constitution.

6. **May the constitution be amended or changed?**

   Yes.

7. **How may it be amended or changed?**

   The people who wrote the Constitution understood that changes might be required for the development of the United States. It was planned that the Constitution might be amended. An amendment to the Constitution may be made by a two-thirds vote of both the Houses of Congress and ratification by three-fourths of the states.

8. **Has the Constitution ever been amended?**

   Yes.

9. **How many amendments have been made to the Constitution?**

   There have been 26 amendments.

10. **What is the 21st Amendment?**

    It repealed the 18th Amendment.

11. **What was the 18th Amendment?**

    Prohibition.

12. **What is the 20th Amendment?**

    It changed the inauguration of the President to January 20 and meeting of Congress to January 3.

13. **What is the 19th Amendment?**

    Women's suffrage.

14. **What are the first ten Amendments to the Constitution called?**

    The Bill of Rights.

15. **What are some of the rights guaranteed by the Bill of Rights?**

    (a) Freedom of press

    (b) Freedom of speech

(c) Freedom of religion

(d) The right to petition

(e) The right to a peaceable assembly

(f) The right to bear arms in self defense

(g) The right to privacy of home

(h) The right to a free, speedy trial

16. What are the three branches of government in the United States?

1. Legislative

2. Executive

3. Judicial

17. What is the legislative branch of the US government and what is its function?

Congress is the legislative branch of the US government and its function is to make the laws.

18. What are the divisions of Congress?

Congress is made up of two houses the House of Representatives and the Senate.

19. Who presides over the House of Representatives?

The presiding officer is a Speaker, who is elected by his or her fellow members. A law passed by Congress in 1947 made the Speaker the successor to the presidency of the United States if both the President and Vice-President are unable to serve.

20. What powers has the House of Representatives?

The House of Representatives originates all bills for raising revenue; it impeaches US officers; it elects the President of the United States if the presidential electors fail to elect one.

21. Who presides over the Senate when the President is tried?

The Chief Justice of the US Supreme Court presides, because the Vice-President may be prejudiced.

22. How many senators are there from each state?

Two. The Senate, which represents the states, has 100 members, 2 from each state.

23. Who are the senators from your state?

24. How many representatives has each state?

The number of representatives for each state is decided on the basis of the population as enumerated in the latest census. There is one representative for each 280,000 people, approximately.

25. How many representatives (congressmen) are there from your state?

26. Who are they?

27. How many representatives are in the House of Representatives?

The House of Representatives has 435 members distributed among the states according to populations.

28. What is the executive branch of the government and what is its function?

The cabinet is the executive branch of the government and its function is to enforce the laws.

29. Who is the Chief Executive of the United States?

The President.

30. How long does the President hold office?

Four years.

31. What are some of the President's powers and duties?

He signs and vetoes bills; he is Commander in Chief of the Army and Navy; he delivers an annual message to Congress; he makes treaties; he appoints certain officers with the consent of the Senate.

32. What is the chief duty of the President?

To enforce the laws.

33. What is the cabinet?

The cabinet is a body of persons who assist the President in his executive duties.

34. Who is the head of the cabinet?

The secretary of state is the head of the cabinet.

35. How do cabinet officers get their positions?

They are appointed by the President with the consent of the Senate.

36. What is the cabinet made up of?

The cabinet is made up of 13 departments:

1. Secretary of State
2. Secretary of the Treasury
3. Secretary of Defense
4. Attorney General
5. Postmaster General
6. Secretary of the Interior
7. Secretary of Agriculture
8. Secretary of Commerce
9. Secretary of Labor
10. Secretary of Health and Human Services
11. Secretary of Education
12. Secretary of Transportation
13. Secretary of Housing and Urban Development

37. What cabinet officer is in charge of naturalization?

The Department of Justice, under the attorney general, now has charge of the Bureau of Naturalization and Immigration.

38. If the President vetoes a bill, does that end it?

No, it doesn't.

39. What happens to it next?

By passing both Houses of Congress by a two-thirds majority, the veto of the President can be overridden.

40. What is a referendum?

A referendum is a method by which the voters are given an opportunity to determine whether a law passed by the legislature should go into effect.

41. What is the Judicial Branch of the US government and what is its function?

The Judicial Branch of the US government includes all of the US courts. They are called Federal Courts. Their function is to explain the laws.

42. What is the highest court in the United States?

The United States Supreme Court.

43. How many judges are there in this court?

It consists of nine judges: the Chief Justice and eight associate justices.

44. Who is the Chief Justice of the Supreme Court?

45. What are some of the courts of your state?

1. Court of Justices of the Peace which handle minor cases
2. District Courts which handle important cases

3. State Supreme Court which handles cases appealed from the lower courts

4. Most states also have Juvenile Courts in which cases involving children are handled.

46. What are the three colors in the American flag and what do they stand for?

The three colors of the flag are red, white, and blue, and they stand for courage, justice, and liberty.

47. How many stripes are in the American flag and what do they stand for?

There are 13 stripes in the American flag, and they stand for the 13 original colonies which became the United States of America.

48. What country did the United States fight against in the Revolutionary War?

Great Britain.

49. Why did the United States fight the Revolutionary War against Great Britain?

Because the United States wanted to have representation in the Parliament instead of just paying taxes to Britain.

50. Who was President during the Civil War?

Abraham Lincoln.

51 Why was the Civil War fought in the United States?

The Civil War was fought to prevent the southern states from breaking away from the Union. The southern states wanted to break away and to maintain slavery.

52. How many states have we now?

There are 50 states.

53. Why do we celebrate the fourth of July?

It is the us Independence Day.

54. What rights would you have as a citizen that you do not have now?

(a) Vote

(b) Hold office

(c) Take up a homestead

(d) Serve on a jury

55. What is polygamy?

Polygamy is having more than one wife or husband at the same time. It is against the law in the United States.

56. What is anarchy?

A complete absence of government. An anarchist is a person who believes that all forms of government interfere with individual liberty and should be replaced by voluntary associations of cooperative groups.

APPENDIX 4
FORMS

This section contains blank copies of many of the most commonly needed immigration forms. Feel free to tear out or photocopy any forms for your personal use only. Be aware that samples of completed forms shown in the main text of this book are provided for general guidance only; you will need to read the forms carefully and complete them according to your own situation, which may not exactly match the fictional situations used in our samples.

All forms, along with complete instructions for completing them, are available from US government offices. Contact the Immigration and Naturalization Service office or US consulate in your area for more information.

Forms provided include:

Form I-131	Application for Travel Document
Form I-130	Petition for Alien Relative
Form DS-230	Application for Immigrant Visa and Alien Registration
Form G-28	Notice of Entry of Appearance as Attorney or Representative
Form EOIR-29	Notice of Appeal to the Board of Immigration Appeals of Decision of District Director
Form I-864	Affidavit of Support
Form I-601	Application for Waiver of Grounds of Excludability
Form I-751	Petition to Remove the Conditions on Residence
Form I-129F	Petition for Alien Fiancé(e)
Form ETA 750	Application for Alien Employment Certification
Form I-140	Immigrant Petition for Alien Worker
Form I-485	Application to Register Permanent Residence or Adjust Status
Form I-526	Immigrant Petition by Alien Entrepreneur
Form IAP-66	Certificate of Eligibility for Exchange Visitor (J-1) Status
Form I-612	Application for Waiver of the Foreign Residence Requirement
Form DS-156	Nonimmigrant Visa Application
Form I-539	Application to Extend/Change Nonimmigrant Status
Form I-129	Petition for a Nonimmigrant Worker
Form I-589	Application for Asylum and for Withholding of Removal

Form EOIR-26	Notice of Appeal to the Board of Immigration Appeals of Decision of Immigration Judge
Form EOIR-27	Notice of Entry of Appearance as Attorney or Representative Before the Board of Immigration Appeals Executive Office for Immigration Review
Form G-325	Biographic Information Sheet
Form I-765	Application for Employment Authorization
Form N-400	Application for Naturalization
Form N-600	Application for Certificate of Citizenship
Form DV-2003	Application for Diversity Visa Lottery
Form G-639	Freedom of Information/Privacy Act Request (very useful for finding out what the Immigration Service knows about you)

U.S. Department of Justice
Immigration and Naturalization Service

OMB No. 1115-0005

Application for Travel Document

START HERE - Please Type or Print

Part 1. Information about you.

Family Name	Given Name	Middle Initial

Address - C/O

Street # and Name		Apt. #
City	State or Province	
Country	Zip/Postal Code	

Date of birth (month/day/year) / /	Country of Birth
Social Security #	A #

Part 2. Application Type (check one).

a. ☐ I am a permanent resident or conditional resident of the United States and I am applying for a Reentry Permit.

b. ☐ I now hold U.S. refugee or asylee status and I am applying for a Refugee Travel Document.

c. ☐ I am a permanent resident as a direct result of refugee or asylee status, and am applying for a Refugee Travel Document.

d. ☐ I am applying for an Advance Parole to allow me to return to the U.S. after temporary foreign travel.

e. ☐ I am outside the U.S. and am applying for an Advance Parole.

f. ☐ I am applying for an Advance Parole for another person who is outside the U.S. *Give the following information about that person:*

Family Name	Given Name	Middle Initial
Date of birth (month/day/year)	Country of Birth	

Foreign Address - C/O

Street # and Name		Apt. #
City	State or Province	
Country	Zip/Postal Code	

Part 3. Processing Information

Date of Intended departure (Month/Day/Year)	Expected length of trip

Are you, or any person included in this application, now in exclusion or deportation proceedings?
☐ No   ☐ Yes, at (give office name) _____

If applying for an Advance Parole Document, skip to Part 7.

Have you ever been issued a Reentry Permit or Refugee Travel Document?
☐ No   ☐ Yes, (give the following for the last document issued to you)

Date Issued	Disposition (attached, lost, etc.)

Form I-131 (Rev. 12/10/91) N

Continued on back.

Part 3. Processing Information. (continued)

Where do you want this travel document sent? (check one)

a. ☐ Address in Part 2. above

b. ☐ American Consulate at (give City and Country, below)

c. ☐ INS overseas office at (give City and Country, below)

City   Country

If you checked b. or c., above, give your overseas address:

Part 4. Information about the Proposed Travel.

Purpose of trip, *If you need more room, continue on a separate sheet of paper*	List the countries you intend to visit.

Part 5. Complete only if applying for a Reentry Permit.

Since becoming a permanent resident (or during the last five years, whichever is less) how much total time have you spent outside the United States?	☐ less than 6 months ☐ 6 months to 1 year ☐ 1 to 2 years	☐ 2 to 3 years ☐ 3 to 4 years ☐ more than 4 years
Since you became a Permanent Resident, have you ever filed a federal income tax return as a nonresident, or failed to file a federal tax return because you considered yourself to be a nonresident? (If yes, give details on a separate sheet of paper).	☐ Yes	☐ No

Part 6. Complete only if applying for a Refugee Travel Document.

Country from which you are a refugee or asylee:

If you answer yes to any of the following sheet of paper, explain on a separate sheet of paper.

Do you plan to travel to the above named country?	☐ Yes	☐ No
Since you were accorded Refugee/Asylee status, have you ever: returned to the above-named country; applied for an/or obtained a national passport, passport renewal, or entry permit into this country; or applied for an/or received any benefit from such country (for example, health insurance benefits)?	☐ Yes	☐ No
Since being accorded Refugee/Asylee status, have you, by any legal procedure or voluntary act, re-acquired the nationality of the above-named country, acquired a new nationality, or been granted refugee or asylee status in any other country?	☐ Yes	☐ No

Part 7. Complete only if applying for an Advance Parole.

On a separate sheet of paper, please explain how you qualify for an Advance Parole and what circumstances warrant issuance of Advance Parole. Include copies of any documents you wish considered(See instructions.)

For how many trips do you intend to use this document?   ☐ 1 trip   ☐ More than 1 trip
If outside the U.S., at right give the U.S. consulate or INS office you wish notified if this application is approved.

Part 8. Signature.   *Read the information on penalties in the instructions before completing this section. You must file this application while in the United States if filing for a reentry permit or refugee travel document.*

I certify under penalty of perjury under the laws of the United States of America that this petition, and the evidence submitted with it, is all true and correct. I authorize the release of any information from my records which the Immigration and Naturalization Service needs to determine eligibility for the benefit I am seeking.

Signature   Date   Daytime Telephone #

Please note: *If you do not completely fill out this form, or fail to submit the required documents listed in the instructions, you may not be found eligible for the requested document and this application will have to be denied.*

Part 9. Signature of person preparing form if other than above. (sign below)

I declare that I prepared this application at the request of the above person and it is based on all information of which I have knowledge.

Signature   Print Your Name   Date

Firm Name   Daytime Telephone #
and Address

OMB #1115-0054

Petition for Alien Relative

DO NOT WRITE IN THIS BLOCK - FOR EXAMINING OFFICE ONLY

A#	Action Stamp	Fee Stamp

Section of Law/Visa Category

- ☐ 201(b) Spouse - IR-1/CR-1
- ☐ 201(b) Child - IR-2/CR-2
- ☐ 201(b) Parent - IR-5
- ☐ 203(a)(1) Unm. S or D - F1-1
- ☐ 203(a)(2)(A)Spouse - F2-1
- ☐ 203(a)(2)(A) Child - F2-2
- ☐ 203(a)(2)(B) Unm. S or D - F2-4
- ☐ 203(a)(3) Married S or D - F3-1
- ☐ 203(a)(4) Brother/Sister - F4-1

Petition was filed on: _____ (priority date)

- ☐ Personal Interview
- ☐ Pet. ☐ Ben. " A" File Reviewed
- ☐ Field Investigation
- ☐ 203(a)(2)(A) Resolved
- ☐ Previously Forwarded
- ☐ I-485 Filed Simultaneously
- ☐ 204(g) Resolved
- ☐ 203(g) Resolved

Remarks:

A. Relationship   You are the petitioner; your relative is the beneficiary.

1. I am filing this petition for my:
☐ Husband/Wife   ☐ Parent   ☐ Brother/Sister   ☐ Child

2. Are you related by adoption?
☐ Yes   ☐ No

3. Did you gain permanent residence through adoption?
☐ Yes   ☐ No

B. Information about you

1. Name (Family name in CAPS)   (First)   (Middle)

2. Address (Number and Street)   (Apt.No.)

(Town or City)   (State/Country)   (Zip/Postal Code)

3. Place of Birth (Town or City)   (State/Country)

4. Date of Birth (Month/Day/Year)

5. Gender ☐ Male ☐ Female

6. Marital Status ☐ Married ☐ Single ☐ Widowed ☐ Divorced

7. Other Names Used (including maiden name)

8. Date and Place of Present Marriage (if married)

9. Social Security Number (if any)   10. Alien Registration Number

11. Name(s) of Prior Husband(s)/Wive(s)   12. Date(s) Marriage(s) Ended

13. If you are a U.S. citizen, complete the following:
My citizenship was acquired through (check one):
- ☐ Birth in the U.S.
- ☐ Naturalization. Give certificate number and date and place of issuance.
- ☐ Parents. Have you obtained a certificate of citizenship in your own name?
  - ☐ Yes. Give certificate number, date and place of issuance.   ☐ No

14a. If you are a lawful permanent resident alien, complete the following: Date and place of admission for, or adjustment to, lawful permanent residence and class of admission.

14b. Did you gain permanent resident status through marriage to a United States citizen or lawful permanent resident?
☐ Yes   ☐ No

C. Information about your relative

1. Name (Family name in CAPS)   (First)   (Middle)

2. Address (Number and Street)   (Apt. No.)

(Town or City)   (State/Country)   (Zip/Postal Code)

3. Place of Birth (Town or City)   (State/Country)

4. Date of Birth (Month/Day/Year)

5. Gender ☐ Male ☐ Female

6. Marital Status ☐ Married ☐ Single ☐ Widowed ☐ Divorced

7. Other Names Used (including maiden name)

8. Date and Place of Present Marriage (if married)

9. Social Security Number (if any)   10. Alien Registration Number

11. Name(s) of Prior Husband(s)/Wive(s)   12. Date(s) Marriage(s) Ended

13. Has your relative ever been in the U.S.?   ☐ Yes   ☐ No

14. If your relative is currently in the U.S., complete the following:
He or she arrived as a::
(visitor, student, stowaway, without inspection, etc.)

Arrival/Departure Record (I-94)   Date arrived (Month/Day/Year)

Date authorized stay expired, or will expire, as shown on Form I-94 or I-95

15. Name and address of present employer (if any)

Date this employment began (Month/Day/Year)

16. Has your relative ever been under immigration proceedings?
☐ No ☐ Yes Where _____ When _____
☐ Removal ☐ Exclusion/Deportation ☐ Recission ☐ Judicial Proceedings

INITIAL RECEIPT	RESUBMITTED	RELOCATED: Rec'd	Sent	COMPLETED: Appv'd	Denied	Ret'd

Form I-130 (Rev. 06/05/02) Y

C. Information about your alien relative (continued)

17. List husband/wife and all children of your relative.

(Name)	(Relationship)	(Date of Birth)	(Country of Birth)

18. Address in the United States where your relative intends to live.

(Street Address)   (Town or City)   (State)

19. Your relative's address abroad. (Include street, city, province and country)

_____   Phone Number (if any)

20. If your relative's native alphabet is other than Roman letters, write his or her name and foreign address in the native alphabet.

(Name)   Address (Include street, city, province and country):

21. If filing for your husband/wife, give last address at which you lived together. (Include street, city, province, if any, and country):

From: (Month) (Year)   To: (Month) (Year)

22. Complete the information below if your relative is in the United States and will apply for adjustment of status

Your relative is in the United States and will apply for adjustment of status to that of a lawful permanent resident at the office of the Immigration and Naturalization Service in _____ . If your relative is not eligible for adjustment of status, he or she

(City)   (State)

will apply for a visa abroad at the American consular post in _____

(City)   (Country)

NOTE: Designation of an American embassy or consulate outside the country of your relative's last residence does not guarantee acceptance for processing by that post. Acceptance is at the discretion of the designated embassy or consulate.

D. Other information

1. If separate petitions are also being submitted for other relatives, give names of each and relationship.

2. Have you ever filed a petition for this or any other alien before? ☐ Yes ☐ No

If "Yes," give name, place and date of filing and result.

WARNING: INS investigates claimed relationships and verifies the validity of documents. INS seeks criminal prosecutions when family relationships are falsified to obtain visas.

PENALTIES: By law, you may be imprisoned for not more than five years or fined $250,000, or both, for entering into a marriage contract for the purpose of evading any provision of the immigration laws. In addition, you may be fined up to $10,000 and imprisoned for up to five years, or both, for knowingly and willfully falsifying or concealing a material fact or using any false document in submitting this petition.

YOUR CERTIFICATION: I certify, under penalty of perjury under the laws of the United States of America, that the foregoing is true and correct. Furthermore, I authorize the release of any information from my records which the Immigration and Naturalization Service needs to determine eligibility for the benefit that I am seeking.

E. Signature of petitioner.

Date   Phone Number

F. Signature of person preparing this form, if other than the petitioner.

I declare that I prepared this document at the request of the person above and that it is based on all information of which I have any knowledge.

Print Name _____   Signature _____   Date _____

Address _____   G-28 ID or VOLAG Number, if any. _____

U.S. Department of State

APPLICATION FOR IMMIGRANT VISA AND ALIEN REGISTRATION

OMB APPROVAL NO. 1405-0015
EXPIRES: 05/31/2004
ESTIMATED BURDEN: 1 HOUR*
(See Page 2)

PART I - BIOGRAPHIC DATA

INSTRUCTIONS: Complete one copy of this form for yourself and each member of your family, regardless of age, who will immigrate with you. Please print or type your answers to all questions. Mark questions that are Not Applicable with "N/A". If there is insufficient room on the form, answer on a separate sheet using the same numbers that appear on the form. Attach any additional sheets to this form.

WARNING: Any false statement or concealment of a material fact may result in your permanent exclusion from the United States.

This form (DS-230 PART I) is the first of two parts. This part, together with Form DS-230 PART II, constitutes the complete Application for Immigrant Visa and Alien Registration.

1. Family Name	First Name	Middle Name

2. Other Names Used or Aliases *(If married woman, give maiden name)*

3. Full Name in Native Alphabet *(If Roman letters not used)*

4. Date of Birth *(mm-dd-yyyy)*	5. Age	6. Place of Birth (City or town) *(Province)* *(Country)*

7. Nationality *(If dual national, give both)*	8. Gender ☐ Male ☐ Female	9. Marital Status ☐ Single *(Never married)* ☐ Married ☐ Widowed ☐ Divorced ☐ Separated Including my present marriage, I have been married_____ times.

10. Permanent address in the United States where you intend to live, if known *(street address including zip code)*. Include the name of a person who currently lives there. Telephone number:	11. Address in the United States where you want your Permanent Resident Card *(Green Card)* mailed, if different from address in item #10 *(include the name of a person who currently lives there)*. Telephone number:

12. Your Present Occupation	13. Present Address *(Street Address) (City or Town) (Province) (Country)* Telephone number: Home Office

14. Name of Spouse *(Maiden or family name)*   First Name   Middle Name

Date *(mm-dd-yyyy)* and place of birth of spouse:

Address of spouse *(If different from your own)*:

Spouse's occupation: Date of marriage *(mm-dd-yyyy)*:

15. Father's Family Name	First Name	Middle Name

16. Father's Date of Birth *(mm-dd-yyyy)*	Place of Birth	Current Address	If deceased, give year of death

17. Mother's Family Name at Birth	First Name	Middle Name

18. Mother's Date of Birth *(mm-dd-yyyy)*	Place of Birth	Current Address	If deceased, give year of death

DS-230 Part I
05-2001

THIS FORM MAY BE OBTAINED FREE AT CONSULAR OFFICES OF THE UNITED STATES OF AMERICA
PREVIOUS EDITIONS OBSOLETE

Page 1 of 4

19. List Names, Dates and Places of Birth, and Addresses of ALL Children.

NAME	DATE (mm-dd-yyyy)	PLACE OF BIRTH	ADDRESS (If different from your own)

20. List below all places you have lived for at least six months since reaching the age of 16, including places in your country of nationality. Begin with your present residence.

CITY OR TOWN	PROVINCE	COUNTRY	FROM/TO (mm-yyyy)

21a. Person(s) named in 14 and 19 who will accompany you to the United States now.

21b. Person(s) named in 14 and 19 who will follow you to the United States at a later date.

22. List below all employment for the last ten years.

EMPLOYER	LOCATION	JOB TITLE	FROM/TO (mm-yyyy)

In what occupation do you intend to work in the United States? _____

23. List below all educational institutions attended.

SCHOOL AND LOCATION	FROM/TO (mm-yyyy)	COURSE OF STUDY	DEGREE OR DIPLOMA

Languages spoken or read: _____

Professional associations to which you belong: _____

24. Previous Military Service ☐ Yes ☐ No

Branch: _____   Dates (mm-dd-yyyy) of Service: _____

Rank/Position: _____   Military Speciality/Occupation: _____

25. List dates of all previous visits to or residence in the United States. (If never, write "never") Give type of visa status, if known. Give INS "A" number if any.

FROM/TO (mm-yyyy)	LOCATION	TYPE OF VISA	"A" NO. (If known)

SIGNATURE OF APPLICANT	DATE (mm-dd-yyyy)

U.S. Department of State
APPLICATION FOR IMMIGRANT VISA AND ALIEN REGISTRATION

OMB APPROVAL NO. 1405-0015
EXPIRES: 05/31/2004
ESTIMATED BURDEN: 1 HOUR*

PART II - SWORN STATEMENT

INSTRUCTIONS: Complete one copy of this form for yourself and each member of your family, regardless of age, who will immigrate with you. Please print or type your answers to all questions. Mark questions that are Not Applicable with "N/A". If there is insufficient room on the form, answer on a separate sheet using the same numbers that appear on the form. Attach any additional sheets to this form. The fee should be paid in United States dollars or local currency equivalent, or by bank draft.

WARNING: Any false statement or concealment of a material fact may result in your permanent exclusion from the United States. Even if you are issued an immigrant visa and are subsequently admitted to the United States, providing false information on this form could be grounds for your prosecution and/or deportation.

This form (DS-230 PART II), together with Form DS-230 PART I, constitutes the complete Application for Immigrant Visa and Alien Registration.

26. Family Name   First Name   Middle Name

27. Other Names Used or Aliases *(If married woman, give maiden name)*

28. Full Name in Native Alphabet *(If Roman letters not used)*

29. Name and Address of Petitioner

Telephone number:

30   United States laws governing the issuance of visas require each applicant to state whether or not he or she is a member of any class of individuals excluded from admission into the United States. The excludable classes are described below in general terms. You should read carefully the following list and answer YES or NO to each category. The answers you give will assist the consular officer to reach a decision on your eligibility to receive a visa.

EXCEPT AS OTHERWISE PROVIDED BY LAW, ALIENS WITHIN THE FOLLOWING CLASSIFICATIONS ARE INELIGIBLE TO RECEIVE A VISA. DO ANY OF THE FOLLOWING CLASSES APPLY TO YOU?

a. An alien who has a communicable disease of public health significance; who has failed to present documentation of having received vaccinations in accordance with U.S. law; who has or has had a physical or mental disorder that poses or is likely to pose a threat to the safety ☐ Yes ☐ No

b. An alien convicted of, or who admits having committed, a crime involving moral turpitude or violation of any law relating to a controlled substance or who is the spouse, son or daughter of such a trafficker who knowingly has benefited from the trafficking activities in the past five years; who has been convicted of 2 or more offenses for which the aggregate sentences were 5 years or more; who is coming to the United States to engage in prostitution or commercialized vice or who has engaged in prostitution or procuring within the past 10 years; who is or has been an illicit trafficker in any controlled substance; who has committed a serious criminal offense in the United States and who has asserted immunity from prosecution; who, while serving as a foreign government official and within the previous 24-month period, was responsible for or directly carried out particularly severe violations of religious freedom; or whom the President has identified as a person who plays a significant role in a severe form of trafficking in persons, who otherwise has knowingly aided, abetted, assisted or colluded with such a trafficker in severe forms of trafficking in persons, or who is the spouse, son or daughter of such a trafficker who knowingly has benefited from the trafficking activities within the past five years. ☐ Yes ☐ No

c. An alien who seeks to enter the United States to engage in espionage, sabotage, export control violations, terrorist activities, the overthrow of the Government of the United States or other unlawful activity; who is a member of or affiliated with the Communist or other totalitarian party; who participated in Nazi persecutions or genocide; who has engaged in genocide; or who is a member or representative of a terrorist organization as currently designated by the U.S. Secretary of State. ☐ Yes ☐ No

d. An alien who is likely to become a public charge. ☐ Yes ☐ No

e. An alien who seeks to enter for the purpose of performing skilled or unskilled labor who has not been certified by the Secretary of Labor; who is a graduate of a foreign medical school seeking to perform medical services who has not passed the NBME exam or its equivalent; or who is a health care worker seeking to perform such work without a certificate from the CGFNS or from an equivalent approved independent credentialing organization. ☐ Yes ☐ No

f. An alien who failed to attend a hearing on deportation or inadmissibility within the last 5 years; who seeks or has sought a visa, entry into the United States, or any immigration benefit by fraud or misrepresentation; who knowingly assisted any other alien to enter or try to enter the United States in violation of law; who, after November 30, 1996, attended in student (F) visa status a U.S. public elementary school or who attended a U.S. public secondary school without reimbursing the school; or who is subject to a civil penalty under INA 274C. ☐ Yes ☐ No

Privacy Act and Paperwork Reduction Act Statements

The information asked for on this form is requested pursuant to Section 222 of the Immigration and Nationality Act. The U.S. Department of State uses the facts you provide on this form primarily to determine your classification and eligibility for a U.S. immigrant visa. Individuals who fail to submit this form or who do not provide all the requested information may be denied a U.S. immigrant visa. If you are issued an immigrant visa and are subsequently admitted to the United States as an immigrant, the Immigration and Naturalization Service will use the information on this form to issue you a Permanent Resident Card, and, if you so indicate, the Social Security Administration will use the information to issue you a social security number and card.

*Public reporting burden for this collection of information is estimated to average 1 hour per response, including time required for searching existing data sources, gathering the necessary data, providing the information required, and reviewing the final collection. In accordance with 5 CFR 1320 5(b), persons are not required to respond to the collection of this information unless this form displays a currently valid OMB control number. Send comments on the accuracy of this estimate of the burden and recommendations for reducing it to: U.S. Department of State (A/RPS/DIR) Washington, D.C. 20520.

g. An alien who is permanently ineligible for U.S. citizenship; or who departed the United States to evade military service in time of war. ☐ Yes ☐ No

h. An alien who was previously ordered removed within the last 5 years or ordered removed a second time within the last 20 years; who was previously unlawfully present and ordered removed within the last 10 years or ordered removed a second time within the last 20 years; who was convicted of an aggravated felony and ordered removed; who was previously unlawfully present in the United States for more than 180 days but less than one year who voluntarily departed within the last 3 years; or who was unlawfully present for more than one year or an aggregate of one year within the last 10 years. ☐ Yes ☐ No

i. An alien who is coming to the United States to practice polygamy; who withholds custody of a U.S. citizen child outside the United States from a person granted legal custody by a U.S. court or intentionally assists another person to do so; who has voted in the United States in ☐ Yes ☐ No

j. An alien who is a former exchange visitor who has not fulfilled the 2-year foreign residence requirement. ☐ Yes ☐ No

k. An alien determined by the Attorney General to have knowingly made a frivolous application for asylum. ☐ Yes ☐ No

l. An alien who has ordered, carried out or materially assisted in extrajudicial and political killings and other acts of violence against the Haitian people; who has directly or indirectly assisted or supported any of the groups in Colombia known as FARC, ELN, or AUC; who through abuse of a governmental or political position has converted for personal gain, confiscated or expropriated property in Cuba, a claim to which is owned by a national of the United States, has trafficked in such property or has been complicit in such conversion, has committed similar acts in another country, or is the spouse, minor child or agent of an alien who has committed such acts; who has been directly involved in the establishment or enforcement of population controls forcing a woman to undergo an abortion against her free choice or a man or a woman to undergo sterilization against his or her free choice; or who has disclosed or trafficked in confidential U.S. business information obtained in connection with U.S. participation in the Chemical Weapons Convention or is the spouse, minor child or agent of such a person. ☐ Yes ☐ No

31. Have you ever been charged, arrested or convicted of any offense or crime?
(If answer is Yes, please explain) ☐ Yes ☐ No

32. Have you ever been refused admission to the United States at a port-of-entry?
(If answer is Yes, please explain) ☐ Yes ☐ No

33a. Have you ever applied for a Social Security Number (SSN)?	33b. CONSENT TO DISCLOSURE: I authorize disclosure of information from this form to the Immigration and Naturalization Service (INS), the Social Security Administration (SSA), such other U.S. Government agencies as may be required for the purpose of assigning me an SSN and issuing me a Social Security card, and I authorize the SSA to share my SSN with the INS.
☐ Yes Give the number _____ ☐ No Do you want the Social Security Administration to assign you an SSN (and issue a card) or issue you a new card (if you have an SSN)? You must answer "Yes" to this question and to the "Consent To Disclosure" in order to receive an SSN and/or card. ☐ Yes ☐ No	☐ Yes ☐ No The applicant's response does not limit or restrict the Government's ability to obtain his or her SSN, or other information on this form, for enforcement or other purposes as authorized by law.

34. WERE YOU ASSISTED IN COMPLETING THIS APPLICATION? ☐ Yes ☐ No
(If answer is Yes, give name and address of person assisting you, indicating whether relative, friend, travel agent, attorney, or other)

DO NOT WRITE BELOW THE FOLLOWING LINE
The consular officer will assist you in answering item 35.
DO NOT SIGN this form until instructed to do so by the consular officer

35. I claim to be:
☐ A Family-Sponsored Immigrant
☐ An Employment-Based Immigrant
☐ A Diversity Immigrant
☐ A Special Category *(Specify)* _____
(Returning resident, Hong Kong, Tibetan, Private Legislation, etc.)

☐ I derive foreign state chargeability under Sec. 202(b) through my _____

☐ Preference: _____
☐ Numerical limitation: _____
(foreign state)

I understand that I am required to surrender my visa to the United States Immigration Officer at the place where I apply to enter the United States, and that the possession of a visa does not entitle me to enter the United States if at that time I am found to be inadmissible under the immigration laws.
I understand that any wilfully false or misleading statement or wilful concealment of a material fact made by me herein may subject me to permanent exclusion from the United States and, if I am admitted to the United States, may subject me to criminal prosecution and/or deportation.
I, the undersigned applicant for a United States immigrant visa, do solemnly swear (or affirm) that all statements which appear in this application, consisting of Form DS-230 Part I and Part II combined, have been made by me, including the answers to items 1 through 35 inclusive, and that they are true and complete to the best of my knowledge and belief. I do further swear (or affirm) that, if admitted into the United States, I will not engage in activities which would be prejudicial to the public interest, or endanger the welfare, safety, or security of the United States; in activities which would be prohibited by the laws of the United States relating to espionage, sabotage, public disorder, or in other activities subversive to the national security; in any activity a purpose of which is the opposition to or the control, or overthrow of, the Government of the United States, by force, violence, or other unconstitutional means.
I understand that completion of this form by persons required by law to register with the Selective Service System (males 18 through 25 years of age) constitutes such registration in accordance with the Military Selective Service Act.
I understand all the foregoing statements, having asked for and obtained an explanation on every point which was not clear to me.

_____
Signature of Applicant

Subscribed and sworn to before me this _____ day of _____ at: _____

_____
Consular Officer

U.S. Department of Justice
Immigration and Naturalization Service

Notice of Entry of Appearance
as Attorney or Representative

Appearance - An appearance shall be filed on this form by the attorney or representative appearing in each case. Thereafter, substitution may be permitted upon the written withdrawal of the attorney or representative of record or upon notification of the new attorney or representative. When an appearance is made by a person acting in a representative capacity, his personal appearance or signature shall constitute a representation that under the provisions of this chapter he is authorized and qualified to represent. Further proof of authority to act in a representative capacity may be required. **Availability of Records** - During the time a case is pending, and except as otherwise provided in 8CFR 103.2(b), a party to a proceeding or his attorney or representative shall be permitted to examine the record of proceeding in a Service office. He may, in conformity with 8 CFR 103.10, obtain copies of Service records or information therefrom and copies of documents or transcripts of evidence furnished by him. Upon request, he/she may, in addition, be loaned a copy of the testimony and exhibits contained in the record of proceeding upon giving his/her receipt for such copies and pledging that it will be surrendered upon final disposition of the case or upon demand. If extra copies of exhibits do not exist, they shall not be furnished free on loan; however, they shall be made available for copying or purchase of copies as provided in 8 CFR 103.10.

In re:	Date / /
	File No.

I hereby enter my appearance as attorney for (or representative of), and at the request of, the following named person(s):

Name	☐ Petitioner ☐ Beneficiary	☐ Applicant

Address (Apt. No.)	(Number & Street)	(City)	(State)	(ZIP Code)

Name	☐ Petitioner ☐ Beneficiary	☐ Applicant

Address (Apt. No.)	(Number & Street)	(City)	(State)	(ZIP Code)

Check applicable Item(s) below:

☐ 1. I am an attorney and a member in good standing of the bar of the Supreme Court of the United States or of the highest court of the following State, territory, insular possession, or District of Columbia

_____   _____ and am not under a court or administrative agency
Name of Court
order suspending, enjoining, restraining, disbarring, or otherwise restricting me in practicing law.

☐ 2. I am an accredited representative of the following named religious, charitable, social service, or similar organization established in the United States and which is so recognized by the Board:

☐ 3. I am associated with _____
the attorney of record who previously filed a notice of appearance in this case and my appearance is at his request.   *(If you check this item, also check item 1 or 2 whichever is appropriate.)*

☐ 4. Others (Explain fully.)

SIGNATURE	COMPLETE ADDRESS
NAME (Type or Print)	TELEPHONE NUMBER

PURSUANT TO THE PRIVACY ACT OF 1974, I HEREBY CONSENT TO THE DISCLOSURE TO THE FOLLOWING NAMED ATTORNEY OR REPRESENTATIVE OF ANY RECORD PERTAINING TO ME WHICH APPEARS IN ANY IMMIGRATION AND NATURALIZATION SERVICE SYSTEM OF RECORDS:

_____
(Name of Attorney or Representative)

THE ABOVE DISCLOSURE IS IN CONNECTION WITH THE FOLLOWING MATTER:

Name of Person Consenting	Signature of Person Consenting	Date

(NOTE: Execution of this box is required under the Privacy Act of 1974 where the person being represented is a citizen of the United States or an alien lawfully admitted for permanent residence.

This form may not be used to request records under the Freedom of information Act or the Privacy Act. The manner of requesting such records is contained in 8CFR 103.10 and 103.20 Et.SEQ.

NOTICE OF APPEAL TO THE BOARD OF IMMIGRATION APPEALS
OF DECISION OF DISTRICT DIRECTOR

In the Matter:	Fee Stamp

File Number: A_____ — _____ — _____

1. I hereby appeal to the Board of Immigration Appeals from the decision of the District Director, _____District, dated _____, in the above entitled case.

2. Specify reasons for this appeal and continue on separate sheets if necessary. If the factual or legal basis for the appeal is not sufficiently described the appeal may be summarily dismissed.

3. I ☐ do ☐ do not desire oral argument before the Board of Immigration Appeals in Falls Church, Virginia.

4. I ☐ am ☐ am not <u>filing a separate written brief or statement.</u>

_____
Signature of Appellant
(or attorney or representative)

_____
(print or type name)

_____
(print or type name)

_____
Date

_____

_____

_____
Address *(number, street, city, state, Zip code)*

FORM EOIR-29
JAN. 89

INSTRUCTIONS

1. **Filing.** This notice of appeal must be filed with the Office of the Immigration and Naturalization Service (INS) having administrative control over the Record of Proceeding within 15 calendar days *(or 18 calendar days if mailed)* after service of the decision of the District Director. The Notice of Appeal is **not** to be forwarded directly to the Board of Immigration Appeals (BIA).

2. **Fees.** A fee of one hundred and ten dollars *($110)* must be paid for filing this appeal. It cannot be refunded regardless of the action taken on the appeal. *(Only a single fee need be paid if two or more persons are covered by a single decision.)* DO NOT MAIL CASH. ALL FEES MUST BE SUBMITTED IN THE EXACT AMOUNT. Payment by check or money order must be drawn on a bank or other institution located in the United States and be payable in United States Currency. If appellant resides in Guam, check or money order must be payable to the "Treasurer of Guam." If appellant resides in the Virgin Islands, checks or money order must be payable to the "Commissioner of Finance of the Virgin Islands." All other appellants must make the check or money order payable to the "Treasurer of the United States." When check is drawn on account of a person other than the appellant, the name and "A" number of the appellant must be entered on the face of the check. If appeal is submitted from outside the United States, remittance may be made by bank international money order or foregoing draft drawn on a financial institution in the United States and payable to the "Treasurer of the United States" in United States currency. Personal checks are accepted subject to collectibility. An uncollected check will render the appeal form and any document issued pursuant thereto invalid.

3. **Counsel.** In presenting and prosecuting this appeal, the INS may be represented by appropriate counsel. An appellant may be represented at no expense to the Government by counsel or other duly authorized representative. A separate notice of appearance must be filed with this notice of appeal.

4. **Briefs.** When a brief is filed, it shall be submitted to the Office of the Immigration and Naturalization Service having administrative control over the Record of Proceeding in this matter within the time designated by the District Director. A copy shall be served on the opposing party. The District Director, or the BIA, for good cause, may extend the time of filing a brief or reply brief. The BIA in its discretion may authorize the filing of briefs with it, in which event the opposing party shall be allowed a specified time to respond.

5. **Oral argument.** No personal appearance by the appellant or counsel is required. The BIA will consider every case on the record submitted, whether or not oral representations are made. Oral argument may be requested. If approved, oral argument in any case should not extend beyond fifteen *(15)* minutes, unless additional time is granted by the BIA pursuant to a request made in advance of the hearing. No interpreters are furnished by the Government for the argument before the BIA.

   An appellant will not be released from detention or permitted to enter the United States to present oral argument to the BIA personally. The appellant, however, may make arrangements to have someone represent him/her before the BIA. Unless such arrangements are made at the time the appeal is taken, the Board will not calendar the case for argument.

6. **Summary dismissal of appeals.** The BIA may deny oral argument and summarily dismiss any appeal in which (i) the party concerned fails to specify the reasons for his/her appeal on the reverse side of this form, (ii) the only reason specified by the party concerned for his/her appeal involves a finding of fact or conclusion of law which was condeded by him/her at the hearing, (iii) the appeal is from an order that grants the party concerned the relief which he/she requested, or (iv) if the BIA is satisfied from a review of the record, that the appeal is frivolous or filed solely for the purpose of delay.

U.S. Department of Justice
Immigration and Naturalization Service

OMB No.1115-0214

Affidavit of Support under Section 213A of the Act

START HERE - Please Type or Print

Part 1. Information on Sponsor (You)

Last Name	First Name	Middle Name

Mailing Address (Street Number and Name)	Apt/Suite Number

City	State or Province

Country	Zip/Postal Code	Telephone Number

Place of Residence if different from above (Street Number and Name)	Apt/Suite Number

City	State or Province

Country	Zip/Postal Code	Telephone Number

Date of Birth (Month, Day, Year)	Place of Birth (City, State, Country)	Are you a U.S. Citizen? ☐ Yes ☐ No

Social Security Number	A-Number (If any)

FOR AGENCY USE ONLY

This Affidavit   Receipt

[ ] Meets

[ ] Does not meet

Requirements of Section 213A

Officer's Signature

Location

Date

Part 2. Basis for Filing Affidavit of Support

I am filing this affidavit of support because *(check one):*

a. ☐ I filed/am filing the alien relative petition.

b. ☐ I filed/am filing an alien worker petition on behalf of the intending immigrant, who is related to me as my _____ .
(relationship)

c. ☐ I have ownership interest of at least 5% of _____ .
(name of entity which filed visa petition)
which filed an alien worker petition on behalf of the intending immigrant, who is related to me as my _____ .
(relationship)

d. ☐ I am a joint sponsor willing to accept the legal obligations with any other sponsor(s).

Part 3. Information on the Immigrant(s) You Are Sponsoring

Last Name	First Name	Middle Name

Date of Birth (Month, Day, Year) / /	Sex: ☐ Male ☐ Female	Social Security Number (If any)

Country of Citizenship	A-Number (If any)

Current Address (Street Number and Name)	Apt/Suite Number	City

State/Province	Country	Zip/Postal Code	Telephone Number

List any spouse and/or children immigrating with the immigrant named above in this Part: *(Use additional sheet of paper if necessary.)*

Name	Relationship to Sponsored Immigrant			Date of Birth			A-Number (If any)	Social Security (If any)
	Spouse	Son	Daughter	Mo.	Day	Yr.		

Form I-864 (Rev. 11/05/01)Y

Part 4. Eligibility to Sponsor

To be a sponsor you must be U.S. citizen or national or lawful permanent resident. If you are not the petitioning relative, you must provide proof of status. To prove status, U.S. citizens or nationals must attach a copy of a document proving status, such as a U.S. passport, birth certificate, or certificate of naturalization, and lawful permanent residents must attach a copy of both sides of their Alien Registration Card (Form I-551).

The determination of your eligibility to sponsor an immigrant will be based on an evaluation of your demonstrated ability to maintain an annual income at or above 125 percent of the Federal poverty line (100 percent if you are a petitioner sponsoring your spouse or child and you are on active duty in the U.S. Armed Forces). The assessment of your ability to maintain an adequate income will include your current employment, household size, and household income as shown on the Federal income tax returns for the 3 most recent tax years. Assets that are readily converted to cash and that can be made available for the support of sponsored immigrants if necessary, including any such assets of the immigrant(s) you are sponsoring, may also be considered.

The greatest weight in determining eligibility will be placed on current employment and household income. If a petitioner is unable to demonstrate ability to meet the stated income and asset requirements, a joint sponsor who can meet the income and asset requirements is needed. Failure to provide adequate evidence of income and/or assets or an affidavit of support completed by a joint sponsor will result in denial of the immigrant's application for an immigrant visa or adjustment to permanent resident status.

A. Sponsor's Employment

I am:
1. ☐ Employed by _____ (Provide evidence of employment)
   Annual salary $ _____ or hourly wage $ _____ (for _____ hours per week)
2. ☐ Self employed _____(Name of business)
   Nature of employment or business _____
3. ☐ Unemployed or retired since _____

B. Sponsor's Household Size

Number

1. Number of persons (related to you by birth, marriage, or adoption) living in your residence, including yourself. *(Do NOT include persons being sponsored in this affidavit.)* _____
2. Number of immigrants being sponsored in this affidavit   *(Include all persons in Part 3.)* _____
3. Number of immigrants   **NOT** living in your household whom you are still obligated to support under a previously signed affidavit of support using Form I-864. _____
4. Number of persons who are otherwise dependent on you, as claimed in your tax return for the most recent tax year. _____
5. Total household size.   *(Add lines 1 through 4.)*   **Total** _____

List persons below who are included in lines 1 or 3 for whom you previously have submitted INS Form I-864, *if your support obligation has not terminated.*

(If additional space is needed, use additional paper)

Name	A-Number	Date Affidavit of Support Signed	Relationship

Part 4. Eligibility to Sponsor *(Continued)*

C. Sponsor's Annual Household Income

Enter total unadjusted income from your Federal income tax return for the most recent tax year below. If you last filed a joint income tax return but are using only your *own* income to qualify, list total earnings from your W-2 Forms, or *if* necessary to reach the required income for your household size, include income from other sources listed on your tax return. If your *individual* income does not meet the income requirement for your household size, you may also list total income for anyone related to you by birth, marriage, or adoption currently living with you in your residence if they have lived in your residence for the previous 6 months, or any person shown as a dependent on your Federal income tax return for the most recent tax year, even if not living in the household. For their income to be considered, household members or dependents must be willing to make their income available for support of the sponsored immigrant(s) and to complete and sign Form I-864A, Contract Between Sponsor and Household Member. A sponsored immigrant/household member only need complete Form I-864A if his or her income will be used to determine your ability to support a spouse and/or children immigrating with him or her.

You must attach evidence of current employment and copies of income tax returns as filed with the IRS for the most recent 3 tax years for yourself and all persons whose income is listed below. See "Required Evidence" in Instructions. Income from all 3 years will be considered in determining your ability to support the immigrant(s) you are sponsoring.

☐ I filed a single/separate tax return for the most recent tax year.
☐ I filed a joint return for the most recent tax year which includes only my own income.
☐ I filed a joint return for the most recent tax year which includes income for my spouse and myself.
    ☐ I am submitting documentation of my individual income (Form W-2 and 1099).
    ☐ I am qualifying using my spouse's income; my spouse is submitting a Form I-864A.

Indicate most recent tax year _____
(tax year)

Sponsor's individual income $_____

or

Sponsor and spouse's combined income $_____

(If spouse's income is to be considered, spouse must submit Form I-864A.)

Income of other qualifying persons.
(List names; include spouse if applicable. Each person must complete Form I-864A.)

_____ $_____

_____ $_____

_____ $_____

Total Household Income $_____

Explain on separate sheet of paper if you or any of the above listed individuals are submitting Federal income tax returns for fewer than 3 years, or if other explanation of income, employment, or evidence is necessary.

D. Determination of Eligibility Based on Income

1.   ☐ I am subject to the 125 percent of poverty line requirement for sponsors.
      ☐ I am subject to the 100 percent of poverty line requirement for sponsors on active duty in the U.S. Armed Forces sponsoring their spouse or child.
2.   Sponsor's total household size, from Part 4.B., line 5   _____ .
3.   Minimum income requirement from the Poverty Guidelines chart for the year of   _____ is $_____
      for this household size.   *(year)*

If you are currently employed and your household income for your household size is equal to or greater than the applicable poverty line requirement (from line D.3.), you do not need to list assets (Part 4.E. and 5) or have a joint sponsor (Part 6) unless you are requested to do so by a Consular or Immigration Officer. You may skip to Part 7, Use of the Affidavit of Support to Overcome Public Charge Ground of Admissibility **Otherwise, you should continue with Part 4.E.**

Part 4. Eligibility to Sponsor   *(Continued)*

E. Sponsor's Assets and Liabilities

Your assets and those of your qualifying household members and dependents may be used to demonstrate ability to maintain an income at or above 125 percent (or 100 percent, if applicable) of the poverty line *if* they are available for the support of the sponsored immigrant(s) and can readily be converted into cash within 1 year. The household member, other than the immigrant(s) you are sponsoring, must complete and sign Form I-864A, Contract Between Sponsor and Household Member. List the cash value of each asset *after* any debts or liens are subtracted. Supporting evidence must be attached to establish location, ownership, date of acquisition, and value of each asset listed, including any liens and liabilities related to each asset listed. See "Evidence of Assets" in Instructions.

Type of Asset	Cash Value of Assets *(Subtract any debts)*
Saving deposits	$
Stocks, bonds, certificates of deposit	$
Life insurance cash value	$
Real estate	$
Other *(specify)*	$
Total Cash Value of Assets	$ _____

Part 5. Immigrant's Assets and Offsetting Liabilities

The sponsored immigrant's assets may also be used in support of your ability to maintain income at or above 125 percent of the poverty line *if* the assets are or will be available in the United States for the support of the sponsored immigrant(s) and can readily be converted into cash within 1 year.

The sponsored immigrant should provide information on his or her assets in a format similar to part 4.E. above. Supporting evidence must be attached to establish location, ownership, and value of each asset listed, including any liens and liabilities for each asset listed. See "Evidence of Assets" in Instructions.

Part 6. Joint Sponsors

If household income and assets do not meet the appropriate poverty line for your household size, a joint sponsor is required. There may be more than one joint sponsor, but each joint sponsor must individually meet the 125 percent of poverty line requirement based on his or her household income and/or assets, including any assets of the sponsored immigrant. By submitting a separate Affidavit of Support under Section 213A of the Act (Form I-864), a joint sponsor accepts joint responsibility with the petitioner for the sponsored immigrant(s) until they become U.S. citizens, can be credited with 40 quarters of work, leave the United States permanently, or die.

Part 7. Use of the Affidavit of Support to Overcome Public Charge Ground of Inadmissibility

Section 212(a)(4)(C) of the Immigration and Nationality Act provides that an alien seeking permanent residence as an immediate relative (including an orphan), as a family-sponsored immigrant, or as an alien who will accompany or follow to join another alien is considered to be likely to become a public charge and is inadmissible to the United States unless a sponsor submits a legally enforceable affidavit of support on behalf of the alien. Section 212(a)(4)(D) imposes the same requirement on employment-based immigrant, and those aliens who accompany or follow to join the employment-based immigrant, if the employment-based immigrant will be employed by a relative, or by a firm in which a relative owns a significant interest. Separate affidavits of support are required for family members at the time they immigrate if they are not included on this affidavit of support or do not apply for an immigrant visa or adjustment of status within 6 months of the date this affidavit of support is originally signed. The sponsor must provide the sponsored immigrant(s) whatever support is necessary to maintain them at an income that is at least 125 percent of the Federal poverty guidelines.

> *I submit this affidavit of support in consideration of the sponsored immigrant(s) not being found inadmissible to the United States under section 212(a)(4)(C) (or 212(a)(4)(D) for an employment-based immigrant) and to enable the sponsored immigrant(s) to overcome this ground of inadmissibility. I agree to provide the sponsored immigrant(s) whatever support is necessary to maintain the sponsored immigrant(s) at an income that is at least 125 percent of the Federal poverty guidelines. I understand that my obligation will continue until my death or the sponsored immigrant(s) have become U.S. citizens, can be credited with 40 quarters of work, depart the United States permanently, or die.*

Part 7. Use of the Affidavit of Support to Overcome Public Charge Grounds   *(Continued)*

Notice of Change of Address.

Sponsors are required to provide written notice of any change of address within 30 days of the change in address until the sponsored immigrant(s) have become U.S. citizens, can be credited with 40 quarters of work, depart the United States permanently, or die. To comply with this requirement, the sponsor must complete INS Form I-865. Failure to give this notice may subject the sponsor to the civil penalty established under section 213A(d)(2) which ranges from $250 to $2,000, unless the failure to report occurred with the knowledge that the sponsored immigrant(s) had received means-tested public benefits, in which case the penalty ranges from $2,000 to $5,000.

> *If my address changes for any reason before my obligations under this affidavit of support terminate, I will complete and file INS Form I-865, Sponsor's Notice of Change of Address, Within 30 days of the change of address. I understand that failure to give this notice may subject me to civil penalties.*

Means-tested Public Benefit Prohibitions and Exceptions.

Under section 403(a) of Public Law 104-193 (Welfare Reform Act), aliens lawfully admitted for permanent residence in the United States, with certain exceptions, are ineligible for most Federally-funded means-tested public benefits during their first 5 years in the United States. This provision does not apply to public benefits specified in section 403(c) of the Welfare Reform Act or to State public benefits, including emergency Medicaid; short-term, non-cash emergency relief; services provided under the National School Lunch and Child Nutrition Acts; immunizations and testing and treatment for communicable diseases; student assistance under the Higher Education Act and the Public Health Service Act; certain forms of foster-care or adoption assistance under the Social Security Act; Head Start programs; means-tested programs under the Elementary and Secondary Education Act; and Job Training Partnership Act programs.

Consideration of Sponsor's Income in Determining Eligibility for Benefits.

If a permanent resident alien is no longer statutorily barred from a Federally-funded means-tested public benefit program and applies for such a benefit, the income and resources of the sponsor and the sponsor's spouse will be considered (or deemed) to be the income and resources of the sponsored immigrant in determining the immigrant's eligibility for Federal means-tested public benefits. Any State or local government may also choose to consider (or deem) the income and resources of the sponsor and the sponsor's spouse to be the income and resources of the immigrant for the purposes of determining eligibility for their means-tested public benefits. The attribution of the income and resources of the sponsor and the sponsor's spouse to the immigrant will continue until the immigrant becomes a U.S. citizen or has worked or can be credited with 40 qualifying quarters of work, provided that the immigrant or the worker crediting the quarters to the immigrant has not received any Federal means-tested public benefit during any creditable quarter for any period after December 31, 1996.

> *I understand that, under section 213A of the Immigration and Nationality Act (the Act), as amended, this affidavit of support constitutes a contract between me and the U.S. Government. This contract is designed to protect the United States Government, and State and local government agencies or private entities that provide means-tested public benefits, from having to pay benefits to or on behalf of the sponsored immigrant(s), for as long as I am obligated to support them under this affidavit of support. I understand that the sponsored immigrants, or any Federal, State, local, or private entity that pays any means-tested benefit to or on behalf of the sponsored immigrant(s), are entitled to sue me if I fail to meet my obligations under this affidavit of support, as defined by section 213A and INS regulations.*

Civil Action to Enforce.

If the immigrant on whose behalf this affidavit of support is executed receives any Federal, State, or local means-tested public benefit before this obligation terminates, the Federal, State, or local agency or private entity may request reimbursement from the sponsor who signed this affidavit. If the sponsor fails to honor the request for reimbursement, the agency may sue the sponsor in any U.S. District Court or any State court with jurisdiction of civil actions for breach of contract. INS will provide names, addresses, and Social Security account numbers of sponsors to benefit- providing agencies for this purpose. Sponsors may also be liable for paying the costs of collection, including legal fees.

Part 7.   Use of the Affidavit of Support to Overcome Public Charge Grounds   *(Continued)*

I acknowledge that section 213A(a)(1)(B) of the Act grants the sponsored immigrant(s) and any Federal, State, local, or private agency that pays any means-tested public benefit to or on behalf of the sponsored immigrant(s) standing to sue me for failing to meet my obligations under this affidavit of support. I agree to submit to the personal jurisdiction of any court of the United States or of any State, territory, or possession of the United States if the court has subject matter jurisdiction of a civil lawsuit to enforce this affidavit of support. I agree that no lawsuit to enforce this affidavit of support shall be barred by any statute of limitations that might otherwise apply, so long as the plaintiff initiates the civil lawsuit no later than ten (10) years after the date on which a sponsored immigrant last received any means-tested public benefits.

Collection of Judgment.

I acknowledge that a plaintiff may seek specific performance of my support obligation. Furthermore, any money judgment against me based on this affidavit of support may be collected through the use of a judgment lien under 28 U.S.C. 3201, a writ of execution under 28 U.S.C. 3203, a judicial installment payment order under 28 U.S.C. 3204, garnishment under 28 U.S.C. 3205, or through the use of any corresponding remedy under State law. I may also be held liable for costs of collection, including attorney fees.

Concluding Provisions.

I, _____ , *certify under penalty of perjury under the laws of the United States that:*

  (a) *I know the contents of this affidavit of support signed by me;*
  (b) *All the statements in this affidavit of support are true and correct;*
  (c) *I make this affidavit of support for the consideration stated in Part 7, freely, and without any mental reservation or purpose of evasion;*
  (d) *Income tax returns submitted in support of this affidavit are true copies of the returns filed with the Internal Revenue Service; and*
  (e) *Any other evidence submitted is true and correct.*

_____   _____
              (Sponsor's Signature)   *(Date)*

Subscribed and sworn to   *(or affirmed)*   before me this

_____ day of _____ , _____
                              (Month)   *(Year)*

at _____ ,

My commission expires on   _____

_____
  (Signature of Notary Public or Officer Administering Oath)

_____
                        (Title)

Part 8.   If someone other than the sponsor prepared this affidavit of support, that person must complete the following:

I certify under penalty of perjury under the laws of the United States that I prepared this affidavit of support at the sponsor's request, and that this affidavit of support is based on all information of which I have knowledge.

Signature	Print Your Name	Date	Daytime Telephone Number

Firm Name and Address

2002 Poverty Guidelines*

Minimum Income Requirement For Use in Completing Form I-864

For the 48 Contiguous States, the District of Columbia, Puerto Rico, the U.S. Virgin Islands, and Guam:

Sponsor's Household Size	100% of Poverty Line For sponsors on active duty in the U.S. Armed Forces who are petitioning for their spouse or child	125% of Poverty Line For all other sponsors
2	$11,940	$14,925
3	15,020	18,775
4	18,100	22,625
5	21,180	26,475
6	24,260	30,325
7	27,340	34,175
8	30,420	38,025
	Add $3,080 for each additional person.	Add $3,850 for each additional person.

For Alaska: / For Hawaii:

Sponsor's Household Size	For Alaska: 100% of Poverty Line For sponsors on active duty in the U.S. Armed Forces who are petitioning for their spouse or child	For Alaska: 125% of Poverty Line For all other sponsors	For Hawaii: 100% of Poverty Line For sponsors on active duty in the U.S. Armed Forces who are petitioning for their spouse or child	For Hawaii: 125% of Poverty Line For all other sponsors
2	$14,930	$18,662	$13,740	$17,175
3	18,780	23,474	17,280	21,600
4	22,630	28,286	20,820	26,025
5	26,480	33,098	24,360	30,450
6	30,330	37,910	27,900	34,875
7	34,180	42,722	31,440	39,300
8	38,030	47,534	34,980	43,725
	Add $3,850 for each additional person.	Add $4,812 for each additional person.	Add $3,540 for each additional person.	Add $4,425 for each additional person.

Means-tested Public Benefits

Federal Means-tested Public Benefits.   To date, Federal agencies administering benefit programs have determined that Federal means-tested public benefits include Food Stamps, Medicaid, Supplemental Security Income (SSI), Temporary Assistance for Needy Families (TANF), and the State Child Health Insurance Program (CHIP).

State Means-tested Public Benefits. Each State will determine which, if any, of its public benefits are means-tested. If a State determines that it has programs which meet this definition, it is encouraged to provide notice to the public on which programs are included. Check with the State public assistance office to determine which, if any, State assistance programs have been determined to be State means-tested public benefits.

Programs Not Included: The following Federal and State programs are *not* included as means-tested benefits: emergency Medicaid; short-term, non-cash emergency relief; services provided under the National School Lunch and Child Nutrition Acts; immunizations and testing and treatment for communicable diseases; student assistance under the Higher Education Act and the Public Health Service Act; certain forms of foster-care or adoption assistance under the Social Security Act; Head Start programs; means-tested programs under the Elementary and Secondary Education Act; and Job Training Partnership Act programs.

* These poverty guidelines remain in effect for use with the Form I-864 Affidavit of Support from April 1, 2002 until new poverty guidelines go into effect in the Spring of 2003.

Application for Waiver of Ground of Excludability

DO NOT WRITE IN THIS BLOCK

Fee Stamp

- ☐ 212 (a) (1)
- ☐ 212 (a) (3)
- ☐ 212 (a) (6)
- ☐ 212 (a) (9)
- ☐ 212 (a) (10)
- ☐ 212 (a) (12)
- ☐ 212 (a) (19)
- ☐ 212 (a) (23)

A. Information about applicant

1. Family Name (Surname In CAPS) (First) (Middle)

2. Address (Number and Street) (Apartment Number)

3. (Town or City) (State/Country) (Zip/Postal Code)

4. Date of Birth *(Month/Day/Year)* 5. INS File Number A-

6. City of Birth 7. Country of Birth

8. Date of Visa Application 9. Visa Applied for at:

10. Applicant was declared inadmissible to the United States for the following reasons: (List acts, convictions, or physical or mental conditions. If applicant has active or suspected tuberculosis, page 2 of this fom must be fully completed.)

11. Applicant was previously in the United States, as follows:

City and State	From (Date)	To (Date)	INS Status

12. Applicant's Social Security Number (if any)

B. Information about relative, through whom applicant claims eligibility for a waiver

1. Family Name (Surname in CAPS) (First) (Middle)

2. Address (Number and Street) (Apartment Number)

3. (Town or City) (State/Country) (Zip/Postal Code)

4. Relationship to applicant 5. INS Status

C. Information about applicant's other relatives in the U.S.
(List only U.S. citizens and permanent residents)

1. Family Name (Surname in CAPS) (First) (Middle)

2. Address (Number and Street) (Apartment Number)

3. (Town or City) (State/Country) (Zip/Postal Code)

4. Relationship to applicant 5. INS Status

1. Family Name (Surname in CAPS) (First) (Middle)

2. Address (Number and Street) (Apartment Number)

3. (Town or City) (State/Country) (Zip/Postal Code)

4. Relationship to applicant 5. INS Status

1. Family Name (Surname in CAPS) (First) (Middle)

2. Address (Number and Street) (Apartment Number)

3. (Town or City) (State/Country) (Zip/Postal Code)

4. Relationship to applicant 5. INS Status

Signature (of applicant or petitioning relative)

Relationship to applicant Date

Signature (of person preparing application, if not the applicant or petitioning relative). I declare that this document was prepared by me at the request of the applicant or petitioning relative, and is based on all information of which I have any knowledge.

Signature

Address Date

FOR INS USE ONLY. DO NOT WRITE IN THIS AREA.	Initial receipt	Resubmitted	Relocated		Completed		
			Received	Sent	Approved	Denied	Returned

Form I-601 (Rev. 01/16/02)Y

To be Completed for Applicants with
Active Tuberculosis or Suspected Tuberculosis

A. Statement by Applicant

Upon admission to the United States I will:

1. Go directly to the physician or health facility named in Section B;

2. Present all X-rays used in the visa medical examination to substantiate diagnosis;

3. Submit to such examinations, treatment, isolation and medical regimen as may be required; and

4. Remain under the prescribed treatment or observation whether on inpatient or outpatient basis, until discharged.

Signature of Applicant

Date

B. Statement by Physician or Health Facility

(May be executed by a private physician, health department, other public or private health facility or military hospital.)

I agree to supply any treatment or observation necessary for the proper management of the alien's tuberculosis condition.

I agree to submit Form CDC 75.18, "Report on Alien with Tuberculosis Waiver," to the health officer named in Section D:

1. Within 30 days of the alien's reporting for care, indicating presumptive diagnosis, test results and plans for future care of the alien; or

2. 30 days after receiving Form CDC 75.18, if the alien has not reported.

Satisfactory financial arrangements have been made. (This statement does not relieve the alien from submitting evidence, as required by consul, to establish that the alien is not likely to become a public charge.)

I represent (enter an "X" in the appropriate box and give the complete name and address of the facility below.)

☐ 1. Local Health Department
☐ 2. Other Public or Private Facility
☐ 3. Private Practice
☐ 4. Military Hospital

Name of Facility (please type or print)

Address (Number and Street)   (Apartment Number)

City, State and Zip Code

Signature of Physician   Date

C. Applicant's Sponsor in the U.S.

Arrange for medical care of the applicant and have the physician complete Section B.

If medical care will be provided by a physician who checked box 2 or 3, in Section B, have Section D completed by the local or State Health Officer who has jurisdiction in the U.S. area where the applicant plans to reside.

If medical care will be provided by a physician who checked box 4, in Section B, forward this form directly to the military facility at the address provided in Section B.

Address in the U.S. where the alien plans to reside.

Address (Number and Street)   (Apartment Number)

City, State and Zip Code

D. Endorsement of Local or State Health Officer

Endorsement signifies recognition of the physician or facility for the purpose of providing care for tuberculosis. If the facility or physician who signed his or her name in Section B is not in your health jurisdiction and not familiar to you, you may want to contact the health officer responsible for the jurisdiction of the facility or physician prior to endorsing.

Endorsed by: Signature of Health Officer

Date

Enter below the name and address of the Local Health Department where the "Notice of Arrival of Alien with Tuberculosis Waiver" should be sent when the alien arrives in the U. S.

Official Name of Department

Address (Number and Street)   (Apartment Number)

City, State and Zip Code

If further assistance is needed, contact the INS office with jurisdiction over the intended place of U.S. residence of the applicant.

Application for Waiver of Ground of Excludability

DO NOT WRITE IN THIS BLOCK

☐ 212 (a) (1)   ☐ 212 (a) (10)

☐ 212 (a) (3)   ☐ 212 (a) (12)

☐ 212 (a) (6)   ☐ 212 (a) (19)

☐ 212 (a) (9)   ☐ 212 (a) (23)

Fee Stamp

A. Information about applicant

1. Family Name (Surname In CAPS)   (First)   (Middle)

2. Address (Number and Street)   (Apartment Number)

3. (Town or City) (State/Country)   (Zip/Postal Code)

4. Date of Birth *(Month/Day/Year)*   5. INS File Number
A-

6. City of Birth   7. Country of Birth

8. Date of Visa Application   9. Visa Applied for at:

10. Applicant was declared inadmissible to the United States for the following reasons: (List acts, convictions, or physical or mental conditions. If applicant has active or suspected tuberculosis, page 2 of this form must be fully completed.)

11. Applicant was previously in the United States, as follows:

City and State   From (Date)   To (Date)   INS Status

12. Applicant's Social Security Number (if any)

B. Information about relative, through whom applicant claims eligibility for a waiver

1. Family Name (Surname in CAPS)   (First)   (Middle)

2. Address (Number and Street)   (Apartment Number)

3. (Town or City) (State/Country)   (Zip/Postal Code)

4. Relationship to applicant   5. INS Status

C. Information about applicant's other relatives in the U.S.
(List only U.S. citizens and permanent residents)

1. Family Name (Surname in CAPS)   (First)   (Middle)

2. Address (Number and Street)   (Apartment Number)

3. (Town or City) (State/Country)   (Zip/Postal Code)

4. Relationship to applicant   5. INS Status

1. Family Name (Surname in CAPS)   (First)   (Middle)

2. Address (Number and Street)   (Apartment Number)

3. (Town or City) (State/Country)   (Zip/Postal Code)

4. Relationship to applicant   5. INS Status

1. Family Name (Surname in CAPS)   (First)   (Middle)

2. Address (Number and Street)   (Apartment Number)

3. (Town or City) (State/Country)   (Zip/Postal Code)

4. Relationship to applicant   5. INS Status

INS Use Only: Additional Information and Instructions

Signature and Title of Requesting Officer

Address   Date

This office will maintain only a folder relating to the applicant pursuant to A.M. 2712.01

AGENCY COPY

OMB No. 1115-0145

Petition to Remove the Conditions on Residence

START HERE - Please Type or Print

Part 1. Information about you.

Family Name	Given Name	Middle Initial

Address - C/O:

Street Number and Name		Apt. #

City	State or Province

Country	ZIP/Postal Code

Date of Birth (month/day/year)	Country of Birth

Social Security # (if any)	A#

Conditional residence expires on (month/day/year)

Mailing address if different from address listed above:

Street Number and Name		Apt. #

City	State or Province

Country	ZIP/Postal Code

FOR INS USE ONLY

Returned	Receipt
Resubmitted	
Reloc Sent	
Reloc Rec'd	
☐ Applicant Interviewed	

Remark

Action

Part 2. Basis for petition (check one).

a. ☐ My conditional residence is based on my marriage to a U.S. citizen or permanent resident, and we are filing this petition together.

b. ☐ I am a child who entered as a conditional permanent resident and I am unable to be included in a Joint Petition to Remove the Conditional Basis of Alien's Permanent Residence (Form 1-751) filed by my parent(s).

My conditional residence is based on my marriage to a U.S. citizen or permanent resident, but I am unable to file a joint petition and I request a waiver because: (check one)

c. ☐ My spouse is deceased.

d. ☐ I entered into the marriage in good faith, but the marriage was terminated through divorce/annulment.

e. ☐ I am a conditional resident spouse who entered into the marriage in good faith, or I am a conditional resident child, who has been battered or subjected to extreme cruelty by my citizen or permanent resident spouse or parent.

f. ☐ The termination of my status and removal from the United States would result in an extreme hardship.

Part 3. Additional information about you.

Other Names Used (including maiden name):	Telephone #

Date of Marriage	Place of Marriage

If your spouse is deceased, give the date of death. (month/day/year)

- Are you in removal or deportation proceedings?   ☐ Yes ☐ No

- Was a fee paid to anyone other than an attorney in connection with this petition?   ☐ Yes ☐ No

To Be Completed by Attorney or Representative, if any

☐ Fill in box if G-28 is attached to represent the applicant

VOLAG#

ATTY State License #

Continued on back.

Form 1-751 (Rev. 06/05/02)Y Page 1

Part 3. Additional information about you. (continued)

- Since becoming a conditional resident, have you ever been arrested, cited, charged, indicted, convicted, fined or imprisoned for breaking or violating any law or ordinace (excluding traffic regulations), or committed any crime for which you were not arrested? ☐ Yes ☐ No

- If you are married, is this a different marriage than the one through which conditional residence status was obtained? ☐ Yes ☐ No

- Have you resided at any other address since you became a permanent resident? *(If yes, attach a list of all addresses and dates.)* ☐ Yes ☐ No

- Is your spouse currently serving with or employed by the U.S. government and serving outside the United States? ☐ Yes ☐ No

Part 4. Information about the spouse or parent through whom you gained your conditional residence.

Family Name	Given Name	Middle Initial	Phone Number

Address		

Date of Birth (month/day/year)	Social Security # (if any)	A#

Part 5. Information about your children. *List all your children. Attach another sheet(s) if necessary.*

Name	Date of Birth (month/day/year)	If in U.S., give A number, current immigration status and U.S. address.	Living with you?
1.			☐ Yes ☐ No
2.			☐ Yes ☐ No
3.			☐ Yes ☐ No
4.			☐ Yes ☐ No

Part 6. Signature. *Read the information on penalties in the instructions before completing this section. If you checked block "a" in Part 2, your spouse must also sign below.*

I certify, under penalty of perjury under the laws of the United States of America, that this petition and the evidence submitted with it is all true and correct. If conditional residence was based on a marriage, I further certify that the marriage was entered into in accordance with the laws of the place where the marriage took place and was not for the purpose of procuring an immigration benefit. I also authorize the release of any information from my records that the Immigration and Naturalization Service needs to determine eligibility for the benefit sought.

Signature	Print Name	Date

Signature of Spouse	Print Name	Date

Please note: If you do not completely fill out this form or fail to submit any required documents listed in the instructions, you cannot be found eligible for the requested benefit and this petition may be denied.

Part 7. Signature of person preparing form, if other than above.

I declare that I prepared this petition at the request of the above person and it is based on all information of which I have knowledge.

Signature	Print Name	Date

Firm Name and Address

U.S. Department of Justice
Immigration and Naturalization Service

Petition for Alien Fiancé(e)

DO NOT WRITE IN THIS BLOCK

Case ID#	**Action Stamp**	**Fee Stamp**
A#		
G-28 or Volag #		
The petition is approved for status under Section 101(a)(15)(k). It is valid for four months from date of action.		AMCON: _____ ☐ Personal Interview ☐ Previously Forwarded ☐ Document Check ☐ Field Investigations
Remarks:		

A. Information about you.

1. Name (Family name in CAPS)   (First)   (Middle)

2. Address (Number and Street)   (Apartment Number)

(Town or City)   (State/Country)   (Zip/Postal Code)

3. Place of Birth (Town or City)   (State/Country)

4. Date of Birth (Mo/Day/Yr)

5. Sex
☑ Male
☑ Female

6. Marital Status
☐ Married   ☐ Single
☐ Widowed   ☐ Divorced

7. Other Names Used (including maiden name)

8. Social Security Number (if any)   **9. Alien Registration Number** (if any)

10. Names of Prior Husband/Wives   **11. Date(s) Marriages(s)**

12. If you are a U.S. citizen, complete the following:
My citizenship was acquired through (check one)

☐ Birth in the U.S.   ☐ Naturalization

Give number of certificate, date and place it was issued

☐ Parents
Have you obtained a certificate of citizenship in your own name?
☐ Yes   ☐ No
If "Yes," give number of certificate, date and place it was issued.

13. Have you ever filed for this or any other alien fiancé(e) before? ☐ Yes   ☐ No
If you checked "yes," give name of alien, place and date of filing, and result.

B. Information about your alien fiancé(e).

1. Name (Family name in CAPS)   (First)   (Middle)

2. Address (Number and Street)   (Apartment Number)

(Town or City)   (State/Country)   (Zip/Postal Code)

3. Place of Birth (Town or City)   (State/Country)

4. Date of Birth (Mo/Day/Yr)

5. Sex
☐ Male
☐ Female

6. Marital Status
☐ Married   ☐ Single
☐ Widowed   ☐ Divorced

7. Other Names Used (including maiden name)

8. Social Security Number (if any)   **9. Alien Registration Number** (if any)

10. Names of Prior Husbands/Wives   **11. Date(s) Marriages(s)**

12. Has your fiancé(e) ever been in the U.S.?
☐ Yes   ☐ No

13. If your fiancé(e) is currently in the U.S., complete the following:
He or she last arrived as a (visitor, student, exchange alien, crewman, stowaway, temporary worker, without inspection, etc.)

Arrival/Departure Record (I-94)   Date arrived (Month/Day/Year)

Date authorized stay expired, or will expire, as shown on Form I-94

INITIAL	RESUBMITTED	RELOCATED		COMPLETED		
		Rec'd	Sent	Approved	Denied	Returned

B. Information about your alien fiancé(e) (Continued)

14. List all children of your alien fiancé(e) (if any)

(Name)	(Date of Birth)	(Country of Birth)	(Present Address)

15. Address in the United States where your fiancé(e) intends to live

(Number and Street)	(Town or City)	(State)

16. Your fiancé(e)'s address abroad

(Number and Street)	(Town or City)	(Province)	(Country)	(Phone Number)

17. If your fiancé(e)'s native alphabet uses other than Roman letters, write his or her name and address abroad in the native alphabet:

(Name)	(Number and Street)	(Town or City)	(Province)	(Country)

18. Is your fiancé(e) related to you? ☐ Yes ☐ No
If you are related, state the nature and degree of relationship, e.g., third cousin or maternal uncle, etc.

19. Has your fiancé(e) met and seen you? ☐ Yes ☐ No

Describe the circumstances under which you met. If you have not personally met each other, explain how the relationship was established, and explain in detail any reasons you may have for requesting that the requirement that you and your fiancé(e) must have met should not apply to you.

20. Your fiancé(e) will apply for a visa abroad at the American Consulate in

(City)	(Country)

(Designation of a consulate outside the country of your fiancé(e)'s last residence does not guarantee acceptance for processing by that consulate. Acceptance is at the discretion of the designated consulate.)

C. Other information

If you are serving overseas in the Armed Forces of the United States, please answer the following:

I presently reside or am stationed overseas and my current mailing address is _____

I plan to return to the United States on or about _____

Penalties: You may, by law, be imprisoned for not more than five years, or fined $250,000, or both, for entering into a marriage contract for the purpose of evading any provision of the immigration laws and you may be fined up to $10,000 or imprisoned up to five years, or both, for knowingly and willfully falsifying or concealing a material fact or using any false document in submitting this petition.

Your Certification:
I am legally able to and intend to marry my alien fiancé(e) within 90 days of his or her arrival in the United States. I certify, under penalty of perjury under the laws of the United States of America, that the foregoing is true and correct. Furthermore, I authorize the release of any information from my records which the Immigration and Naturalizaton Service needs to determine eligibility for the benefit that I am seeking.

Signature _____ (Date)_____ (Phone Number)_____

Signature of Person Preparing Form, If Other Than Above:

I declare that I prepared this document at the request of the person above and that it is based on all information of which I have any knowledge.

Print Name _____ (Address)_____ (Signature) _____ (Date)_____

G-28 ID _____   Volag _____

U.S. DEPARTMENT OF LABOR
Employment and Training Administration

APPLICATION
FOR
ALIEN EMPLOYMENT CERTIFICATION

IMPORTANT: READ CAREFULLY BEFORE COMPLETING THIS FORM

PRINT legibly in ink or use a typewriter. If you need more space to answer questions in this form, use a separate sheet. Identify each answer with the number of the corresponding question. SIGN AND DATE each sheet in original signature.

To knowingly furnish any false information in the preparation of this form and any supplement thereto or to aid, abet, or counsel another to do so is a felony punishable by $10,000 fine or 5 years in the penitentiary, or both (18 U.S.C. 1001)

PART A. OFFER OF EMPLOYMENT

1. Name of Alien   (Family name in capital letter, First, Middle, Maiden)

2. Present Address of Alien   (Number, Street, City and Town, State ZIP code or Province, Country)

3. Type of Visa   (If in U.S.)

The following information is submitted as an offer of employment.

4. Name of Employer   (Full name of Organization)

5. Telephone

6. Address   (Number, Street, City and Town, State ZIP code)

7. Address Where Alien Will Work   (if different from item 6)

8. Nature of Employer's Business Activity	9. Name of Job Title	10. Total Hours Per Week		11. Work Schedule (Hourly)	12. Rate of Pay	
		a. Basic	b. Overtime	a.m. / p.m.	a. Basic $ per _____	b. Overtime $ per hour

13. Describe Fully the job to be Performed   (Duties)

14. State in detail the MINIMUM education, training, and experience for a worker to perform satisfactorily the job duties described in item 13 above.

15. Other Special Requirements

EDU-CATION (Enter number of years)	Grade School	High School	College	College Degree Required (specify)
				Major Field of Study

TRAIN-ING	No. Yrs.	No. Mos.	Type of Training

EXPERI-ENCE	Job Offered		Related Occupation	Related Occupation (specify)
	Number Yrs. / Mos.	Yrs. / Mos.		

16. Occupational Title of Person Who Will Be Alien's Immediate Supervisor

17. Number of Employees Alien Will Supervise

ENDORSEMENTS (Make no entry in section - for Government use only)

Date Forms Received	
L.O.	S.O.
R.O.	N.O.
Ind. Code	Occ. Code
Occ. Title	

Replaces MA 7-50A, B and C (Apr. 1970 edition) which is obsolete.

18. COMPLETE ITEMS ONLY IF JOB IS TEMPORARY				19. IF JOB IS UNIONIZED (Complete)	
a. No. of Openings To Be Filled By Aliens Under Job Offer	b. Exact Dates You Expect To Employ Alien			a. Number of Local	b. Name of Local
	From	To			
					c. City and State

20. STATEMENT FOR LIVE-AT-WORK JOB OFFERS (Complete for Private Household ONLY)

a. Description of Residence		b. No. Persons residing at Place of Employment				c. Will free board and private room not shared with anyone be provided?	("X" one)
("X" one)	Number of Rooms	Adults		Children	Ages		☐ YES ☐ NO
☐ House			BOYS				
☐ Apartment			GIRLS				

21. DESCRIBE EFFORTS TO RECRUIT U.S. WORKERS AND THE RESULTS. (Specify Sources of Recruitment by Name)

22. Applications require various types of documentation. Please read Part II of the instructions to assure that appropriate supporting documentation is included with your application.

23. EMPLOYER CERTIFICATIONS

By virtue of my signature below, I HEREBY CERTIFY the following conditions of employment.

a. I have enough funds available to pay the wage or salary offered the alien.

b. The wage offered equals or exceeds the prevailing wage and I guarantee that, if a labor certification is granted, the wage paid to the alien when the alien begins work will equal or exceed the prevailing wage which is applicable at the time the alien begins work.

c. The wage offered is not based on commissions, bonuses, or other incentives, unless I guarantee a wage paid on a weekly, bi-weekly, or monthly basis.

d. I will be able to place the alien on the payroll on or before the date of the alien's proposed entrance into the United States.

e. The job opportunity does not involve unlawful discrimination by race, creed, color, national origin, age, sex, religion, handicap, or citizenship.

f. The job opportunity is not:

(1) Vacant because the former occupant is on strike or is being locked out in the course of a labor dispute involving a work stoppage.

(2) At issue in a labor dispute involving a work stoppage.

g. The job opportunity's terms, conditions and occupational environment are not contrary to Federal, State or local law.

h. The job opportunity has been and is clearly open to any qualified U.S. worker.

24. DECLARATIONS

DECLARATION OF EMPLOYER ➤ Pursuant to 28 U.S.C. 1746, I declare under penalty of perjury the foregoing is true and correct.

SIGNATURE	DATE

NAME (Type or Print)	TITLE

AUTHORIZATION OF AGENT OF EMPLOYER ➤ I HEREBY DESIGNATE the agent below to represent me for the purposes of labor certification and I TAKE FULL RESPONSIBILITY for accuracy of any representations made by my agent.

SIGNATURE OF EMPLOYER	DATE

NAME OF AGENT (Type or Print)	ADDRESS OF AGENT (Number, Street, City, State, ZIP code)

PART B. STATEMENT OF QUALIFICATIONS OF ALIEN

FOR ADVICE CONCERNING REQUIREMENTS FOR ALIEN EMPLOYMENT CERTIFICATION: If alien is in the U.S., contact nearest office of Immigration and Naturalization Service. If alien is outside U.S., contact nearest U.S. Consulate.

IMPORTANT: READ ATTACHED INSTRUCTIONS BEFORE COMPLETING THIS FORM.

Print legibly in ink or use a typewriter. If you need more space to fully answer any questions on this form, use a separate sheet. Identify each answer with the number of the corresponding question. Sign and date each sheet.

1. Name of Alien (Family name in capital letters)	First name	Middle name	Maiden name

2. Present Address (No., Street, City or Town, State or Province and ZIP code)	Country	3. Type of Visa (If in U.S.)

4. Alien's Birthdate (Month, Day, Year)	5. Birthplace (City or Town, State or Province)	Country	6. Present Nationality or Citizenship (Country)

7. Address in United States Where Alien Will Reside

8. Name and Address of Prospective Employer if Alien has job offer in U.S.	9. Occupation in which Alien is Seeking Work

10. "X" the appropriate box below and furnish the information required for the box marked

		City in Foreign Country	Foreign Country
a. ☐	Alien will apply for a visa abroad at the American Consulate in ⟶		
b. ☐	Alien is in the United States and will apply for adjustment of status to that of a lawful permanent resident in the office of the Immigration and Naturalization Service at ⟶	City	State

11. Names and Addresses of Schools, Colleges and Universities Attended (Include trade or vocational training facilities)	Field of Study	FROM Month	FROM Year	TO Month	TO Year	Degrees or Certificates Received

SPECIAL QUALIFICATIONS AND SKILLS

12. Additional Qualifications and Skills Alien Possesses and Proficiency in the use of Tools, Machines or Equipment Which Would Help Establish if Alien Meets Requirements for Occupation in Item 9.

13. List Licenses (Professional, journeyman, etc.)

14. List Documents Attached Which are Submitted as Evidence that Alien Possesses the Education, Training, Experience, and Abilities Represented

Endorsements	DATE REC. DOL
(Make no entry in this section - FOR Government Agency USE ONLY)	O.T. & C.

(Items continued on next page)

15. WORK EXPERIENCE. List all jobs held during the last three (3) years. Also, list any other jobs related to the occupation for which the alien is seeking certification as indicated in item 9.

a. NAME AND ADDRESS OF EMPLOYER

NAME OF JOB	DATE STARTED Month	Year	DATE LEFT Month	Year	KIND OF BUSINESS

DESCRIBE IN DETAIL THE DUTIES PERFORMED, INCLUDING THE USE OF TOOLS, MACHINES OR EQUIPMENT	NO. OF HOURS PER WEEK

b. NAME AND ADDRESS OF EMPLOYER

NAME OF JOB	DATE STARTED Month	Year	DATE LEFT Month	Year	KIND OF BUSINESS

DESCRIBE IN DETAIL THE DUTIES PERFORMED, INCLUDING THE USE OF TOOLS, MACHINES OR EQUIPMENT	NO. OF HOURS PER WEEK

c. NAME AND ADDRESS OF EMPLOYER

NAME OF JOB	DATE STARTED Month	Year	DATE LEFT Month	Year	KIND OF BUSINESS

DESCRIBE IN DETAIL THE DUTIES PERFORMED, INCLUDING THE USE OF TOOLS, MACHINES OR EQUIPMENT	NO. OF HOURS PER WEEK

16. DECLARATIONS

DECLARATION OF ALIEN ➤ ➤ Pursuant to 28 U.S.C. 1746, I declare under penalty of perjury the foregoing is true and correct.

SIGNATURE OF ALIEN	DATE

AUTHORIZATION OF AGENT OF ALIEN ➤ ➤ I hereby designate the agent below to represent me for the purposes of labor certification and I take full responsibility for accuracy of any representations made by my agent.

SIGNATURE OF ALIEN	DATE

NAME OF AGENT (Type or print)	ADDRESS OF AGENT (No., Street, City, State, ZIP code)

U.S. Department of Justice
Immigration and Naturalization Service

OMB No.1115-0061

Immigrant Petition for Alien Worker

START HERE - Please Type or Print

FOR INS USE ONLY

Receipt

Part 1.   Information about the person or organization filing this petition.

If an individual is filing, use the top name line. Organizations should use the second line.

Family Name	Given Name	Middle Initial

Company or Organization

Address - Attn:

Street Number and Name		Room
City	State or Province	
Country	Zip/Postal Code	

E-mail Address:

IRS Tax #	Social Security # (if any)

Part 2.   Petition type.

1. This petition is being filed for (check one)

a. ☐ An alien of extraordinary ability

b. ☐ An outstanding professor or researcher

c. ☐ A multinational executive or manager

d. ☐ A member of the professions holding an advanced degree or an alien of exceptional ability (who is**NOT** seeking a National Interest Waiver.)

e. ☐ A skilled worker (requiring at least two years of specialized training or experience) or professional (Item F- no longer available)

g. ☐ Any other worker (requiring less than two years of training or experience)

i. ☐ An alien applying for a national interest waiver (who **IS**   a member of the professions holding an advanced degree or an alien of exceptional ability)

Classification

☐ 203 (b)(1)(A) Alien of Extraordinary Ability

☐ 203 (b)(1)(B) Outstanding Professor or Researcher

☐ 203 (b)(1)(C) Multi-national executive or manager

☐ 203 (b)(2) Member of professional w/adv. degree or of exceptional ability

☐ 203 (b)(3)(A)(i) Skilled Worker

☐ 203 (b)(3)(A)(ii) Professional

☐ 203 (b)(3)(A)(iii) Other worker

Certification

☐ National Interest Waiver (NIW)

☐ Schedule A, Group I

☐ Schedule A, Group II

Priority Date	Consulate

Remarks

Action Block

Part 3.   Information about the person you are filing for.

Family Name	Given Name	Middle Initial

Address - C/O

Street # and Name		Apt. #
City	State or Province	
Country	Zip/Postal Code	

E-mail Address:

Date of Birth (Month/Day/Year) / /	Country of Birth
Social Security # (if any)	A# (if any)

If in the U.S.	Date of Arrival (Month/Day/Year)	I-94#
	Current Nonimmigrant Status	Expires on (Month/Day/Year)

Form I-140 (Rev. 12/04/01)N

Part 4. Processing Information.

Please complete the following for the person named in Part 3: (Check one)

☐ Alien will apply for a visa abroad at the American
   Consulate in: City: _____   Foreign Country: _____

☐ Alien is in the United States and will apply for adjustment of status to that of lawful permanent resident.

Alien's Country of Nationality: _____

Alien's country of current residence or, if now in the U.S., last permanent residence abroad: _____

If you provided a U.S. address in Part 3, print the person's foreign address: _____

If the person's native alphabet is other than Roman letters, write the person's foreign name and address in the native alphabet:

Are you filing any other petitions or applications with this one?	☐ No	☐ Yes-attach an explanation
Is the person you are filing for in removal proceedings?	☐ No	☐ Yes-attach an explanation
Has any immigrant visa petition ever been filed by or on behalf of this person?	☐ No	☐ Yes-attach an explanation

If you answered yes to any of these questions, please provide the case number, office location, date of decision and disposition of the decision on a separate piece of paper.

Part 5. Additional information about the petitioner.

Type of petitioner (Check one)

☐ Employer   ☐ Self   ☐ Other (Explain, e.g., Permanent Resident, U.S. Citizen or any other person filing on behalf of the alien.)

If a company, give the following: Type of business		NAICS Code:						
Date Established	Current # of employees	Gross Annual Income	Net Annual Income					
If a individual, give the following: Occupation		Annual Income						

PART 6. Basic information about the proposed employment.

Job title		SOC Code						
Nontechnical description of job								

Address where the person will work if different from address in Part 1.

Is this a full-time position?:	☐ Yes	☐ No (hours per week _____)	Wages per week $
Is this a permanent position?:	☐ Yes ☐ No	Is this a new position? ☐ Yes ☐ No	

Part 7. Information on the spouse and all children of the person you are filing for.

List husband/wife and all children related to the individual for whom the petition is being filed.   Provide an attachment of additional family members, if needed.

(Name)	(Relationship)	(Date of Birth)	(Country of Birth)

Part 8. Signature.

Read the information on penalties in the instructions before completing this section. If someone helped you prepare this petition, he or she must complete Part 9.

I certify, under penalty of perjury under the laws of the United States of America, that this petition and the evidence submitted with it are all true and correct. I authorize the release of any information from my records which the Immigration and Naturalization Service needs to determine eligibility for the benefit I are seeking.

Petitioner's Signature	Print Name	Date	Daytime Telephone No.

E-mail Address:

Please Note: *If you do not completely fill out this form or fail to submit required documents listed in the instructions, you may not be found eligible for the requested benefit and this petition may be denied*

Part 9. Signature of person preparing form, if other than above. *(Sign below)*

I declare that I prepared this petition at the request of the above person and it is based on all information of which I have knowledge.

Signature	Print Name	Date	Daytime Telephone No.

Firm's Name
and Address

E-mail Address:

To Be Completed by *Attorney or Representative, if any.*

☐ Fill in box if G-28 is attached to represent the petitioner.

VOLAG No.   ATTY State License No.

Attorney or Representative Signature:

Note: In the event of a Request for Evidence (RFE) may the INS contact you by Fax or E-mail: ☐ Yes   ☐ No

Fax Number: E-mail Address:

U.S. Department of Justice
Immigration and Naturalization Service

OMB No. 1115-0053
Form I-485, Application to Register Permanent Residence or Adjust Status

START HERE - Please Type or Print

Part 1. Information about you.

Family Name	Given Name	Middle Initial

Address - C/O

Street Number and Name		Apt. #

City

State	Zip Code

Date of Birth (month/day/year) / /	Country of Birth
Social Security #	A # (if any)
Date of Last Arrival (month/day/year)	I-94 #
Current INS Status	Expires on (month/day/year)

Part 2. Application Type.   *(Check one)*

I am applying for adjustment to permanent resident status because

a. ☐ an immigrant petition giving me an immediately available immigrant visa number has been approved. (Attach a copy of the approval notice-- or a relative, special immigrant juvenile, or special immigrant military visa petition filed with this application that will give you an immediately available visa number, if approved.)

b. ☐ My spouse or parent applied for adjustment of status or was granted lawful permanent residence in an immigrant visa category that allows derivative status for spouses and children.

c. ☐ I entered as a K-1 fiance(e) of a U.S. citizen whom I married within 90 days of entry, or I am the K-2 child of such a fiance(e) [Attach a copy of the fiance(e) petition approval notice and the marriage certificate.]

d. ☐ I was granted asylum or derivative asylum status as the spouse or child of a person granted asylum and am eligible for adjustment.

e. ☐ I am a native or citizen of Cuba admitted or paroled into the U.S. after January 1, 1959, and thereafter have been physically present in the U.S. for at least one year.

f. ☐ I am the husband, wife, or minor unmarried child of a Cuban described in (e) and am residing with that person, and was admitted or paroled into the U.S. after January 1, 1959, and thereafter have been physically present in the U.S. for at least on year.

g. ☐ I have continuously resided in the U.S. since before January 1, 1972.

h. ☐ Other basis of eligibility. Explain. (If additional space is needed, use a separate piece of paper.)

_____

I am already a permanent resident and am applying to have the date I was granted permanent residence adjusted to the date I originally arrived in the U.S. as a nonimmigrant or parolee, or as of May 2, 1964, whichever date is later, and: *(Check one)*

i. ☐ I am a native or citizen of Cuba and meet the description in (e), above.

j. ☐ I am the husband, wife or minor unmarried child of a Cuban, and meet the description in (f), above.

Continued on back.

Form I-485 (Rev. 02/07/00)N Page 1

Part 3. Processing Information

A. City/Town/Village of Birth	Current occupation
Your mother's first name	Your father's first name

Give your name exactly how it appears on your Arrival/Departure Record (Form I-94)

Place of last entry into the U.S. (City/State)	In what status did you last enter? *(Visitor, Student, exchange alien, crewman, temporary worker, without inspection, etc.)*
Were you inspected by a U.S. Immigration Officer? ☐ Yes ☐ No	
Nonimmigrant Visa Number	Consulate where Visa was issued
Date Visa was issued (month/day/year) Sex: ☐ Male ☐ Female	Marital Status ☐ Married ☐ Single ☐ Divorced ☐ Widowed

Have you ever before applied for permanent resident status in the U.S.?   ☐ No   ☐ Yes If you checked "Yes," give date and place of filing and final disposition.

B. List your present husband/wife, all of your sons and daughters (if you have none, write "none". If additional space is needed, use separate paper).

Family Name	Given Name	Middle Initial	Date of Birth (month/day/year)
Country of Birth	Relationship	A #	Applying with you? ☐ Yes ☐ No
Family Name	Given Name	Middle Initial	Date of Birth (month/day/year)
Country of Birth	Relationship	A #	Applying with you? ☐ Yes ☐ No
Family Name	Given Name	Middle Initial	Date of Birth (month/day/year)
Country of Birth	Relationship	A #	Applying with you? ☐ Yes ☐ No
Family Name	Given Name	Middle Initial	Date of Birth (month/day/year)
Country of Birth	Relationship	A #	Applying with you? ☐ Yes ☐ No
Family Name	Given Name	Middle Initial	Date of Birth (month/day/year)
Country of Birth	Relationship	A #	Applying with you? ☐ Yes ☐ No

C. List your present and past membership in or affiliation with every political organization, association, fund, foundation, party, club, society, or similar group in the United States or in other places since your 16th birthday. Include any foreign military service in this part. If none, write "none". Include the name(s) of organization(s), location(s), dates of membership from and to, and the nature of the organization(s). If additional space is needed, use a separate piece of paper.

Part 3. Processing Information   *(Continued)*

Please answer the following questions. (If your answer is "Yes" on any one of these questions, explain on a separate piece of paper. Answering "Yes" does not necessarily mean that you are not entitled to register for permanent residence or adjust status).

1. Have you ever, in or outside the U.S.:
    a. knowingly committed any crime of moral turpitude or a drug-related offense for which you have not been arrested? ☐ Yes ☐ No
    b. been arrested, cited, charged, indicted, fined, or imprisoned for breaking or violating any law or ordinance, excluding traffic violations? ☐ Yes ☐ No
    c. been the beneficiary of a pardon, amnesty, rehabilitation decree, other act of clemency or similar action? ☐ Yes ☐ No
    d. exercised diplomatic immunity to avoid prosecution for a criminal offense in the U.S.? ☐ Yes ☐ No

2. Have you received public assistance in the U.S. from any source, including the U.S. government or any state, county, city, or municipality (other than emergency medical treatment), or are you likely to receive public assistance in the future? ☐ Yes ☐ No

3. Have you ever:
    a. within the past 10 years been a prostitute or procured anyone for prostitution, or intend to engage in such activities in the future? ☐ Yes ☐ No
    b. engaged in any unlawful commercialized vice, including, but not limited to, illegal gambling? ☐ Yes ☐ No
    c. knowingly encouraged, induced, assisted, abetted or aided any alien to try to enter the U.S. illegally? ☐ Yes ☐ No
    d. illicitly trafficked in any controlled substance, or knowingly assisted, abetted or colluded in the illicit trafficking of any controlled substance? ☐ Yes ☐ No

4. Have you ever engaged in, conspired to engage in, or do you intend to engage in, or have you ever solicited membership or funds for, or have you through any means ever assisted or provided any type of material support to, any person or organization that has ever engaged or conspired to engage, in sabotage, kidnapping, political assassination, hijacking, or any other form of terrorist activity? ☐ Yes ☐ No

5. Do you intend to engage in the U.S. in:
    a. espionage? ☐ Yes ☐ No
    b. any activity a purpose of which is opposition to, or the control or overthrow of, the Government of the United States, by force, violence or other unlawful means? ☐ Yes ☐ No
    c. any activity to violate or evade any law prohibiting the export from the United States of goods, technology or sensitive information? ☐ Yes ☐ No

6. Have you ever been a member of, or in any way affiliated with, the Communist Party or any other totalitarian party? ☐ Yes ☐ No

7. Did you, during the period March 23, 1933 to May 8, 1945, in association with either the Nazi Government of Germany or any organization or government associated or allied with the Nazi Government of Germany, ever order, incite, assist or otherwise participate in the persecution of any person because of race, religion, national origin or political opinion? ☐ Yes ☐ No

8. Have you ever engaged in genocide, or otherwise ordered, incited, assisted or otherwise participated in the killing of any person because of race, religion, nationality, ethnic origin, or political opinion? ☐ Yes ☐ No

9. Have you ever been deported from the U.S., or removed from the U.S. at government expense, excluded within the past year, or are you now in exclusion or deportation proceedings? ☐ Yes ☐ No

10. Are you under a final order of civil penalty for violating section 274C of the Immigration Act for use of fraudulent documents or have you, by fraud or willful misrepresentation of a material fact, ever sought to procure, or procured, a visa, other documentation, entry into the U.S., or any other immigration benefit? ☐ Yes ☐ No

11. Have you ever left the U.S. to avoid being drafted into the U.S. Armed Forces? ☐ Yes ☐ No

12. Have you ever been a J nonimmigrant exchange visitor who was subject to the two-year foreign residence requirement and not yet complied with that requirement or obtained a waiver? ☐ Yes ☐ No

13. Are you now withholding custody of a U.S. Citizen child outside the U.S. from a person granted custody of the child? ☐ Yes ☐ No

14. Do you plan to practice polygamy in the U.S.? ☐ Yes ☐ No

Part 4. Signature. *(Read the information on penalties in the instructions before completing this section. You must file this application while in the United States.)*

I certify, under penalty of perjury under the laws of the United States of America, that this application and the evidence submitted with it is all true and correct. I authorize the release of any information from my records which the INS needs to determine eligibility for the benefit I am seeking.

Selective Service Registration. The following applies to you if you are a man at least 18 years old, but not yet 26 years old, who is required to register with the Selective Service System: I understand that my filing this adjustment of status application with the Immigration and Naturalization Service authorizes the INS to provide certain registration information to the Selective Service System in accordance with the Military Selective Service Act. Upon INS acceptance of my application, I authorize INS to transmit to the Selective Service System my name, current address, Social Security number, date of birth and the date I filed the application for the purpose of recording my Selective Service registration as of the filing date. If, however, the INS does not accept my application, I further understand that, if so required, I am responsible for registering with the Selective Service by other means, provided I have not yet reached age 26.

Signature	Print Your Name	Date	Daytime Phone Number

Please Note: If you do not completely fill out this form, or fail to submit required documents listed in the instructions, you may not be found eligible for the requested document and this application may be denied.

Part 5. Signature of person preparing form if other than above. *(Sign Below)*

I declare that I prepared this application at the request of the above person and it is based on all information of which I have knowledge.

Signature	Print Your Name	Date	Daytime Phone Number

Firm Name and Address

U.S. Department of Justice
Immigration and Naturalization Service

OMB #1115-0081

Immigrant Petition by Alien Entrepreneur

START HERE - Please Type or Print

Part 1.   Information about you.

Family Name	Given Name	Middle Initial

Address - In Care of:

Street # and Name		Apt #

City or town	State or Province

Country	Zip or Postal Code

Date of Birth (Month/Day/Year)	Country of Birth

Social Security #	A#

If in the U.S	Date of Arrival (Month/Day/Year)	I-94#
	Current Nonimmigrant Status	Expires on (Month/Day/Year)

Part 2.   Application type (Check one).

a. ☐ This petition is based on an investment in a commercial enterprise in a targeted employment area for which the required amount of capital invested has been adjusted downward.

b. ☐ This petition is based on an investment in a commercial enterprise in an area for which the required amount of capital invested has been adjusted upward.

c. ☐ This petition is based on an investment in a commercial enterprise which is not in either a targeted area or in an upward adjustment area.

Part 3.   Information about your investment.

Name of Commercial Enterprise Invested In

Street Address

Phone #	Business Organized as (Corporation, partnership, etc ...)

Kind of Business
(Example: Furniture Manufacturer)

Date established (Month/Day/Year)	IRS Tax #
Date of your initial investment (Month/Day/Year)	Amount of your initial investment
Your total capital investment in enterprise to date $	Percentage of enterprise you own

If you are not the sole investor in the new commercial enterprise, list on separate paper the names of all other parties (natural and non-natural) who hold a percentage share of ownership of the new enterprise and indicate whether any of these parties is seeking classifications as an alien entrepreneur. Include the name, percentage of ownership and whether or not the person is seeking classification under section 203(b)(5).

If you indicated in Part 2 that the enterprise was in a targeted employment area or in an upward adjustment area, give the location at right.   County   State

_____ _____

Continued on back.

FOR INS USE ONLY

Returned	Receipt
————	
Resubmitted	
————	
Reloc Sent	
————	
Reloc Rec'd	
————	

☐ Applicant Interviewed

Action Block

To Be Completed by
Attorney or Representative, if any
☐ Fill in box if G-28 is attached to represent the applicant

VOLAG#

ATTY State License #

Form I-526 (Rev. 11/30/01)Y Page 1

Part 4. Additional information about the enterprise.

Type of enterprise *(check one):*

- [ ] new commercial enterprise resulting from the creation of a new business.
- [ ] new commercial enterprise resulting from the purchase of an existing business.
- [ ] new commercial enterprise resulting from a capital investment in an existing business.

Assets:

Total amount in U.S. bank account	$ _____
Total value of all assets purchased for use in the enterprise	$ _____
Total value of all property transferred from abroad to the new enterprise	$ _____
Total of all debt financing	$ _____
Total stock purchases	$ _____
Other (explain on separate paper)	$ _____
Total	$ _____

Income:

When you made investment	Gross $ _____	Net	$ _____
Now	Gross $ _____	Net	$ _____

Net worth When you made investment $ _____   Now $ _____

Part 5. Employment creation information.

Number of full-time employees In Enterprise in U.S. (excluding you, spouse, sons and daughters)

When you made your initial investment _____   Now _____   Difference _____

How many of these new jobs were created by your investment? _____   How many additional now jobs will be created by your additional investment? _____

What is your position, office or title with the new commercial enterprise?

_____

Briefly describe your duties, activities and responsibilities.

_____

_____

Your Salary _____   Cost of Benefits _____

Part 6. Processing information.

Check One:

- [ ] The person named in Part 3 is now in the U.S. and an application to adjust status to permanent resident will be filed if this petition is approved.
- [ ] If the petition is approved, and the person named in Part 3 wishes to apply for an immigrant visa abroad, complete the following for that person:

Country of Nationality : _____

Country of current residence or , if now in the U.S., last permanent residence abroad: _____

If you provided a U.S. address in Part 3, print the person's foreign address: _____

If the person's native alphabet is other than Roman letters, write the foreign address in the native alphabet:

Is an application for adjustment of status attached to this petition?	[ ] Yes		[ ] No
Are you in exclusion or deportation proceedings?	[ ] Yes (If yes, explain on separate paper)		[ ] No
Have you ever worked in the U.S. without permission?	[ ] Yes (Explain on separate paper)		[ ] No

Part 7. Signature. *Read the information on penalties in the instrucitons before completing this section.*

I certify under penalty of perjury under the laws of the United States of America that this petition, and the evidence submitted with it, is all true and correct. I authorize the release of any information from my records which the Immigration and Naturalization Service needs to determine eligibility for the benefit I am seeking.

Signature _____   Date _____

Please Note: *If you do not completely fill out this form, or fail to submit required documents listed in the instructions, you may not be found eligible for the requested document and this application may be denied.*

Part 8. Signature of person preparing form, if other than above. (Sign below)

I declare that I prepared this application at the request of the above person and it is based on all information of which I have knowledge.

Signature _____   Print Your Name _____   Date _____

Firm Name and Address _____

United States Information Agency
EXCHANGE VISITOR PROGRAM SERVICES, GC/V
CERTIFICATE OF ELIGIBILITY FOR EXCHANGE VISITOR (J-1) STATUS

( ) Male
( ) Female

THE PURPOSE OF THIS FORM IS TO:

1. _____
   (FAMILY NAME OF EXCHANGE VISITOR)   (FIRST NAME)   (MIDDLE NAME)

born _____ _____ _____
   (Mo) (Day) (Yr)   (City)   (Country)

a citizen of _____ _____ a legal permanent resident of _____
                        (Country)   (Code)

_____ _____ whose position in that country is _____
           (Country)   (Code)

_____
                              (Pos. Code)

U.S. address

1 ( ) Begin a new program ( ) Accompanied by
       _____ immediate family members

2 ( ) Extend an on-going program.

3 ( ) Transfer to a different program.

4 ( ) Replace a lost IAP-66 form;
       amend a previous IAP-66 form.

5 ( ) Permit visitor's immediate family
       (____ members) to enter U.S. separately

6 ( ) Reinstatement request to USIA.

2. Will be sponsored by_____
   _____to participate in Exchange Visitor Program No. _____ _____ _____ which is still valid and is officially described as follows.

3. This form covers the period from ____ ____ ____ to ____ ____ ____ Exchange Visitor are permitted to travel abroad & maintain status (e.g. obtain a new visa) under duration of the program as indicated by the dates on this form.

4. The category of this visitor is 1( ) Student, 2( ) Trainee, 3 ( ) Teacher, 4 ( ) Professor, 5 ( ) International Visitor, 6 ( ) Alien Physician, 7 ( ) Government Visitor, 8 ( ) Research Scholar, 9 ( ) Short-Term Scholar, 10 ( ) Specialist, 11 ( ) Camp Counselor. The specific field of study, research, training or professional activity is_____verbally described as follows:
   (Subj/Field Code)

   12 ( ) Summer Travel/Work

5. During the period covered by this for, the total estimated financial support (in U.S. $) is to be provided to the exchange visitor by:

   a. ( ) The Program Sponsor in item 2 above $ _____

   This Program Sponsor has ☐ has not ☐ (check one) received funding for international exchange from one or more U.S. Government Agency(ies) to support this exchange visitor. If any U.S. Government Agency(ies) provided funding, indicate the Agency(ies) by code below.

   Financial support from organizations other than the sponsor will be provided by one or more of the following:

   b1.( ) U.S. Government Agency(ies) _____ (Agency Code). $ _____ ; b2._____ (Agency Code). $ _____
   c1.( ) International Organization(s) _____ (Int. Org. Code).$ _____ ; c2._____ (Int. Org. Code). $ _____
   d. ( ) The Exchange Visitor's Government $ _____
   e. ( ) The binational Commission of the visitor's Country $ _____   (If necessary, use above spaces
   f. ( ) All other organizations providing support $ _____   for funding by multiple U.S.
   g. ( ) Personal funds $ _____   Agencies or Intl. Organizations)

6. I.N.S. OR U.S.I.A USE

7. _____
   (Name of Official Preparing Form)   (Title)

   _____
   (Address)

   _____
   (Signature of Responsible Officer or Alternate R.O)   (Date)

PRELIMINARY ENDORSEMENT OF CONSULAR OR IMMIGRATION OFFICER REGARDING SECTION 212 (e) OF THE I.N.S.

1. (Name) _____
   (Title) _____

have determined that this alien in the above program.

1. ( ) is not subject to the two year residence requirement
2. ( ) is subject based on - A ( ) government financing and/or
                            B ( ) the Exchange visitor skills list and/or
                            C ( ) PL-94 484 as amended

_____ _____
(Signature of Officer)   (Date)
The United States information Agency reserves the right to make the final determination

8. STATEMENT OF RESPONSIBLE OFFICER FOR RELEASING SPONSOR (FOR TRANSFER OF PROGRAM)

Date _____ Transfer of this exchange visitor from program No._____ sponsored by _____ to the program specified in item (2) is necessarily or highly desirable and is in conformity with the objectives of the Mutual Educational and Cultural Exchange Act of 1961.

_____
(Signature of Officer)   (Date)

IAP-66 (1-97)

Application for Waiver of the Foreign Residence Requirement of Section 212(e) of the Immigration and Nationality Act, as amended

U. S. Department of Justice
Immigration and Naturalization Service

This application must be typewritten or printed legibly in black ink with block letters.

Fee Stamp

1. Name (Last in CAPS)	First	Middle	If you are a married woman, give your maiden

2. Mailing Address (Apt. No.)	(Number and Street)	(Town or City)	(State or Province)	(Country)	(Zip Code, if in U.S.)
Present or last U.S. residence	(Number and Street)	(City)	(State)		(ZIP Code)

3. Date of Birth	Country of Birth	Country of Nationality	Country of Last Foreign Residence

Alien Registration Number, If Known

4. I believe I am subject to the foreign residence requirements because: (Check appropriate box(es))

A. ☐ I participated in an exchange program which was financed by an agency of the U.S. Government or the government of the country of my nationality or last foreign residence for the purpose of promoting international educational, and cultural exchange.

B. ☐ An agency of the Government of the U.S. or the government of the country of my nationality or last foreign residence gave me a grant (such as a Fullbright grant), stipend or allowance for the purpose of participation in an exchange program. Name of U.S. Government agency or foreign country _____.

C. ☐ I became an exchange visitor after the Secretary of State designated the country of my nationality or last foreign residence as clearly requiring the services of persons with my specialized knowledge or skill.

D. ☐ I entered the United States as, or my status was changed to that of, an exchange visitor on or after January 10, 1977 to participate in graduate medical education or training.

5. I am applying for waiver of the foreign residence requirement on the ground that: (Check appropriate box(es))

A. ☐ My departure from the United States would impose exceptional hardship on my United States citizen or lawful permanent resident spouse or child.

B. ☐ I cannot return to the country of my nationality or last foreign residence because I would be subject to persecution on account of race, religion or political opinion.

IMPORTANT: If you have checked "A" under number 5, you must attach to this application a statement dated and signed by you giving a *detailed explanation* of the basis for your belief that compliance by you with the two-year foreign residence requirement of Section 212(e) of the Immigration and Nationality Act, as amended, would impose exceptional hardship on your spouse or child who is a citizen of the United States or a lawful permanent resident thereof. Without such statement your application is incomplete. You must include in the statement all pertinent information concerning the income and savings of yourself and your spouse. There should also be attached such documentary evidence as may be available to support the allegations of hardship.

If you have checked "B" under number 5, you must attach a statement dated and signed by you setting forth in detail the reason(s) you believe that you cannot return to the country of your nationality or last foreign residence because you would be subject to persecution on account of race, religion or political opinion. There should also be attached such documentary evidence as may be available to support the allegations of persecution.

6. If married, check appropriate box(es): (See Instruction No. 4)

A. ☐ My spouse is included in this application.   B. ☐ My spouse is filing a separate application for waiver.

RECEIVED	TRANS. IN	RET'D TRANS. OUT	COMPLETED

7. List all program numbers and names of *all* program sponsors.

8. Major field of activity (*Check one*)

☐ (1) Agriculture	☐ (4) Engineering	☐ (7) Natural And Physical Sciences
☐ (2) Business Administration	☐ (5) Humanities	☐ (8) Social Sciences
☐ (3) Education	☐ (6) Medicine	☐ (9) Other

9. Occupation

10. Date and port of last arrival in the United States as participant in a designated exchange program.

---

11. If you are now abroad, give date of departure from U.S.

12. Number of prior marriages of applicant _____

If married, number of prior marriages of applicant's spouse _____

13. Name of spouse	Date and Country of birth	Nationality	Country of last foreign residence

14. Names of children	Date and Country of birth	Nationality	Country of last foreign residence

---

15. If you checked "A" under number 5 on page 1 of this form, furnish the following information concerning your spouse or one of your children who is a citizen of the United States and who you believe would suffer exceptional hardship if you resided outside the United States for 2 years following your departure from this country.

If United States citizenship of spouse or child was acquired through naturalization, give the following:

Name of United States citizen spouse or child:	United States citizenship of spouse or child was acquired through (*check one*)
	☐ Birth in the United States ☐ Naturalization ☐ Parent(s)

Number of naturalization certificate	Date of naturalization	Place of naturalization

If United States citizenship of spouse or child was acquired through parent(s), has spouse or child obtained a certificate of citizenship?

If so, give number of certificate _____ If not, submit evidence in accordance with instruction 6(a) (2).

---

16. If you checked "A" under number 5 on page 1 of this form, and you do not have a spouse or child who is a citizen of the United States, furnish the following information concerning your spouse or one of your children who is a lawful permanent resident of the United States and who you believe would suffer exceptional hardship if you resided outside the United States for two years following your departure from this country.

Name of lawful resident alien spouse or child:	Alien Registration Number

Date, place and means of admission for lawful permanent residence:

I certify under penalty of perjury under the laws of the United States of America that the foregoing is true and correct.

Executed on _____ _____ _____
                    (Date)   (Place)   (Signature of applicant)

Signature of person preparing form, if other than applicant: I declare that this document was prepared by me at the request of the applicant and is based on all information of which I have any knowledge:

_____
(Signature)

_____ _____ _____
(Address of person preparing form, if other than applicant)   (Date)   (Occupation)

U.S. Department of State

NONIMMIGRANT VISA APPLICATION

Approved OMB 1405-0018
Expires 08/31/2004
Estimated Burden 1 hour
See Page 2

PLEASE TYPE OR PRINT YOUR ANSWERS IN THE SPACE PROVIDED BELOW EACH ITEM

DO NOT WRITE IN THIS SPACE

B-1/B-2 MAX	B-1 MAX	B-2 MAX

1. SURNAMES *(As in Passport)*

OTHER _____ MAX

Visa Classification

2. FIRST AND MIDDLE NAMES *(As in Passport)*

MULT OR _____

Number of Applications

3. OTHER SURNAMES USED *(Maiden, Religious, Professional, Aliases)*

MONTHS _____

Validity

4. OTHER FIRST AND MIDDLE NAMES USED

ISSUED/REFUSED

ON _____ BY _____

5. DATE OF BIRTH *(mm-dd-yyyy)*   6. PASSPORT NUMBER

UNDER SEC.   214(b)   221(g)

OTHER _____ INA

7. PLACE OF BIRTH

Country   City   State/Province

REFUSAL REVIEWED BY _____

8. NATIONALITY   9. SEX
☐ Male
☐ Female
10. NATIONAL IDENTIFICATION NUMBER

11. MARITAL STATUS
☐ Married   ☐ Single (Never Married)   ☐ Widowed   ☐ Divorced   ☐ Separated

12. HOME ADDRESS *(Include apartment number, street, city, state or province, postal zone, and country)*

13. HOME TELEPHONE NUMBER   14. E-MAIL ADDRESS

15. PRESENT OCCUPATION *(If retired, write "retired")*

25. DO YOU INTEND TO WORK IN THE U.S.?
☐ YES ☐ NO
If YES, give name and complete address of U.S. employer.

16. NAME AND STREET ADDRESS OF PRESENT EMPLOYER OR SCHOOL
(Postal box number unacceptable)

17. BUSINESS TELEPHONE NUMBER   18. BUSINESS FAX NUMBER

26. DO YOU INTEND TO STUDY IN THE U.S.?
☐ YES ☐ NO
If YES, give name and complete address of school.

19. WHAT IS THE PURPOSE OF YOUR TRIP?

20. AT WHAT ADDRESS WILL YOU STAY IN THE U.S.?

27. HAVE YOU EVER BEEN IN THE U.S.?
☐ YES ☐ NO
WHEN? _____

21. WHEN DO YOU INTEND TO ARRIVE IN THE U.S.?

FOR HOW LONG? _____

22. HOW LONG DO YOU INTEND TO STAY IN THE U.S.?

DO NOT WRITE IN THIS SPACE

23. WHO WILL PAY FOR YOUR TRIP?

37 mm x 37 mm

PHOTO

24. NAMES AND RELATIONSHIPS OF PERSONS TRAVELING WITH YOU
(NOTE: A separate application for a visa must be made for each traveler, regardless of age.)

staple or glue photo here

DS-156
08-2001

PREVIOUS EDITIONS OBSOLETE

Page 1 of 2

28. HAVE YOU EVER BEEN ISSUED A U.S. VISA?

☐ YES ☐ NO

WHEN? _____

WHERE? _____

WHAT TYPE OF VISA? _____

29. HAVE YOU EVER BEEN REFUSED A U.S. VISA?

☐ YES ☐ NO

WHEN? _____

WHERE? _____

WHAT TYPE OF VISA? _____

30. HAS YOUR U.S. VISA EVER BEEN CANCELLED OR REVOKED?

☐ YES ☐ NO

WHEN? _____

WHERE? _____

31. HAS ANYONE EVER FILED AN IMMIGRANT VISA PETITION ON YOUR BEHALF?

☐ YES ☐ NO

32. ARE ANY OF THE FOLLOWING PERSONS IN THE U.S., OR DO THEY HAVE U.S. LEGAL PERMANENT RESIDENCE OR U.S. CITIZENSHIP?
Mark YES or NO and indicate that person's status in the U.S. *(i.e., U.S. legal permanent resident. U.S. citizen, visiting, studying, working, etc.).*

☐ YES ☐ NO Husband/ Wife _____   ☐ YES ☐ NO Fiance/ Fiancee _____   ☐ YES ☐ NO

☐ YES ☐ NO Father/ Mother _____   ☐ YES ☐ NO Son/ Daughter _____   Brother/ Sister _____

33. IMPORTANT: ALL APPLICANTS MUST READ AND CHECK THE APPROPRIATE BOX FOR EACH ITEM.

A visa may not be issued to persons who are within specific categories defined by law as inadmissible to the United States *(except when a waiver is obtained in advance)*. Is any of the following applicable to you?

- Have you ever been arrested or convicted for any offense or crime, even though subject of a pardon, amnesty or other similar legal action? Have you ever unlawfully distributed or sold a controlled substance (drug), or been a prostitute or procurer for prostitutes? ☐ YES ☐ NO

- Have you ever been refused admission to the U.S., or been the subject of a deportation hearing, or sought to obtain or assist others to obtain a visa, entry into the U.S., or any other U.S. immigration benefit by fraud or willful misrepresentation or other unlawful means? Have you attended a U.S. public elementary school on student (F) status or a public secondary school after November 30, 1996 without reimbursing the school? ☐ YES ☐ NO

- Do you seek to enter the United States to engage in export control violations, subversive or terrorist activities, or any other unlawful purpose? Are you a member or representative of a terrorist organization as currently designated by the U.S. Secretary of State? Have you ever participated in persecutions directed by the Nazi government of Germany; or have you ever participated in genocide? ☐ YES ☐ NO

- Have you ever violated the terms of a U.S. visa, or been unlawfully present in, or deported from, the United States? ☐ YES ☐ NO

- Have you ever withheld custody of a U.S. citizen child outside the United States from a person granted legal custody by a U.S. court, voted in the United States in violation of any law or regulation, or renounced U.S. citizenship for the purpose of avoiding taxation? ☐ YES ☐ NO

- Have you ever been afflicted with a communicable disease of public health significance or a dangerous physical or mental disorder, or ever been a drug abuser or addict? ☐ YES ☐ NO

A YES answer does not automatically signify ineligibility for a visa, but if you answered YES to any of the above, or if you have any questions about the above, a personal appearance at this office is recommended. If an appearance is not possible at this time, attach a statement of facts in your case to this application.

34. WAS THIS APPLICATION PREPARED BY ANOTHER PERSON ON YOUR BEHALF? ☐ YES ☐ NO

(If answer is YES, then have that person complete item 35.)

35. Application Prepared By: NAME: _____

ADDRESS: _____

Relationship to Applicant: _____

Signature of Person Preparing Form: _____ DATE *(mm-dd-yyyy)* _____

36. I certify that I have read and understood all the questions set forth in this application and the answers I have furnished on this form are true and correct to the best of my knowledge and belief. I understand that any false or misleading statement may result in the permanent refusal of a visa or denial of entry into the United States. I understand that possession of a visa does not automatically entitle the bearer to enter the United States of America upon arrival at a port of entry if he or she is found inadmissible.

APPLICANT'S SIGNATURE _____

DATE *(mm-dd-yyyy)* _____

U.S. Department of Justice
Immigration and Naturalization Service

Application to Extend/Change Nonimmigrant Status

START HERE - Please Type or Print

Part 1. Information about you.

Family Name	Given Name	Middle Initial

Address-
In Care of-

Street Number and Name		Apt. #

City	State	Zip Code	Daytime Phone#

Country of Birth	Country of Citizenship

Date of Birth / / (MM/DD/YYYY)	Social Security # (if any)	A# (if any)

Date of Last Arrival Into the U.S.	I-94#

Current Nonimmigrant Status	Expires on (MM/DD/YYYY)

Part 2. Application type. *(See instructions for fee.)*

1. I am applying for: *(Check one.)*
   a. ☐ An extension of stay in my current status
   b. ☐ A change of status. The new status I am requesting is: _____
   c. ☐ Other: *(Describe grounds of eligibility.)* _____
2. Number of people included in this application: *(Check one.)*
   a. ☐ I am the only applicant
   b. ☐ Members of my family are filing this application with me.

   The Total number of people included in this application is: _____
   (complete the supplement for each co-applicant)

Part 3. Processing Information.

1. I/We request that my/our current or requested status be extended until (MM/DD/YYYY):_____
2. Is this application based on an extension or change of status already granted to your spouse, child or parent?
   ☐ No ☐ Yes receipt # _____
3. Is this application based on a separate petition or application to give your spouse, child or parent an extension or change of status? ☐ No ☐ Yes, filed with this I-539.
   ☐ Yes, filed previously and pending with INS. INS receipt number:_____
4. If you answered "Yes" to Question 3, give the petitioner or applicant:

   _____

   If the application is pending with INS, also give the following information.

Office filed at _____	Filed on (MM/DD/YYYY)

Part 4. Additional Information.

1. For applicant #1, provide passport information:

   Country of Issuance

   Valid to: (MM/DD/YYYY)
   / /

2. Foreign Address: Street Number and Name _____ Apt# ___

City or Town	State or Province

Country	Zip/Postal Code

FOR INS USE ONLY

Returned	Receipt

Date

Resubmitted

Date

Reloc Sent

Date

Reloc Rec'd

Date

☐ Applicant Interviewed on

Date

☐ *Extension Granted to (Date):*
_____

Change of Status/Extension Granted
New Class: From *(Date):* _____
_____ To *(date):* _____

If denied:
☐ Still within period of stay
☐ S/D to: _____
☐ Place under docket control

Remarks:

Action Block

To be completed by
Attorney or Representative, **if any**

☐ Fill in box if G-28 is attached to represent represent the applicant

ATTY State License #

Form I-539 (Rev. 09/04/01)N - Prior Versions May be Used Until 12/31/2001

Part 4. Additional Information.

3. Answer the following questions. If you answer "YES" to any question, explain on separate sheet of paper.	Yes	No
a. Are you, or any other person included on the application, an applicant for an immigrant visa?		
b. Has an immigrant petition ever been filed for you or for any other person included in this application?		
c. Has a form I-485, Application to Register Permanent Residence or Adjust Status, ever been filed by you or by any other person included in this application?		
d. Have you, or any other person included in this application, ever been arrested or convicted of any criminal offense since last entering the U.S.?		
e. Have you, or any other person included in this application done anything that violated the terms of the nonimmigrant status you now hold?		
f. Are you, or any other person included in this application, now in removal proceedings?		
g. Have you, or any other person included in this application, been employed in the U.S. since last admitted or granted an extension or change of status?		

- If you answered "YES" to Question 3f, give the following information concerning the removal proceedings on the attached page entitled **"Part 4. Additional information. Page for answers to 3f and 3g."** Include the name of the person in removal proceedings and information on jurisdiction, date proceedings began and status of proceedings.

- If you answered "No" to question 3g, fully describe how you are supporting yourself on the attached page entitled **'Part 4. Additional information. Page for answers to 3f and 3g."** Include the source, amount and basis for any income.

- If you answered "Yes" to Question 3g, fully describe the employment on the attached page entitled **'Part 4. Additional information. Page for answers to 3f and 3g."** Include the name of the person employed, name and address of the employer, weekly income and whether the employment was specifically authorized by INS.

Part 5. Signature *(Read the information on penalties in the instruction before completing this section. You must file this application while in the United States.)*

I certify, under penalty of perjury under the laws of the United States of America, that this application and the evidence submitted with it, is all true and correct. I authorize the release of any information from my record which the Immigration and Naturalization Service needs to determine eligibility for the benefit I am seeking.

Signature	Print your name	Date

Please note: *If you do not completely fill out this form, or fail to submit required documents listed in the instructions, you may not be found eligible for the requested benefit and this application will have to be denied.*

Part 6. Signature of person preparing form if other than above. *(Sign below)*

I declare that I prepared this application at the request of the above person and it is based on all information of which I have knowledge.

Signature	Print your name	Date
Firm Name and Address	Daytime Phone Number *(Area Code and Number)*	
	Fax Number *(Area Code and Number)*	

(Please remember to enclose the mailing label with your application)

Part 4. Additional information. Page for answers to 3f and 3g.

If you answered "Yes" to Question 3f in Part 4 on page 3 of this form, give the following information concerning the removal proceedings. Include the name of the person in removal proceedings and information on jurisdiction, date proceedings began and status of proceedings.

If you answered "No" to Question 3g in Part 4 on page 3 of this form, fully describe how you are supporting yourself. Include the source, amount and basis for any income.

If you answered "Yes" to Question 3g in Part 4 on page 3 of this form, fully describe the employment. Include the name of the person employed, name and address of the employer, weekly income and whether the employment was specifically authorized by INS.

Supplement-1
Attach to Form I-539 when more than one person is included in the petition or application.
(List each person separately. Do not include the person you named on the form).

Family Name	Given Name	Middle Name	Date of Birth (MM/DD/YYYY)
Country of Birth	Country of Citizenship	Social Security # (if any)	A# (if any)
Date of Arrival (MM/DD/YYYY)		I-94#	
Current Nonimmigrant Status		Expires on (MM/DD/YYYY)	
Country where passport issued		Expiration Date (MM/DD/YYYY)	

Family Name	Given Name	Middle Name	Date of Birth (MM/DD/YYYY)
Country of Birth	Country of Citizenship	Social Security # (if any)	A# (if any)
Date of Arrival (MM/DD/YYYY)		I-94#	
Current Nonimmigrant Status		Expires on (MM/DD/YYYY)	
Country where passport issued		Expiration Date (MM/DD/YYYY)	

Family Name	Given Name	Middle Name	Date of Birth (MM/DD/YYYY)
Country of Birth	Country of Citizenship	Social Security # (if any)	A# (if any)
Date of Arrival (MM/DD/YYYY)		I-94#	
Current Nonimmigrant Status		Expires on (MM/DD/YYYY)	
Country where passport issued		Expiration Date (MM/DD/YYYY)	

Family Name	Given Name	Middle Name	Date of Birth (MM/DD/YYYY)
Country of Birth	Country of Citizenship	Social Security # (if any)	A# (if any)
Date of Arrival (MM/DD/YYYY)		I-94#	
Current Nonimmigrant Status		Expires on (MM/DD/YYYY)	
Country where passport issued		Expiration Date (MM/DD/YYYY)	

Family Name	Given Name	Middle Name	Date of Birth (MM/DD/YYYY)
Country of Birth	Country of Citizenship	Social Security # (if any)	A# (if any)
Date of Arrival (MM/DD/YYYY)		I-94#	
Current Nonimmigrant Status		Expires on (MM/DD/YYYY)	
Country where passport issued		Expiration Date (MM/DD/YYYY)	

If you need additional space, attach a separate sheet(s) of paper.

Place your name, A # if any, date of birth, form number and application date at the top of the sheet(s) of paper.

U.S. Department of Justice
Immigration and Naturalization Service

OMB No. 1115-0168
Petition for a Nonimmigrant Worker

START HERE - Please Type or Print.

Part 1. Information about the employer filing this petition.
is an individual, use the top name line. Organizations should use the second line.

Family Name	Given Name	Middle Initial

Company or Organization Name

Address - Attn:

Street Number and Name		Apt. #

City	State or Province	

Country	Zip/Postal Code

IRS Tax #

Part 2. Information about this Petition.
(See instructions to determine the fee)

1. **Requested Nonimmigrant classification:**
   (write classification symbol at right) _____

2. **Basis for Classification** *(check one)*
   a. ☐ New employment
   b. ☐ Continuation of previously approved employment without change
   c. ☐ Change in previously approved employment
   d. ☐ New concurrent employment

3. **Prior Petition.** If you checked other than "New Employment" in item 2 (above) give the most recent prior petition numbers for the worker(s): _____

4. **Requested Action:** *(check one)*
   a. ☐ Notify the office in Part 4 so the person(s) can obtain a visa or be admitted (NOTE: a petition is not required for an E-1, E-2, or R visa)
   b. ☐ Change the person(s) status and extend their stay since they are all now in the U.S. in another status (see instructions for limitations). This is available only where you check "New Employment" in item 2, above.
   c. ☐ Extend or amend the stay of the person(s) since they now hold this status.

   Total number of workers in petition:
   (See instructions for where more than one worker can be included.) _____

Part 3. Information about the person(s) you are filing for.
Complete the blocks below. Use the continuation sheet to name each person included in this petition.

If an entertainment group, give their group name.

Family Name	Given Name	Middle Initial

Date of Birth (Month/Day/Year) / /	Country of Birth	

Social Security #	A #

If in the United States, complete the following:

Date of Arrival (Month/Day/Year)	I-94 #

Current Nonimmigrant Status	Expires (Month/Day/Year)

Continued on back.

Form I-129 (Rev. 12/10/01)Y

FOR INS USE ONLY

Returned	Receipt
_____	
_____	

Resubmitted
_____
_____

Reloc Sent
_____
_____

Reloc Rec'd
_____
_____

Interviewed
☐ Petitioner
☐ Beneficiary

Class: _____
# of Workers: _____
Priority Number: _____
Validity Dates: From _____
To _____

☐ **Classification Approved**
☐ Consulate/POE/PFI Notified

At: _____
☐ Extension Granted
☐ COS/Extension Granted

Partial Approval (explain)

Action Block

To be Completed by Attorney or Representative, if any
☐ Fill in box if G-28 is attached to represent the applicant

VOLAG#

ATTY State License #

Part 4. Processing Information

a. If the person named in Part 3 is outside the U.S. or a requested extension of stay or change of status cannot be granted, give the U.S. consulate or inspection facility you want to be notified if this petition is approved.

Type of Office (check one):	☐ Consulate	☐ Pre-flight inspection	☐ Port of Entry
Office Address (City)			U.S. State or Foreign Country

Person's Foreign Address

b. Does each person in this petition have a valid passport?
    ☐ Not required to have passport   ☐ No - explain on separate paper   ☐ Yes

c. Are you filing any other petitions with this one?   ☐ No   ☐ Yes - How many? _____

d. Are applications for replacement/Initial I-94's being filed with this petition?   ☐ No   ☐ Yes - How many? _____

e. Are applications by dependents being filed with this petition?   ☐ No   ☐ Yes - How many? _____

f. Is any person in this petition in exclusion or deportation proceedings?   ☐ No   ☐ Yes - explain on separate paper

g. Have you ever filed an immigrant petition for any person in this petition?   ☐ No   ☐ Yes - explain on separate paper

h. If you indicated you were filing a new petition in Part 2, within the past 7 years has any person in this petition:

    1) ever been given the classification you are now requesting?   ☐ No   ☐ Yes - explain on separate paper

    2) ever been denied the classification you are now requesting?   ☐ No   ☐ Yes - explain on separate paper

i. If you are filing for an entertainment group, has any person in this petition not been with the group for at least 1 year?   ☐ No   ☐ Yes - explain on separate paper

Part 5. Basic Information about the proposed employment and employer. *Attach the supplement relating to the classification you are requesting.*

Job Title	Nontechnical Description of Job

Address where the person(s) will work if different from the address in Part 1.

Is this a full-time position? ☐ No - Hours per week ☐ Yes	Wages per week or per year
Other Compensation *(Explain)*	Value per week or per year	Dates of Intended employment From: To:
Type of Petitioner - *Check* ☐ U.S. citizen or permanent resident ☐ Organization ☐ Other - explain on separate paper		
Type of business		Year established
Current number of employees	Gross Annual Income	Net Annual Income

Part 6. Signature. *Read the information on penalties in the instructions before completing this section.*

I certify, under penalty of perjury under the laws of the United States of America, that this petition, and the evidence submitted with it, is all true and correct. If filing this on behalf of an organization, I certify that I am empowered to do so by that organization. If this petition is to extend a prior petition, I certify that the proposed employment is under the same terms and conditions as in the prior approved petition. I authorize the release of any information from my records, or from the petitioning organization's records, which the Immigration and Naturalization Service needs to determine eligibility for the benefit being sought.

Signature and title	Print Name	Date

Please note: If you do not completely fill out this form and the required supplement, or fail to submit required documents listed in the instructions, then the person(s) filed for may not be found eligible for the requested benefit, and this petition may be denied.

Part 7. Signature of person preparing form if other than above.

I declare that I prepared this application at the request of the above person and it is based on all information of which I have knowledge.

Signature	Print Name	Date

Firm Name
and Address

Application for Asylum and for Withholding of Removal

Start Here- Please Type or Print. USE BLACK INK. SEE THE SEPARATE INSTRUCTION PAMPHLET FOR INFORMATION ABOUT ELIGIBILITY AND HOW TO COMPLETE AND FILE THIS APPLICATION. (Note: There is NO filing fee for this application.)

Please check the box if you also want to apply for withholding of removal under the Convention Against Torture. ☐

PART A.I.   INFORMATION ABOUT YOU

1. Alien Registration Number(s)(A #'s) *(if any)*	2. Social Security No. *(if any)*

3. Complete Last Name	4. First Name	5. Middle Name

6. What other names have you used *(Include maiden name and aliases.)*

7. Residence in the U.S.	Telephone Number
C/O	
Street Number and Name	Apt. No.
City State	ZIP Code

8. Mailing Address in the U.S., if other than above	Telephone Number
Street Number and Name	Apt. No.
City State	ZIP Code

9. Sex ☐ Male ☐ Female   10. Marital Status: ☐ Single ☐ Married ☐ Divorced ☐ Widowed

11. Date of Birth *(Mo/Day/Yr)* / /	12. City and Country of Birth

13. Present Nationality *(Citizenship)*	14. Nationality at Birth	15. Race, Ethnic or Tribal Group	16. Religion

17.   *Check the box, a through c that applies:*   a. ☐ I have never been in immigration court proceedings.

b. ☐ I am now in immigration court proceedings.   c. ☐ I am **not** now in immigration court proceedings, but I have been in the past.

18. *Complete 18 a through c.*
a. When did you last leave your country? *(Mo/Day/Yr)* _____   b. What is your current I-94 Number, if any? _____

c. Please list each entry to the U.S. beginning with your most recent entry.
   List date (Mo/Day/Yr), and your status for each entry. (Attach additional sheets as needed)

Date _____	Place _____	Status _____	Date Status Expires _____
Date _____	Place _____	Status _____	
Date _____	Place _____	Status _____	
Date _____	Place _____	Status _____	

19. What country issued your last passport or travel document	20. Passport # Travel Document #	21. Expiration Date *(Mo/Day/Yr)* / /

22. What is your native language?	23. Are you fluent in English? ☐ Yes ☐ No	24. What other languages do you speak fluently?

FOR EOIR USE ONLY	FOR INS USE ONLY
	Action:
	Interview Date: _____
	Decision:
	__ Approval Date _____
	__ Denial Date: _____
	__ Referral Date: _____
	Asylum Officer ID# _____

Form I-589 (Rev. 10/18/01)N

PART A.II. INFORMATION ABOUT YOUR SPOUSE AND CHILDREN

Your Spouse   ☐ I am not married. (Skip to *Your Children,* below)

1. Alien Registration Number (A#) *(If Any)*	2. Passport/ID Card No. *(If any)*	3. Date of Birth *(Mo/Day/Yr)*	4. Social Security No. *(If any)*
5. Complete Last Name	6. First Name	7. Middle Name	8. Maiden Name
9. Date of Marriage *(Mo/Day/Yr)*	10. Place of Marriage	11. City and Country of Birth	

12. Nationality *(Citizenship)*	13. Race, Ethnic or Tribal Group	14. Sex ☐ Male ☐ Female

15. Is this person in the U.S.?   ☐ Yes *(Complete blocks 16 to 24)*   ☐ No *(Specify location)*

16. Place of last entry in U.S.?	17. Date of last entry in the U.S. *(Mo/Day/Yr)*	18. I-94 No. *(If any)*	19. Status when last admitted *(Visa type, if any)*
20. What is your spouse's current status?	21. What is the expiration date of his/her authorized stay, if any? *(Mo/Day/Yr)*	22. Is your spouse in immigration court proceedings? ☐ Yes ☐ No	23. If previously in the U.S., date of previous arrival *(Mo/Day/Yr)*

24. If in the U.S., is your spouse to be included in this application? *(Check the appropriate box.)*

☐ Yes *(Attach one (1) photograph of your spouse in the upper right hand corner of page 9 on the extra copy of the application submitted for this person.)*
☐ No

Your Children.   Please list **ALL** of your children, regardless of age, location, or marital status.

☐ I do not have any children *(Skip to Part A.III., **Information about Your Background.**)*
☐ I do have children. Total number of children _____

(Use Supplement A Form I-589 or attach additional pages and documentation if you have more than four (4) children.)

1. Alien Registration Number (A#) *(if any)*	2. Passport/ID Card No.*(If any)*	3. Marital Status *(Married Single, Divorced, Widowed)*	4. Social Security No. *(if any)*
5. Complete Last Name	6. First Name	7. Middle Name	8. Date of Birth *(Mo/Day/Yr)*

9. City and Country of Birth	10. Nationality *(Citizenship)*	11. Race, Ethnic or Tribal Group	12. Sex ☐ Male ☐ Female

13. Is this child in the U.S.?   ☐ Yes *(Complete Blocks 14 to 21)*   ☐ No *(Specify Location)*

14. Place of last entry in the U.S.?	15. Date of last entry in the U.S.? *(Mo/Day/Yr)*	16. I-94 No. *(If any)*	17. Status when last admitted *(Visa type, if any)*
18. What is your child's current status?	19. What is the expiration date of his/her authorized stay, if any? *(Mo/Day/Yr)*	20. Is your child in immigration court proceedings? ☐ Yes ☐ No	

21. If in the U.S., is this child to be included in this application?   *(Check the appropriate box.)*

☐ Yes *(Attach one (1) photograph of your child in the upper right hand corner of page 9 on the extra copy of the application submitted for this person)*
☐ No

PART A.II. INFORMATION ABOUT YOUR SPOUSE AND CHILDREN Continued

1. Alien Registration Number (A#) (if any)	2. Pass/ID Card No. (if any)	3. Marital Status (Married Single, Divorced, Widowed)	4. Social Security No. (if any)
5. Complete Last Name	6. First Name	7. Middle Name	8. Date of Birth (Mo/Day/Year)
9. City and Country of Birth	10. Nationality (Citizenship)	11. Race, Ethnic or Tribal Group	12. Sex ☐ Male ☐ Female

13. Is this child in the U.S.? ☐ Yes (Complete blocks 14 to 21)   ☐ No (Specify Location)

14. Place of last entry in the U.S.?	15. Date of last entry in the U.S.? (Mo/Day/Yr)	16. I-94 No. (If any)	17. Status when last admitted
18. What is your child's current status?	19. What is the expiration date of his/her authorized stay, (if any) (Mo/Day/Yr)	20. Is your child in immigration court proceedings? ☐ Yes ☐ No	

21. If in the U.S., is this child to be included in this application? (Check the appropriate box)

☐ Yes (Attach one (1) photograph of your child in the upper right hand corner of page 9 on the extra copy of the application submitted for this person.)
☐ No

1. Alien Registration Number (A#)(If any)	2. Passport/ID Card No. (If any)	3. Marital Status (Married, Single, Divorced, Widowed)	4. Social Security No.
5. Complete Last Name	6. First Name	7. Middle Name	8. Date of Birth (Mo/Day/Yr)
9. City and Country of Birth	10. Nationality (Citizenship)	11. Race, Ethnic or Tribal Group	12. Sex ☐ Male ☐ Female

13. Is this Child in the U.S.? ☐ Yes (Complete blocks 14 to 21)   ☐ No (Specify Location)

14. Place of last entry in the U.S.?	15. Date of last entry in the U.S.? (Mo/Day/Yr)	16. I-94 No. (If any)	17. Status when last admitted (Visa type, if any)
18. What is your child's current status?	19. What is the expiration date of his/her authorized stay, if any?	20. Is your child in immigration court proceedings? ☐ Yes ☐ No	

21. If in the U.S., is this child to be included in this application? (Check the appropriate box)

☐ Yes (Attach one (1) photograph of your child in the upper right hand corner of page 9 on the extra copy of the application submitted for this person.)
☐ No

1. Alien Registration Number (A#) (If any)	2. Passport/ID Card No. (If any)	3. Marital Status (Married Single, Divorced, Widowed)	4. Social Security No. (If any)
5. Complete Last Name	6. First Name	7. Middle Name	8. Date of Birth (Mo/Day/Yr)
9. City and Country of Birth	10. Nationality	11. Race, Ethnic or Tribal Group	12. Sex ☐ Male ☐ Female

13. Is the child in the U.S.? ☐ Yes (Complete blocks 14 to 21)   ☐ No (Specify Location)

14. Place of last entry in the U.S.?	15. Date of last entry in the U.S.? (Mo/Day/Yr)	16. I-94 No. (If any)	17. Status when last admitted (Visa type, if any)
18. What is your child's current status?	19. What is the expiration date of his/her authorized stay, if any?(Mo/Day/Yr)	20. Is your child in immigration court proceedings ☐ Yes ☐ No	

21. If in the U.S., is this child to be included in this application? (Check the appropriate box)

☐ Yes (Attach one (1) photograph of your child in the upper right hand corner of page 9 on the extra copy of the application submitted for this person.)
☐ No

PART A.III.   INFORMATION ABOUT YOUR BACKGROUND

1. Please list your last address where you lived before coming to the U.S. If this is not the country where your fear persecution, also list the last address in the country where you fear persecution. *(List Address, City/Town, Department, Province, or State, and Country.) (Use Supplement B Form I-589 or additional sheets of paper if necessary.)*

Number and Street *(Provide if available)*	City/Town	Department, Province or State	Country	Dates From *(Mo/Yr)* To *(Mo/Yr)*	

2. Provide the following information about our residences during the last five years. List your present address first. *(Use Supplement Form B or additional sheets of paper if necessary.)*

Number and Street	City/Town	Department, Province or State	Country	Dates From *(Mo/Yr)* To *(Mo/Yr)*	

3. Provide the following information about your education, beginning with the most recent. *(Use Supplement B Form I-589 or additional sheets of paper if necessary.)*

Name of School	Type of School	Location *(Address)*	Attended From *(Mo/Yr)* To *(Mo/Yr)*	

4. Provide the following information about your employment during the last five years. List your present employment first. *(Use Supplement Form B or additional sheets of paper if necessary.)*

Name and Address of Employer	Your Occupation	Dates From *(Mo/Yr)* To *(Mo/Yr)*	

5. Provide the following information about your parents and siblings (brother and sisters). Check box if the person is deceased *(Use Supplement B Form I-589 or additional sheets of paper if necessary.)*

Name	City/Town and Country of Birth	Current Location	
Mother		☐ Deceased	
Father		☐ Deceased	
Siblings		☐ Deceased	
		☐ Deceased	

PART B. INFORMATION ABOUT YOUR APPLICATION

(Use Supplement B Form I-589 or attach additional sheets of paper as needed to complete your responses to the questions contained in PART B.)

When answering the following questions about your asylum or other protection claim (withholding of removal under 241(b)(3) of the Act or withholding of removal under the Convention Against Torture) you should provide a detailed and specific account of the basis of your claim to asylum or other protection. To the best of your ability, provide specific dates, places, and descriptions about each event or action described. You should attach documents evidencing the general conditions in the country from which you are seeking asylum or other protection and the specific facts on which you are relying to support your claim. If this documentation is unavailable or you are not providing this documentation with your application, please explain why in your responses to the following questions. Refer to Instructions, Part 1: Filing Instructions, Section II, "Basis of Eligibility," Parts A-D, Section V, "Completing the Form," Part B, and Section VII, "Additional Documents the You Should Submit" or more information on completing this section of the form.

1. Why are you applying for asylum or withholding of removal under section 241(b)(3) of the Act, or for withholding of removal under the Convention Against Torture? Check the appropriate box(es) below and then provide detailed answers to questions A and B below.

    I am seeking asylum or withholding of removal based on

    ☐ Race
    ☐ Religion
    ☐ Nationality
    ☐ Political opinion
    ☐ Membership in a particular social group
    ☐ Torture Convention

    A. Have you, your family, or close friends or colleagues ever experienced harm or mistreatment or threats in the past by anyone?

    ☐ No ☐ Yes   If your answer is "Yes," explain in detail:

    1) What happened;
    2) When the harm or mistreatment or threats occurred;
    3) Who caused the harm or mistreatment or threats; and
    4) Why you believe the harm or mistreatment or threats occurred.

    B. Do you fear harm or mistreatment if you return to your home country?

    ☐ No ☐ Yes   If your answer is "Yes," explain in detail:

    1) What harm or mistreatment you fear;
    2) Who you believe would harm or mistreat you; and
    3) Why you believe you would be harmed or mistreated.

PART B. INFORMATION ABOUT YOUR APPLICATION Continued

2. Have you or your family members ever been charged, arrested, detained, interrogated, convicted and sentenced, or imprisoned in any country other than the United States?

☐ No ☐ Yes If "Yes," explain the circumstances and reasons for action.

3.A. Have you or your family members ever belonged to or been associated with any organizations or groups in your home country, such as, but not limited to, a political party, student group, labor union, religious organization, military or paramilitary group, civil patrol, guerrilla organization, ethnic group, human rights group, or the press or media?

☐ No ☐ Yes If "Yes," describe for each person the level of participation, any leadership or other positions held, and the length of time you or your family members were involved in each organization or activity.

B. Do you or your family members continue to participate in any way in these organizations or groups?

☐ No ☐ Yes If "Yes," describe for each person, you or your family members' current level of participation, any leadership or other positions currently held, and the length of time you or your members have been involved in each organization or group.

4. Are you afraid of being subjected to torture in your home country or any other country to which you may be returned?

☐ No ☐ Yes If "Yes," explain why you are afraid and describe the nature of the torture you fear, by whom, and why it would be inflicted.

PART C. ADDITIONAL INFORMATION ABOUT YOUR APPLICATION

(Use Supplement B Form I-589 or attach additional sheets of paper as needed to complete your responses to the questions contained in Part C.)

1. Have you, your spouse, your child(ren), your parents, or your siblings ever applied to the United States Government for refugee status, asylum, or withholding of removal? ☐ No ☐ Yes

    If "Yes" explain the decision and what happened to any status you, your spouse, your child(ren), your parents, or your siblings received as a result of that decision. Please indicate whether or not you were included in a parent or spouse's application. If so, please include your parent or spouse's A-number in your response. If you have been denied asylum by an Immigration Judge or the Board of Immigration Appeals, please describe any change(s) in conditions in your country or your own personal circumstances since the date of the denial that may affect your eligibility for asylum.

2. A.   After leaving the country from which you are claiming asylum, did you or your spouse or child(ren), who are now in the United States, travel through or reside in any other country before entering the United States? ☐ No ☐ Yes

    B.   Have you, your spouse, your child(ren), or other family members such as your parents or siblings ever applied for or received any lawful status in any country other than the one from which you are now claiming asylum? ☐ No ☐ Yes

    If "Yes" to either or both questions (2A and/or 2B), provide for each person the following: the name of each country and the length of stay; the person's status while there; the reasons for leaving; whether the person is entitled to return for lawful residence purposes; and whether the person applied for refugee status or for asylum while there, and, if not, why he or she did not do so.

3. Have you, your spouse, or child(ren) ever ordered, incited, assisted, or otherwise participated in causing harm or suffering to any person because of his or her race, religion, nationality, membership in a particular social group or belief in a particular political opinion?

    ☐ No   ☐ Yes If "Yes," describe in detail each such incident and your own or your spouse's or child(ren)'s involvement.

PART C.   ADDITIONAL INFORMATION ABOUT YOUR APPLICATION Continued

4. After you left the country where you were harmed or feared harm, did you return to that country?

☐ No   ☐ Yes   If "Yes," describe in detail the circumstances of your visit (for example, the date(s) of the trip(s), the purpose(s) of the trip(s), and the length of time you remained in that country for the visit(s)).

5. Are you filing the application more than one year after your last arrival in the United States?

☐ No   ☐ Yes   If "Yes," explain why you did not file within the first year after you arrived. You should be prepared to explain at your interview or hearing why you did not file your asylum application within the first year after you arrived. For guidance in answering this question, see Instructions, Part 1: Filing Instructions, Section V. "Completing the Form," Part C.

6. Have you or any member of your family included in the application ever committed any crime and/or been arrested, charged, convicted and sentenced for any crimes in the United States?

☐ No   ☐ Yes   If "Yes," for each instance, specify in your response what occurred and the circumstances; dates; length of sentence received; location; the duration of the detention or imprisonment; the reason(s) for the detention or conviction; any formal charges that were lodged against you or your relatives included in your application; the reason(s) for release. Attach documents referring to these incidents, if they are available, or an explanation of why documents are not available.

PART D.   YOUR SIGNATURE

After reading the information regarding penalties in the instructions, complete and sign below. If someone helped you prepare this application, he or she must complete Part E.

I certify, under penalty of perjury under the laws of the United States of America, that this application and the evidence submitted with it are all true and correct. Title 18, United States Code, Section 1546, provides in part; "Whoever knowingly makes under oath, or as permitted under penalty of perjury under section 1746 of Title 28, United States Code, knowingly subscribes as true, any false statement with respect to a material fact in any application, affidavit, or knowingly presents any such application, affidavit, or other document required by the immigration laws or regulations prescribed thereunder, or knowingly presents any such application, affidavit, or other document containing any such false statement or which fails to contain any reasonable basis in the law or fact - shall be fined in accordance with this title or imprisoned not more than five years, or both." I authorize the release of any information from my record which the Immigration and Naturalization Service needs to determine eligibility for the benefit I am seeking.

> Staple your photograph here or the photograph of the family member to be included on the extra copy of the application submitted for that person.

WARNING: Applicants who are in the United States illegally are subject to removal if their asylum or withholding claims are not granted by an Asylum Officer or an Immigration Judge. Any information provided in completing this application may be used as a basis for the institution of, or as evidence in, removal proceedings even if the application is later withdrawn. Applicants determined to have knowingly made a frivolous application for asylum will be permanently ineligible for any benefits under the Immigration and Nationality Act. See 208(d)(6) of the Act and 8 CFR 208.20.

Print Complete Name	Write your name in your native alphabet

Did your spouse, parent, or child(ren) assist you in completing this application?   ☐ No   ☐ Yes   *(If "Yes," list the name and relationship.)*

_____   _____   _____   _____
(Name)   *(Relationship)*   *(Name)*   *(Relationship)*

Did someone other than your spouse, parent, or child(ren) prepare this application?   ☐ No ☐ Yes *(If "Yes," complete Part E)*

Asylum applicants may be represented by counsel. Have you been provided with a list of persons who may be available to assist you, at little or no cost, with your asylum claim?   ☐ No   ☐ Yes

Signature of Applicant   *(The person in Part A.I.)*

[_____]   _____
Sign your name so it all appears within the brackets   Date *(Mo/Day/Yr)*

PART E.   DELCLARATION OF PERSON PREPARING FORM IF OTHER THAN APPLICANT, SPOUSE, PARENT OR CHILD

I declare that I have prepared this application at the request of the person named in Part D, that the responses provided are based on all information of which I have knowledge, or which was provided to me by the applicant and that the completed application was read to the applicant in his or her native language or a language he or she understands for verification before he or she signed the application in my presence. I am aware that the knowing placement of false information on the Form I-589 may also subject me to civil penalties under 8 U.S.C. 1324(c).

Signature of Preparer	Print Complete Name		
Daytime Telephone Number	Address of Preparer: Street Number and Name		
Apt. No.	City	State	ZIP Code

PART F.   TO BE COMPLETED AT INTERVIEW OR HEARING

You will be asked to complete this Part when you appear before an Asylum Officer of the Immigration and Naturalization Service (INS), or an Immigration Judge of the Executive Office for Immigration Review (EOIR) for examination.

I swear (affirm) that I know the contents of this application that I am signing, including the attached documents and supplements, that they are all true to the best of my knowledge taking into account correction(s) numbered _____ to _____ that were made by me or at my request

Signed and sworn to before me by the above named applicant on:

_____   _____
Signature of Applicant   Date *(Mo/Day/Yr)*

_____   _____
Write Your Name in Your Native Alphabet   Signature of Asylum Officer or Immigration Judge

1. List Name(s) and "A" Number(s) of all Respondent(s)/Applicant(s):

For Official Use Only

Staple Check or Money Order Here. Include Name(s) and "A" number(s) on the face of the check or money order.

! WARNING: Names and "A" Number of **everyone** appealing the Immigration Judge's decision must be written in item #1.

2. I am the ☐ Respondent/Applicant ☐ INS *(Mark only one box.)*

3. I am ☐ DETAINED ☐ NOT DETAINED *(Mark only one box.)*

4. My last hearing was at _____ *(Location, City, State)*

5. What decision are you appealing?

Mark only one box below. If you want to appeal more than one decision, you must use more than one Notice of Appeal (Form EOIR-26).

☐ I am filing an appeal from the Immigration Judge's decision *in **merits** proceedings* (example: removal, deportation, exclusion, asylum, etc.) dated _____ .

☐ I am filing an appeal from the Immigration Judge's decision *in **bond** proceedings* dated

_____ .

☐ I am filing an appeal from the Immigration Judge's decision ***denying a motion to reopen or a motion to reconsider*** dated _____ .

(Please attach a copy of the Immigration Judge's decision you are appealing.)

OMB# 1125-0002; Expires 12/31/02

Form EOIR-26
Revised Sept. 2002

6. | State in detail the reason(s) for this appeal. Please refer to the Instructions at part F for further guidance. You are not limited to the space provided below; use more sheets of paper if necessary. Write your name(s) and "A" number(s) on every sheet.

(Attach additional sheets if necessary)

! WARNING: You must clearly explain the specific facts and laws on which you base your appeal of the Immigration Judge's decision. The Board may summarily dismiss your appeal if it cannot tell from this Notice of Appeal, or any statements attached to this Notice of Appeal, why you are appealing.

7. Do you desire oral argument before the Board of Immigration Appeals? ❑ Yes ❑ No

8. Do you intend to file a separate written brief or statement after filing this Notice of Appeal? ❑ Yes ❑ No

! WARNING: If you mark "Yes" in item #8, you will be expected to file a written brief or statement after you receive a briefing schedule from the Board. The Board may summarily dismiss your appeal if you do not file a brief or statement within the time set in the briefing schedule.

9. | SIGN HERE ➡ | X _____   _____
Signature of Person Appealing   Date
(or attorney or representative)

Form EOIR-26
Revised Sept. 2002

Internet Version

10.

Mailing Address of Respondent(s)/Applicant(s)
_____
(Name)
_____
(Street Address)
_____
(Apartment or Room Number)
_____
(City, State, Zip Code)
_____
(Telephone Number)

11.

Mailing Address of Attorney or Representative for the Respondent(s)/Applicant(s)
_____
(Name)
_____
(Street Address)
_____
(Suite or Room Number)
_____
(City, State, Zip Code)
_____
(Telephone Number)

NOTE: You must notify the Board within five (5) working days if you move to a new address. You must use an alien's Change of Address Form (Form EOIR-33/BIA).

NOTE: If an attorney or representative signs this appeal for you, he or she must file *within this appeal*, a Notice of Entry of Appearance as Attorney or Representative Before the Board of Immigration Appeals (Form EOIR-27).

12.

PROOF OF SERVICE
(You Must Complete This)

I _____ mailed or delivered a copy of this Notice of Appeal
                           (Name)

on _____ to _____
            (Date)   (Opposing Party)

at _____
                    (Address of Opposing Party)

SIGN HERE ➡ X _____
                                    Signature

NOTE: If you are the Respondent or Applicant, the "Opposing Party" is the District Counsel for the INS.

NOTE: If you do not complete this section properly, your appeal will be rejected or dismissed.

WARNING: If you do not attach the fee or a completed Fee Waiver Request, (Form EOIR-26A) to this appeal, your appeal will be rejected or dismissed.

❑ Read all of the General Instructions
❑ Provided all of the requested information
❑ Completed this form in English
❑ Provided a certified English translation for all non-English attachments

HAVE YOU?

❑ Signed the form
❑ Served a copy of this form and all attachments on the opposing party
❑ Completed and signed the Proof of Service
❑ Attached the required fee or Fee Waiver Request

Form EOIR-26
Revised Sept. 2002

Internet Version

NOTICE OF ENTRY OF APPEARANCE AS ATTORNEY OR REPRESENTATIVE
BEFORE THE BOARD OF IMMIGRATION APPEALS
EXECUTIVE OFFICE FOR IMMIGRATION REVIEW

TYPE OF PROCEEDING:

[ ] Deportation   [ ] Bond Redetermination   [ ] Disciplinary

[ ] Removal   [ ] Motion to Reopen/Reconsider

[ ] Exclusion   [ ] Rescission

DATE

ALIEN NUMBER(S) (list lead alien number and all family member alien numbers if applicable)

I hereby enter my appearance as attorney or representative for, and at the request of, the following named person(s):

NAME   (First)   (Middle Initial)   (Last)

ADDRESS   (Number & Street)   (Apt. No.)   (City)   (State)   (Zip Code)

Please check one of the following:

[ ]   1.   I am a member in good standing of the bar of the highest court(s) of the following State(s), possession(s), Territory(ies), Commonwealth(s), or the District of Columbia:

Name(s) of Court(s)   *State Bar No. (if applicable)*

_____   _____

_____   _____

(Please use space on reverse side to list additional jurisdictions.)

I [ ] am not (or [ ] am - explain fully on reverse side) subject to any order of any court or administrative agency disbarring, suspending, enjoining, restraining, or otherwise restricting me in the practice of law and the courts listed above comprise all of the jurisdictions other than federal courts where I am licensed to practice law.

[ ]   2.   I am an accredited representative of the following qualified non-profit religious, charitable, social service, or similar organization established in the United States, so recognized by the Executive Office for Immigration Review (provide name of organization): _____

[ ]   3.   I am a law student or law graduate, reputable individual, accredited official, or other person authorized to represent individuals pursuant to 8 C.F.R. § 292. (Explain fully on reverse side.)

I have read and understand the statements provided on the reverse side of this form that set forth the regulations and conditions governing appearances and representation before the Board of Immigration Appeals. I declare under penalty of perjury under the laws of the United States of America that the foregoing is true and correct.

SIGNATURE OF ATTORNEY OR REPRESENTATIVE   EOIR ID#   TELEPHONE NUMBER (Include Area Code)   DATE

NAME OF ATTORNEY OR REPRESENTATIVE (TYPE OR PRINT)   ADDRESS   [ ] Check here if this is a new address.

Certificate of Service

I _____ mailed or delivered a copy of the foregoing on _____ to the Immigration
    (Name)   (Date)

and Naturalization Service at _____
                  (Address)

X _____
    Signature of Attorney or Representative

OMB#1125-0005

FORM EOIR-27
August 99

(Note: Alien may be required to sign Acknowledgement and Consent on reverse side of this form.)

I HEREBY ACKNOWLEDGE THAT THE ABOVE-NAMED ATTORNEY OR REPRESENTATIVE REPRESENTS ME IN THESE PROCEEDINGS AND I CONSENT TO DISCLOSURE TO HIM/HER OF ANY RECORDS PERTAINING TO ME WHICH APPEAR IN ANY EOIR SYSTEM OF RECORDS.

NAME OF PERSON CONSENTING	SIGNATURE OF PERSON CONSENTING	DATE

(NOTE: *The Privacy Act of 1974 requires that if the person being represented is or claims to be a citizen of the United States or an alien lawfully admitted for permanent residence, he/she must sign this form.*)

APPEARANCES - An appearance shall be filed on EOIR Form-27 by the attorney or representative appearing in each case before the Board of Immigration Appeals (see 8 C.F.R. § 3.38((g)), even though the attorney or representative may have appeared in the case before the Immigration Judge or the Immigration and Naturalization Service. When an appearence is made by a person acting in a representative capacity, his/her personal appearance or signature shall constitute a representation that, under the provisions of 8 C.F.R. Chapter 3, he/she is authorized and qualified to represent individuals. Thereafter, substitution or withdrawal may be permitted upon the approval of the Board of a request by the attorney or representative of record in accordance with Matter of Resales, 19 I&N Dec. 655 (1988). Further proof of authority to act in a representative capacity may be required.

REPRESENTATION - A person entitled to representation may be represented by any of the following:

(1) Attorneys in the United States as defined in 8 C.F.R. § 1.1(f).

(2) Law students and law graduates not yet admitted to the bar as defined in 8 C.F.R. § 292.1(a)(2).

(3) Reputable individuals as defined in 8 C.F.R. § 292.1(a)(3).

(4) Accredited representative as defined in 8 C.F.R. § 292.1(a)(4).

(5) Accredited officials as defined in 8 C.F.R. § 292.1(a)(5).

THIS FORM MAY NOT BE USED TO REQUEST RECORDS UNDER THE FREEDOM OF INFORMATION ACT OR THE PRIVACY ACT. THE MANNER OF REQUESTING SUCH RECORDS IS CONTAINED IN 28 C.F.R. §§ 16.1-16.11 AND APPENDICES.

Public reporting burden for the collection of information is estimated to average 6 minutes per response, including the time for reviewing the data needed, completing and reviewing the collection of information, and record-keeping. Send comments regarding this burden estimate or any other aspect of this information collection including suggestions for reviewing this burden to the Executive Office for Immigration Review, 5107 Leesburg Pike, Suite 2400, Falls Church, VA 22041.

(Please attach additional sheets of paper as necessary.)

*U.S. GPO: 2000-461-076/21608

OMB No. 1115-0066
BIOGRAPHIC INFORMATION

(Family name) (First name) (Middle name)	☐ MALE ☐ FEMALE	BIRTHDATE (Mo.-Day-Yr.)	NATIONALITY	FILE NUMBER A
ALL OTHER NAMES USED (Including names by previous marriages)		CITY AND COUNTRY OF BIRTH		SOCIAL SECURITY NO. (If any)

	FAMILY NAME	FIRST NAME	DATE, CITY AND COUNTRY OF BIRTH (If known)	CITY AND COUNTRY OF RESIDENCE.
FATHER				
MOTHER (Maiden name)				

HUSBAND (If none, so state) OR WIFE	FAMILY NAME (For wife, give maiden name)	FIRST NAME	BIRTHDATE	CITY & COUNTRY OF BIRTH	DATE OF MARRIAGE	PLACE OF MARRIAGE

FORMER HUSBANDS OR WIVES (if none, so state)

FAMILY NAME (For wife, give maiden name)	FIRST NAME	BIRTHDATE	DATE & PLACE OF MARRIAGE	DATE AND PLACE OF TERMINATION OF MARRIAGE

APPLICANT'S RESIDENCE LAST FIVE YEARS. LIST PRESENT ADDRESS FIRST.

STREET AND NUMBER	CITY	PROVINCE OR STATE	COUNTRY	FROM MONTH	FROM YEAR	TO MONTH	TO YEAR
						PRESENT TIME	

APPLICANT'S LAST ADDRESS OUTSIDE THE UNITED STATES OF MORE THAN ONE YEAR

STREET AND NUMBER	CITY	PROVINCE OR STATE	COUNTRY	FROM MONTH	FROM YEAR	TO MONTH	TO YEAR

APPLICANT'S EMPLOYMENT LAST FIVE YEARS. (IF NONE, SO STATE) LIST PRESENT EMPLOYMENT FIRST

FULL NAME AND ADDRESS OF EMPLOYER	OCCUPATION (SPECIFY)	FROM MONTH	FROM YEAR	TO MONTH	TO YEAR
				PRESENT TIME	

Show below last occupation abroad if not shown above. (Include all information requested above.)

THIS FORM IS SUBMITTED IN CONNECTION WITH APPLICATION FOR ☐ NATURALIZATION ☐ OTHER (SPECIFY): ☐ STATUS AS PERMANENT RESIDENT	SIGNATURE OF APPLICANT	DATE
Submit both copies of this form.	IF YOUR NATIVE ALPHABET IS IN OTHER THAN ROMAN LETTERS, WRITE YOUR NAME IN YOUR NATIVE ALPHABET IN THIS SPACE:	

PENALTIES: SEVERE PENALTIES ARE PROVIDED BY LAW FOR KNOWINGLY AND WILLFULLY FALSIFYING OR CONCEALING A MATERIAL FACT.

APPLICANT   BE SURE TO PUT YOUR NAME AND ALIEN REGISTRATION NUMBER IN THE BOX OUTLINED BY HEAVY BORDER BELOW.

COMPLETE THIS BOX (Family name)	(Given name)	(Middle name)	(Alien registration number)

Form G-325 (Rev. 09/11/00)Y

Do Not Write in This Block.

Remarks	Action Stamp	Fee Stamp
A#		

Applicant is filing under §274a.12 _____

☐ Application Approved. Employment Authorized / Extended *(Circle One)*   until _____ (Date).
_____ (Date).

Subject to the following conditions: _____

☐ Application Denied.
   ☐ Failed to establish eligibility under 8 CFR 274a.12 (a) or (c).
   ☐ Failed to establish economic necessity as required in 8 CFR 274a.12(c)(14), (18) and 8 CFR 214.2(f)

I am applying for:
   ☐ Permission to accept employment.
   ☐ Replacement *(of lost employment authorization document)*.
   ☐ Renewal of my permission to accept employment *(attach previous employment authorization document)*.

1. Name (Family Name in CAPS)　(First)　(Middle)

2. Other Names Used (Include Maiden Name)

3. Address in the United States (Number and Street)　(Apt. Number)

   (Town or City)　(State/Country)　(ZIP Code)

4. Country of Citizenship/Nationality

5. Place of Birth (Town or City)　(State/Province)　(Country)

6. Date of Birth　7. Sex ☐ Male ☐ Female

8. Marital Status ☐ Married ☐ Single ☐ Widowed ☐ Divorced

9. Social Security Number (Include all Numbers you have ever used) (if any)

10. Alien Registration Number (A-Number) or I-94 Number (if any)

11. Have you ever before applied for employment authorization from INS?
   ☐ Yes (If yes, complete below)　☐ No
   Which INS Office?　Date(s)

   Results (Granted or Denied - attach all documentation)

12. Date of Last Entry into the U.S. (Month/Day/Year)

13. Place of Last Entry into the U.S.

14. Manner of Last Entry (Visitor, Student, etc.)

15. Current Immigration Status (Visitor, Student, etc.)

16. Go to Part 2 of the Instructions, Eligibility Categories. In the space below, place the letter and number of the category you selected from the instructions (For example, (a)(8), (c)(17)(iii), etc.).

Eligibility under 8 CFR 274a.12

(   ) (   ) (   )

Certification.

Your Certification: I certify, under penalty of perjury under the laws of the United States of America, that the foregoing is true and correct. Furthermore, I authorize the release of any information which the Immigration and Naturalization Service needs to determine eligibility for the benefit I am seeking. I have read the Instructions in Part 2 and have identified the appropriate eligibility category in Block 16.

Signature　Telephone Number　Date

Signature of Person Preparing Form, If Other Than Above: I declare that this document was prepared by me at the request of the applicant and is based on all information of which I have any knowledge.

Print Name　Address　*Signature*　Date

Initial Receipt	Resubmitted	Relocated		Completed		
		Rec'd	Sent	Approved	Denied	Returned

(a)(3)--Refugee. File your EAD application with either a copy of your Form I-590, Registration for Classification as Refugee, approval letter or a copy of a Form I-730, Refugee/Asylee Relative Petition, approval notice.

(a)(4)--Paroled as a Refugee. File your EAD application with a copy of your Form I-94, Departure Record.

(a)(5)--Asylee, (granted asylum). File your EAD application with a copy of the INS letter granting you asylum. It is not necessary to apply for an EAD as an asylee until 90 days before the expiration of your current EAD.

(a)(6)--K-1 Nonimmigrant Fiancé(e) of U.S. Citizen or K-2 Dependent. File your EAD application if you are filing within 90 days from the date of entry. This EAD cannot be renewed. Any EAD application other than for a replacement must be based on your pending application for adjustment under (c)(9). FEE REQUIRED.

(a)(7)--N-8 or N-9 Nonimmigrant. File your EAD application with the required evidence listed in Part 3.

(a)(8)--Citizen of Micronesia or the Marshall Islands or Palau. File your EAD application if you were admitted to the United States as a citizen of the Federated States of Micronesia (CFA/FSM) or of the Marshall Islands (CFA/MIS) pursuant to agreements between the United States and the former trust territories.

(a)(10)--Granted Withholding of Deportation. File your EAD application with a copy of the Immigration Judge's order. It is not necessary to apply for a new EAD until 90 days before the expiration of your current EAD.

(a)(11)--Deferred Enforced Departure (DED)/Extended Voluntary Departure. File your EAD application with evidence of your identity and nationality.

(a)(12)--Temporary Protected Status (TPS). File your EAD application with Form I-821, Application for Temporary Protected Status. FEE REQUIRED.

(a)(13)--Family Unity Program. File your EAD application with a copy of the approval notice, if you have been granted status under this program. You may choose to file your EAD application concurrently with your Form I-817, Application for Voluntary Departure under the Family Unity Program. The INS may take up to 90 days from the date upon which you are granted status under the Family Unity Program to adjudicate your EAD application. If you were denied Family Unity status solely because your legalized spouse or parent first applied under the Legalization/SAW programs after May 5, 1988, file your EAD application with a new Form I-817 and a copy of the original denial. However, if your EAD application is based on continuing eligibility under (c)(12), please refer to Deportable Alien Granted Voluntary Departure. FEE REQUIRED.

(c)(1)--Dependent of A-1 or A-2 Foreign Government Officials. File your EAD application with a Form I-566, Application for Employment by Spouse or Unmarried Dependent Son or Daughter of A-1 or A-2 Official or Employee of Diplomatic or Consular Establishment or G-4 Officer or Employee of International Organization, with the Department of State endorsement.

(c)(2)--Dependent of CCNAA E-1 Nonimmigrant. File your EAD application with the required certification from the American Institute in Taiwan if you are the spouse, or unmarried child, of an E-1 employee of the Coordination Council for North American Affairs. FEE REQUIRED.

(c)(3)(i)--F-1 Student Seeking Optional Practical Training in an Occupation Directly Related to Studies. File your EAD application with a Certificate of Eligibility of Nonimmigrant (F-1) Student Status (Form I-20 A-B/I-20 ID) endorsed by a designated school official within the past 30 days. FEE REQUIRED.

(c)(3)(ii)--F-1 Student Offered Off-Campus Employment under the Sponsorship of a Qualifying International Organization. File your EAD application with the international organization's letter of certification that the proposed employment is within the scope of its sponsorship and a Certificate of Eligibility of Nonimmigrant (F-1) Student Status--For Academic and Language Students (Form I-20 A-B/I-20 ID) endorsed by the designated school official within the past 30 days. FEE REQUIRED.

(c)(3)(iii)--F-1 Student Seeking Off-Campus Employment Due to Severe Economic Hardship. File your EAD application with Form I-20 A-B/I-20 ID, Certificate of Eligibility of Nonimmigrant (F-1) Student Status--For Academic and Language Students; Form I-538, Certification by Designated School Official, and any evidence you wish to submit, such as affidavits, which detail the unforeseen economic circumstances that cause your request, and evidence you have tried to find off-campus employment with an employer who has filed a labor and wage attestation. FEE REQUIRED.

(c)(4)--Dependent of G-1, G-3 or G-4 Nonimmigrant. File your EAD application with a Form I-566, Application for Employment by Spouse or Unmarried Dependent Son or Daughter of A-1 or A-2 Official or Employee of Diplomatic or Consular Establishment or G-4 Officer or Employee of International Organization, with the Department of State endorsement if you are the dependent of a qualifying G-1, G-3 or G-4 officer of, representative to, or employee of an international organization and you hold a valid nonimmigrant status.

(c)(5)--J-2 Spouse or Minor Child of an Exchange Visitor. File your EAD application with a copy of your J-1's (principal alien's) Certificate of Eligibility for Exchange Visitor (J-1) Status (Form IAP-66). You must submit a written statement, with any supporting evidence showing, that your employment is not necessary to support the J-1 but is for other purposes. FEE REQUIRED.

(c)(6)--M-1 Student Seeking Practical Training after Completing Studies. File your EAD application with a completed Form I-538, Application by Nonimmigrant Student for Extension of Stay, School Transfer, or Permission to Accept or Continue Employment, Form I-20 M-N, Certificate of Eligibility for Nonimmigrant (M-1) Student Status--For Vocational Students endorsed by the designated school official within the past 30 days. FEE REQUIRED.

(c)(7)--Dependent of NATO Personnel. File your EAD application with a letter from the Department of Defense or NATO/SACLANT verifying your principal alien's status, your status, and your relationship to your principal alien. FEE REQUIRED.

(c)(8)--Asylum Applicant under the ABC Settlement Agreement. If you are an El Salvadoran or Guatemalan national eligible for benefits under the ABC settlement agreement, American Baptist Churches v. Thornburgh, 760 F. Supp. 796 (N.D. Cal. 1991), there are special instructions applicable to filing your Form I-765 which supplement these instructions. These instructions and the application can be obtained by asking for an "ABC packet" at your local INS office or by calling 1-800-755-0777.

(c)(9)--Adjustment Applicant. File your EAD application with a copy of the receipt notice or other evidence that your Form I-485, Application for Permanent Residence, is pending. You may file Form I-765 together with your Form I-485. FEE REQUIRED.

(c)(10)--Applicant for Suspension of Deportation. File your EAD application with evidence that your Form I-256A, Application for Suspension of Deportation, is pending. FEE REQUIRED.

(c)(ll)--Paroled in the Public Interest. File your EAD application if you were paroled into the United States for emergent reasons or reasons strictly in the public interest. FEE REQUIRED.

(c)(12)--Deportable Alien Granted Voluntary Departure. File your EAD application with a copy of the order or notice granting voluntary departure, and evidence establishing your economic need to work. FEE REQUIRED.

(c)(14)--Deferred Action. File your EAD application with a copy of the order, notice or document placing you in deferred action and evidence establishing economic necessity for an EAD. FEE REQUIRED.

(c)(16)--Adjustment Applicant Based on Continuous Residence Since January 1, 1972. File your EAD application with your Form I-485, Application for Permanent Residence; a copy of your receipt notice; or other evidence that the Form I-485 is pending. FEE REQUIRED.

(c)(17)(i)--B-1 Nonimmigrant who is the personal or domestic servant of a nonimmigrant employer. File your EAD application with:
· Evidence from your employer that he or she is a B, E, F, H, I, J, L, M, O, P, R or TN nonimmigrant and you were employed for at least one year by the employer before the employer entered the United States or your employer regularly employs personal and domestic servants and has done so for a period of years before coming to the United States; and
· Evidence that you have either worked for this employer as a personal or domestic servant for at least one year or, evidence that you have at least one year's experience as a personal or domestic servant; and
· Evidence establishing that you have a residence abroad which you have no intention of abandoning. FEE REQUIRED.

(c)(17)(ii)--B-1 Nonimmigrant Domestic Servant of a U.S. Citizen. File your EAD application with:
· Evidence from your employer that he or she is a U.S. Citizen; and
· Evidence that your employer has a permanent home abroad or is stationed outside the United States and is temporarily visiting the United States or the citizen's current assignment in the United States will not be longer than four (4) years; and
· Evidence that he or she has employed you as a domestic servant abroad for at least six (6) months prior to your admission to the United States. FEE REQUIRED.

(c)(17)(iii)--B-1 Nonimmigrant Employed by a Foreign Airline. File your EAD application with a letter, from the airline, fully describing your duties and indicating that your position would entitle you to E nonimmigrant status except for the fact that you are not a national of the same country as the airline or because there is no treaty of commerce and navigation in effect between the United States and that country. FEE REQUIRED.

(c)(18)--Final Order of Deportation. File your EAD application with a copy of the order of supervision and a request for employment authorization which may be based on, but not limited to the following:
· Existence of economic necessity to be employed;
· Existence of a dependent spouse and/or children in the United States who rely on you for support; and
· Anticipated length of time before you can be removed from the United States. FEE REQUIRED.

(c)(l9)--Applying for Temporary Protected Status (TPS)/Temporary Treatment Benefits. File your EAD application with your TPS application, Form I-821. If you are using this application to register for TPS and do not want to work in the United States, you must submit a letter indicating this application is for registration purposes only. No fee is required to register. FEE REQUIRED.

Print clearly or type your answers using **CAPITAL** letters. Failure to print clearly may delay your application. Use black or blue ink.

Part 1. Your Name *(The Person Applying for Naturalization)*

Write your INS "A"- number here:

A _ _ _ _ _ _ _ _ _

FOR INS USE ONLY

A. Your current legal name.

Family Name *(Last Name)*

Given Name *(First Name)*   Full Middle Name   *(If applicable)*

Bar Code	Date Stamp

B. Your name <u>exactly</u> as it appears on your Permanent Resident Card.

Family Name *(Last Name)*

Given Name *(First Name)*   Full Middle Name   *(If applicable)*

Remarks

C. If you have ever used other names, provide them below.

Family Name *(Last Name)*	Given Name *(First Name)*	Middle Name

D. Name change *(optional)*

Please read the Instructions before you decide whether to change your name.

1. Would you like to legally change your name? ☐ Yes ☐ No
2. If "Yes," print the new name you would like to use. Do not use initials or abbreviation when writing your new name.

Family Name *(Last Name)*

Given Name *(First Name)*   Full Middle Name

Action

Part 2. Information About Your Eligibility   *(Check Only One)*

I am at least 18 years old **AND**

A. ☐ I have been a Lawful Permanent Resident of the United States for at least 5 years.

B. ☐ I have been a Lawful Permanent Resident of the United States for at least 3 years, AND I have been married to and living with the same U.S. citizen for the last 3 years AND my spouse has been a U.S. citizen for the last 3 years.

C. ☐ I am applying on the basis of qualifying military service.

D. ☐ Other *(Please explain)* _____

A. Social Security Number

[_____]

B. Date of Birth *(Month/Day/Year)*

_/_/_____

C. Date You Became a Permanent Resident   *(Month/Day/Year)*

_ _ _ _ _ _ _

D. Country of Birth

[_____]

E. Country of Nationality

[_____]

F. Are either of your parents U.S. citizens? *(if yes, see Instructions)*   ☐ Yes   ☐ No

G. What is your current marital status?   ☐ Single, Never Married   ☐ Married   ☐ Divorced   ☐ Widowed

☐ Marriage Annulled or Other *(Explain)* _____

H. Are you requesting a waiver of the English and/or U.S. History and Government requirements based on a disability or impairment and attaching a Form N-648 with your application?   ☐ Yes   ☐ No

I. Are you requesting an accommodation to the naturalization process because of a disability or impairment? *(See Instructions for some examples of accommodations.)*   ☐ Yes   ☐ No

If you answered "Yes", check the box below that applies:

☐ I am deaf or hearing impaired and need a sign language interpreter who users the following language: _____

☐ I use a wheelchair.

☐ I am blind or sight impaired.

☐ I will need another type of accommodation. Please explain: _____

_____

_____

Part 4. Addresses and Telephone Numbers

A. Home Address - Street Number and Name *(Do NOT write a P.O. Box in this space)*

[_____]   Apartment Number [_____]

City	County	State	ZIP Code	Country

B. Care of

[_____]   Mail Address - Street Number and Name *(If different from home address)*   [_____]   Apartment Number [_____]

City	State	ZIP Code	Country

C. Daytime Phone Number *(If any)*

[_____]

Evening Phone Number *(If any)*

[_____]

E-mail Address *(If any)*

[_____]

Note: The categories below are those required by the FBI. See Instructions for more information.

A. Gender

☐ Male ☐ Female

B. Height

| Feet | Inches |

C. Weight

| | Pounds |

D. Race

☐ White ☐ Asian or Pacific Islander ☐ Black ☐ American Indian or Alaskan Native ☐ Unknown

E. Hair color

☐ Black ☐ Brown ☐ Blonde ☐ Gray ☐ White ☐ Red ☐ Sandy ☐ Bald (No Hair)

F. Eye color

☐ Brown ☐ Blue ☐ Green ☐ Hazel ☐ Gray ☐ Black ☐ Pink ☐ Maroon ☐ Other

Part 6. Information About Your Residence and Employment

A. Where have you lived during the last 5 years? Begin with where you live now and then list every place you lived for the last 5 years. If you need more space, use a separate sheet of paper.

Street Number and Name, Apartment Number, City, State, Zip Code and Country	Dates *(Month/Year)*	
	From	To
Current Home Address - Same as Part 4.A	__ __ __ __ __ __	Present
	__ __ __ __ __ __	__ __ __ __ __ __
	__ __ __ __ __ __	__ __ __ __ __ __
	__ __ __ __ __ __	__ __ __ __ __ __
	__ __ __ __ __ __	__ __ __ __ __ __

B. Where have you worked (or, if you were a student, what schools did you attend) during the last 5 years? Include military service. Begin with your current or latest employer and then list every place you have worked or studied for the last 5 years. If you need more space, use a separate sheet of paper.

Employer or School Name	Employer or School Address *(Street, City and State)*	Dates *(Month/Year)*		Your Occupation
		From	To	
		__ __ __ __ __ __	__ __ __ __ __ __	
		__ __ __ __ __ __	__ __ __ __ __ __	
		__ __ __ __ __ __	__ __ __ __ __ __	
		__ __ __ __ __ __	__ __ __ __ __ __	
		__ __ __ __ __ __	__ __ __ __ __ __	

Part 7. Time Outside the United States	Write your INS "A"- number here:
(Including Trips to Canada, Mexico, and the Caribbean Islands)	A _ _ _ _ _ _ _ _ _ _ _

A. How many total days did you spend outside of the United States during the past 5 years? ☐ days

B. How many trips of 24 hours or more have you taken outside of the United States during the past 5 years? ☐ trips

C. List below all the trips of 24 hours or more that you have taken outside of the United States since becoming a Lawful Permanent Resident. Begin with your most recent trip. If you need more space, use a separate sheet of paper.

Date You Left the United States (Month/Day/Year)	Date You Returned to the United States (Month/Day/Year)	Did Trip Last 6 Months or More?	Countries to Which You Traveled	Total Days Out of the United States
_ _ _ _ _ _ _	_ _ _ _ _ _ _	☐ Yes ☐ No		
_ _ _ _ _ _ _	_ _ _ _ _ _ _	☐ Yes ☐ No		
_ _ _ _ _ _ _	_ _ _ _ _ _ _	☐ Yes ☐ No		
_ _ _ _ _ _ _	_ _ _ _ _ _ _	☐ Yes ☐ No		
_ _ _ _ _ _ _	_ _ _ _ _ _ _	☐ Yes ☐ No		
_ _ _ _ _ _ _	_ _ _ _ _ _ _	☐ Yes ☐ No		
_ _ _ _ _ _ _	_ _ _ _ _ _ _	☐ Yes ☐ No		
_ _ _ _ _ _ _	_ _ _ _ _ _ _	☐ Yes ☐ No		
_ _ _ _ _ _ _	_ _ _ _ _ _ _	☐ Yes ☐ No		
_ _ _ _ _ _ _	_ _ _ _ _ _ _	☐ Yes ☐ No		

Part 8. Information About Your Marital History

A. How many times have you been married (including annulled marriages)? ☐ If you have NEVER been married, go to Part 9.

B. If you are married, give the following information about your spouse:

1. Spouse's Family Name *(Last Name)* Given Name *(First Name)* Full Middle Name *(If applicable)*

2. Date of Birth *(Month/Day/Year)* 3. Date of Marriage *(Month/Day/Year)* 4. Spouse's Social Security Number

5 Home Address - Street Number and Name Apartment Number

City State ZIP Code

Form N-400 (Rev. 05/31/01)N Page 4

Write your INS "A"- number here:

A ___ ___ ___ ___ ___ ___ ___ ___

C. Is your spouse a U.S. citizen? ☐ Yes ☐ No

D. If your spouse is a U.S. citizen, give the following information:

   1. When did your spouse become a U.S. citizen? ☐ At Birth ☐ Other

   If "Other," give the following information:

   2. Date your spouse became a U.S. citizen

   ___ ___ ___ ___ ___ ___ ___ ___

   3. Place your spouse became a U.S. citizen *(Please see Instructions)*

                           City and State

E. If your spouse is NOT a U.S. citizen, give the following information:

   1. Spouse's Country of Citizenship

   2. Spouse's INS "A"- Number *(If applicable)*

   A ___ ___ ___ ___ ___ ___ ___ ___

   3. Spouse's Immigration Status

   ☐ Lawful Permanent Resident ☐ Other _____

F. If you were married before, provide the following information about your prior spouse. If you have more than one previous marriage, use a separate sheet of paper to provide the information requested in questions 1-5 below.

   1. Prior Spouse's Family Name *(Last Name)* | Given Name *(First Name)* | Full Middle Name *(If applicable)*

   2. Prior Spouse's Immigration Status

   ☐ U.S. Citizen

   ☐ Lawful Permanent Resident

   ☐ Other _____

   3. Date of Marriage *(Month/Day/Year)*

   ___ ___ ___ ___ ___ ___ ___ ___

   4. Date Marriage Ended *(Month/Day/Year)*

   ___ ___ ___ ___ ___ ___ ___ ___

   5. How Marriage Ended

   ☐ Divorce ☐ Spouse Died ☐ Other _____

G. How many times has your current spouse been married (including annulled marriages)? ☐

   If your spouse has EVER been married before, give the following information about your spouse's prior marriage.
   If your spouse has more than one previous marriage, use a separate sheet of paper to provide the information requested in questions 1 - 5 below.

   1. Prior Spouse's Family Name *(Last Name)* | Given Name *(First Name)* | Full Middle Name *(If applicable)*

   2. Prior Spouse's Immigration Status

   ☐ U.S. Citizen

   ☐ Lawful Permanent Resident

   ☐ Other _____

   3. Date of Marriage *(Month/Day/Year)*

   ___ ___ ___ ___ ___ ___ ___ ___

   4. Date Marriage Ended *(Month/Day/Year)*

   ___ ___ ___ ___ ___ ___ ___ ___

   5. How Marriage End

   ☐ Divorce ☐ Spouse Died ☐ Other _____

Write your INS "A"- number here:

A _ _ _ _ _ _ _ _ _

A. How many sons and daughters have you had? For more information on which sons and daughters you should include and how to complete this section, see the Instructions.

B. Provide the following information about all of your sons and daughters. If you need more space, use a separate sheet of paper.

Full name of Son or Daughter	Date of Birth (Month/Day/Year)	INS "A"- number (if child has one)	Country of Birth	Current Address (Street, City, State & Country)
	_ _ _ _ _ _ _	A _ _ _ _ _ _ _ _		
	_ _ _ _ _ _ _	A _ _ _ _ _ _ _ _		
	_ _ _ _ _ _ _	A _ _ _ _ _ _ _ _		
	_ _ _ _ _ _ _	A _ _ _ _ _ _ _ _		
	_ _ _ _ _ _ _	A _ _ _ _ _ _ _ _		
	_ _ _ _ _ _ _	A _ _ _ _ _ _ _ _		
	_ _ _ _ _ _ _	A _ _ _ _ _ _ _ _		
	_ _ _ _ _ _ _	A _ _ _ _ _ _ _ _		

Part 10. Additional Questions

Please answer questions 1 through 14. If you answer "Yes" to any of these questions, include a written explanation with this form. Your written explanation should (1) explain why your answer was "Yes," and (2) provide any additional information that helps to explain your answer.

A. General Questions

1. Have you **EVER** claimed to be a U.S. citizen *(in writing or any other way)?* ☐ Yes ☐ No

2. Have you **EVER** registered to vote in any Federal, state, or local election in the United States? ☐ Yes ☐ No

3. Have you **EVER** voted in any Federal, state, or local election in the United States? ☐ Yes ☐ No

4. Since becoming a Lawful Permanent Resident, have you **EVER** failed to file a required Federal, state, or local tax return? ☐ Yes ☐ No

5. Do you owe any Federal, state, or local taxes that are overdue? ☐ Yes ☐ No

6. Do you have any title of nobility in any foreign country? ☐ Yes ☐ No

7. Have you ever been declared legally incompetent or been confined to a mental institution within the last 5 years? ☐ Yes ☐ No

B. Affiliations

8. a. Have you **EVER** been a member of or associated with any organization, association, fund, foundation, party, club, society, or similar group in the United States or in any other place? ☐ Yes ☐ No

b. If you answered "Yes," list the name of each group below. If you need more space, attach the names of the other group(s) on a separate sheet of paper.

Name of Group	Name of Group
1.	6.
2.	7.
3.	8.
4.	9.
5.	10.

9. Have you **EVER** been a member of or in any way associated *(either directly or indirectly)* with:

a. The Communist Party? ☐ Yes ☐ No

b. Any other totalitarian party? ☐ Yes ☐ No

c. A terrorist organization? ☐ Yes ☐ No

10. Have you **EVER** advocated *(either directly or indirectly)* the overthrow of any government by force or violence? ☐ Yes ☐ No

11. Have you **EVER** persecuted *(either directly or indirectly)* any person because of race, religion, national origin, membership in a particular social group, or political opinion? ☐ Yes ☐ No

12. Between March 23, 1933, and May 8, 1945, did you work for or associate in any way *(either directly or indirectly)* with:

a. The Nazi government of Germany? ☐ Yes ☐ No

b. Any government in any area (1) occupied by, (2) allied with, or (3) established with the help of the Nazi government of Germany? ☐ Yes ☐ No

c. Any German, Nazi, or S.S. military unit, paramilitary unit, self-defense unit, vigilante unit, citizen unit, police unit, government agency or office, extermination camp, concentration camp, prisoner of war camp, prison, labor camp, or transit camp? ☐ Yes ☐ No

C. Continuous Residence

Since becoming a Lawful Permanent Resident of the United States:

13. Have you **EVER** called yourself a "nonresident" on a Federal, state, or local tax return? ☐ Yes ☐ No

14. Have you **EVER** failed to file a Federal, state, or local tax return because you considered yourself to be a "nonresident"? ☐ Yes ☐ No

D. Good Moral Character

For the purposes of this application , you must answer "Yes" to the following questions, if applicable, even if your records were sealed or otherwise cleared or if anyone, including a judge, law enforcement officer, or attorney, told you that you no longer have a record.

15. Have you **EVER** committed a crime or offense for which you were NOT arrested? ☐ Yes ☐ No

16. Have you **EVER** been arrested, cited, or detained by any law enforcement officer (including INS and military officers) for any reason? ☐ Yes ☐ No

17. Have you **EVER** been charged with committing any crime or offense? ☐ Yes ☐ No

18. Have you **EVER** been convicted of a crime or offense? ☐ Yes ☐ No

19. Have you **EVER** been placed in an alternative sentencing or a rehabilitative program (for example: diversion, deferred prosecution, withheld adjudication, deferred adjudication)? ☐ Yes ☐ No

20. Have you **EVER** received a suspended sentence, been placed on probation, or been paroled? ☐ Yes ☐ No

21 Have you **EVER** been in jail or prison? ☐ Yes ☐ No

If you answered "Yes" to any of questions 15 through 21, complete the following table. If you need more space, use a separate sheet of paper to give the same information.

Why were you arrested, cited, detained, or charged?	Date arrested, cited, detained, or charged *(Month/Day/Year)*	Where were you arrested, cited, detained or charged? *(City, State, Country)*	Outcome or disposition of the arrest, citation, detention or charge *(No charges filed, charges dismissed, jail, probation, etc.)*

Answer questions 22 through 33. If you answer "Yes" to any of these questions, attach (1) your written explanation why your answer was "Yes," and (2) any additional information or documentation that helps explain your answer.

22. Have you **EVER**:

    a. been a habitual drunkard? ☐ Yes ☐ No

    b. been a prostitute, or procured anyone for prostitution? ☐ Yes ☐ No

    c. sold or smuggled controlled substances, illegal drugs or narcotics? ☐ Yes ☐ No

    d. been married to more than one person at the same time? ☐ Yes ☐ No

    e. helped anyone enter or try to enter the United States illegally? ☐ Yes ☐ No

    f. gambled illegally or received income from illegal gambling? ☐ Yes ☐ No

    g. failed to support your dependents or to pay alimony? ☐ Yes ☐ No

23. Have you **EVER** given false or misleading information to any U.S. government official while applying for any immigration benefit or to prevent deportation, exclusion, or removal? ☐ Yes ☐ No

24. Have you **EVER** lied to any U.S. government official to gain entry or admission into the United States? ☐ Yes ☐ No

E. Removal, Exclusion, and Deportation Proceedings

25. Are removal, exclusion, rescission or deportation proceedings pending against you? ☐ Yes ☐ No

26. Have you **EVER** been removed, excluded, or deported from the United States? ☐ Yes ☐ No

27. Have you **EVER** been ordered to be removed, excluded, or deported from the United States? ☐ Yes ☐ No

28. Have you **EVER** applied for any kind of relief from removal, exclusion, or deportation? ☐ Yes ☐ No

F. Military service

29. Have you **EVER** served in the U.S. Armed Forces? ☐ Yes ☐ No

30. Have you **EVER** left the United States to avoid being drafted into the U.S. Armed Forces? ☐ Yes ☐ No

31. Have you **EVER** applied for any kind of exemption from military service in the U.S. Armed Forces? ☐ Yes ☐ No

32. Have you **EVER** deserted from the U.S. Armed Forces? ☐ Yes ☐ No

G. Selective Service Registration

33. Are you a male who lived in the United States at any time between your 18th and 26th birthdays
in any status except as a lawful nonimmigrant? ☐ Yes ☐ No

If you answered "NO", go on to question 34.

If you answered "YES", provide the information below.

If you answered "YES", but you did NOT register with the Selective Service System and are still under 26 years of age, you
must register before you apply for naturalization, so that you can complete the information below:

Date Registered (Month/Day/Year) [   ] Selective Service Number [_ _ _ _ _ _ _ _]

If you answered "YES", but you did NOT register with the Selective Service and you are now 26 years old or older, attach a
statement explaining why you did not register.

H. Oath Requirements *(See Part 14 for the text of the oath)*

Answer questions 34 through 39. If you answer "No" to any of these questions, attach (1) your written explanation why the answer was
"No" and (2) any additional information or documentation that helps to explain your answer.

34. Do you support the Constitution and form of government of the United States? ☐ Yes ☐ No

35. Do you understand the full Oath of Allegiance to the United States? ☐ Yes ☐ No

36. Are you willing to take the full Oath of Allegiance to the United States? ☐ Yes ☐ No

37. If the law requires it, are you willing to bear arms on behalf of the United States? ☐ Yes ☐ No

38. If the law requires it, are you willing to perform noncombatant services in the U.S. Armed Forces? ☐ Yes ☐ No

39. If the law requires it, are you willing to perform work of national importance under civilian
direction? ☐ Yes ☐ No

Part 11. Your Signature

I certify, under penalty of perjury under the laws of the United States of America, that this application, and the evidence submitted with it, are all true and correct. I authorize the release of any information which INS needs to determine my eligibility for naturalization.

Your Signature

Date *(Month/Day/Year)*

_ _ _ _ _ _ _ _

Part 12. Signature of Person Who Prepared This Application for You   *(If Applicable)*

I declare under penalty of perjury that I prepared this application at the request of the above person. The answers provided are based on information of which I have personal knowledge and/or were provided to me by the above named person in response to the *exact questions* contained on this form.

Preparer's Printed Name

Preparer's Signature

Date *(Month/Day/Year)*

_ _ _ _ _ _

Preparer's Firm or Organization Name   *(If applicable)*

Preparer's Daytime Phone Number

Preparer's Address - Street Number and Name

City

State

ZIP Code

Do Not Complete Part 13 and 14 Until an INS Officer Instructs You To Do So

Part 13. Signature at Interview

I swear (affirm) and certify under penalty of perjury under the laws of the United States of America that I know that the contents of this application for naturalization subscribed by me, including corrections numbered 1 through _____ and the evidence submitted by me numbered pages 1 through _____, are true and correct to the best of my knowledge and belief.

Subscribed to and sworn to (affirmed) before me

Officer's Printed Name or Stamp

Date *(Month/Day/Year)*

Complete Signature of Applicant

Officer's Signature

Part 14. Oath of Allegiance

If your application is approved, you will be scheduled for a public oath ceremony at which time you will be required to take the following oath of allegiance immediately prior to becoming a naturalized citizen. By signing below, you acknowledge your willingness and ability to take this oath:

I hereby declare, on oath, that I absolutely and entirely renounce and abjure all allegiance and fidelity to any foreign prince, potentate, state, or sovereignty, of whom or which I have heretofore been a subject or citizen;

that I will support and defend the Constitution and laws of the United States of America against all enemies, foreign and domestic;
that I will bear true faith and allegiance to the same;
that I will bear arms on behalf of the United States when required by the law;
that I will perform noncombatant service in the Armed Forces of the United States when required by the law;
that I will perform work of national importance under civilian direction when required by the law; and
that I take this obligation freely, without any mental reservation or purpose of evasion; so help me God.

Printed Name of Applicant

Complete Signature of Applicant

U.S. Department of Justice
Immigration and Naturalization Service

**Application for
Certificate of Citizenship**

FEE STAMP

Take or mail this application to:
IMMIGRATION AND NATURALIZATION SERVICE

(Print or type)

Date ___ / / _____

_____ *nee* _____
(Full, True Name, without Abbreviations)   (Maiden name, if any)

_____
(Apartment number, Street address, and, if appropriate, "in care of")

ALIEN REGISTRATION

NO._____

_____
(City)   (County)   (State)   (ZIP Code)

_____
(Telephone Number)

(SEE INSTRUCTIONS. BE SURE YOU UNDERSTAND EACH QUESTION BEFORE YOU ANSWER IT.)

I hereby apply to the Commissioner of Immigration and Naturalization for a certificate showing that I am a citizen of the United States of America.

(1) I was born in _____ on ___ / / _____
                  (City) (State or country)   (Month) (Day) (Year)

(2) My personal description is: Gender;_____; height_____ feet _____ inches;

Marital status: ☐ Single; ☐ Married; ☐ Divorced; ☐ Widow(er).

(3) I arrived in the United States at _____ on _____
                                      (City and State)   (Month) (Day) (Year)

under the name _____ by means of _____
                                                          (Name of ship or other means of arrival)

☐ on U.S. Passport No. _____ issued to me at _____ on ___ / / _____
                                                                            (Month) (Day) (Year)

☐ on an Immigrant Visa ☐ Other (specify) _____

(4) FILL IN THIS BLOCK ONLY IF YOU ARRIVED IN THE UNITED STATES BEFORE JULY 1, 1924.

(a) My last permanent foreign residence was _____
                                              (City)   (Country)

(b) I took the ship or other conveyance to the United States at _____
                                                                 (City)   (Country)

(c) I was coming to _____ at _____
                     (Name of person in the United States)   (City and State where this person was living)

(d) I traveled to the United States with _____
                                          (Name of passengers or relatives with whom you traveled, and their relationship to you, if any)

(5) Have you been out of the United States since you first arrived? ☐ Yes ☐ No; If "Yes" fill in the following information for every absence.

DATE DEPARTED	DATE RETURNED	Name of airlines or other means used to return to the United States	Port of return to the United States

(6) I _____ filed a petition for naturalization. *(If "have", attach full explanation.)*
       (have)   (have not)

TO THE APPLICANT. - Do not write between the double lines below. Continue on next page.

ARRIVAL RECORDS EXAMINED	ARRIVAL RECORD FOUND

Card index _____   Place _____ Date _____

Index books _____   Name _____

Manifests _____   Manner_____

_____   Marital status _____ Age _____

_____   _____
                            (Signature of person making search)

(CONTINUE HERE)

(7) I claim United States citizenship through my   *(check whichever applicable)*   ☐ **father;**   ☐ **mother;**   ☐ **both parents;**

☐ **adoptive parent(s);**   ☐ **husband**

(8) My father's name is _____ ; he was born on _____

(Month)   (Day)   (Year)

at _____ ; and resides at _____

(City)   (State or Country)   (Street address, city, and State or country. If dead, write

He became a citizen of the United States by ☐ birth; ☐ naturalization on _____

(Month)   (Day)   (Year)

"dead" and date of death.)

in the _____ Certificate of Naturalization No. _____

(Name of court, city, and State)

☐ through his parent(s), and _____ issued Certificate of Citizenship No. A or AA _____

(was)   (was not)

(If known) His former Alien Registration No. was _____

He _____ lost United States citizenship. *(If citizenship lost, attach full explanation)*

(has) (has not)

He resided in the United States from _____ to _____ ; from _____ to _____ ; from _____ to _____

(Year)   (Year)   (Year)   (Year)   (Year)   (Year)

from _____ to _____ ; from _____ to _____ ; I am the child of his _____ marriage.

(Year)   (Year)   (Year)   (Year)   (1st, 2d, 3d, etc.)

(9) My mother's present name is _____ ; her maiden name was _____ ;

she was born on _____ ; at _____ ; she resides

(Month)   (Day)   (Year)   (City)   (State or country)

at _____ She became a citizen of the

(Street address, city, and State or country. If dead, write "dead" and date of death.)

United States by ☐ birth; ☐ naturalization under the name of _____

on _____ in the _____

(Month) (Day) (Year)   (Name of court, city, and State)

Certificate of Naturalization No. _____ ☐ through her parent(s), and _____ issued Certificate

(was)(was not)

of Citizenship No. A or AA _____ (If known) Her former Alien Registration No. was _____

She _____ lost United States citizenship. *(If citizenship lost, attach full explanation)*

(has) (has not)

She resided in the United States from _____ to _____ ; from _____ to _____ ; from _____ to _____ ;

(Year)   (Year)   (Year)   (Year)   (Year)   (Year)

from _____ to _____ ; from _____ to _____ ; I am the child of her _____ marriage.

(Year)   (Year)   (Year)   (Year)   (1st, 2d, 3d, etc.)

(10) My mother and my father were married to each other on _____ at _____

(Month)(Day)(Year)   (City)   (State or country)

(11) If claim is through adoptive parent(s):

I was adopted on _____ in the _____

(Month)(Day)(Year)   (Name of Court)

at _____ by my _____ who were not United States citizens at that time.

(City or town)(State)(Country)   (mother, father, parents)

(12) My _____ served in the Armed Forces of the United States from _____ to _____ and _____

(father) (mother)   (Date)   (Date)   (was) (was not)

honorably discharged.

(13) I _____ lost my United States citizenship. *(If citizenship lost, attach full explanation.)*

(have) (have not)

(14) I submit the following documents with this application:

Nature of Document   *Names of Persons Concerned*

_____   _____

_____   _____

_____   _____

_____   _____

_____   _____

(15) Fill in this block if your brother, sister, mother or father ever applied to the INS for a certificate of citizenship.

NAME OF RELATIVE	RELATIONSHIP	DATE OF BIRTH	WHEN APPLICATION SUBMITTED	CERTIFICATE NO. AND FILE NO., IF KNOWN, AND LOCATION OF OFFICE

(16) Fill in this block only if your are now or ever have been a married woman. I have been married_____ time(s), as follows: *(1, 2, 3, etc.)*

DATE MARRIED	NAME OF HUSBAND	CITIZENSHIP OF HUSBAND	IF MARRIAGE HAS BEEN TERMINATED:	
			Date Marriage Ended	How Marriage Ended *(Death or divorce)*

(17) Fill in this block only if you claim citizenship through a husband. *(Marriage must have occurred prior to September 22, 1922.)*

Name of citizen husband _____ ;he was born on _____

(Give full and complete name) _(Month) (Day) (Year)_

at _____ ;and resides at _____ He became a citizen of the

(City) (State or country) _(Street address, city, and State or country. If dead, write "dead" and date of death.)_

United States by ☐ birth; ☐naturalization on _____ in the _____ Certificate of

(Month)(Day)(Year) _(Name of court, city, and State)_

Naturalization No._____ ; ☐ through his parent(s), and _____ issued Certificate of Citizenship No. A or AA

(was)(was not)

_____ . He _____ since lost United States citizenship. *(If citizenship lost, attach full explanation.)*

(has)(has not)

I am of the _____ race. Before my marriage to him, he was married_____ time(s), as follows:

(1, 2, 3, etc.)

DATE MARRIED	NAME OF WIFE	IF MARRIAGE HAS BEEN TERMINATED:	
		Date Marriage Ended	How Marriage Ended *(Death or divorce)*

(18) Fill in this block only if you claim citizenship through your stepfather. *(Applicable only if mother married U.S. Citizen prior to September 22, 1922.)*

The full name of my stepfather is _____ ; he was born on _____ at _____ ;

(Month)(Day)(Year) _(City)(State or country)_

and resides at _____ He became a citizen of the United States by ☐birth;

(Street address, city, and State or country. If dead, write "dead" and date of death.)

☐ naturalization on _____ in the _____ Certificate of Naturalization No. _____ ;

(Month)(Day)(Year) _(Name of court, city, and State)_

☐ through his parent(s), and _____ issued Certificate of Citizenship No. A or AA _____ He _____ since lost United

(was)(was not) _(has)(has not)_

States citizenship. *(If citizenship lost, attach full explanation.)* He and my mother were married to each other on _____ at _____

(Month)(Day)(Year) _(City and State or_

My mother is of the _____ race. She _____ issued Certificate of Citizenship No. A _____

country) _(was) (was not)_

Before marrying my mother, my stepfather was married _____ time(s), as follows:

(1, 2, 3, etc.)

DATE MARRIED	NAME OF WIFE	IF MARRIAGE HAS BEEN TERMINATED:	
		Date Marriage Ended	How Marriage Ended *(Death or divorce)*

(19) I _____ previously applied for a certificate of citizenship on_____ , at _____

(have) (have not) _(Date)_ _(Office)_

(20) Signature of person preparing form, if other than applicant. I declare that this document was prepared by me at the request of the applicant and is based on all information of which I have any knowledge.

SIGNATURE:

ADDRESS: | DATE:

(SIGN HERE) _____

(Signature of applicant or parent or guardian)

AFFIDAVIT

I, the _____ , do swear
(Applicant, parent, guardian)
that I know and understand the contents of this application, signed by me, and

of attached supplementary pages numbered (   ) to (   ), inclusive

that the same are true to the best of my knowledge and belief: and that

corrections numbered (   )to (   ) were made by me or at my request.

_____
(Signature of applicant, parent, guardian)

Subscribed and sworn to before me upon applicant examination of the applicant

(parent, guardian) at _____

this _____ day of _____, _____

and continued solely for:

_____
(Officer's Signature and Title)

REPORT AND RECOMMENDATION ON APPLICATION

On the basis of the documents, records, and persons examined, and the identification upon personal appearance of the underage beneficiary, I find that
all the facts and conclusions set forth under oath in this application are _____ true and correct; that the applicant did _____ derive or acquire United
States citizenship on _____ , through
(month) (Day)(Year)

and that (s)he_____been expatriated since that time. I recommend that this application be_____ and that
(has) (has not)   (granted) (denied)
_____ Certificate of citizenship be _____ issued in the name of _____
(A) (AA)
In addition to the documents listed in Item 14, the following documents and records have been examined:

Person Examined	Address	Relationship to Applicant	Date Testimony Heard
_____	_____	_____	_____
	_____		
_____	_____	_____	_____
	_____		

Supplementary Report(s) No.(s)_____ Attached.

Date _____, _____

_____
(Officer's Signature and Title)

I do_____ concur in the recommendation.

Date _____ , _____

_____
(Signature of District Director or Officer in Charge)

DV-2003 ENTRY FORM

1. **FULL NAME:** _____
   LAST(surname/family)   FIRST   MIDDLE

2. **DATE OF BIRTH:** _____
   Day, Month, Year

   PLACE OF BIRTH: _____
   City/Town, District/Country/Province, Country

3. **APPLICANT'S NATIVE COUNTRY IF DIFFERENT FROM COUNTRY OF BIRTH:**

   _____

4. **NAME, DATE AND PLACE OF BIRTH OF THE APPLICANT'S SPOUSE AND CHILDREN (IF ANY):**

Spouse's Name	Date of birth (day/Month/yr)	Place of birth
Child's Name	Date of birth (day/Month/yr)	Place of birth
Child's Name	Date of birth (day/Month/yr)	Place of birth
Child's Name	Date of birth (day/Month/yr)	Place of birth

   Attach information on additional child(ren) as necessary

5. **FULL MAILING ADDRESS:** _____

   _____

   _____

   _____

   PHONE NUMBER: _____

6. **PHOTOGRAPH:**

   Attach a recent (less than 6 months old)
   1.5 inches (37mm) square photograph (not
   a photocopy) with the applicant's name
   printed on the back. By using clear tape
   (no staples or paperclips).

   SIGNATURE: _____
   (Failure to PERSONALLY sign the entry will disqualify the applicant.)

U.S. Department of Justice

Immigration and Naturalization Service

OMB No. 1115-0087

Freedom of Information/Privacy Act Request

The completion of this form is optional.
Any written format for Freedom of Information or Privacy Act requests is acceptable

START HERE - Please Type or Print and read instructions on reverse before completing this form.

1. Type of Request: *(Check appropriate box)*

   ☐   Freedom of Information Act (FOIA) *(complete all items except 7)*

   ☐   Privacy Act (PA) *(item 7 must be completed in addition to all other applicable items)*

   ☐   Amendment *(PA only, Item 7 must be completed in addition to all other applicable items)*

2. Requester Information:

Name of Requester:		Daytime Telephone:
Address *(Street Number and Name):*		Apt. No
City:	State:	Zip Code:

By my signature, I consent to the following:

Pay all costs incurred for search, duplication, and review of materials up to $25.00, when applicable.   *(See Instructions)*

*Signature of requester:*_____

   ☐   Deceased Subject - **Proof of death must be attached.**   *(Obituary, Death Certificate or other proof of death required)*

3. Consent to Release Information.   *(Complete if name is different from Requester)(Item 7 must be completed)*

Print Name of Person Giving Consent:	Signature of Person Giving Consent:

By my signature, I consent to the following: *(check applicable boxes)*

   ☐   Allow the Requester named in item 2 to see ☐ all of my records or ☐ a portion of my record. If a portion, specify
   what part *(i.e. copy of application)*

   (Consent is required for records for United States Citizens (USC) and Lawful Permanent Residents (LPR)

4. Action Requested *(Check One):*   ☐   Copy   ☐   In-Person Review

5. Information needed to search for records;
   Specific information, document(s), or record(s) desired: *(Identify by name, date, subject matter, and location of information)*

   Purpose: *(Optional: you are not required to state the purpose for your request; however, doing so may assist the INS in
   locating the records needed to respond to your request.)*

6. Data NEEDED on SUBJECT of Record: *(If data marked with asterisk (*) is not provided records may not be located)*

* Family Name	Given Name:		Middle Initial:
* Other names used, if any:	* Name at time of entry into the U.S.:		I-94 Admissions #:
* Alien Registration #:	* Petition or Claim Receipt #:	* Country of Birth:	* Date of Birth or Appx. Year / /
Names of other family members that may appear on requested record(s) *(i.e., Spouse, Daughter, Son):*			
Country of Origin *(Place of Departure):*	Port-of-Entry into the U.S.		Date of Entry:
Manner of Entry: *(Air, Sea, Land)*	Mode of Travel: *(Name of Carrier)*		SSN:
Name of Naturalization Certifications:		Certificate #:	Naturalization Date:
Address at the time of Naturalization:		Court and Location:	

Form G-639 (Rev. 7-25-00)N

7. Verification of Subject's Identity: *(See Instructions for Explanation)(Check One Box)*

☐ In-Person with ID ☐ Notarized Affidavit of Identity ☐ Other *(Specify)* _____

Signature of Subject of Record: _____ Date: _____

_____ Telephone No.:

NOTARY *(Normally needed from individuals who are the subject of the records sought)(See below)*
or a sworn declaration under penalty of perjury.
Subscribed and sworn to before me this _____ day of _____ in the Year _____

Signature of Notary _____ My Commission Expires _____

OR

If a declaration is provided in lieu of a notarized signature, at a minimum, the following: (Include Notary Seal or Stamp in this Space)

If executed outside the United States: "I declare (certify, verify, or state) under penalty of perjury under the laws of the United States of America that the foregoing is true and correct.

Signature:_____

If executed within the United States, its territories, possessions, or commonwealths: "I declare (certify, verify, or state) under penalty of perjury that the foregoing is true and correct.

Signature:_____

Freedom of Information/Privacy Act Request

INSTRUCTIONS

Please read ALL Instructions carefully before completing this form.
Applicants making false statements are subject to criminal penalties (Pub.L. 93-579.99 Stat. (5 U.S.C. 552a(i)(3)).

Are There Cases When You do not Use This Form?

Do not use this form:

(1) To determine status of pending applications, write to the office where the application was filed or call the nearest INS office;

(2) For Consular notification of visa petition approval, use Form I-824 (Application for Action on an Approved Application or Petition);

(3) For the return of original documents, use Form G-884 (Request for Return of Original Documents);

(4) For records of naturalization prior to September 27, 1906, write to the clerk of court where naturalization occurred; or

(5) For information on INS manifest arrivals prior to December 1982, write to the National Archives.

How Can You Obtain Copies of Records from INS?

Persons requesting a search for access to INS records under the Freedom of Information or Privacy Acts may submit the completed application to the INS office nearest the applicant's place of residence. Requests may be submitted in person or by mail. If an application is mailed, the envelope should be clearly marked "Freedom of Information" or "Privacy Act Request." The INS Internet address is: http://www.ins.usdoj.gov.

What Information is Needed to Search for Records?

Please Note: Failure to provide complete and specific information as requested in Item 5 of the form, may result in a delay in processing or inability to locate the record(s) or information requested. You may access "http://www.access.gpo.gov/su-docs" for a description of DOJ/INS systems of records.

Verification of Identity in Person.

Requesters appearing in person for access to their records may identify themselves by showing a document bearing a photograph (such as an Alien Registration Card, Form I-551, Citizen Identification Card, Naturalization Certificate, or passport) or two items which bear their name and address (such as a driver's license and voter's registration).

Verification of Identity by Mail.

Requesters wanting access to their records shall identify themselves by name, current address, date and place of birth, and alien or employee identification number. A notarized example of their signatures or sworn declaration under penalty of perjury must also be provided (this Form G-639 or a DOJ Form 361, Certification of Identity, may be used for this purposes).

Verification of Identity of Guardians.

Parents or legal guardians must establish their own identity as parents or legal guardians and the identity of the child or other person being represented.

Authorization or Consent.

Other parties requesting nonpublic information about an individual usually must have the consent of that individual on Form G-639 or by an authorizing letter, together with appropriate verification of identity of the record subject. Notarized or sworn declaration is required from a record subject who is a lawful permanent resident or U.S. citizen, and for access to certain Legalization files.

Can My Request be Expedited?

To have your request processed ahead of ones received earlier you must show a compelling need for the information.

How Do You Show a Compelling Need?

A requester who seeks expedited processing must explain in detail the basis of the need and should submit a statement certified to be true and correct to the best of your knowledge and belief. You must also establish one or more of the following exists:

(1) Circumstances in which the lack of expedited processing could reasonably be expected to pose an imminent threat to the life or physical safety of an individual, or result in the loss of substantial due process rights;

(2) An urgency to inform the public about an actual or alleged federal government activity, if made by a person primarily engaged in disseminating information; or

(3) A matter of widespread and exceptional media interest in which there exists possible questions about the government's integrity which affect public confidence.

Fees.

Except for commercial requesters, the first 100 pages of reproduction and two hours of search time will be furnished without charge. Thereafter, for requests processed under the Privacy Act, there may be a fee of $ .10 per page for photocopy duplication. For requests processed under the Freedom of Information Act, there may be a fee for quarter hours of time spent for searches and for review of records. Search fees are at the following rates per quarter hour: $4.00 clerical; $7.00 professional/computer operator; and $ 10.00 managerial. Other costs for searches and duplication will be charged at the actual direct cost. Fees will only be charged if the aggregate amount of fees for searches, copy and/or review is more than $14.00. If the total anticipated fees amount to more than $250.00, or the same requester has failed to pay fees in the past, an advance deposit may be requested. Fee waivers or reductions may be requested for a request that clearly will benefit the public and is not primarily in the personal or commercial interest of the requester. Such requests should include a justification.

When Must I Submit Fees?

Do not send money with this request. When requested to do so, submit fees in the exact amount. Payment may be in the form of a check or a United States Postal money order (or, if form is submitted from outside the United States, remittance may be made by bank international money order or foreign draft drawn on a financial institution in the United States) made payable, in United States currency, to the "Immigration and Naturalization Service". A requester residing in the U.S. Virgin Islands shall make his/her remittance payable to "Commissioner of Finance of the Virgin Islands," and, if residing in Guam, to "Treasurer, Guam". **DO NOT SEND CASH AT ANYTIME.**

A charge of $30.00 will be imposed if a check in payment of a fee is not honored by the bank on which it is drawn. Every remittance will be accepted subject to collection.

Routine Uses.

Information will be used to comply with requests for information under 5 U.S.C. 552 and 552a; information provided to other agencies may be for referrals, consultations, and/or to answer subsequent inquiries concerning specific requests.

Effect of Not Providing Requested Information.

Furnishing the information requested on this form is voluntary. However, failure to furnish the information may result in the inability of INS to comply with a request when compliance will violate other policies or laws.

General Information.

The Freedom of Information Act (5 U.S.C. 552) allows requesters to have access to Federal agency records, except those which have been exempted by the Act.

Privacy Act Statement.

Authority to collect this information is contained in Title 5 U.S.C. 552 and 552a. The purpose of the collection is to enable INS to locate applicable records and to respond to requests made under the Freedom of Information and Privacy Acts.

The Privacy Act of 1974. (5 U.S.C. 552a).

With certain exceptions, the Privacy Act of 1974 permits individuals (U.S. citizens or permanent resident aliens) to gain access to information pertaining to themselves in Federal agency records, to have a copy made of all or any part thereof, to correct or amend such records, and to permit individuals to make requests concerning what records pertaining to themselves, are collected, maintained, used or disseminated. The Act also prohibits disclosure of individuals' records without their written consent, except under certain circumstances as prescribed by the Privacy Act.

Public Reporting Burden.

Under the Paperwork Reduction Act (5 U.S.C. 1320), a person is not required to respond to a collection of information unless it displays a currently valid OMB control number. We try to create forms and instructions that are accurate, can be easily understood, and which impose the least possible burden on you to provide us with information. Often this is difficult because some immigration laws are very complex. The estimated average time to complete and file this application is 15 minutes per response, including the time for reviewing the instructions, searching existing data sources, gathering and maintaining the data needed, and completing and reviewing the collection of information. If you have comments regarding the accuracy of this estimate, or suggestions for making this form simpler you may write to the Immigration and Naturalization Service, HQPDI, 425 I Street, N.W., Room 4307r, Washington, DC 20536; OMB No. 1115-0087.